Landlord and Tenant

's are to be retu~

QUESTIONS & ANSWERS SERIES

Company Law

Constitutional and Administrative Law

Conveyancing

Criminal Law

EC Law

Employment Law

English Legal System

Equity and Trusts

Evidence

Family Law

Land Law

Landlord and Tenant

Law of Contract

Law of Torts

Other titles in preparation

QUESTIONS &
ANSWERS

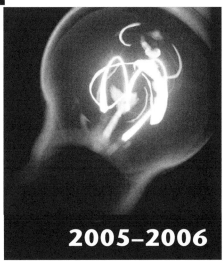

2005–2006

Landlord and Tenant

THIRD EDITION

Mark Pawlowski

LLB(Hons), BCL(Oxon), ACIArb, Barrister
Professor of Property Law, University of Greenwich

James Brown

LLB(Hons), ACIArb, Barrister
Senior Lecturer in Law, London Metropolitan University

OXFORD
UNIVERSITY PRESS

OXFORD
UNIVERSITY PRESS

Great Clarendon Street, Oxford OX2 6DP

Oxford University Press is a department of the University of Oxford.
It furthers the University's objective of excellence in research, scholarship,
and education by publishing worldwide in

Oxford New York

Auckland Cape Town Dar es Salaam Hong Kong Karachi Kuala Lumpur
Madrid Melbourne Mexico City Nairobi New Delhi Shanghai Taipei Toronto

With offices in

Argentina Austria Brazil Chile Czech Republic France Greece
Guatemala Hungary Italy Japan South Korea Poland Portugal
Singapore Switzerland Thailand Turkey Ukraine Vietnam

Oxford is a registered trade mark of Oxford University Press
in the UK and in certain other countries

Published in the United States
by Oxford University Press Inc., New York

First published 1995
Second edition 2000
Third edition 2005

British Library Cataloguing in Publication Data

Data available

Library of Congress Cataloging in Publication Data

Data available

ISBN 0–19–927731–1

3 5 7 9 10 8 6 4 2

Typeset by RefineCatch Ltd, Bungay, Suffolk
Printed in Great Britain by
Ashford Colour Press, Gosport, Hants

Contents

The Q&A Series

Key features

The Q&A series provides full coverage of key subjects in a clear and logical way. This new edition contains the following features:

- Question
- Commentary
- Bullet point list
- Suggested answer
- Further reading
- Diagrams

Preface

It has been a pleasure to produce a third edition of this book at the invitation of our publishers. During the past four years since completing the text for the last edition, there have been several important developments in the field of leasehold law. Most recently, the Regulatory Reform (Business Tenancies) (England and Wales) Order 2003 came into effect on June 1, 2004, making important procedural changes to the workings of the business tenancy code under Pt II of the Landlord and Tenant Act 1954. In the light of these changes, we have made substantial revisions to **Chapter 13** on Business Tenancies, including a new question on the extent to which these reforms reflect the Law Commission's original proposals contained in its 1992 Report, 'Business Tenancies: A Periodic Review of the Landlord and Tenant Act 1954 Pt II' (Law Com. No. 208, 1992): see, **Question 4**.

Significant developments are also taking place in the residential rented-sector with the publication of the Law Commission's Report, 'Renting Homes' (Law Com. No. 284) in November 2003 putting forward major proposals for the overhauling of the assured/assured shorthold, secure and introductory tenancy regimes by the introduction of a simplified type I and type II occupational agreement scheme. In view of the importance of these recommendations, we have created a new question in **Chapter 15** (see, **Question 3**) requiring the reader to comment on the Commission's thinking and underlying rationale in introducing the new scheme. Significant procedural changes have also been made to the statutory frameworks governing leasehold reform and the levying of service charges under the Commonhold and Leasehold Reform Act 2002 which has necessitated substantial revision of **Chapter 12** on Leasehold Enfranchisement (see, **Questions 1** and **2**) and the inclusion of an entirely new question on service charges in **Chapter 8**: see, **Question 5**.

The current law on forfeiture of leases looks also likely (at last) to undergo fundamental change with the recent publication (in January 2004) of the Law Commission's Consultation Paper on 'Termination of Tenancies for Tenant Default' (Law Com. CP No. 174). This has precipitated a revised answer to **Question 3, in Chapter 9**, incorporating the latest proposals. Sadly, however, little progress has been made in the field of leasehold dilapidations since our last edition in 2000 when we commented on the Commission's proposals for reform contained in its

Report, 'Landlord and Tenant, Responsibility for State and Condition of Property' (Law Com. No. 238, 1996).

On a different note, the impact of the Human Rights Act 1998 (which came into force on October 2, 2000) cannot now be ignored in the landlord and tenant context and, consequently, we have included a question in **Chapter 10** (see, **Question 5**) examining the human rights case law affecting residential possession proceedings. It is apparent, however, that the overall impact of the 1998 Act on landlord and tenant relations is likely to be only marginal.

We have also taken the opportunity in this latest edition to add an entirely new chapter (**Chapter 3**) on Types of Tenancies and Leases in order to provide our readers with questions on the nature of tenancies at will, tenancies at sufferance, concurrent leases and tenancies by estoppel. There is also a useful question concerning the possible rationalisation of occupational rights in leasehold law.

We have also added (and substantially revised) a number of questions to cover other developments in the case law. For example, we have included a new question on the lease/licence distinction in order to accommodate the recent ruling in *National Car Parks Ltd v. Trinity Development Co. (Banbury) Ltd* [2001] 2 EGLR 43: **Chapter 2, Question 5**. The subject of non-derogation from grant has seen several cases modifying the rule in *Port v. Griffith* [1938] 1 All ER 295 regarding the letting of adjacent premises to a competitor of the tenant: **Chapter 5, Question 5**. There is a new question on leasehold dilapidations highlighting several new decisions on whether the repairing covenant covers purely anticipatory or preventative works and whether a tenant has an implied licence to enter upon the landlord's premises in order to carry out repairs which are the landlord's responsibility: see **Chapter 7, Question 7**. There has also been a new line of cases concerning the application of the House of Lords' decision in *Mannai Investment Co. Ltd v. Eagle Star Life Assurance Co. Ltd* [1997] 2 WLR 945 to the validity of s.20 notices served on assured shorthold tenants under the Housing Act 1988: see, **Chapter 11, Question 4**. Several recent cases have also emerged on the nature of the landlord's intended building works which qualify under s.30(1)(f) of the Landlord and Tenant Act 1954, which has prompted us to add a new question in **Chapter 13** (**Question 8**). In total, we have created 13 new questions for this new edition.

This latest publication also reflects the 'new look' Q & A series initiated by the current publishers. In addition, therefore, to the inclusion of the bullet points of key issues, we have also provided guides for additional reading at the end of each chapter.

We are very grateful to the staff at Oxford University Press, in particular, Rebecca Webb, the Assistant Commissioning Editor for Law, for all their efforts in bringing this latest edition to print so quickly. We also wish to thank our respective partners, Lidia and Rachel, who have had to endure our undergoing the 'writing process' yet again. Not least, we owe a debt of gratitude to our students who continue to provide us with inspiration and enthusiasm for our subject.

We have endeavoured to present the law accurately in our suggested answers as at 1 October 2004.

Mark Pawlowski
James Brown

To my wife, Lidia de Barbaro

Mark

To my mother, Rosemary Elizabeth

James

Abbreviations

CLY	Current Law Yearbook
Conv	Conveyancer and Property Lawyer
EG	Estates Gazette
EGLR	Estates Gazette Law Reports
JHL	Journal of Housing Law
L & TR	Landlord and Tenant Law Reports
L & T Rev	Landlord and Tenant Review
LQR	Law Quarterly Review
NLJ	New Law Journal
RRLR	Rent Review and Lease Renewal
PLJ	Property Law Journal
SJ	Solicitors Journal

Table of Cases

Table of Statutes

International Legislation

Table of Rules and Regulations

Introduction

This book has been written by two university lecturers who, apart from teaching landlord and tenant law at degree level to both law and non-law students, have also practised in this field for many years. Its aim is to give students detailed examples of suggested solutions to examination questions in landlord and tenant law, and to further their understanding and appreciation of the subject. It is also an attempt to give guidance on examination technique.

In landlord and tenant law, as with other law subjects, there exists no substitute for hard work. You will not pass the examination if you do not know the substance of the course. A student who hopes to do well must attend lectures and seminars and read the recommended textbooks and source materials (e.g., cases, statutes and articles). Knowledge of source material is vital to achieving good class 2:1 answers. For example, read the judgments of the cases, not just the headnotes! Devote time during the week to *reading* your lecture notes. As an aid to understanding and learning each topic, you may find it useful to draw a flowchart summarising how the various aspects of cases and statutory provisions within a topic fit together. Essentially, our advice is to think in terms of the examination *right from the start* of your course, and not just during the last few weeks when you hope to 'cram' everything into a brief revision period. Plan your learning strategy well in advance so that your revision topics cover material you have already learnt and understood in depth during the months prior to the examination.

A good idea when you begin your course is to ensure that you thoroughly understand your syllabus. Check the various topics and, as the course progresses, earmark the key areas which are likely to come up and in which you feel you can do well in the examination. We would like to stress the importance of looking at past papers at an early stage in your course so that you 'get a feel' for the examiner's style and what standard of knowledge is expected of you. Past papers are usually available from your university/college bookshop or library. We also cannot stress enough the importance of attending any revision classes held by your subject lecturer. Such classes are likely to contain invaluable hints. You can expect any topical (controversial) subjects to be included in the examination (see, e.g., Question 4, **Chapter 13** and Question 3, **Chapter 15**).

Acquiring knowledge and understanding the subject is only part of the process of achieving success in examinations. To do well and to guarantee success, it is also necessary to *apply* your knowledge correctly to the question set. This book contains examination questions and answers covering several possible question variations within each topic. There is a mixture of problem and essay-type questions, both of which require a logical and structured approach which many students find difficult. The essay-type question may ask you to explain the meaning of a particular doctrine or principle (i.e., purely factual), or it may ask you to discuss a certain proposition which, sometimes, will be derived from a quotation. In either case, you should produce a well-structured answer explaining the meaning or significance of the doctrine, principle or proposition and its origin in common law, equity or statute, and cases which illustrate its application to the branch of law concerned (see, e.g., Question 3, **Chapter 1**).

The problem type of question requires different skills. You may well be asked to advise one (or more) of the parties, or merely to discuss the legal consequences of the facts raised in the question. In either case, you should devote some time to reading the question very carefully. Do not stray outside the boundaries of the question — irrelevant material will not gain you any marks! Answer the question set, not the question you wish had been set! Avoid long-windedness and waffle — your answer should be a clear, succinct piece of advice referring to the relevant case law and statutory provisions (see, e.g., Question 1, **Chapter 4**). Essentially, your initial task will be to identify the key issues and set out the fundamental principles involved. You must then apply your knowledge of the law to the specific issues posed, raising alternative arguments as part of a logical sequence of reasoning. Remember that the examiner is testing your ability to understand the issues and lucidly argue the case from the point of view of your client(s) on the established law. Make sure you have grasped the legal significance of all the factual data. There will usually be little in the way of superfluous material. A good tip (often used by the writers when reading solicitors' instructions) is to use a highlighting pen to pick out the salient factual points. Virtually all landlord and tenant law problems contain data which are time-significant. For example, the date of a residential letting may be crucial to determining whether the tenancy falls within the security of tenure provisions of the Rent Act 1977 or Pt I of the Housing Act 1988 (see, e.g., Question 1, **Chapter 10**). You should, therefore, pay particular attention to dates and times.

The examination paper will require you to answer a certain number of questions in a limited period of time. The questions, with possibly some exceptions, will carry equal marks. Read the instructions at the top of the examination paper carefully. Read the individual questions carefully. In your institution, you may be given a period of reading time prior to the actual start of the examination itself. Use this time wisely. Read the *whole* of the examination paper before selecting the questions you want to answer. Try to identify which areas of the syllabus are covered by which questions. Analyse the problem questions — jot down, as part of your rough work, what the examiner is looking for in your answer. Plan your answers — make a list of key cases and/or statutory provisions. You may be very thankful for this list during the examination when, for example, you are under pressure to complete an answer. Check the rubric — do not 'discuss' if you are asked to 'compare and contrast'. Above all, do not panic if some of the questions seem unfamiliar to you on first reading. Read the question(s) again and a few pennies may start to drop! Keep calm and do not be put off by the person sitting in front of you who has already started scribbling furiously. The chances are that he or she has not spent sufficient time digesting the question before putting pen to paper. Sadly, the writers commonly find the first side of an examination script contains nothing of any real relevance. Invariably, this turns out to be a script from a candidate who started writing from the first moment, allowing very little time for prior thought.

One of the great dangers during an examination is to spend too much time on any question. If you are running out of time, then complete your answer in note form. This will, at least, gain you some marks. A good tip is to mark down on your rough paper the various times at which you should be starting each question. If you stick to the timetable, you will avoid over-running and save yourself a lot of nerves!

We have already mentioned that your answers should be clear and concise. One common error among students is to write down the nature of every case that happens to deal with the topic concerned and then recite all the facts that he or she can remember. This will, undoubtedly, fill a lot of space on your answer booklet but will not gain you much respect from the examiner. You should cite only relevant cases, and no more facts should be stated than are absolutely essential to establish the relevance of each case. Remember, the more relevant authority you cite properly, the better your answer. If you cannot recall the name of the case, use some such phrase as 'in a decided case' or 'in a recent case'. Some questions, however, may hinge on only one or two cases where it may be appropriate to consider the facts in more detail (see, e.g., Question 4, **Chapter 9**). If you are citing a statute, be precise and try to refer to the section number(s).

As a matter of good style, use paragraphs to separate the various sections of your answer and write simple, straightforward sentences as much as possible. Sometimes, it may be useful to identify the fundamental problem in your opening paragraph (see, e.g., Question 2, **Chapter 2**). A clear conclusion is also helpful in your final paragraph (see, e.g., Question 2, **Chapter 6**). If the question specifically asks you to 'advise' one (or more) of the parties, it is sometimes useful actually to give the advice required in your concluding sentence (see, e.g., Question 4(b), **Chapter 7**). Another good tip regarding style (often ignored by students) is to underline the title of statutes or the name of cases. From our own experience, this makes the examiner's job much easier because he or she can see at a glance whether or not the relevant material has been covered in your script. In fact, anything that makes your paper easier to read will be much appreciated! Always write as neatly as you can; space out your answers sensibly; number your answers (including each part) clearly; begin a new answer on a fresh page. If you *plan* your answer carefully before putting pen to paper, you should be able to produce a well-written, tidy script. Increasingly, external examiners are stressing the importance of good presentation not only in students' assessed course-work but also in examinations. In order to do yourself justice, you should always try to get the examiner on your side by following the basic rules regarding legibility, spelling and presentation outlined above.

If you are dyslexic, or suffer from some other impairment which may affect your ability to write, do not hesitate to mention this to your personal tutor at an early stage in your course. You should not feel any shame in claiming any allowance to which you may be entitled (e.g., extra time, use of a word-processor, private room etc.). If you suffer from 'exam stress' generally, you should contact your student counsellor, who will be able to provide you with various strategies for coping with exam nerves. He or she will know a great deal about exam worries and how to overcome them. If you have any personal, financial or other problems which might affect your exam performance, you should also make these known to your tutor at an early stage. At the very least, a sympathetic ear may go some way towards relieving your anxieties.

A final word — try and keep up with recent cases and articles in your chosen revision topics. You should, for example, consult the *Estates Gazette, Landlord and Tenant Review, Property Law Journal* and the *Conveyancer and Property Lawyer* on a regular basis to see whether there have been any new developments in the case law and academic literature. Your examiner will obviously be impressed if you can show you are acquainted with any recent developments.

Good luck in your endeavours!

The landlord and tenant relationship

Introduction

In this chapter, we have included four questions on a variety of subjects (i.e., leases and licences, certainty of term, and the formalities of a lease) which loosely come under the heading of 'the landlord and tenant relationship'.

The lease/licence distinction has produced a welter of case law and academic discussion in articles and elsewhere — it is, therefore, a popular topic with examiners, especially now with the House of Lords ruling in *Bruton* v *London and Quadrant Housing Trust* [2000] 1 AC 406 (see Question 1(a)).

Certainty of term has also been the subject of interesting case law (*Prudential Assurance Co. Ltd* v *London Residuary Body* [1992] 3 WLR 279, overruling *In Re Midland Railway Co.'s Agreement* [1971] Ch 725 and *Ashburn Anstalt* v *Arnold* [1989] Ch 1 on this point). You may, therefore, expect a question on this topic which may be coupled with the doctrine of repugnancy (see, e.g., *Centaploy Ltd* v *Matlodge Ltd* [1974] Ch 1): Question 4.

The subject of the formalities of a lease has become complicated by the fact that there are now two separate statutory provisions governing the validity of contracts for the disposition of interests in land. The Law of Property Act 1925, s. 40, continues to apply to contracts for the grant of a lease entered into before 27 September 1989. Note that a party to an oral agreement for the grant of a lease (entered into before this date) may be able to enforce the same in equity if he or she can establish a sufficient act of part performance made on the faith of the agreement (*Steadman* v *Steadman* [1976] AC 536). The Law of Property (Miscellaneous Provisions) Act 1989, s. 2, now governs contracts made on or after 27 September 1989. Under s. 2, a contract for the sale or other disposition of an interest in land can only be made in writing, and therefore the doctrine of part performance has been effectively abolished in relation to contracts made after this date. You should also be familiar with the provisions of the Law of Property Act 1925, ss. 52, 53 and 54, and the Court of Appeal decision in *Crago* v *Julian* [1992] 1 WLR 372, to the effect that the assignment of any tenancy at law (including an oral periodic tenancy) will not be valid unless made by deed (save in the case of assignments by operation of law: *Parc Battersea Ltd* v *Hutchinson* [1999] 2 EG 149).

Landlord and tenant courses vary as to the emphasis they give to the various subject areas dealt with in this chapter. The best advice we can give you is to be guided by your lecturer as to how much time you should devote to any one or more of these topics in preparing for your exam.

Q Question 1

(a) Assess critically the legal significance of the House of Lords' ruling in *Bruton v London and Quadrant Housing Trust* (2000).

(b) Tom, Dick and Harriet are three law students who have recently approached Acrecrest Estates Ltd with a view to renting a flat for their use during the next academic session. They have each been handed a separate (but identical) document for signature headed 'Licence Agreement', which states that 'the Licensor shall grant and the Licensee shall accept a licence to share with two others each to be separately licensed by the Licensor and to the intent that the Licensee shall not have exclusive possession of the premises, for a term of 6 months at a monthly licence fee of £240'. Tom, Dick and Harriet are unhappy about the document they have been asked to sign and seek your advice as to their legal position.

Advise Tom, Dick and Harriet.

Commentary

The first part of this question requires a critical analysis of the surprising decision of the House of Lords in *Bruton*. Unfortunately, you will not score good marks if you simply regurgitate the facts of the case and outline the ruling. The question asks you to *assess critically* the legal significance of the decision, so you must be prepared to give an incisive commentary on the case. Show the examiner that you have read (and understood) some of the academic literature on the decision: see, for example, Pawlowski, M. and Greer, S., 'Leases, Licences and Contractual Tenancies' (2000) 9(1) Nott LJ 85.

Part (b) treads more familiar territory and gives you ample opportunity to regurgitate the House of Lords decision in *AG Securities v Vaughan/Antoniades v Villiers* [1990] 1 AC 417, and the subsequent Court of Appeal decision in *Duke v Wynne* [1990] 1 WLR 766.

There is a wealth of reading on the subject of the lease/licence distinction in the context of multiple flat-sharing arrangements. Of particular interest are; Harpum, C., 'Leases, Licences, Sharing and Shams' [1989] CLJ 19; Hill, J., 'Shared Accommodation and Exclusive Possession' (1989) 52 MLR 408 and Murdoch, S., 'The Lease/Licence Distinction' [1989] EG 8911, 22.

- Test of exclusive possession confirmed in *Bruton* (2000), but grant of a tenancy may be displaced if there are 'special circumstances': *Street v Mountford* (1985)

- *Bruton* decision criticised for creating a hybrid personal tenancy and for failing to extend the category of special circumstances to include organisations offering accommodation to the homeless

- Comparison between *AG Securities* v *Vaughan* and *Antoniades* v *Villiers* (1990) — are the agreements independent or interdependent?

- Four unities of a joint tenancy present so likely that the licence agreements are a sham: *Aslan* v *Murphy (No. 1)/Aslan* v *Murphy (No. 2)/Duke* v *Wynne* (1990)

·Ọ· Suggested answer

(a) The House of Lords in *Bruton* has confirmed the principle that an agreement will confer on the occupier the status of a tenant if it gives a right to exclusive possession for a term, notwithstanding that the agreement was intended by the parties to create only a licence. Thus in *Bruton* itself, the agreement gave the occupant a right to exclusive possession because there was nothing to suggest that the occupant was to share possession with the Housing Trust or any other party. Mr Bruton did not fall to be classified as a lodger in the *Street* v *Mountford* sense since the Housing Trust had not retained an unlimited right to enter the accommodation for the purpose of providing attendance or services: see, *Westminster City Council* v *Clarke* [1992] AC 288 (HL), where the licence agreement was upheld on the basis that the council could change the subject accommodation without notice or require the occupant to share with any other person, and the council's representative was entitled to enter the property at any time pursuant to the terms of the agreement. An express reservation of *limited* rights to enter for certain defined purposes only (as in *Bruton*) served only to fortify the conclusion that the Housing Trust had granted exclusive possession. The grant of a tenancy will be displaced only where there are 'special circumstances' which are capable of negativing this result: see *Street* v *Mountford* [1985] AC 809, *per* Lord Templeman.

The cental issue in *Bruton*, therefore, was whether the fact that the Housing Trust was a charitable organisation charged with the function of providing short-term accommodation for the homeless pursuant to a licence agreement with the Council (which by its terms prohibited the grant of any tenancies) was sufficient to constitute special circumstances so as to displace the presumption of a tenancy. On this point, the House of Lords, following the earlier Court of Appeal decision in *Family Housing Association* v *Jones* [1990] 1 WLR 779 (which was largely indistinguishable from *Bruton* on the facts), rejected the notion that performance of socially valuable functions could amount to circumstances capable of negativing the general rule in favour of a tenancy. Moreover, the fact that the Housing Trust had agreed with the Council not to create tenancies (and that it had no estate out of which it could grant them) was considered immaterial where the agreement had clearly conferred exclusive possession on the occupier.

The House of Lords' ruling has been criticised on a number of grounds. First, it rejects the notion that a more flexible approach (exemplified by earlier case law, in particular, *Westminster City Council* v *Clarke* [1992] AC 288 (HL) and *Camden London Borough Council* v *Shortliffe Community Housing* (1992) 25 HLR 330) is more appropriate in determining the rights of the parties in the context of public sector housing for the homeless. Secondly, it is apparent in *Bruton* that the Housing Trust, being itself only a licensee of the property, could never have had the power to exclude the Council from possession and, consequently, was not in a position to confer such a right on Mr Bruton. This, it is submitted, is a compelling argument and one that should have been decisive of the appeal. The point was addressed by Millet LJ in the Court of Appeal in *Bruton* [1998] QB 834, at 845, where his Lordship concluded that 'if the grantor has no power to exclude the true owner from possession, he has no power to grant a legal right to exclusive possession and his grant cannot take effect as a tenancy'. Thirdly, the House of Lords, it is submitted wrongly, refused to extend the category of 'special circumstances' to include organisations offering accommodation to the homeless. In this connection, Lord Templeman in *Street* instanced the situation where the occupier is an 'object of charity' as displacing the intention to create a tenancy. This would have provided a 'neat solution' (see Cowan, D., [1993] Conv 157, at 160) to the problem of admitting evidence of background features (characterised also as a category of exceptional circumstances relying on the intention of the parties not wishing to enter into legal relationships) in determining the issue of exclusive possession.

The effect of the House of Lords ruling is that a grantor may create a tenancy despite having no proprietary interest in the land and irrespective of any factors giving rise to a tenancy by estoppel. This is a startling proposition, not least because it assumes the existence of a lease which does not have any proprietary characteristics. The recent decision of Neuberger J in *PW & Co.* v *Milton Gate Investments Ltd* [2003] EWHC 1994 (Ch) is of particular interest in this context. Although no reference is made to the *Bruton* decision, it is apparent that the judgment reflects the traditional view of the lease as conferring a property right in land. In particular, it was emphasised that (1) the relationship of landlord and tenants depends on privity of estate and (2) the general principle of freedom of contract is limited inevitably in landlord and tenant law by the proprietary nature of a lease. This led his Lordship to conclude in *Milton Gate* that a subtenancy cannot subsist without a reversionary interest to support it. In other words, the person who grants the tenancy must have some greater interest in the land so that there is something which will revert back to him at the end of the tenancy. This traditional line of reasoning is, however, difficult to reconcile with the *Bruton* ruling which presupposes that the rights of the parties may be governed purely by contractual agreement. If Mr Bruton's tenancy did not give rise to a proprietary interest, the question is, what is it? If Mr Bruton's tenancy is purely contractual then surely the very essence of a tenancy, namely, exclusive possession, is lacking unless exclusive possession in this context may now mean exclusive possession as between grantor and grantee only. The conclusion must be that the House of Lords has unwittingly created an entirely new species of tenancy which is purely contractual in nature, personal to the contracting parties, and which cannot be assigned to or bind third parties. But the whole point of the lease/licence distinction is to draw a clear dividing line between personal and proprietary rights. It is now very difficult to distinguish between a contractual tenancy and a licence since both operate *in personam* and create no interest in land.

(b) The grant of exclusive possession remains the governing factor in determining whether or not an occupier is a tenant or a licensee: *Street* v *Mountford* [1985] AC 809. The labelling of the agreement (as either a tenancy or a licence) is not conclusive as the courts are more concerned with the reality (or substance) of the agreement rather than the parties' expressed intentions. A licence will be upheld, however, where the parties' intentions (as manifested by the agreement) clearly negate the right of exclusive possession and accord with the reality of the arrangement: *National Car Parks Ltd* v *Trinity Development Co. (Banbury) Ltd* [2001] 2 EGLR 43, affirmed on appeal: [2001] EWCA Civ 1686. The fact, therefore, that each of the three documents put forward by Acrecrest Estates Ltd are headed 'Licence Agreement' will not be conclusive since the court will be obliged to consider the substance of what has been agreed and not merely the form. In essence, the question is whether, as a matter of law, the three separate agreements will confer joint exclusive possession on Tom, Dick and Harriet, or merely a right to share the flat as licensees. The point was considered in the House of Lords decision in *AG Securities* v *Vaughan/Antoniades* v *Villiers* [1990] 1 AC 417, involving two separate appeals.

In *Vaughan*, four individual occupants each had a short-term licence agreement granting a right to use the flat in common with others with a like right and expressly negativing a right to exclusive possession of any part of the flat. The licence agreements began at different dates, were for different periods and varied to some extent in the rents charged. The four occupants had replaced earlier ones when vacancies occurred. On these facts, the House of Lords held that the agreements were *independent* of each other and did not confer a right to exclusive possession on any one occupant but merely a right to share the flat with others. Because the agreements had been made on different dates and with different terms and rents, they could not be construed as creating a joint tenancy (i.e., in the absence of the four unities for a joint tenancy).

In *Antoniades*, on the other hand, the occupants were a young man and his girlfriend who wanted to live in the flat as husband and wife. The couple had each signed an agreement which stated that it conferred a personal licence only and expressly negatived the grant of exclusive possession. The agreements were, in fact, modelled on those in the earlier case of *Somma* v *Hazelhurst* [1978] 1 WLR 1014. The House of Lords held that the two agreements were *interdependent* in that it was unreal to regard them as separate and independent licences. The couple had applied jointly to rent the flat and sought and enjoyed joint exclusive occupation of the whole flat. The result was, therefore, a joint tenancy protected by the Rent Act 1977. See also *Duke* v *Wynne* [1990] 1 WLR 766, where the Court of Appeal stressed that the labelling which parties agree to attach to their agreements is never conclusive.

Thus, where there is a steady turnover of occupants who move in at different times and pay different rents and stay for different periods, the agreements are likely to be classified as genuine and conferring 'licence' status only. (This, however, is subject to the argument that there may be a tenancy of an individual bedroom coupled with the right to share the communal parts of the flat, a point not canvassed in *Vaughan*.)

Alternatively, agreements which arise where the occupants seek accommodation together (as in the present case) and sign separate but identical agreements at the same time, paying the same rent and for the same period of time, would, it is submitted, almost certainly point to a sham and confer joint tenancy status on the occupants. One difficulty, however, may relate to the payment of rent. In *Mikeover Ltd* v *Brady* [1989] 3 All ER 618, the court held that the obligation to pay separate monthly sums, being several (as opposed to joint obligations) destroyed unity of interest in order to create a joint tenancy.

Subject to this point, the advice to Tom, Dick and Harriet is to sign the agreements on the basis that they will acquire a joint tenancy of the flat. The fact that they purport to agree to a sharing of the flat with each other will not affect their statutory protection (*Aslan* v *Murphy (No. 1)/Aslan* v *Murphy (No. 2)/Duke* v *Wynne* [1990] 1 WLR 766). In this case all three sharers will be treated as tenants. The position would be different, however, if one of the sharers had been named as tenant with the others merely contributing to the rent. Here, the natural inference would be that what was intended was a contractual flat-sharing arrangement under the tenancy of one of them only (*Monmouth Borough Council* v *Marlog* [1994] 44 EG 240).

Q Question 2

In November 2003, Mandy advertised on her local parish church noticeboard for a tenant for her vacant property at 16 Bumble Road, Bigglestown. John, having seen the advertisement, wrote to Mandy expressing an interest in the property.

In December 2003, Mandy met John and took him round to view the house. Mandy told him that the letting was his for £55 per week and that he could move in, in three months' time. John agreed to these terms.

After the expiration of the three months, John telephoned Mandy to inform her that he was ready to move into the property. Mandy replied, 'Sorry, I've changed my mind about the letting, and anyway I've sold the house with vacant possession to David for £85,000'.

Advise John as to his rights (if any) in relation to the property.

Commentary

This is a tricky question concerned with the formalities of a lease and the enforceability of an agreement for a lease against a third party. To score high marks, your answer should display a detailed knowledge of the relevant statutory provisions and case law.

You may find it useful to begin with a brief introduction identifying the legal issues and explaining the relevancy of the rules governing the formalities of leases. This will then pave the way for a more detailed analysis of the problem.

- John's tenancy not a legal lease because it does not take effect in possession — s. 54(2) does not apply

- Valid lease in equity if enforceable by a decree of specific performance: *Walsh* v *Lonsdale* (1882)

- Compliance with s. 2(5)(a) of the Law of Property (Miscellaneous Provisions) Act 1989 — requirement of writing not necessary in case of contracts for short leases made pursuant to s. 54(2) of the 1925 Act

- John's equitable lease binding on David if it has been duly registered — effect of non-registration is that David will take free of John's interest regardless of David's knowledge: *Midland Bank Trust Co. Ltd* v *Green* (1981)

☼ Suggested answer

This question is concerned with the law governing the formalities for the creation of leases. The Law of Property Act 1925, s. 52(1), states that 'all conveyances of land or of any interest therein are void for the purposes of conveying or creating a legal estate unless made by deed'. By virtue of s. 205(1)(ii) of the 1925 Act, a conveyance of land includes a legal lease. A lease may, however, be valid at law even though not created by deed. Section 54(2) of the 1925 Act provides an exception to s. 52(1) in that any lease which takes effect in possession for a term not exceeding three years at the best rent which can reasonably be obtained without taking a fine, is exempted from the requirement of a deed and will take effect as a legal lease.

A lease will normally arise where a landowner (the landlord) grants to another (the tenant) the right exclusively to possess land for a fixed or ascertainable period while himself retaining a reversionary estate (i.e., a freehold estate, or a leasehold estate of longer duration than that demised to the tenant).

Even though it is possible for a landlord to grant a tenant a lease in return for no consideration in the form of a rent or premium (see *Ashburn Anstalt* v *Arnold* [1989] Ch 1), the vast majority of leases are granted in return for the payment of a rental sum by the tenant. (The term 'rent' has been defined as 'a payment which a tenant is bound by his contract to make to his landlord for the use of the land', *per* Lord Denning MR in *CH Bailey* v *Memorial Enterprises Ltd* [1974] 1 WLR 728.) In so far as the tenant provides consideration for the use and occupation of the land, there necessarily arises a contract between landlord and tenant. Thus, a void lease at law (i.e., not complying with the legal formality of a deed under s. 52(1)) may still take effect as a contract for a lease which equity may enforce by means of a decree of specific performance.

It can be assumed that both Mandy and John intended to enter into landlord and tenant relations and create a weekly periodic tenancy in favour of John at an agreed rental of £55 per week. A weekly tenancy will be presumed from the fact that the agreed rental is referable to a weekly period (*Adler* v *Blackman* [1953] 1 QB 146). At first glance, it may appear that John's tenancy takes effect as a legal lease under the exception contained in s. 54(2). In this connection, it has been held that periodic tenancies (e.g., weekly, monthly, yearly etc.) fall within the s. 54(2) exemption as being for less than three years (*Re Knight, Re ex parte Voisey* (1882) 21 Ch D 442). The difficulty, however, in the present case is that John's tenancy does not 'take effect in possession', in so far as it was agreed that John would not move in immediately but in three months' time. Accordingly, the tenancy does not fall within the s. 54(2) concession and is void at law in the absence of a deed.

Does John have an equitable lease (i.e., recognised in equity)? An equitable lease, from the perspective of the common law, is a mere contract for an estate in land, but in equity it is treated in many ways as being 'as good as a lease' (see *Walsh* v *Lonsdale* (1882) 21 Ch D 9). This is because a contract for a lease may be enforceable in equity by a decree of specific performance. To be so enforceable, however, the contract must comply with the requisite legal formalities as to writing.

A contract for the sale or other disposition of an interest in land (e.g., a contract to enter into a lease) must either be reduced to a written document, all its terms contained therein, and signed by both parties, or merely be evidenced in writing and signed by the person to be charged. If the contract was made before 27 September 1989, the latter rule applies by virtue of the Law of Property Act 1925, s. 40. If, on the other hand, the contract is made on or after this date, the former rule applies by virtue of the Law of Property (Miscellaneous Provisions) Act 1989, s. 2. (Section 40 also permits an oral contract to be enforced by virtue of the doctrine of part performance: see, e.g., *Steadman* v *Steadman* [1976] AC 536.)

The oral agreement in the present case was made in December 2003, and hence the provisions of s. 2 of the 1989 Act will apply. The absence of any signed written instrument containing all the terms of the proposed tenancy suggests that the agreement is void for want of formality, but reference should be made to s. 2(5)(a) of the 1989 Act which provides that the requirement of a written instrument is obviated in the case of contracts for short leases made pursuant to s. 54(2) of the 1925 Act.

Assuming, therefore, that John's oral agreement is valid despite the lack of writing, the question arises as to whether it is enforceable against David as an assignee of the reversion. It is unclear whether the house forms registered or unregistered land. If the house is registered, David, as assignee, will only be bound by John's equitable lease if John had registered the same against Mandy's reversionary title prior to the sale of the house by means of a notice on the register. (There is no suggestion that John moved into occupation of the house prior to the completion of the sale to David so as to render his interest an 'unregistered interest which overrides' under the Land Registration Act 2002, Schedule 3, para. 2). If, on the other hand, the house is unregistered, John's agreement for a lease, being an 'estate contract', was registrable as a Class C(iv) land charge under the Land Charges Act 1972. The effect of non-registration of the contract as against Mandy's title, prior to the sale of the freehold to David, will be that David (as a purchaser) will take the freehold estate free of John's interest, irrespective of whether he (David) actually knew of the equitable lease or not (*Midland Bank Trust Co. Ltd* v *Green* [1981] AC 513).

Q Question 3

In 2003, Arnold entered into partnership with his brother, Jake, for the purpose of carrying out public relations work. The partnership was called 'Communicate Associates'. In the same year, Communicate Associates purchased the freehold title to some office space.

In 2004, Arnold and Jake fell into disagreement and decided that, while they would formally carry on the partnership from the office premises for fiscal reasons, the day to day running of the business would be Arnold's responsibility. To make full use of the office premises, however, it was agreed that the partnership would grant Jake a lease of half of the office space, from which Jake would run another business in his own right. Both parties agreed and executed a lease (in 2004) which contained the following wording:

> . . . that the Lessee shall from this day be entitled to exclusively possess the premises demised herein for five years, or in any event until such time as the Communicate Associates partnership . . . shall cease to exist . . . at a rental of £16,000 per year . . . payable on the unusual quarter days.

Since taking up possession, Jake has been paying Communicate Associates £1,000 per month rental in advance, which Arnold has paid into the business account of Communicate Associates.

Jake is keen to demonstrate that the 2004 lease is void and that there exists instead a periodic monthly tenancy because, by so doing, he would be able to escape liability to pay the higher rent under the lease.

Advise Jake.

Commentary

This question is concerned with the doctrine of certainty of term (*Prudential Assurance Co. Ltd v London Residuary Body* [1992] 3 WLR 279) and the law relating to the capacity of a party to grant a lease of land to himself (*Rye v Rye* [1962] AC 496 and the Law of Property Act 1925, s. 72). The facts do not readily bring these issues to mind and so, if you have not carefully revised the case law and statutory provisions, the question may prove somewhat baffling!

- Grant of lease to Jake alone permissible under s. 72(4) of the Law of Property Act 1925: *Rye* v *Rye* (1962) does not apply

- But lease void for uncertainty of term: *Prudential Assurance Co. Ltd* v *London Residuary Body* (1992)

- Effect of void lease is that Jake holds under less onerous monthly periodic tenancy arising by implication of law from payment and acceptance of monthly rent: *Alder* v *Blackman* (1946)

- Such periodic tenancy valid at law despite absence of deed or writing: s. 54(2) of the Law of Property Act 1925

⚡ Suggested answer

In order to succeed in his contention, Jake must establish that the 2004 lease is void and that, as a matter of law, he holds the premises under a periodic (monthly) tenancy at the lower rent of £1,000 per month.

It is trite law that there must exist two separate parties to a lease (i.e., it is not possible for a person to grant a lease of land to himself). Although the Law of Property Act 1925, s. 72(3) expressly states that 'a person may convey land to or vest land in himself' (for this purpose, a legal lease is a 'conveyance' of land within the meaning of s. 205(1) of the 1925 Act), the subsection has been judicially interpreted as not having this effect (*Rye v Rye* [1962] AC 496). In this case, Lord Denning held that it was impossible for a person to grant a lease to himself, invoking the maxim *nemo potest esse tenens et dominus* (a person cannot be, at the same time, both landlord and tenant of the same premises). In *Rye*, the appellant and his brother acquired a freehold property which they co-owned in equity as tenants in common. The brothers were in partnership as solicitors and agreed that the firm should be run from the premises they had purchased. As a firm, they agreed to pay themselves an annual rent of £500. The House of Lords held that no lease was ever created because the same parties existed on either side of the landlord and tenant relationship. However, Lord Denning did expressly confirm that two lessors could properly grant a lease to one of themselves because, in such an arrangement, there would exist different individuals on either side of the lease. Such an arrangement would be a conveyance pursuant to s. 72(4) of the 1925 Act and the covenants contained in the agreement would be enforceable under s. 82(1) of the 1925 Act just as if the lessee had covenanted with the lessors alone.

The decision in *Rye* was applied in *Ingram* v *Inland Revenue Commissioners* [1997] 4 All ER 395, where the Court of Appeal held that the purported grant of a lease by a nominee to his principal was of no effect since a person could not contract with himself.

In the present case, Jake and Arnold have granted a lease to Jake alone. This is permissible under s. 72(4) of the 1925 Act and the lease cannot, therefore, be attacked on this ground.

Crucial to the existence of a valid lease is the requirement that the term of the lease is for a certain or an ascertainable period. A classic illustration of this doctrine is to be found in the case of *Lace* v *Chantler* [1944] KB 368, where a tenancy 'for the duration of the war' was held invalid as being for an uncertain term. It is interesting to observe that there was, in fact, an exchange of a weekly sum in that case and, consequently, the court was able to infer the existence of a weekly periodic tenancy independently of the void lease at law. (The case, in fact, prompted the enactment of the Validation of War Time Leases Act 1944, which rendered such leases valid as leases for 10-year terms determinable by a month's notice on either side given after the end of hostilities as fixed by Order in Council.) The current leading authority is *Prudential Assurance Co. Ltd* v *London Residuary Body* [1992] 3 WLR 279, in which the House of Lords, overruling *Re Midland Railways Co.'s Agreement* [1971] Ch 725, re-affirmed that the doctrine applies to both fixed and periodic tenancies.

If the 2004 lease is void for uncertainty of term, Jake will be in a position to claim that there exists (between himself and the partnership) a less onerous monthly periodic tenancy arising by implication of law from the payment and acceptance of a monthly rent. (See *Adler* v *Blackman* [1946] 1 QB 146, where the landlord granted a one-year term at a rent of £2 per week. On the expiry of the fixed term the tenant held over, continuing to pay £2 a week. It was held that the tenant was a weekly tenant.)

Such a periodic tenancy will be valid at law (despite the absence of a deed or writing) because it will fall within the Law of Property Act 1925, s. 54(2), which applies to leases taking effect in possession for a term of less than three years (this includes periodic tenancies: *Re Knight, Re ex parte Voisey* (1882) 21 Ch D 442) at the best rent obtainable.

Is, however, the 2004 lease void for uncertainty of term? The doctrine of certainty of term dictates that the maximum period for which a lease is to run must be calculable with certainty. In the *Prudential* case (see above) the landlords demised the land until such time as it was required by the landlords for the purposes of widening the highway. The House of Lords held that no estate in land had been granted because the purported lease was uncertain as to duration. However, in view of the tenant's entry into possession of the land and payment of a yearly rent, the court was able to infer the creation of a yearly tenancy on such terms as were not inconsistent with the void lease at law. (See also, *Doe d Warner* v *Browne* (1908) 8 East 165 and *Doe d Rigge* v *Bell* (1793) 5 Durn & E 471.)

In the present case, the 2004 lease provides that Jake should be entitled to exclusive possession of the premises 'for five years, or in any event until such time as the Communicate Associates partnership . . . shall cease to exist'. If the term granted was simply for five years, the lease would, undoubtedly, be certain as to its duration as from the outset and, hence, valid. However, the additional words 'or in any event until such time as the . . . partnership shall cease', render the lease uncertain as to its maximum duration since it is unknown when the partnership (and hence the lease) will end. The lease is, therefore, void for uncertainty. (If the lease was expressed in terms of a five-year term, subject to a power of the landlord to determine earlier upon the partnership ceasing during the term, this would be valid because from its outset the maximum duration of the lease would be certain (i.e., a determinable certain term of five years).

Assuming, therefore, that the monthly tenancy governs the relationship between Jake and the partnership, Jake is under no obligation to pay the higher rent under the void lease since this would be inconsistent with the terms of the periodic tenancy.

Q Question 4

To what extent does the doctrine of certainty of term apply to periodic tenancies? What is the 'doctrine of repugnancy' in this context? (Illustrate your answer by reference to the decided cases.)

Commentary

The doctrine of certainty in relation to periodic tenancies was discussed by the House of Lords in *Prudential Assurance Co. Ltd* v *London Residuary Body* [1992] 3 WLR 279. For a good summary of the law of certainty of term in the context of the *Prudential* case, see Biles, M., 'One Thing is Certain and the Rest is Lies' (1994) NLJ, 4 February, 156.

- Application of certainty of term doctrine to periodic tenancies — decision in *Re Midland Railway* (1971) overruled in *Prudential Assurance* (1992)

- Periodic tenancy saved from uncertainty because each party has power by notice to quit to determine at the end of any period of the tenancy

- Doctrine of repugnancy prohibits a total fetter on either party's right to serve notice to quit: *Centaploy Ltd* v *Matlodge Ltd* (1974) and *Cheshire Lines Committee* v *Lewis & Co* (1880)

- Partial fetters, however, not considered to be repugnant: *Re Midland Railway* (1971). Ultimately, it is a matter of construing the lease: *Breams Property Investment Co. Ltd* v *Stroulger* (1948)

:Q̇: Suggested answer

The common law has always required that, for a lease to be valid, its maximum duration must be ascertained, or ascertainable, at the time when it comes into effect. The famous case on this point is *Lace* v *Chantler* [1944] KB 368, where the Court of Appeal ruled that a lease which had been granted 'for the duration of the war' was void for uncertainty.

The doctrine appears to come unstuck when applied to periodic tenancies where, in reality, the maximum duration is not clear from the outset and simply depends on when, or whether, one of the parties serves a notice to quit. An illusion of certainty can be achieved, however, by arguing that the maximum term is ascertainable in that its duration can be fixed by an act of one of the parties. The difficulty with this approach is that the right of one (or both) of the parties to serve notice may be contractually tied to an event which may or may not happen. In *Re Midland Railway Co.'s Agreement* [1971] Ch 725, the Court of Appeal recognised this difficulty and concluded that the requirement of certainty of term had no direct relevance to periodic tenancies.

This view, however, was exploded by the House of Lords in *Prudential Assurance Co. Ltd* v *London Residuary Body* [1992] 3 WLR 279. In this case, the House of Lords, overruling the *Re Midland Railway* case on this point, held that it was a requirement of *all* leases and tenancy agreements that the term created was of certain duration. Lord Templeman, who gave the leading speech, reasoned that a periodic tenancy is saved from being uncertain because each party has power by notice to determine at the end of any period of the tenancy. The relevant term continues until determined as if both parties made a new agreement at the end of each period for a new term for the next ensuing period. It is interesting to note, however, that Lord Browne-Wilkinson observed that no satisfactory rationale for the rule existed and expressed the hope that the Law Commission would look at the subject afresh to see whether there was, in fact, any good reason for maintaining the rule which operates to defeat in many cases the contractually agreed arrangements between the parties. In the *Prudential* case itself, the parties had, in fact, intended to create a lease on terms that it should continue until the subject land was required by the landlord for the purposes of the widening of a highway. In the result, this purported lease was held void for uncertainty and the land was deemed to be held on a yearly tenancy created by virtue of the tenant's possession and payment of a yearly rent. Moreover, since the term preventing the landlord from determining the tenancy until the land was required for road widening purposes was inconsistent with the right of either party under a yearly tenancy to terminate it on notice, it was considered repugnant to such periodic tenancy and of no effect.

The doctrine of repugnancy is closely related to the rule regarding certainty of term. The basic proposition is that a clause totally precluding a party from determining a periodic tenancy is repugnant to the nature of such a tenancy and void. A leading case is *Centaploy Ltd* v *Matlodge Ltd* [1974] Ch 1, where an agreement to let a garage contained the following words: 'Received the sum of £12, being one week's rent . . . and to continue until determined by the lessee . . .' Whitford J held that the document provided for a weekly tenancy and, although the term making the tenancy determinable only by the lessee did not make the periodic tenancy thus created void for uncertainty, nevertheless, a term whereby a landlord would never have the right to terminate a periodic tenancy was repugnant to the nature of such a tenancy and void. The practical significance of this finding was that, despite the terms of the agreement, the landlord was free to serve a notice to quit on the tenant bringing the weekly tenancy to an end.

A partial fetter, however, on the right to serve a notice to quit will not be considered as repugnant to the grant of a periodic tenancy. Thus, in *Re Midland Railway Co.'s Agreement* (above), it was suggested by Russell LJ (at p. 733) that a curb for 10, 20 or 50 years should not be rejected as repugnant to the concept of a periodic tenancy.

In *Cheshire Lines Committee* v *Lewis & Co.* (1880) 50 LJ QB 121, the claimants, a railway company, let premises to the defendants on a weekly tenancy to be determined by a week's notice on either side. The parties entered into a collateral agreement that the tenant could occupy the premises 'until the railway company require to pull them down'. The Court of Appeal held that this collateral agreement was void as being repugnant to a periodic tenancy. The case may be contrasted with *Breams Property Investment Co. Ltd* v *Stroulger* [1948] 2 KB 1, where various agreements for quarterly tenancies contained a clause to the effect that the landlords would not, during the period of three years from the beginning of the tenancies, serve notice to quit on the tenants except in the event of the landlords requiring the premises for their own occupation and use. The Court of Appeal held that, as the clause merely attached a condition to the quarterly right to give notice (by suspending it during the first three years of the tenancies except in the event of the landlords requiring possession for their own use), it was not repugnant to the nature of a quarterly tenancy. In effect, the doctrine of repugnancy was side-stepped by construing the lease in a particular way.

Q Question 5

In January 2003, Leisure Car Parks Ltd (Leisure) entered into a written agreement with Goodtown Developments Co. Ltd (Goodtown) to operate a car park adjacent to a shopping precinct in Banbury, Oxfordshire. The agreement was headed 'Licence Agreement' and, by its terms, Leisure agreed to pay to Goodtown, in respect of this right, a percentage of its net profits earned from the business. Clause 2 thereof provided that the agreement would continue in force from year to year until determined by either party upon two months' written notice.

Clause 4 provided: 'This licence is not intended by either party to confer upon the licensee any right or interest in the nature of a tenancy and gives no proprietary right or interest to the licensee in the licensed premises.'

Clause 7 provided: 'The licensee shall not to impede in any way the exercise of any of the licensor's rights of possession and control in respect of the licensed premises.'

Clause 8 provided: 'The licensee shall indemnify the licensor against occupier's liability and shall contribute to the cost of security in respect of the licensed premises provided by the licensor.'

Earlier this year, Goodtown gave Lesiure two months' notice in writing terminating the agreement. Leisure contends that the notice is ineffective because, upon its true construction, the agreement created a tenancy protected by Pt II of the Landlord and Tenant Act 1954. Advise Leisure.

Commentary

This is a relatively straightforward question as to whether the agreement, upon its true construction, constitutes a tenancy or a licence. It will require you to examine the House of Lords' ruling in *Street* v *Mountford* [1985] AC 809, as well as subsequent case law, in particular, *Shell-Mex & BP Ltd* v *Manchester Garages Ltd* [1971] 1 WLR 612, *Esso Petroleum Co. Ltd* v *Fumegrange Ltd* [1994] 2 EGLR 90 and, most recently, *National Car Parks Ltd* v *Trinity Development Co. (Banbury) Ltd* [2001] 2 EGLR 43 (affirmed on appeal: (2001) EWCA Civ 1686). The key to answering this question well is to focus not only on the actual terms of the agreement, but also on what the agreement does not say!

- Consider the test of exclusive possession put forward in *Street* v *Mountford* (1985). Does the agreement, upon its true construction, confer exclusive possession?

- The agreement does not reserve any right of entry, nor contain any covenant for quiet enjoyment or repair. Significantly also, there is no power of re-entry (forfeiture) upon breach by the grantee, normally to be found in a tenancy: *Shell-Mex & BP Ltd* v *Manchester Garages Ltd* (1971)

- Clause 7 not a reservation of rights in favour of grantor but consistent with Goodtown retaining possession and control of the property: *Esso Petroleum Co. Ltd* v *Fumegrange Ltd* (1994). Consider the factual matrix

- Clauses 4 and 8 consistent with a licence agreement. Express statements of intention relevant if consistent with the agreement as a whole: *National Car Parks Ltd* v *Trinity Development Co. (Banbury) Ltd* (2001)

�💡 Suggested answer

There is no doubt that the agreement is for a periodic term and at a rent. (Although the word 'rent' is not used in the agreement, the provision for the payment of a percentage of the net profits in consideration of operating the car park will be treated as rent.) The central issue, therefore is whether, upon its true construction, the agreement grants Leisure exclusive possession of the car park — if it does, it will qualify as a tenancy. If not, it will rank merely as a licence. Ultimately, this is a question of law: *Street* v *Mountford* [1985] AC 809.

Although clause 4 indicates the intention of the parties not to create a tenancy, this is by no means conclusive. What must be considered is the *legal* effect of the agreement and not what the parties expressed themselves as intending to make. The correct approach, therefore, is to consider the substance rather than the form of the document so that the actual labels put upon the agreement will not be determinative. The fact, therefore, that the agreement is headed a licence agreement and that the parties are referred to as licensor and licensee will not (by themselves) materially assist in determining the true nature of the parties' contract. Instead, the agreement as a whole must be looked at in order to see what indications can be found pointing towards either a tenancy or licence.

Crucial to this approach is the requirement that a tenancy must confer exclusive possession on the occupier. Exclusive possession has been defined as the ability on the part of the tenant to exclude all persons, including the landlord, from the demised premises: *Essex Plan Ltd* v *Broadminister* [1988] 2 EGLR 73. In this connection, I note that the agreement does not contain any reservation of rights of entry onto the car park in favour of the grantor, Goodtown. This is significant in so far as the reservation of such rights is usually indicative of a tenancy — such rights of entry would be unnecessary if the grantor had an unrestricted right of access apart from the agreement: *Addiscombe Garden Estates Ltd* v *Crabbe* [1958] 1 QB 513. Clause 7 of the agreement, in my view, simply reinforces the tenor of the agreement (in particular, clause 4) that Goodtown has retained rights of possession and control over the property in question which the grantee is obliged not to impede. This clearly points to the agreement being a licence since the document is consistently framed so as not to give Leisure exclusive possession.

It is also significant that the agreement does not contain any term for quiet enjoyment of the premises enjoyed by the grantee, Leisure. This too is consistent with the agreement being a licence since a covenant for quiet enjoyment presupposes that the occupier has exclusive possession of the property. Nor, for that matter, is there any provision requiring Leisure to repair and maintain the property consistently with a tenancy: *Delneed* v *Chin* [1987] 1 EGLR 75. Perhaps, most importantly of all, there is no mention in the agreement of a right of re-entry upon Leisure's breach of any of the terms of the agreement. Here again, a right of re-entry (or forfeiture) is consistent with a tenancy and wholly inappropriate in the context of a genuine licence: *Shell-Mex & BP Ltd* v *Manchester Garages Ltd* [1971] 1 WLR 612, *per* Buckley LJ at 618.

Clause 7 of the agreement is, in my view, indicative of the degree of control that Goodtown has effectively retained over the premises despite the conferment of the right to operate the car park in favour of Leisure. Although it is apparent that Leisure is to manage and administer the car park during the currency of the agreement, it is also clear that, in all other respects, Goodtown has retained rights of possession and control over the site. In *Esso Petroleum Co. Ltd* v *Fumegrange Ltd* [1994] 2 EGLR 90, for example, involving the occupation of two service stations, the licence agreement referred to the owner's 'right of possession and control of the service station' and required the occupier not to impede in any way the exercise of that right. These rights were held to be quite inconsistent with an exclusive right to possession of the stations. In particular, the degree of physical control by the owner was very significant. The owner could make alterations to the premises, install a car wash (as was in fact done at one of the stations) and make changes to the layout of the occupier's shop. These rights and powers of the owner were looked at together and cumulatively and were wholly inconsistent with the grant of a tenancy. Both the terms of the agreement in that case and the surrounding factual matrix pointed to that conclusion. (See also, *McCarthy* v *Bence* [1990] 1 EGLR 1, where the owner took a 'keen and positive interest' in the land occupied by the licensee.)

Ultimately, therefore, the question is whether Leisure has been granted a right to keep out Goodtown. It is significant that no language is used in the agreement that assumes Leisure's right of exclusive possession. In fact, the document does not in form grant Leisure any rights at all. It simply imposes obligations, including an obligation to operate the car park and to account for a percentage of the net profit. Most significantly, however, as mentioned earlier, it includes an obligation on Leisure not to impede Goodtown's right to possession and control of the premises. Interestingly, in a case involving a similarly worded agreement, both the judge at first instance and the Court of Appeal held that the absence of any conferment of exclusive possession was fatal to the agreement being treated as a tenancy: *National Car Parks Ltd* v *Trinity Develoment Co. (Banbury) Ltd* [2001] 2 EGLR 43: affirmed on appeal at [2001] EWCA Civ 1686. In that case also the agreement expressly stated that it was not intended to confer any rights in the nature of a tenancy and that the occupier would not impede the owner's right to possession and control of the property. The court found that this indicated that the grantor had retained possession of the premises as opposed to granting exclusive possession with retained rights of access. This was despite the fact that the occupier in that case was obliged under the agreement to provide maintenance, insurance and security for the premises, which were all factors not inconsistent with a tenancy.

Turning to clause 4 and 8 of the agreement, these are clearly consistent with the view that Leisure has no right to exclusive possession. On this point, the Court of Appeal in the *National Car Parks* case held that *Street* v *Mountford* had not ruled out the possibility of examining clauses that expressly stated that the agreement was a licence. Such statements were relevant if they reflected what was in the minds of the parties when the agreement was made. Clauses 4 and 8 do not, therefore, fall to be ignored if they are consistent with the parties' agreement as a whole.

Finally, reference may be made to *Dresden Estates Ltd* v *Collinson* [1987] 1 EGLR 45, where the Court of Appeal, applying the *Addiscombe* decision, concluded that the inclusion of a term stating that exclusive possession was not granted, together with the right to move the occupier to other premises, were strong indications pointing towards a licence. In that case, unlike here, there were also a number of provisions normally found in tenancies (in particular, the grant of a limited right of way for the owners to enter for the purpose of carrying out work) which pointed to a tenancy. The task of the court was, therefore, made more difficult in view of the fact that there was a conflict in the agreement between provisions suggesting a tenancy and those pointing to a licence. The Court of Appeal, however, looking at the agreement as a whole, concluded that the indications were in favour of a licence. In particular, the provision by which the occupier could be required to move to other premises was considered wholly inconsistent with a right to exclusive possession.

In the instant case, my view is that all the provisions of the agreement point clearly in favour of a genuine licence so that, regrettably, Leisure has no protection under the 1954 Act as a business tenant.

Further reading

Bright, S., 'Exclusive Possession, True Agreement and Tenancy by Estoppel' (1998) 114 LQR 345.

Bright, S., 'Leases, Exclusive Possession and Estates' (2000) 116 LQR 7.

Haley, M., 'Licences of Business Premises: Principle and Practicality' [2001] 65 Conv 348.

Harwood, M., 'Leases: Are They Still Not Really Real?' [2000] LS 503.

Morgan, J., 'Whether a Licence Agreement is a Lease: The Irrelevance of the Grantor's Lack of Title' [1999] 63 Conv 517.

Morgan, J., 'Exclusive Possession and the Tenancy by Estoppel: "A Familiar Problem in an Unusual Setting" [1999] 63 Conv 493.

Pawlowski, M., 'Contractual Intention and the Nature of Leases' (2004) 120 LQR 222.

Pawlowski, M. and Greer, S., 'Leases, Licences and Contractual Tenancies' (2000) 9(1) Nott LJ 85.

Pawlowski, M., and Brown J., 'Bruton: A New Species of Tenancy?' (2000) 4 L & T Rev 119.

Richards, E., 'Tenancy Tests' (2001) SJ 1088.

Wilkinson, H.W., 'The Lease-licence Distinction Again?' (2001) NLJ 1489.

Types of leases and tenancies

Introduction

Leases (or tenancies) are categorised as being either specific (fixed term) or periodic. With fixed term tenancies, the duration of the tenancy is fixed for a definite period of time starting from the commencement date of the term. Periodic tenancies, on the other hand, simply continue from period to period until determined at the end of a given period by a notice to quit served by either party on the other. Periodic tenancies can be weekly, monthly, quarterly or yearly. It is fundamental, however, to the operation of any periodic tenancy that either party has the ability to serve a notice to quit terminating the tenancy. As we have seen, any provision which completely fetters this right is void (see, Question 4, in the preceding chapter). Fixed term tenancies may also take a number of different forms:

- Tenancy determinable with a life. By virtue of s. 149(6) of the Law of Property Act 1925, such a lease is converted into one for a fixed term of 90 years. In *Skipton Building Society* v *Clayton* (1993) 66 P & CR 223, it was held that the occupiers of a flat who, in return for some money, had been granted a licence to occupy the flat rent-free for the rest of their lives had, in reality, been given a lease and not a licence and that the lease was caught by s. 149(6) and duly converted into a 90-year term on the basis that the words 'at a rent or in consideration of a fine' in the subsection included the payment of a premium, which was held to have been paid on the facts.

- Concurrent lease (or lease of the reversion). This arises where the landlord grants a lease to T1 and subsequently grants a lease to T2 of the same premises for a term to commence before the expiry of the lease in favour of T1. So long as the leases are concurrent, the disposition in favour of T2 operates as a part assignment of the landlord's reversion entitling T2 to the rent reserved in T1's lease and the benefit of the covenants given by T1. If T1's lease is prematurely determined before T2's lease has expired, T2 will be entitled to possession of the premises. However, forfeiture (see, **Chapter 9**) by the landlord of T2's lease cannot affect T1, for although T1's lease is akin to a subtenancy, it is not derived out of T2's lease: see, Question 3(a).

- Perpetually renewable lease. If a lease contains an option to renew in favour of the tenant under which the new lease is to include the option to renew, a perpetually renewable lease will exist and, in accordance with Schedule 15 to the Law of Property Act 1922, will be converted into a 2,000 year term determinable by the tenant by 10 days' notice expiring on any date upon which the original lease would have expired if it had not been renewed: *Caerphilly Concrete Products Ltd* v *Owen* [1972] 1 WLR 372.

Apart from fixed and periodic tenancies, there are also a number of other types of tenancy. These include tenancies at will and tenancies at sufferance: see, Question 3(c). With the introduction of the purely personal tenancy by the House of Lords in *Bruton* v *London & Quadrant Housing Trust* [2000] 1 AC 406, (see **Chapter 2**), the dividing line between leases and licences has become even more difficult to draw, particularly when comparisons are made with other forms of occupational interests in leasehold law. The tenancy at will, for example, lies somewhere between the tenancy (in the orthodox sense) and a mere licence to occupy. Like a tenancy, it confers on the occupier exclusive possession albeit that a purely personal relationship is created between the parties and, as with a contractual licence, no estate in land arises so that the tenancy is incapable of assignment or sub-letting. Similarly, the tenancy at sufferance creates no 'tenancy' in any strict legal sense although the relationship does entitle the landlord to demand rent for use and occupation. In reality, there is little to distinguish between these various types of occupation and this (in turn) has prompted the question whether the time has now come to abandon fine distinctions in favour of a more rational scheme of occupational rights in leasehold law: see, Question 1.

Tenancies by estoppel have been the subject of several important cases in the last few years. They represent somewhat of an anomaly in landlord and tenant law in so far as they involve the recognition of a leasehold relationship in circumstances where the landlord has no (or an imperfect) title to the property concerned. The tenancy by estoppel falls to be distinguished from an 'estoppel-based tenancy' which arises in a quite different context: see Question 2.

Q Question 1

'In truth, there is little to distinguish the contractual licence from a personal (*Bruton*) tenancy or, indeed, a tenancy at will or sufferance. Given the close similarities between these various interests, there is considerable scope for abandoning fine distinctions in favour of a more rational structure involving the grant of either personal or proprietary occupational rights in land'.

Discuss this statement.

Commentary

This is a difficult question for the uninitiated, not least because you are asked to put forward an alternative solution to the current myriad of occupational rights affecting leasehold law. The temptation is to simply outline each type of occupational right in isolation without making any meaningful comparisons. Remember, the examiner's thesis is that a 'more rational structure' is needed, so explain why this might be so and how this could be achieved. There is no doubt that the question requires a good understanding of the subject, particularly the nature of a *Bruton*-type tenancy and its inter-relationship with contractual licences. Begin with *Bruton* and the distinction between proprietary and non-proprietary tenancies. Then consider how the tenancy at will and tenancy at sufferance fit into the picture. Finally, identify some common threads with a view to showing how a simplified structure would work. There is no doubt that the weaker student will struggle with this question, but for those of you who have prepared well, it is an opportunity to show the examiner your critical awareness of the current law.

- Exclusive possession governing test for determining whether an occupational right constitutes a tenancy — *Street* v *Mountford* (1985)

- *Bruton* hybrid tenancy creating a type of quasi-estate conferring only a limited form of exclusive possession between grantor and grantee

- Similarities between tenancy at will and contractual licence and the diminishing significance of the tenancy at will in both the residential and commercial rented sector

- Tenancy at sufferance also an anomalous hybrid resembling contractual licence and tenancy at will

- A simplified structure based on personal and proprietary occupational rights; the former conferring exclusive occupation (akin to a licence) and the latter giving rise to exclusive possession with all the other hallmarks of a leasehold estate.

:Q: Suggested answer

It was, of course, Lord Templeman in *Street* v *Mountford* [1985] AC 809 who enunciated the three hallmarks of a tenancy, namely, (1) exclusive possession (2) for a fixed or periodic term and (3) at a rent. In reality, however, it is the requirement of exclusive possession which is the decisive factor in determining whether an occupier is a tenant unless there are special circumstances (identified in *Street*) which negate the existence of a tenancy. The reservation of a rent was held to be not strictly necessary in *Ashburn Anstalt* v *Arnold* [1989] Ch 1 and it is apparent that the existence of a term is not conclusive given that a contractual licence will normally confer on the occupier the right to occupy land for a stated period.

What does the conferment of a legal right to exclusive possession actually mean? Most commentators agree that it is the right to exclude the world (including the landlord) which distinguishes the right of exclusive *possession* from the right of exclusive *occupation*. In other words, the vital difference is that in acquiring exclusive possession, the occupier is deemed to acquire dominion over the land (i.e., a monopoly of control), which gives him the authority to exercise the rights of an owner of the land consistent with the acquisition of a legal estate. In *Bruton*, however, the House of Lords alluded to the existence of a hybrid tenancy which does not confer exclusive possession against the whole world but only against the grantor. The problem here is that, if a *Bruton*-type tenancy is not 'good against all the world', there seems little to distinguish it from a contractual licence which also confers purely personal rights as between the parties. In fact, both operate *in personam* and create no proprietary interest in land. Neither bind third parties. The former gives the tenant exclusive possession but only as against the grantor, whilst the latter confers no exclusive possession but merely exclusive occupation. What is evident is that the dividing line between personal and proprietary rights has become difficult to draw since leases are no longer necessarily proprietary and may be purely personal.

As with other tenancies, tenancies at will often arise by contract, but even though there is the conferment of exclusive possession, no 'estate' in land is created as the tenancy is not, in any sense, a 'term of years' within the meaning of s. 205(1)(xxvii) of the Law of Property Act 1925. Such a tenancy can be determined by the landlord making an unequivocal demand for possession, usually in writing or by the commencement of proceedings for possession. However, except for exclusive possession, there are a number of striking similarities between tenancies at will and contractual licences. As with a licence, a tenancy at will creates a purely personal relationship between the parties. In neither case is an estate in land created, although a tenant at will may have tenure in the sense that he holds the land from the landlord. Neither a licensee nor a tenant at will can assign or sublet to a third party. In both cases, the occupier is not classified as a trespasser because he occupies with the consent of the owner. In view of these similarities, it has been suggested judicially that, in reality, the tenant at will is simply a person with a licence to occupy: *Irish Shell and BP Ltd* v *John Costello Ltd* [1984] IR 511, at 523, per McCarthy J. Although the fundamental difference between the two forms of occupancy is that a contractual licence gives rise to a mere right of occupation (as opposed to exclusive possession), the practical significance of this distinction is now much diminished given that a contractual licensee has been held to be entitled to recover possession against a trespasser: *Manchester Airport plc* v *Dutton* [2000] QB 133. Moreover, its role within the residential sector has declined with the growing importance of the licence and assured shorthold regime as alternative (and more popular) methods of landholding. Coupled with this is the fact that the courts are now much less inclined to infer a residential tenancy at will from the parties' intentions: *Sopwith* v *Stuchbury* (1985) 17 HLR 50 and *Sharp* v *McArthur and Sharp* (1987) 19 HLR 364.

Equally, in the commercial context, with the growing trend towards contracting out of Pt II of the Landlord and Tenant Act 1954 (made even easier now under the Regulatory Reform (Business Tenancies) (England and Wales) Order 2003), which came into force on 1 June 2004), the parties have less desire to use the mechanism of the tenancy at will so as to avoid business security, particularly as there may be a real risk that the tenancy will be struck down as a sham. It is apparent, therefore, that the function and purpose of the tenancy at will (both in the residential and commercial context) has become increasingly limited to providing the occupier with a form of intermediate status pending the grant of a more enduring interest. Even here, however, where the occupier goes into possession pending negotiations for a lease or where he holds over after the expiry of an existing lease, the contractual licence may be an equally 'apt legal mechanism' (see *Heslop* v *Burns* [1974] 1 WLR 1241, 1253, per Scarman LJ) to protect the occupier during the period of transition.

A tenancy at sufferance denotes the relationship of owner and occupier where the tenant holds over on the expiry of his lease and the landlord has neither consented nor expressed objection. The absence of the landlord's consent negatives any relationship of tenure and, therefore, the so-called 'tenant' has no tenancy in any true sense. For this reason, a tenant at sufferance cannot create any form of tenancy out of his own interest nor, it seems, maintain an action for trespass. Moreover, he is under no obligation to pay rent, but the landlord may demand money for use and occupation. It is apparent, therefore, that a tenancy at sufferance is another anomalous hybrid having some of the hallmarks of an occupational licence, yet also resembling a tenancy at will in so far as the landlord may sue for possession without demand. Ultimately, however, because the tenant holds over without the consent of the landlord, he falls to be classified as a form of tolerated trespasser.

The upshot of the forgoing is that the distinction between proprietary and non-proprietary rights has become increasingly blurred in landlord and tenant law. The suggested solution is to return to a simplified structure involving personal occupational rights (akin to licences) on the one hand, and proprietary occupational rights (conferring an estate in land) on the other. The former would confer on the occupier the benefit of personal occupation either at the will of the owner or for a stated period (fixed or periodic) depending on the form of contract entered into between the parties. The occupier would enjoy exclusive occupation but not exclusive possession (in the traditional sense). In other words, the occupational right would not create any estate in land capable of assignment or binding third parties. This accords with the current status of the contractual licence which does not create a property interest in land: *Ashburn Anstalt* v *Arnold* [1989] Ch 1. It would be possible, under such a new scheme, to abandon also the notion of the tenancy at sufferance by recognising that a tenant who holds over after the expiry of his lease does so under a non-proprietary right determinable at the will of the landlord. This would be akin to the bare licence to occupy recognising that, if the landlord does not expressly object to continued occupation, he is deemed to consent until such time as his (implied) permission is revoked. By contrast, a proprietary occupational right would create in favour of the occupier an estate in land and, consequently, the right to exclusive possession of the property against all the world. Such right (being a lease or tenancy) would be capable of assignment and have all the other hallmarks of a leasehold estate.

Under such a proposed structure, there would be no room for hybrids since the governing factor distinguishing the two types of occupational right would be the presence (or absence) of exclusive possession. This, as has been demonstrated, reflects the current test for distinguishing between a lease and a licence. Ultimately, it is this element of territorial control or excludability which characterises estate ownership under English law. As the question suggests, a restructuring of occupational rights into a simplified two-tier hierarchy of personal and proprietary interests would bring about a much needed return to this orthodoxy.

Q Question 2

(a) What is the nature and effect of a tenancy by estoppel?

(b) John is the freehold owner of a building which comprises a number of flats. He resides in another part of the building and, therefore, qualifies as a resident landlord so that his tenants will *prima facie* be excluded from statutory protection under Pt I of the Housing Act 1988. Last month, however, he let one of the flats to Judy using an assured tenancy agreement under which the tenant was declared to have all the rights and incidents of an assured tenant under the 1988 Act. How, if at all, will this affect Judy's legal status as tenant of the flat?

Commentary

The first part of this question is relatively straightforward requiring the student to outline the meaning and practical workings of a tenancy by estoppel. Apart from explaining how the tenancy arises, a good answer will also detail the limits of the principle and whether such a tenancy can confer statutory protection under the residential and business tenancy codes: *Stratford v Syrett* [1958] 1 QB 107 and *Bell v General Accident Fire & Life Assurance Corporation Ltd* [1998] 17 EG 144. See also Question 1(a), **Chapter 16**.

The second part of the question is far more difficult since it raises the interesting issue of whether the concept of an estoppel can be used to confer on an occupier security of tenure which he (or she) would not otherwise enjoy under the appropriate statutory code. The point arose in *Daejan Properties Ltd v Mahoney* [1995] 2 EGLR 75 and, more recently, in

Wroe v. Exmos Cover Ltd [2000] 15 EG 155 concerning an estoppel-based tenancy (as opposed to a tenancy by estoppel). The question, therefore, focuses on the distinction between these two types of tenancy. You are, of course, unlikely to be faced with a difficult question of this sort in the exam unless it has been covered by your tutor in lectures or seminars.

- Tenancy by estoppel operates as a rule of evidence which precludes the parties from denying the existence of a tenancy granted by a landlord who has no (or a defective) title to the property

- Application of the doctrine to all types of tenancy (residential and commercial)

- The effect of such a tenancy on both the landlord and tenant and persons claiming under a title paramount

- Nature of an estoppel-based tenancy which can be used to confer statutory rights on a tenant who would not otherwise qualify under the relevant statutory code

- Explanation of *Daejan Properties Ltd* v *Mahoney* (1995) and *Wroe* v *Exmos Cover Ltd* (2000)

- Difference between conferring tenancy *status* on Judy which is prohibited by the 1988 Act and estopping John from arguing that she has the same statutory rights *as if* the Act applied

:Q: **Suggested answer**

(a) The doctrine of estoppel precludes a party who has induced another to rely upon his representation from denying the truth of the facts represented. For the purposes of landlord and tenant law, this means that neither landlord nor tenant can question the validity of the lease, once possession has been taken up. Thus, even if the landlord had no authority to grant the lease, the tenant cannot deny any of his leasehold obligations to the landlord by arguing that the grant was not effectively made. Similarly, the landlord is prevented from setting up his own want or defect in title as a ground for repudiating the lease. A tenancy by estoppel, therefore, arises in the limited circumstances where a landlord purports to grant a tenancy in respect of property to which he has no or an imperfect title. In this sense, the estoppel operates as a rule of evidence in that it precludes the parties from denying the existence of a tenancy on the basis of the landlord's grant or representation: *Bruton* v *London Quadrant Housing Trust* [1998] QB 834, 840, (CA), per Millett LJ.

The doctrine applies to all types of tenancy, including periodic tenancies, tenancies at will and at sufferance, statutory tenancies under the Rent Act 1977 (*Stratford* v *Syrett* [1958] 1 QB 107), business tenancies under Pt II of the Landlord and Tenant Act 1954

(*Bell* v *General Accident Fire & Life Assurance Corporation* [1998] 1 EGLR 69) and even licences. Moreover, the doctrine has application whether the tenancy was created orally, in writing or by deed and operates not only as between the parties to the purported grant, but also so as to bind their successors in title. Thus, a tenancy by estoppel can be devolved and alienated in the same way as any other tenancy.

A tenancy by estoppel does not, however, bind a person claiming under a title paramount (the true owner of the land) unless there is evidence that he has accepted the tenant as his tenant: *Chatsworth Properties Ltd* v *Effiom* [1971] 1 WLR 144. But if the tenant is evicted by the true owner, he can claim damages for the eviction against his landlord provided there is an express covenant for quiet enjoyment covering interruption by title paramount. If, on the other hand, the landlord acquires the legal estate out of which the tenancy could be created (for example, where he purchases the freehold title), this 'feeds the estoppel' and the tenancy becomes good in interest. On this occurrence, the tenant acquires a legal tenancy as founded upon the landlord's newly acquired legal estate. A good example is where a purchaser of land is allowed into possession prior to completion/registration (i.e., before the legal title is vested in him). If, prior to the vesting of any such title but during the currency of his possession, the purchaser grants a lease to another, the lease will take effect as a tenancy by estoppel even though the purchaser holds no formal legal title to the property. When the purchaser's transaction is later completed and registered, the legal title passes and the estoppel is said to be 'fed' and the leasehold title is perfected. However, during the interim period prior to completion, the tenancy by estoppel binds both the landlord and the tenant and their successors in title (if any). An interesting illustration of these principles is to found in the recent case of *Rother District Investments Ltd* v *Corke* [2004] 13 EG 128, where the landlord had purported to forfeit a sublease even though its title to the headlease was unregistered. Despite having no title to forfeit, the court held that the claimant was estopped from denying the forfeiture. Moreover, upon the claimant becoming registered as proprietor of the headlease, the act of forfeiture was retrospectively validated as a forfeiture by estoppel — the doctrine of 'feeding the estoppel' was held to apply to such a situation.

(b) A related doctrine is the estoppel-based tenancy which arises when a landlord makes a positive assurance to the tenant that the latter has or will acquire the rights of a tenant in the property to which the landlord has good title. An estoppel equity will arise in favour of the tenant if he (or she) can establish the requisite element of detrimental reliance so as to render it unconscionable for the landlord to assert his strict legal rights inconsistently with his assurance.

The second part of the question, therefore, raises the issue of whether John is estopped from denying the existence of an assured tenancy in favour of Judy despite his privileged status as a resident landlord under the 1988 Act. The point arose in *Daejan Properties Ltd* v *Mahoney* [1955] 2 EGLR 75, where the Court of Appeal drew a distinction between a landlord's representation that 'the Act shall apply' (which would be objectionable as an attempt to confer on the court a jurisdiction that went beyond the legislature) and a representation on the part of the landlord that 'I will *treat* you as having the same rights *as if* the Act applied'. In that case, the Court held that the tenant could not have become a statutory tenant by estoppel because any such estoppel would have compelled the landlord to recognise a state of affairs which Parliament itself had forbidden. In this connection, the Rent Act 1977 had clearly prescribed the way in which a statutory tenancy could arise or be transmitted and none of those prescribed methods applied to the tenant (Miss Mahoney). The doctrine of estoppel could not be invoked to render valid a transaction which the legislature had enacted was to be invalid, nor could it give the court jurisdiction which was denied to it by statute: *J & F Stone Lighting & Radio Ltd* v *Levitt* [1947] AC 209. Accordingly, the landlord could not be estopped from denying that Miss Mahoney was in law a statutory tenant. However, this did not preclude the court from accepting that the landlord had estopped itself from denying that Miss Mahoney (and her mother) would be *treated* by the landlord *as if* they were joint tenant statutory tenants. Such an approach did not offend any principle of public policy because it was implicit in it that the parties were *not*, strictly speaking, joint tenants but would simply be treated as if they were. As one eminent commentator has observed (R.E. Megarry, (1951) 67 LQR 505, at p. 506), commenting on the earlier decision in *Rogers v. Hyde* [1951] 2 KB 923:

> . . . even if the premises or letting is outside the Acts, why should not the landlord by contract give the tenant the same protection as if the Acts applied?

Further support for this approach can be found in *Wroe* v *Exmos Cover Ltd* [2000] 15 EG 155, a case dealing with commercial premises, where it was opined that, in relation to security of tenure, there was no reason why the landlord should not agree to treat the tenant as having the same protection as he (or she) would have if the tenancy fell within the statute, and no reason why the tenant should not be able to rely on an estoppel to the same effect provided that the requirements for such an estoppel were satisfied. On this analysis, John may well be estopped from denying the existence of an assured tenancy in favour of Judy. Although the 1988 Act prohibits the conferment of assured tenancy status on a tenant whose landlord qualifies as a resident landlord under the relevant statutory exclusion, this is not fatal to Jane's claim that she should be treated as if she were an assured tenant under the Act. The doctrine of estoppel could not be invoked in these circumstances so as to render valid the assured tenancy agreement which the statute has, on grounds of public policy, enacted to be invalid. However, this would not, it is submitted, preclude Judy from successfully asserting that John, by his representation (on which she presumably relied), had estopped himself from denying that she would be treated as if she were an assured tenant with all the corresponding statutory rights (in relation to security of tenure, succession and rent control) afforded to such a tenant. Although not an assured tenant as such, she would fall to be treated as if she were by virtue of John's representation implicit from the nature and content of the (assured) tenancy agreement executed by the parties.

Both the *Daejan* and *Wroe* cases illustrate that an estoppel-based tenancy may not legitimately be used to confer tenancy *status* if this is prohibited by the relevant statutory code. On the other hand, there is nothing, it seems, to prevent such an estoppel operating so as to deny the landlord from arguing that the tenant is to have the same statutory *rights* (in relation to security, rent control, etc) as if the appropriate statute applied.

Q Question 3

(a) You act for Mr Smith, who is the tenant of 15 Wellington Avenue. He holds under a lease, dated 1 January 1920, for a term of 99 years from 25 December 1919. Viscount Marmaduke, the freeholder, granted recently a second lease of the property to Acrecrest Holdings Ltd for a term of 21 years subject to and with the benefit of the existing lease granted to Mr Smith. Consider the position of the parties under these two leases.

(b) Sam is the freehold owner of a lock-up shop in Richmond, Surrey. In September 2002, he granted Sally a five-year tenancy of the premises. The parties expressly excluded Pt II of the Landlord a[nd Tenant Act 1954 (affording] security of tenure to business tenants) so tha[t] continuance of the tenancy after the expiry [...] rently two years left to run on her tenancy. A [...] to grant Jeremy a five-year subtenancy of t[...] arrears with his rent and Sally wants to forfe[...] default. Advise Sally.

(c) Albert holds over after the expiry of his 14-year lease. At first, his landlord, Nigel, is unaware of Albert's continued possession but later he writes to Albert saying that he is prepared to allow him to continue as tenant but fails to mention for what period he is to hold under him. Later, Albert tenders a quarter's rent which is duly accepted by Albert. Consider Albert's current legal status and that existing during each stage of his period of holding over.

Commentary

This question is divided into three parts. Part (a) asks you to explain the nature and effect of a concurrent lease (also known sometimes as a lease of the reversion, which is not to be confused with a reversionary lease!). The leading authority on this topic is *London & County (A & D) Ltd* v *Wilfred Sportsman Ltd* [1971] Ch 764.

Part (b) is concerned with the principle that the relationship of landlord and tenant depends on privity of estate existing between the parties (*Milmo* v *Carreras* [1946] KB 306). It also requires you to mention the case of *Parc Battersea Ltd* v *Hutchinson* [1999] 22 EG 149: see further, Brown, J., 'Avoiding Pt II of the Landlord and Tenant Act 1954 by Default' [1999] RRLR 246. The point here is that the purported subtenancy is void and will operate as an assignment by operation of law of the remainder of Sally's interest in the premises. The subtenancy cannot subsist because it has been granted for a term longer than Sally's expired residue of her head tenancy.

Part (c) requires you to examine Albert's status following the expiry of his fixed term lease. Initially, he will qualify as a tenant at sufferance. When Nigel signifies his consent to his continued occupation, Albert will become a tenant at will. Once a quarter's rent is tendered and accepted, he will be a periodic (quarterly) tenant.

Where you find a question in multiple parts such as this, you can assume that each section carries equal marks unless, of course, there is a contrary indication in the rubric. If the question carries equal marks, it goes without saying that you should devote equal attention to each part so as to produce a balanced answer attracting a fair division of the allocated marks.

- Nature of a concurrent lease — the interrelationship between Mr Smith's earlier lease and the later lease in favour of Acrecrest Holdings Ltd: *London & County (A & D) Ltd* v *Wilfred Sportsman Ltd* (1971)

- Acrecrest entitled to possession of premises if Mr Smith's lease prematurely determined, but forfeiture of Acrecrest's concurrent lease will not affect Mrs Smith's lease which is not treated as a subtenancy

- Effect of purported grant of subtenancy to Jeremy for a term greater than Sally's headlease: *Milmo* v *Carreras* (1946)

- Because Sally has no reversionary interest, she cannot claim rent or forefeit against Jeremy, who becomes tenant under the headlease for the duration of Sally's unexpired term

- Initially Albert is a tenant at sufferance and his legal status will thereafter depend on Nigel's responses

- Nigel's consent gives rise to a tenancy at will followed by a periodic tenancy once Nigel accepts rent referable to a quarterly period

:Ö: Suggested answer

(a) The second lease of the property to Acrecrest Holdings Ltd is classified as a concurrent lease (or a lease of the reversion as it is also sometimes known). This type of lease arises where a landlord grants a lease to T1 and subsequently grants a lease to T2 of the same premises for a term to commence before the expiry of the lease in favour of T1. The two leases, even though staggered in time, run concurrently with or parallel to one another.

So long as the two leases are concurrent (as in the question), the disposition in favour of Acrecrest Holdings Ltd operates as a part assignment of Viscount Marmaduke's reversion entitling Acrecrest to the rent reserved in Smith's (earlier) lease and the benefit of the covenants given by Mr Smith: *London & County (A & D) Ltd* v *Wilfred Sportsman* Ltd [1971] Ch 764. If Mr Smith's lease is prematurely determined before Acrecrest's concurrent lease has expired, Acrecrest will be entitled to possession of the premises. Moreover, if Acrecrest's lease is forfeited by the landlord, this will not affect Mr Smith' status as tenant for, although his lease is akin to a subtenancy, it is not derived out of Acrecrest's lease. In other words, the two leases are independent of each other.

A concurrent lease is a useful device whereby, for a definite period, T2 becomes a temporary owner of the reversionary estate of the landlord. I am not told of Marmaduke's purpose for creating a concurrent lease in favour of Acrecrest. Such a lease may, however, provide security in favour of T2 for a fixed period in return for T2 advancing credit or other commercial benefit to the landlord. Thus, a landlord, in return for money borrowed from T2, may grant a concurrent lease whereby T2 is entitled to the benefit of the rental payments issuing out of the land paid by T1: *Re Moore and Hulm's Contract* [1912] 2 Ch 105 and *Adelphi (Estates) Ltd* v *Christie* (1983) 47 P & CR 650).

(b) In this case, Sally was granted (in September 2002) a tenancy of the house for a term of five years. She, in turn, has recently purported to grant a a five-year sub-tenancy to Jeremy (i.e., for a term longer than the unexpired residue of the headlease). The rule in *Milmo* v *Carreras* [1946] KB 306 dictates that, where a tenant by a document in the form of a sublease divests himself of his entire leasehold interest (which will occur when a mesne landlord transfers to his subtenant an estate as great as or greater than his own), the relationship of landlord and tenant cannot exist between him and the purported subtenant. The sublease will, in fact, operate as an assignment by operation of law of the remainder of the tenant's interest in the premises. This is what has effectively happened in this case with the result that no privity of estate exists between Sally and her purported subtenant, Jeremy.

In the absence of any reversionary interest vested in Sally, she has no right to possession of the premises. This is because after the execution of the purported sublease, she effectively became an assignor of the headlease to the property. The assignment of Sally's headlease by operation of law will also mean that Jeremy will be bound by the provisions and limitations contained in the headlease — one of them being that Pt II of the 1954 Act should not apply. Jeremy, therefore, is without protection under Pt II and will be required to give up possession on the expiry date of the lease (i.e., in 2007): *Parc Battersea Ltd* v *Hutchinson* [1999] 22 EG 149. In the meantime, he will be obliged to pay the rent reserved under the headlease to Sam, the head landlord. He will also be obliged to perform all the other tenant's covenants contained therein for the duration of Sally's unexpired term.

(c) Upon the expiry of Albert's fixed term lease, he will continue in occupation of the premises initially as a tenant at sufferance. This denotes the relationship of owner and occupier where a tenant holds over and the landlord has neither consented nor expressed objection. The legal effects of the relationship will depend on subsequent events. Thus, if the landlord requires the tenant to quit, the latter becomes a trespasser and (by the doctrine of trespass by relation) the landlord can claim mesne profits from the date that the tenant's possession ceased to be lawful until possession is delivered up. Nigel, however, has not requested Albert to leave. On the contrary, he has written to him stating he is prepared to allow him to continue in occupation as tenant. Since Nigel has now signified his consent to Albert's occupation, the latter becomes a tenant at will even though the conduct of the parties allows for no inference as to the quantum of Albert's interest (i.e., Nigel has failed, in his letter, to mention for what period he is to hold under him). A tenancy at will confers on Albert a right of exclusive possession although no estate in land is created as the tenancy is not a 'term of years' within the meaning of s. 205(1)(xxvii) of the Law of Property Act 1925. Such a tenancy can be determined by the landlord making an unequivocal demand for possession, usually in writing or by the commencement of proceedings for possession. Once again, Nigel has not done this but, instead, accepted a quarter's rent from Albert. If, as here, rent is deliberately tendered and accepted by reference to a particular period (quarterly in Albert's case), the tenant becomes a periodic tenant. Albert's current status, therefore, is that of a quarterly tenant.

A further alternative (although not arising on these facts) is that, if the landlord simply acquiesces in the tenant's continued occupation, the former will be statute barred if he fails to re-assert his title within 12 years from the date that the tenant's possession ceased to be lawful: s. 15 of the Limitation Act 1980.

Further reading

Pawlowski, M., 'Occupational Rights in Leasehold Law: Time for Rationalisation?' [2002] Conv. 550.

Pawlowski, M. and Brown J., 'Tenancies at Will — Still a Useful Device?' (2001) 68 PLJ 21.

Pawlowski, M., 'Tenancies by Estoppel' (1998) SJ 248.

Pawlowski, M. and Brown J., 'Tenancies by Estoppel and Estoppel-based Tenancies' [2000] RRLR 207.

Enforceability of covenants

Introduction

Who can enforce a covenant in a lease, and against whom? This is a difficult topic because it abounds with technical rules and the student may be obliged to consider the liability of a number of different parties (i.e., original tenant, original landlord, assignee of lease, assignee of reversion, a surety).

The law now differs depending on whether the lease was granted before, or on or after 1 January 1996, when the Landlord and Tenant (Covenants) Act 1995 came into force. One of the main provisions of the 1995 Act, which applies to *all* leases (including those entered into before 1 January 1996), requires that if the landlord wishes to sue the original tenant for fixed charges (i.e., arrears of rent, service charges or liquidated damages, including interest on any of these sums) he must give notice of his intention to do so within six months of the liability arising: s. 17. Another important provision under the 1995 Act, which is common to both old and new leases, relates to the former tenant's entitlement to an 'overriding lease'. The Act entitles the former tenant, if he satisfies an obligation of an assignee following assignment, to call for the grant to him (within 12 months) of an overriding lease from the landlord for a term equal to the unexpired residue of the actual lease (plus a nominal reversion). This has the effect of inserting the former tenant as an intermediate landlord between the landlord and the defaulting assignee. The advantage of the overriding lease to the former tenant is that he will be able to forfeit the assignee's interest and regain possession of the demised premises with a view to marketing them. The rationale behind the overriding lease is, therefore, to give the former tenant the opportunity to recoup his expenditure in discharging his liability to the landlord. If you are faced with a question involving a pre-1996 lease, it is important that you make mention of these changes brought about by the 1995 Act. See Question 1 and 3.

With regard to leases created on or after 1 January 1996, the position is now governed by the 1995 Act. The basic principle under the Act is that, on assignment, the original tenant will be automatically released from his liabilities and only the tenant for the time being will be liable to the landlord. There is a notable situation, however, in which the former tenant will continue to be liable under the covenants in the lease following an assignment. This is where the landlord requires the tenant to enter into an authorised guarantee agreement (AGA), whereby the tenant guarantees performance of the covenants in the lease by his immediate assignee. The AGA must release the tenant from liability under the agreement on a further assignment of the lease. If the tenant is not so released, the agreement is not an AGA and is void under the Act. See Question 2(a) and 4.

It is frequently overlooked that the privity of contract rule applies to landlords just as it does to tenants. Thus, in relation to pre-1996 leases, the original landlord will remain liable to the tenant on his covenants (express or implied) in the lease despite an assignment of the lease. It is also well-established that the original landlord, although he can no longer sue, can still be sued after the reversion has been assigned: *Re King, (dec'd), Robinson* v *Gray* [1963] Ch 459. Under the 1995 Act, in respect of post-1996 leases, the landlord may seek to be released from his covenants in the lease when he assigns the reversion by serving notice on the tenant giving details of the proposed assignment and indicating that he wishes to be released. The tenant then has four weeks within which to object to the proposed release. If he does not object within that period then, on completion of the assignment, the landlord will be released. If there is an objection (e.g., the tenant may fear that the premises will decline under the new landlord), the landlord can apply to the county court for a declaration that it is reasonable for him to be released. See Question 2(b).

The provisions of the 1995 Act apply to original tenants and landlords, and also to those who become tenants or landlords by virtue of an assignment of the tenancy or reversion.

You should also be aware that the Contracts (Rights of Third Parties) Act 1999 may be relevant in the leasehold context. The Act provides that a third party may enforce directly a contractual term where the contract expressly provides that right, or where the contractual term confers a benefit on him. The Act, therefore, allows for the inclusion of sub-tenants, as a named class of future persons, as the beneficiaries of covenants in a headlease granted after the Act became law. In other words, the sub-tenant may be able to enforce the head landlord's covenants directly against the superior landlord: see further, Porter, R., 'Third Party Benefits', [1999] EG 9950, 72–73. We have included an essay-type question on the 1999 Act in this chapter: see Question 5.

Our advice is to plan your answer carefully, since problem questions in this area seek to test not only your knowledge of the principles but also your ability to write clearly and concisely. If you are thinking of taking up a career at the bar, a problem question on this highly technical topic is definitely for you! Good luck!

Q Question 1

In 1986, Bakewell Ltd was granted a 30-year lease of a shop in Eltham, London. Two years later, Bakewell Ltd requested consent to an assignment of the unexpired residue of the lease to Babyfoods Ltd. Pursuant to a term of the licence to assign granted by the landlord, Mr Brown entered into a covenant with the landlord to guarantee payment of the rent by Babyfoods Ltd.

In 1990, the landlord sold the freehold of the shop to Property Developments Ltd. Babyfoods Ltd recently went into liquidation owing £15,000 rent,
the rent having been increased on review in 1997 (i.e., since the assignment of the
lease).

Advise Bakewell Ltd as to its rights and liabilities in respect of the shop. How
would your advice differ (if at all) if the lease had been granted to Bakewell Ltd for
a term of 10 years (as opposed to 30 years)?

Commentary

This is, without doubt, a difficult question. Even the bright and well-motivated student
will find it challenging! It raises a number of complex issues relating to a pre-1996 lease
(i.e., prior to the commencement of the 1995 Act) and you will need a clear head to tackle
this question successfully. The secret is to plan your answer carefully, jotting down the key
points and case names (i.e., what should be included). Use this rough plan to balance the
material in your answer so as to avoid writing excessively on one point to the detriment
of others. For a good summary of the subject, see Murdoch, S., 'Tenants, Assignees and
Sureties' (1984) 272 EG 732 and 857. See also Pawlowski, M., *Leasing Commercial Premises*,
London: *Estates Gazette*, 2002 Ch. 6, for a good summary of the interrelation between the
common law and the Landlord and Tenant (Covenants) Act 1995.

As to the second part of the question, the widely held view, prior to the decision in *City of
London Corporation* v *Fell* [1993] 3 WLR 1164, was that the liability of an original tenant did
not cease on the expiry of the contractual term of the lease but extended into any statutory
continuation of the tenancy under the Landlord and Tenant Act 1954, Pt II. See, Pawlowski,
M., 'Liability of an Original Tenant and his Surety' [1990] EG 9050, 38. The principal
authority relied upon for this view was the judgment of Nourse J in *GMS Syndicate Ltd* v *Gary
Elliott Ltd* [1982] Ch 1.

In *City of London Corporation* v *Fell*, Mr Desmond Perrett QC at first instance (in which
one of the writers appeared as counsel for the City of London: [1992] 3 All ER 224) held
that the obligations of the respondents, as original tenants, ceased on the expiration of
the contractual term and did not extend into the period of the statutory continuation
of the tenancy under Pt II of the 1954 Act. The Court of Appeal ([1993] 2 All ER 449)
confirmed this decision, holding that where an original tenant had assigned the tenancy
before the end of the contractual term, 'the tenancy' (which s. 24(1) of the 1954 Act
provides shall not come to an end) could only mean the tenancy of the assignee. Thus, if
the original tenant contracted to pay rent only during the contractual term (as in *Fell*), the
landlord could not recover from him any rent payable in respect of any period after
that date. The House of Lords ([1993] 3 WLR 1164) reiterated this principle, concluding
that there is nothing in Pt II of the 1954 Act to impose liability on an original tenant
who has ceased to have any interest in the demised premises. For a short note on the House
of Lords decision, see 'Liability of an Original Tenant' (Legal Notes) [1993] EG 9349, 112.

Contrast, however, *Herbert Duncan Ltd* v *Cluttons* [1993] 2 All ER 449, where the word 'term' was expressly defined to include 'any period of holding over or extension thereof whether by statute or common law'.

Lastly, our suggested answer contains a reference to *Kumar* v *Dunning* [1987] 3 WLR 1167 and the doctrine of subrogation. If you are mystified as to what this doctrine entails, see Brown, J., and Pawlowski, M., 'Rights of Subrogation and Non-Payment of Rent' [1994] 14/4 RRLR, 22.

Because of the complexity of the factual data in questions of this sort, we would strongly recommend that you prepare a simple diagram identifying the various parties as a prelude to answering the question:

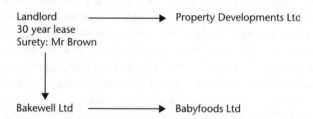

- **Bakewell Ltd continues to be liable on all the covenants in the lease as original tenant notwithstanding (1) assignment of the term to Babyfoods Ltd and (2) assignment of reversionary interest to Property Developments Ltd**

- **Bakewell Ltd also remains liable on the covenant to pay rent despite increase of rent on review: s. 18 of the 1995 Act**

- **An implied right of indemnity (under both statute and the common law) exists against Babyfoods Ltd as assignee in default**

- **The benefit of Mr Brown's surety covenant will pass to Property Developments Ltd: *Kumar* v *Dunning* (1987). If Bakewell Ltd discharges the rent arrears, it will be entitled to the benefit of Mr Brown's surety covenant under the doctrine of subrogation**

- **Effect of Babyfood Ltd's liquidation — this does not end the term so liability of Bakewell Ltd continues despite liquidation. Consider also effect of liquidation on Mr Brown's surety covenant**

- **If lease granted for a 10-year term only, Bakewell Ltd's liability as original tenant will be limited to the contractual term of the lease, unless covenant to pay rent expressly defines term to include any statutory continuation thereof under the Landlord and Tenant Act 1954: *City of London Corporation* v *Fell* (1993) and *Herbert Duncan Ltd* v *Cluttons* (1993)**

·Ò· **Suggested answer**

In view of Babyfoods Ltd's liquidation, it is likely that Property Developments Ltd will pursue Bakewell Ltd for the arrears of rent. (It appears that an original tenant has no power to force the landlord to sue the current assignee in breach before pursuing its remedy against it: *Norwich Union Life Insurance* v *Low Profile Fashions* (1992) 64 P & CR 187.)

As original tenant, Bakewell Ltd is liable on all the covenants in the lease for the duration of the term, and such liability will continue notwithstanding the assignment of the term to Babyfoods Ltd. The Landlord and Tenant (Covenants) Act 1995 does not abrogate the privity of contract rule in respect of leases granted before 1 January 1996. Since Bakewell Ltd's lease was granted in 1986, it would not have been released from its obligations under the lease upon the assignment to Babyfoods Ltd.

Bakewell Ltd's liability will also continue despite an assignment of the freehold reversionary interest in the shop to Property Developments Ltd. Under the Law of Property Act 1925, s. 141, the obligation to pay rent (and the benefit of other tenant's covenants which have reference to the subject matter of the lease) runs with the freehold reversion. Thus, Property Developments Ltd may sue to recover the arrears of rent from Bakewell Ltd notwithstanding the assignment of the freehold.

However, the effect of s. 141 is that, once the reversion has been assigned, it is only the assignee of the reversion who can sue on the real covenants in the lease, whether the breach took place before or after the date of the assignment (*Re King, Deceased, Robinson* v *Gray* [1963] Ch 459 and *London & County (A & D) Ltd* v *Wilfred Sportsman Ltd* [1971] Ch 764, *per* Russell LJ, at pp. 782–4). Moreover, in *Arlesford Trading Co. Ltd* v *Servansingh* [1971] 1 WLR 1080, it was held that the ability to enforce the covenants in the lease against the original tenant passed to the assignee of the reversion although there had never been privity of estate between the parties. In that case (as in the facts here), the original tenant had assigned the lease before the new landlord had acquired the reversion so that the two had never been in any direct relationship of landlord and tenant.

The position prior to the enactment of the Landlord and Tenant (Covenants) Act 1995 was that the liability of the original tenant continued even where the terms of the lease were subsequently varied by the original landlord and an assignee of the lease. In *Selous Street Properties Ltd* v *Oronel Fabrics Ltd* (1984) 270 EG 643 and 743, for example, the landlord brought an action for arrears of rent against the original tenants, who contested their liability on the ground that the rent review (under which the unpaid rent arose) had been carried out on a basis different from that to which the original tenants had agreed. The court held that any increase in the rental value of the premises for rent review purposes did not discharge the liability of the original tenant. The assignee stood in the shoes of the original tenant and was the owner of the whole leasehold estate and, hence, could deal with it so as to alter it or its terms: see also *GUS Management Ltd* v *Texas Homecare Ltd* [1993] 27 EG 130. The principle was also applied in *Centrovincial Estates plc* v *Bulk Storage Ltd* (1983) 268 EG 59, where it was held that the original tenant was liable to pay rent at the rate fixed under a rent review clause even though this took place after it had parted with the lease. Similarly, in *Friends' Provident Life Office* v *British Railways Board* [1996] 1 All ER 336, a substantial increase in rent did not affect the original tenant's liability. The 1995 Act has altered the law by providing (in s. 18) that no former tenant (or his surety) is liable to pay any sum resulting from a 'relevant variation' to the terms of the lease effected after the enactment of the Act (i.e., 1 January 1996). Essentially, the liability of former tenants (and their sureties) will be increased by subsequent variations only if either (1) it is contemplated in the lease, or (2) it is permitted under the general law. An increase in rent under a rent review clause is not covered by the exclusion in s. 18 because the former tenant would have agreed to such a covenant and the covenant itself would not have been altered. Accordingly, Bakewell Ltd will remain liable on the covenant to pay rent, notwithstanding the increase of rent on review since the assignment of the lease.

To what extent may Bakewell Ltd seek to claim an indemnity in respect of the arrears of rent against its assignee? In the absence of an express indemnity covenant, there is implied into any assignment for valuable consideration a covenant under which the assignee will indemnify the assignor in respect of any liability incurred for any breach of covenant committed during the remainder of the term (Law of Property Act 1925, s. 77(1)(c) (unregistered land) and Land Registration Act 1925, s. 24(1)(b) (registered land)) (both then applicable). The effect of these provisions is that Bakewell Ltd will have a right of indemnity against its immediate assignee (Babyfoods Ltd) in respect of the £15,000 rent arrears it may be called upon to pay to Property Developments Ltd: *Scottish and Newcastle plc* v *Raquz* [2003] EWCA Civ 1070. The indemnity may not be worth very much in view of Babyfoods Ltd's liquidation but Bakewell Ltd should make a formal claim in the liquidation in case the company has any assets worth realising.

In addition to this statutory right, Bakewell Ltd will also have an implied right of indemnity at common law against the assignee in breach (*Moule* v *Garrett* (1872) LR 7 Ex 101; *Selous Street Properties Ltd* v *Oronel Fabrics Ltd* (1984) 270 EG 643 and 743 and *Re Healing Research Trustee Co. Ltd* (1992) 2 EGLR 231).

In *Kumar* v *Dunning* [1987] 3 WLR 1167, it was held that the benefit of a surety covenant may pass to an assignee of the reversion: see also, *P & A Swift Investments Ltd* v *Combined English Stores Group plc* [1988] 3 WLR 313. Accordingly, in the present case, Property Developments Ltd may seek to claim the arrears of rent from Mr Brown subject to the point that any variation in the terms of the lease between the landlord and the tenant which could prejudice the surety will discharge the latter from his obligations (*Holme* v *Brunskill* (1878) 3 QBD 495).

It also appears from the *Kumar* case that, if Bakewell Ltd is called upon to pay the rent, then it would be entitled to the benefit of Mr Brown's surety covenant under the doctrine of subrogation. In other words, it would be able to recover the rent arrears from Mr Brown by being subrogated to the rights of the landlord under the surety covenant.

Upon the liquidation of Babyfoods Ltd, the lease will vest in the liquidator of the company, who may disclaim the lease under the Insolvency Act 1986, s. 178. If the bankruptcy (or liquidation) is that of an *assignee* of the lease (as in the present case), the disclaimer will not end the term and the liability of the original tenant will not be discharged, although it will determine the assignee's interest in the term, which continues to subsist although apparently having no owner until a vesting order is made (*Warnford Investments Ltd* v *Duckworth* [1979] Ch 127; *WH Smith Ltd* v *Wyndham Investments Ltd* [1994] EGCS 94 and *Hindcastle Ltd* v *Barbara Attenborough Associates Ltd* [1996] 1 All ER 737 (HL)). Under the Insolvency Act 1986, s. 181, Bakewell Ltd may apply to the court for an order vesting the lease in its name.

A disclaimer of the lease will also not affect the obligations to the landlord of a surety of the original (insolvent) tenant. Under s. 178(4) of the 1986 Act, the interest of the insolvent tenant in the disclaimed property is determined by the disclaimer and the lease extinguished so far as he is concerned, but the lease is deemed to continue in respect of the rights and obligations of other persons: *Hindcastle Ltd* v *Barbara Attenborough Associates Ltd* [1996] 1 All ER 737 (HL), overruling *Stacey* v *Hill* [1901] 1 QB 660. (See [1997] Conv 24 for a commentary on the House of Lords ruling.) However, where it is the *assignee* who is in liquidation, the effect of a disclaimer on the assignee's guarantor will depend on the wording of the guarantee covenant. If Mr Brown's obligations (set out in the licence to assign) are stated to be independent of the covenants of Babyfoods Ltd, then it is clear that they will survive the disclaimer and Mr Brown will continue to be liable. If, however, the liability of Mr Brown is stated to arise only on a *default* of Babyfoods Ltd, then the situation is different. The decision in *Warnford Investments* makes it clear that, after a disclaimer, the assignee has no liability to pay the rent reserved by the lease. So, in *Murphy* v *Sawyer-Hoare* (1993) 27 EG 127, the liability of the assignee's surety arose upon the default of the assignee. After the date of the disclaimer, there could be no such default so it was held that the surety had no liability from then on. This would not, of course, absolve Mr Brown from the £15,000 arrears of rent due up to the date of the disclaimer.

What if the lease had been granted for only a 10-year term? If this were the case, the issue would be whether Bakewell Ltd's liability was limited to the contractual term of the lease (which would have expired in 1996), or whether it extended into the statutory continuation of the tenancy (being a business tenancy) under the Landlord and Tenant Act 1954, s. 24. A great deal will depend upon the wording of the original tenant's covenant to pay rent in the lease and the definition of the word 'term' in the reddendum. In *City of London Corporation* v *Fell* [1993] 3 WLR 1164, the House of Lords held that an original tenant's liability did not extend beyond the original contractual term. However, in *Herbert Duncan Ltd* v *Cluttons* [1993] 2 All ER 449, the wording of the lease expressly defined the term to include 'any period of holding over or extension thereof whether by statute or common law'. The Court of Appeal held that, where the term expressly covers any continuation, the original tenant cannot escape liability beyond the term date.

Q Question 2

(a) In what circumstances may a landlord require the tenant to enter into an authorised guarantee agreement under the Landlord and Tenant (Covenants) Act 1995? [15 marks]

(b) The Earl of Leamington holds the freehold title to a pet shop in Coventry. The current tenant is Bernard, who holds a 10-year lease which was granted to him in 1997. The lease includes a covenant on the part of the landlord to maintain a policy of insurance in relation to the demised premises with the Balmoral Insurance Co. Ltd and to pay them the yearly insurance premium of £750. There is also a landlord's personal covenant to remedy any building defects in the premises.

The Earl now wishes to sell his freehold reversionary interest to a property investment company and seeks your advice as to how (if at all) he may be released from his insurance and personal liability under the lease upon assignment of the reversion. Advise him. [10 marks]

Commentary

This is a two-part question on the workings of the 1995 Act. The first part requires you to give an overview of the mechanics of the authorised guarantee agreement (AGA). Try to be succinct and informative in your answer. Don't dwell on one aspect to the exclusion of other important points. Imagine you are giving a short seminar presentation to your fellow students on this topic. Your objective is to demonstrate to the examiner that you have a good basic understanding of how the AGA operates in practice.

The second part of the question requires an examination of the rules which permit an original landlord to seek a release from his covenants under the lease in accordance with the statutory procedure laid down by the 1995 Act. The question whether or not a landlord's personal covenant is released under the 1995 Act was considered in *BHP Petroleum Great Britain* v *Chesterfield Properties* [2002] 1 All ER 821.

- Former tenant remains liable for defaults of immediate assignee if landlord has benefit of AGA. Landlord may require AGA from former tenant either (1) automatically as one of the conditions for assignment set out in the lease or (2) because it is reasonable to do so

- Default notice procedure (under s. 17 of the 1995 Act) will apply and former tenant may seek indemnity or call for an overriding lease

- Landlord can apply to be released from his insurance covenant upon assignment of reversion by serving notice on tenant. If Bernard objects, Earl can apply to court for an order for release on the ground that Bernard's objections are unreasonable

- If Earl unsuccessful, he will continue to remain liable to Bernard as original landlord (by virtue of privity of contract) despite sale of reversion. But further opportunity to seek release upon any future assignment of the reversion. Personal covenant outside scope of 1995 Act.

⠐Q⠐ Suggested answer

(a) The Landlord and Tenant (Covenants) Act 1995 introduced a new regime of landlord and tenant covenant liability into leases granted on or after 1 January 1996. It also modified existing leases from that date by introducing procedures (notably, the s. 17 notice procedure and overriding leases) to assist former tenants with continuing leasehold liability.

The basic principle under the Act is that, on assignment, the former tenant will be automatically released from his liabilities and only the tenant for the time being will be liable to the landlord. However, under a lease granted after 1 January 1996, a former tenant will remain liable for the defaults of his immediate assignee if the landlord obtains an authorised guarantee agreement (AGA) from him guaranteeing performance of the tenant's covenants by his immediate assignee. The landlord may require such an agreement from the former tenant either (1) automatically as one of the conditions for assignment set out in the covenant in the lease, or (2) because it is reasonable to do so.

Under (1), the parties to a new lease are given the right (under the 1995 Act) to agree in advance the conditions which the former tenant or prospective assignee must meet as a precondition of the landlord's consent to the assignment. A typical condition may be that the assignee must have net profits before tax in its most recent accounts of at least three times the rent, or that the assignee must provide a rent deposit or guarantor. Another condition may be that the former tenant enter into an AGA. So far as the latter is concerned, any form of commercial guarantee is permissible under the Act, so long as no term of the guarantee prevents the former tenant's statutory rights to be released from the guarantee upon a further assignment by his immediate assignee. (To the extent that the former tenant is not so released, the agreement is not an AGA and is void under the Act.)

As to (2), this will apply where the landlord's consent is required to the assignment and the landlord gives the consent on condition that the former tenant enters into an AGA. The condition must be lawfully imposed, and so this situation will arise in either of two cases:

(a) where the lease contains an absolute prohibition against assignment, but the landlord decides in his discretion to permit the assignment if the former tenant offers a guarantee; or

(b) (more commonly) where the lease requires the landlord's consent which cannot be unreasonably withheld (whether as a result of s. 19(1) of the Landlord and Tenant Act 1927 or because of an express proviso to that effect) and it is reasonable for the landlord to require a guarantee from the former tenant as a condition of granting his consent. Whether it is reasonable for the landlord to insist on an AGA as a precondition of granting consent will depend on all the circumstances of the case. These circumstances remain uncertain in the absence of any judicial guidance (to date) on this issue: but see *Wallis Fashion Group Ltd* v *General Accident Life Assurance Ltd* [2000] 27 EG 145 in the context of a business tenancy renewal. It is also unclear to what extent the landlord can insist on additional security (e.g., in the form of a rent deposit) from the prospective assignee.

It is important to stress that the former tenant's liability under the AGA is entirely different from his previous liability as tenant under the lease before the assignment. The tenant liability is released and replaced by a new liability which is that of a surety only under the AGA. Thus, his liability will be discharged, for example, upon a subsequent variation of the lease terms.

The default notice procedure under s. 17 of the 1995 Act applies in the context of recovering arrears of rent, service charge and liquidated damages (including interest thereon) from the former tenant under his liability arising by virtue of an AGA. Equally, the former tenant is entitled to call for an overriding lease if he satisfies his immediate assignee's obligations under the lease by virtue of his AGA commitment. Apart from this, the original tenant may (under an old tenancy only) still seek an indemnity for his expenditure from his immediate assignee (under s. 77 of the Law of Property Act 1925 or s. 24 of the Land Registration Act 1925), or (in respect of old and new tenancies) from the assignee in breach by way of indemnity under the common law rule in *Moule* v *Garrett* (1872) LR 7 EX 101.

(b) Prior to the introduction of the 1995 Act, the original landlord remained liable on his real covenants in the lease throughout the whole term despite any assignment of his reversionary interest. This, in effect, mirrored the position of the original tenant under the privity of contract doctrine.

Given that tenants do not generally have any control over the assignment of the landlord's interest, a landlord who assigns his reversion post-1995 Act is not subject to the automatic release of his covenants like the original tenant. Instead, the landlord can apply to be released by serving a notice under s. 8 of the Act on the tenant either before or within four weeks after the assignment. If a tenant objects, the landlord can apply to court seeking a declaration that his release is reasonable. If there is no objection, the landlord will be released on completion of the assignment. But in the event that the landlord does not apply for a release or accepts the tenant's objection, or the court does not declare the release to be reasonable, the landlord will remain liable on his covenants following the assignment. He will, however, have another opportunity to apply for a release when there is a further assignment of the reversion by his assignee: s. 7 of the 1995 Act.

In the present case, the lease is a post–1995 Act lease (i.e., created after 1 January 1996) and so is caught by the new regime under the Act. Although, as we have seen, there is no mechanism for automatic release in the event of a landlord wishing to assign his reversion, the Earl can apply by notice under s. 8 to the tenant, Bernard, seeking a release from his leasehold liablities. If Bernard objects, the Earl should be advised to apply to the court for an order for release on the ground that Bernard's objections are unreasonable. This will depend on all the circumstances of the case. However, it has been held recently that a personal covenant on the part of the landlord (which does not pass to the landlord's assignee under the 1995 Act) cannot be the subject of a release by virtue of a s. 8 notice. In *BHP Petroleum Great Britain* v *Chesterfield Properties* [2002] 1 All ER 821, the original landlord (as here) covenanted to remedy any building defects in the property. The covenant was expressed to be personal and, hence, was held not to be not transmissible under the 1995 Act. The landlord served a s. 8 notice and assigned the lease. The tenant did not object to the release of this covenant but later claimed that the original landlord remained liable when a defect was found. The Court of Appeal held that, by serving a s. 8 notice, the landlord was released from all 'landlord covenants', which were expressed in the 1995 Act to be performed by a person who was 'for the time being' the landlord of the premises. Accordingly, the release could only apply to transmissible covenants. The upshot, therefore, is that the Earl will remain liable under his personal covenant despite the assignment of his reversion. (Interestingly, in this context, a covenant will be personal if 'expressed to be personal' by reason of explicit or implicit language, taking account of the language of the tenancy as a whole: *First Penthouse Ltd* v *Channel Hotels and Properties Ltd* [2003] EWHC 2713 (Ch).)

If the Earl is unsuccessful in obtaining a release of the insurance covenant, he will also continue to remain liable under this covenant to Bernard as original landlord (by virtue of privity of contract) despite the sale of his freehold interest. He should be advised, however, to obtain a covenant from the purchaser (to be included in the deed of assignment) to the effect that the latter will inform him of any future assignment of the reversion, thus affording the Earl with another opportunity to seek a release of his liabilities at a future date.

Q Question 3

(a) In 1992, Hogan Estates Ltd granted to Tomkins Ltd a 20-year commercial lease of 200 sq. m. of office space at a rent of £12,000 per year, payable on the usual quarter days. The directors of Tomkins Ltd are Bob and Jane, who covenanted with Hogan Estates Ltd to pay all losses, costs, damage and expenses occasioned to the landlord by the non-payment of rent or breach of any obligation by the tenant.

In 1993, Hogan Estates Ltd sold their reversionary interest to the Duke of Hackney without expressly assigning the benefit of the surety covenant. A year later, Tomkins Ltd ran into financial difficulties and stopped paying the rent. There is now £6,000 due, representing two quarters' rent unpaid. The Duke has made several formal demands for the rent from Tomkins Ltd but these have been to no avail. The Duke does not wish to forfeit the lease, but is keen to recover the rent from Bob and Jane.
Advise the Duke of Hackney.   [10 marks]

(b) In 1990, Fox Property Ltd granted Simon a 14-year lease of commercial premises at a rent of £8,000 per year payable in quarterly instalments.

In 1992, Simon assigned the lease to Brook Ltd. In 1995, Brook Ltd assigned the lease to Sherry, and she in turn (in 1998) assigned the lease to Tony. The lease expired in 2004 and Tony vacated the premises having failed to pay the last two instalments of rent due (i.e., £4,000). Tony has recently been declared bankrupt and has no assets of any value. Since Fox Property Ltd are unlikely to recover any of the unpaid rent from Tony as creditors in his bankruptcy, they have decided to pursue Simon instead for the rent arrears.   [15 marks]
Advise Simon.

Commentary

Part (a) is concerned with the liability of a surety under a guarantee covenant and, in particular, the extent to which the benefit of such a covenant is capable of passing to an assignee landlord in the absence of any express assignment of the benefit. A good knowledge of case law is essential in order to achieve a high mark (see, *Kumar* v *Dunning* [1987] 3 WLR 1167; *P & A Swift Investments* v *Combined English Stores Group plc* [1988] 3 WLR 313 and *Coronation Street Industrial Properties Ltd* v *Ingall Industries* [1989] 1 WLR 304). For further reading, see Brown, J., 'The Enforceability of Surety Covenants' [1994] 14/2 RRLR, 18.

Part (b) is concerned with the liability of an original tenant and his assignees for non-payment of rent and, in particular, the ability of an original tenant to claim an indemnity from subsequent assignees of the term.

Questions on enforceability of covenants may be factually complex, involving not only the original landlord and tenant but also subsequent assignees of the term and (possibly) the reversion. Here again, it is worth spending a few minutes drawing a simple diagram to help you identify the respective parties. For the purposes of part (b), we would suggest something along the following lines:

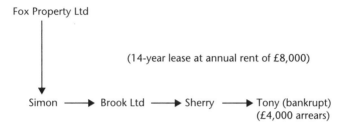

- Benefit of surety covenant passes to the Duke (in the absence of an express assignment) because the tenant's covenant (to which it relates) is a covenant to pay rent which touches and concerns the land. Consider the test in *P & A Swift Investments Ltd* v *Combined English Stores Group plc* (1988)

- Simon (as original tenant) liable on all covenants in the lease for the duration of the term notwithstanding the assignment of his interest

- Fox Property Ltd must give notice to Simon to recover the arrears within six months of the liability arising: s. 17 of the 1995 Act. If Simon discharges this liability, he will be entitled to call for an overriding lease within 12 months

- Alternatively, Simon may seek indemnity against either Tony (the assignee in default) under the rule in *Moule* v *Garrett* or Brook Ltd (the immediate assignee) by virtue of s. 77(1) of the Law of Property Act 1925

- Since Tony is bankrupt, Simon should pursue an indemnity against Brook Ltd without necessity of serving a s. 17 notice: *M.W. Kellog Ltd* v *F. Tobin* (1999)

:Q: Suggested answer

(a) In this case, Hogan Estates Ltd have sold their reversionary interest to the Duke of Hackney without expressly assigning the benefit of the surety covenant. The question therefore arises whether the Duke (as an assignee of the reversion) may enforce this covenant against the two sureties, Bob and Jane.

Bob's and Jane's liability under their surety covenant, being only secondary, is dependent upon liability being established against the party primarily in default (i.e., Tomkins Ltd). In this connection, by virtue of the (then in force) Law of Property Act 1925, s. 141(1), the Duke has inherited the benefit of (and right to sue upon) all those tenant's covenants which have 'reference to the subject-matter of the lease', including the covenant to pay rent. Thus, the Duke can sue Tomkins Ltd (as original tenant) for the rental sums owing, the only difficulty being that the company is in financial difficulties and, accordingly, unlikely to meet the sum due. (The privity of contract rule applies to the present case since the lease was granted in 1992, prior to the enactment of the Landlord and Tenant (Covenants) Act 1995.)

But has the benefit of the surety covenant passed to the Duke? In the absence of an express assignment of the benefit of the covenant (complying with the formalities laid down in the Law of Property Act 1925, s. 136(1)) it might seem, at first glance, that the Duke has not inherited the benefit of the right to sue upon this covenant. However, authority suggests that, in certain circumstances, it is possible for an assignee landlord to acquire the benefit of a surety covenant, even though given to a predecessor in title, in circumstances where there has been no express assignment, and thus enforce the same against the surety in question (*Kumar* v *Dunning* [1987] 3 WLR 1167; *P & A Swift Investments Ltd* v *Combined English Stores Group plc* [1988] 3 WLR 313 and *Coronation Street Industrial Properties Ltd* v *Ingall Industries plc* [1989] 1 WLR 304).

In the *Swift* case, the House of Lords held that a benefit under a covenant could be enforced by the assignee of the reversion without express assignment if the covenant touched and concerned the land. Whether a covenant touched and concerned the land depended on the covenant satisfying three conditions, namely: (i) that it was beneficial only to the reversioner for the time being; (ii) that it affected the nature, quality, mode of user or value of the reversioner's land; and (iii) that it was not personal in nature. If those three conditions were satisfied, a covenant for the payment of a sum of money could touch and concern the land if it was connected with something to be done on, to, or in relation to the land. A covenant by a surety guaranteeing that a tenant's covenants which touched and concerned the land would be performed and observed was itself a covenant which touched and concerned the land. Accordingly, in that case, the assignee landlord was entitled to recover unpaid rent from the surety.

In the present case, the tenant's covenant is a covenant to pay a sum of money (i.e., rent). This covenant, clearly, 'touches and concerns' the land (i.e., the freehold reversionary estate) and the surety covenant appears to meet all the above requirements (i.e., it is not expressed to be exclusively for the personal benefit of Hogan Estates Ltd, it clearly affects the nature, quality, mode of user or value of the reversioner's land and, as a covenant, is beneficial to the reversioner for the time being). The benefit of the surety covenant has, therefore, passed to the Duke, who may thus hold Bob and Jane to account for the arrears of rent of Tomkins Ltd.

(b) The original parties to the lease are Fox Property Ltd (as landlord) and Simon (as tenant). Simon, as original tenant, is as a matter of contract legally liable on all the covenants in the lease (including the covenant to pay rent) for the duration of the term, even where he subsequently assigns his interest. The position is unaffected by the Landlord and Tenant (Covenants) Act 1995 since, here again, the lease was granted (in 1990) prior to the enactment of the Act (i.e., 1 January 1996). The doctrine of privity of contract continues to apply to old tenancies granted before this date. Invariably the tenant will covenant expressly on behalf of himself and his successors in title, but even where this is not the case he will be deemed to do so in respect of those covenants which relate to the land (e.g., a covenant to pay rent) by virtue of the Law of Property Act 1925, s. 79(1), unless a contrary intention appears in the lease.

It follows, therefore, that Simon (as original tenant) remains liable to Fox Property Ltd in contract to pay the rent throughout the term of the lease, irrespective of the subsequent assignments of the leasehold term. In this connection, it has been held that the original tenant has no power to force the landlord to sue the current assignee in breach before pursuing his remedy against him (*Norwich Union Life Insurance* v *Low Profile Fashions* (1992) 64 P & CR 187).

In order, however, for Fox Property Ltd to recover the arrears of rent from Simon, it must give notice of its intention to do so within six months of the liability arising: s. 17 of the Landlord and Tenant (Covenants) Act 1995. This provision, which applies to all tenancies (including those entered into before 1 January 1996), requires that if the landlord wishes to sue the original tenant for fixed charges (i.e., arrears of rent, service charge or liquidated damages, including interest thereon) it must give the requisite notice within the prescribed time-limit. Failure to do so means that the landlord loses the right to recover from the original tenant to the extent that the sums fell due more than six months prior to any notice served. Another important provision under the 1995 Act, which is common to both old and new leases, relates to the former tenant's entitlement to an overriding lease. The Act entitles Simon, if he satisfies Tony's financial obligations to the landlord, to call for the grant to him (within 12 months) of an overriding lease from Fox Property Ltd for a term equal to the unexpired residue of the current lease (plus a nominal reversion). This would have the effect of inserting Simon as an intermediate landlord between Fox Property Ltd and the defaulting assignee, Tony. Although this may ultimately enable Simon to recoup his expenditure in discharging his liability to the landlord, it also has several disadvantages, namely, the overriding lease will attract stamp duty and, by taking up such a lease, Simon may become liable for significant landlord's covenants (e.g., to repair, insure, perform maintenance services, etc.).

As between Fox Property Ltd and the subsequent assignees (Brook Ltd, Sherry and Tony), there exists privity of estate while each assignee is in possession. Thus, since Tony is the current assignee in possession, privity of estate exists between him and the original landlord. (There is no longer any relationship of estate as between Fox Property Ltd and Brook Ltd or Sherry.) As the current assignee of the lease, Tony can sue or be sued on the covenants in the lease which relate to the land demised (e.g., a covenant to pay rent) under the rule in *Spencer's Case* (1583) 5 Co. Rep 16a. The difficulty here is that Tony is bankrupt and has no assets of any value with which to meet the arrears of rent.

If Simon is liable for all the rent owing from Tony (for the reasons mentioned earlier), it may be possible for him to claim reimbursement, by way of indemnity. Such an indemnity may arise in several ways, namely: (i) by way of an express covenant for indemnity; (ii) by way of implication under statute (the Law of Property Act 1925, s. 77(1)(c)); or (iii) by implication under the rule in *Moule* v *Garrett* (1872) LR 7 Ex 101.

As to (i), a tenant, on assigning the unexpired residue of the term, may oblige his assignee to enter into an express covenant for indemnity with him. Clear words are required to achieve this (see, e.g., *Butler Estates Co.* v *Bean* [1942] 1 KB 1). In the present case, however, it seems that Simon has not extracted any such express right of indemnity from his assignee, Brook Ltd.

As to (ii), there is implied into any assignment for value a covenant under which the assignee will indemnify the assignor in respect of any liability incurred for any breach of covenant committed during the remainder of the term (s. 77(1)(c) of the 1925 Act (unregistered land) and the Land Registration Act 1925, s. 24(1)(b) (registered land)): (both then applicable). The effect of s. 77(1) is that the original tenant will have a right of indemnity against his immediate assignee and each subsequent assignor will also have a similar right of indemnity against his assignee, thereby creating a chain of indemnity covenants: *Scottish & Newcastle plc* v *Raquz* [2003] EWCA Civ 1070. Thus, it is open to Simon to claim an indemnity from his immediate assignee (Brook Ltd) for the rent arrears owed by Tony. Similarly, Brook Ltd could claim an indemnity from its immediate asignee, Sherry, who in turn could seek reimbursement from Tony. In this connection, it has been held that an assignee who accepts the liabilities and responsibilities attached to the lease gives valuable consideration for the assignment within the meaning of s. 77(1) of the 1925 Act (*Johnsey Estates Ltd* v *Lewis Manley (Engineering) Ltd* (1987) 284 EG 1240).

As to (iii), in addition to the statutory right under s. 77(1), the original tenant has an implied right of indemnity at common law against the assignee in breach (see, e.g., *Selous Street Properties Ltd* v *Oronel Fabrics Ltd* (1984) 270 EG 643 and 743, where the original tenant was held entitled to be indemnified by the current assignee in breach under the principle in *Moule* v *Garrett*, above, and to be subrogated to the rights of the landlord against such assignee). The rule would therefore permit Simon to sue Tony directly so as to recoup the arrears which Simon is contracturally liable to pay to Fox Property Ltd.

Since Tony is not worth suing, Simon's practical recourse is by way of indemnity against Brook Ltd under s. 77(1) of the 1925 Act. In this connection, the original tenant is not required to serve a s. 17 notice on his assignee in order to recover payments from him *M. W. Kellog Ltd* v *F. Tobin* [1999] L & TR 513.

Q Question 4

In 1997, Blake Ltd granted Peter a 12-year lease of a restaurant in Pimlico, London. The annual rent was £80,000 per annum payable in quarterly instalments. The lease contained a forfeiture clause allowing the landlord to re-enter upon the premises in the event of rent default or any other tenant's breach of covenant. The lease also contained a tenant's qualified covenant against assignment. This covenant stated, *inter alia*, that the prior written consent of the landlord was required in the event of an assignment, and that the tenant enter into an authorised guarantee agreement with the landlord guaranteeing performance of the tenant's covenants in the lease by the tenant's assignee, as a precondition of granting such consent.

In 1998, with the prior written consent of Blake Ltd, Peter assigned the unexpired residue of the lease to Boris. Peter also entered into an authorised guarantee agreement with Blake Ltd, thereby standing as guarantor for Boris's leasehold obligations. Since taking up possession, Boris has been operating a Polish restaurant from the premises.

In 2004, Boris's restaurant business came upon hard times. Custom fell away and Boris was plunged into insolvency. As a consequence, Boris has fallen into arrears with the rent due under the lease. The last quarterly instalment received by Blake Ltd was in March 2004. No payments have been received since this quarter.

Consider how the Landlord and Tenant (Covenant) Act 1995 will affect the rights and remedies of Blake Ltd against Peter. (Peter has not been given any written warning or other indication of the fact that Boris has fallen into rent arrears).

Commentary

This question focuses specifically on the changes to the law effected by the Landlord and Tenant (Covenants) Act 1995. A good answer will mention briefly the old law relating to the original tenant's liability under the privity of contract rule, and the changes which have been introduced by the 1995 Act (i.e., the abolition of the doctrine of privity, the introduction of authorised guarantee agreements, the default notice procedure and overriding leases).

Your answer will inevitably concentrate on detailing the relevant provisions of the Act. This is an easy question provided you have mastered how the Act operates in practice. For further reading, see Elvidge, S. and Williams, P., 'Overriding Importance' [1996] EG 9647 132 and Walter, P., 'The Landlord and Tenant (Covenants) Act 1995: A Legislative Folly' [1996] Conv. 432.

- Peter not released from the tenant's covenants upon assignment of the lease to Boris because he is subject to an AGA

- Blake Ltd must, however, serve Peter with notice of the rent arrears complying with s. 17 of the 1995 Act. Failure to do so within six months renders the arrears irrecoverable

- This will not preclude Blake Ltd from recovering more recent arrears provided s. 17 notice served within the prescribed time-limit. If Peter discharges this liability, he will be entitled to claim on overriding lease

- Consider effect of overriding lease on parties, especially Peter's ability to seek possession of the premises by instigating forfeiture proceedings against Boris. If successful, Peter will be able to obtain a new tenant for the premises

ːQ̈ː Suggested answer

It is important to note at the outset that Peter's lease was granted in 1997 (i.e., after the coming into force of the Landlord and Tenant (Covenants) Act 1995 on 1 January 1996). For new leases entered into on or after 1 January 1996, the Act provides that that all leasehold covenants, irrespective of whether they 'touch and concern' the land, are fully enforceable between landlord and tenant, except where the covenant is expressed to be purely personal. The basic rule is that a tenant is liable on the covenants in the lease only while he remains tenant — upon assignment of the lease, he is automatically discharged from further liability under the lease. The Act therefore effectively abolishes the enduring contractual liability of original tenants, but only in respect of new leases granted on or after 1 January 1996. While a tenant will automatically be released on assignment of the term in most cases (see s. 5 of the 1995 Act), the landlord can require the outgoing tenant to give a guarantee as to future performance of the tenant's obligations by its immediate assignee. In this connection, the Act states that the assigning tenant may be required to enter into an authorised guarantee agreement (AGA) with the landlord as a condition of granting consent to the assignment: s. 16.

The Act also introduced several new measures which apply to both old (i.e., granted before 1 January 1996) and new leases. Of particular significance in the present context is the introduction of the 'default notice' and 'overriding lease' procedures: see ss. 17–20. The default notice procedure is designed as an 'early warning system' for former tenants (and guarantors: see *Cheverell Estates Ltd* v *Harris* [1998] 02 EG 127) who may be obliged to make good to the landlord the financial default of the current tenant. In this connection, s. 17 of the Act states that the landlord must serve on such a party a default notice detailing any fixed charges unpaid by the current tenant, within six months of the relevant sums falling due. These fixed charges are defined in the Act as rent arrears, service charges, insurance fees, and liquidated damages (including interest thereon). In order, therefore, for a landlord to be able to recover any such charges either from an original tenant in an old lease (under the doctrine of privity of contract), or as against a former tenant in a new lease who has entered into an AGA, he must first serve the requisite s. 17 notice in respect of each payment within six months of the charge falling due. (It is noteworthy, however, that a single notice could cover more than one payment, provided that each sum was due less than six months previously.) In the event that the landlord fails to serve such a notice within six months, the charge becomes irrecoverable.

Hand-in-glove with the default notice procedure, the 1995 Act introduced the novel concept of the overriding lease, which is intended to benefit former original tenants (who may be liable for the current tenant's default under the doctrine of privity of contract) and former tenants in new leases (who may be so obliged under an AGA). The Act states that former tenants (or their guarantors) who have paid up under a default notice have 12 months from the date of payment in which to claim 'an overriding lease' from the landlord. Such a lease is inserted above the existing lease, thus creating a direct landlord and tenant relationship between the former tenant (or guarantor) and the assignee in default. In other words, the claimant of the overriding lease becomes the current assignee's landlord and can determine what action, including forfeiture, to take against him. Such an overriding lease will generally be on the same terms as the defaulting tenant's lease, and of a term equivalent to the residue of such lease save that a small reversionary period (typically, three days) will be added. The main advantage, therefore, of acquiring an overriding lease is that the former tenant (or his guarantor) can regain possession of the premises (through forfeiture proceedings) with a view to marketing the property afresh in order to recoup the monies paid to the landlord in discharging its liability under a s. 17 notice.

In the present case, because Peter's lease is a new lease under the Act, the enduring contractual liability of Peter, as original tenant, has been effectively abolished. However, Peter still remains liable to underwrite the financial default and other leasehold obligations of Boris by virtue of his liability under the AGA, which he entered into with Blake Ltd as a condition of the latter granting consent to the assignment. This, in principle, is quite lawful, and indeed encouraged by the Act. However, Peter can be held liable for Boris's rent arrears only upon receipt of a valid s. 17 notice claiming the arrears due. We are told that Blake Ltd received the last quarterly payment in respect of rent in March 2004. Blake Ltd can pursue Peter for those rent arrears only if it gave Peter the appropriate notice within six months of that charge becoming due. In this respect, s. 17 provides a statutory limitation period of six months in relation to landlords who are seeking to claim arrears of rent or other fixed charges from former tenants/guarantors. Since Blake Ltd has clearly not served any such notice on Peter, it will be barred from recovering those arrears from him. This, however, will not preclude Blake Ltd from recovering more recent rent arrears provided it serves the requisite s. 17 notice within the prescribed time-limit. Should Peter then discharge his liability in respect of those arrears to the landlord, he will be able to claim an overriding lease of an equivalent length of the residue of the current lease, plus three days.

Save as to this, the overriding lease will be on the same terms and conditions as the existing lease.

Peter will be liable on the overriding lease for the rent to Blake Ltd, and will become Boris's landlord. If Boris fails to pay the rent to Peter (as his new landlord) then Peter will be able to seek possession of Boris's lease by instigating forfeiture proceedings against him for non-payment of rent. This is possible because we are informed that Boris's lease (and, consequently, the overriding lease) contains a forfeiture clause, which allows the landlord to re-enter the premises in the event, *inter alia*, of non-payment of rent. If Peter does seek to forfeit Boris's lease, the waiver rules relating to forfeiture will apply as normal, as will the rules relating to relief against forfeiture for non-payment of rent: see ss. 138 and 139 of County Courts Act 1984. If Peter is successful in his forfeiture action against Boris, he will be in a position to obtain a new tenant for the restaurant premises by either subletting or assigning the same with Blake Ltd's consent in accordance with the terms of his overriding lease.

Q Question 5

What impact does the Contracts (Rights of Third Parties) Act 1999 have on the enforceability of covenants in commercial leases? Give specific examples to illustrate your answer.

Commentary

The 1999 Act came into force on 11 November 1999 and does not have retrospective effect, although it was subject to a six-month opt-in period (i.e., it applied to all contracts entered into on or after 11 May 2000, but contracts entered into from 11 November 1999 to 10 May 2000 could be made subject to the Act if the parties so agreed).

The question requires you to give an overview of the Act and, more specifically, to give examples of how the legislation may affect the enforceability of leasehold covenants in commercial leases. One obvious example relates to covenants by subtenants which may be for the benefit of superior landlords, or covenants given by superior landlords (e.g., to provide maintenance services for the benefit of tenants) which may be enforced by subtenants. In addition, the Act is likely to affect covenants which are taken to benefit adjoining owners or other tenants in a development. You will also score higher marks if you are able to show how the 1999 Act operates in conjunction with the Landlord and Tenant (Covenants) Act 1995 — by no means an easy task, if your knowledge of the 1995 Act is only superficial! For a good critical appraisal of the 1999 Act in the context of property transactions generally, see Nash, S., and Krieger, A., 'Limitations of the Act' [2000] EG 172.

- Consider the doctrine of privity of contract and the rationale for introducing the 1999 Act

- Effect of 1999 Act on ability of third party to enforce a contract. In particular, ability of a subtenant to directly enforce a superior landlord's covenants contained in a headlease

- Conversely, superior landlord may now enforce covenants in a sublease expressed to be for his benefit. Similarly, covenants may now be enforceable by tenants *inter se* (e.g., tenants in a shopping centre)

- Problems of inter-relationship between 1999 Act and Landlord and Tenant (Covenants) Act 1995

- Likely that superior landlords and subtenants will wish to exclude operation of the 1999 Act, especially in the commercial sector

:Q: Suggested answer

The doctrine of privity of contract provides that a contract under English law cannot generally confer rights or impose obligations arising under it on persons who are not parties to the contract. In essence, it prevents someone, not a party to the contract, from taking its benefit; and it also protects that person from burdens being imposed on him, without his consent, by the parties to the contract. The rule has given rise to much criticism because, in principle, there is no reason why rights in favour of non-parties should not be created, if the parties so desire.

The 1999 Act allows a third party to enforce a term of a contract, despite not being a party to it, if the contract expressly provides that he may, or purports to confer a benefit on him. The third party need not be individually named in the contract and need not even be in existence at the time the contract is made, provided he is identified by description. For example, a covenant in a lease purporting to confer benefits on subtenants can now be enforceable by any subtenant of the demised property. The intention of the Act is, therefore, to place the third party in the same position as if he had been a party to the contract, so that he has all the same remedies as the contracting parties and is subject to all the same restrictions and exclusions. So far as the parties themselves are concerned, they have all the defences against claims by the third party that they would have had if he had been a party to the contract. They are not, however, entitled to rescind the contract or vary its terms so as to deprive the third party of its benefit, without obtaining the third party's consent. It is, however, possible to exclude the application of the Act by agreement.

Under the Landlord and Tenant (Covenants) Act 1995, a subtenant has no ability directly to enforce a superior landlord's covenant contained in a headlease which is a new tenancy (i.e., granted on or after 1 January 1996). (If the headlease is an old tenancy, the subtenant can directly enforce the superior landlord's covenants, provided they relate to the sublet premises.) The 1999 Act now permits direct enforcement of such covenants (e.g., a covenant to insure or repair the building) by a subtenant, provided the lease expressly so provides or the covenant in question purports to confer such a benefit on him: s. 1. In the latter case, however, the subtenant will not be able to enforce the covenant if, on a proper construction of the headlease, it appears that the head landlord and head tenant did not intend the covenant to be enforceable by the subtenant. Quite apart from this, it is also open to the parties to state expressly that they do not want any other persons (e.g., subtenants) to have a right to enforce any part of the headlease. As already mentioned, in order to have the right of enforcement under s. 1, the third party must be identified expressly in the contract either by name, or as a member of a class or as answering a particular description, although it need not be in existence at the time the contract is entered into.

Under s. 3(5) of the 1995 Act, a superior landlord is able to enforce a covenant restricting user against a subtenant, but not any other covenant. In *Amsprop Trading Ltd* v *Harris Distribution Ltd* [1997] 1 WLR 1025, for example, it was held that, although the sublease expressly referred to the superior landlords as persons for whose benefit the repairing covenants in the sublease were given, the covenants were not made with the superior landlords and, accordingly, the latter could not enforce them directly against the subtenant. Under the 1999 Act, however, subleases can now contain covenants (e.g., to repair or permit access) expressed to be for the benefit of any superior landlord, which can then be directly enforceable against the subtenant. Although the same effect can be achieved by imposing direct covenants in the licence to sublet, the new Act provides a much simpler mechanism for direct enforcement as between superior landlord and subtenant.

Under the 1999 Act, it is also possible for covenants in relation to say, nuisance, noise, etc. by one tenant to be taken for the benefit of other tenants in a development such as a shopping centre. Prior to the Act, such covenants would normally only have been enforceable by virtue of a letting scheme (*Williams* v *Kiley (t/a CK Supermarkets Ltd)* [2003] 06 EG 147) or a building scheme under the rule in *Elliston* v *Reacher* [1908] 2 Ch 374. An example of the problems associated with the enforcement of leasehold covenants in the context of a shopping centre is to be found in the case of *Co-operative Insurance Society* v *Argyll Stores (Holdings) Ltd* [1997] 3 All ER 297, where the House of Lords held that a covenant in a lease of retail premises to keep open for trading during business hours was not, other than in exceptional circumstances, specifically enforceable by a landlord: see, Bailey, P., 'When Shops Go AWOL' [1997] EG 9723, pp. 137–39. More strikingly, in *Transworld Land Co.* v *J. Sainsbury plc* [1990] 2 EGLR 255, the landlord sought to claim damages in respect of the adverse effect on other tenants of J. Sainsbury having closed their store in the landlord's shopping centre: see also, *Costain Property Developments Ltd* v *Finlay & Co. Ltd* [1989] 1 EGLR 237. Clearly, a simpler route to the enforcement of the keep-open covenant in the *Transworld* case would have been for the other tenants within the centre to be able to claim their trading losses against Sainsbury directly. The 1999 Act now makes this possible.

The interrelation between the 1995 and 1999 Acts is likely to give rise to some problems in the future. What, for example, is the position if a tenant, who undertakes a repairing obligation for the benefit of other tenants in a development, subsequently assigns his lease? Under the 1995 Act, he will be released (in the absence of an authorised guarantee agreement) from further performance of the tenant's covenants in the lease. He cannot, therefore, be sued by other tenants on the repairing covenant after the assignment. But what is the position of the assignee? Under the 1995 Act, the landlord can enforce the covenant against him, but what about the other tenants? Under the 1999 Act, they are able to enforce the covenant against 'the promisor', defined in s. 1(7) as 'the *party to the contract* against whom the term is enforceable by the third party'. The obvious difficulty here is that the assignee is not a party to the contract (i.e., the lease) but has merely acquired the leasehold estate by assignment. One solution to this problem is to ensure that the assignee covenants (in the licence to assign) not only with the landlord but also with other tenants to observe the tenant's covenants in the lease. This, of course, involves reverting to the pre-1999 Act practice of requiring direct covenants from the assignee.

As mentioned earlier, it is permissible for the parties expressly to contract out of the Act for contracts made on or after 11 May 2000. This, it is suggested, is likely to be common practice in the leasehold context. For example, a superior landlord granting a headlease will usually be reluctant to undertake onerous obligations (e.g., to repair) to a class of subtenants. This reluctance is all the more likely given that the 1999 Act does not specifically state whether or not rights acquired pursuant to it are assignable. The danger here is that the superior landlord may have little or no control over who is within the potential class. It also seems unlikely that subtenants would wish to expose themselves to greater liability under their covenants in favour of superior landlords. Practically speaking, therefore, the new Act may have only limited impact on commercial leases. In the majority of new leases, the expectation amongst practitioners is that there will be an express clause excluding the operation of the Act. By contrast, in the residential field, the enforcement of nuisance and noise covenants will be more relevant to adjoining tenants in, say, a block of flats, and so a decision to retain the provisions of the Act is more likely.

Further reading

Butler, J., and Williams, H., 'Under Guarantee' [2002] EG 142.

Butler, J., and Williams, H., 'Limited Liability' [2002] EG 220.

Dear, B., 'Time for Clarity in AGA Saga' [2000] EG 167.

Draper, M., 'Personal Covenants' (2002) SJ 314.

Draper, M., 'Enforceability of Lease Covenants' (2000) SJ 638.

Elvidge, S., and Williams, P., 'Overriding Importance' [1996] EG 132.

Murdoch, S., 'Sweetshop Revenge' [2003] EG 150.

Murdoch, S., 'The Spirit of the Act' [2001] EG 171.

Wilkinson, H.W., 'Non-receipt but Valid Service' (2001) NLJ 275.

Walter, P., 'The Landlord and Tenant (Covenants) Act 1995: A Legislative Folly' [1996] 60 Conv 432.

Woodhead, S., 'Life After Disclaimer' [2004] EG 146.

Implied and usual covenants

Introduction

In this chapter, we have included five questions covering the following topics:

(a)   the landlord's implied covenant for quiet enjoyment;

(b)   the landlord's implied covenant not to derogate from grant;

(c)   unlawful eviction and harassment;

(d)   usual covenants;

(e)   a tenant's denial of his landlord's title.

(Implied obligations to repair are covered in **Chapter 7** under the heading 'Leasehold Dilapidations'.)

Problem questions on quiet enjoyment and non-derogation from grant are popular with examiners. Since the publication of the 2nd edition of this book, there have been several important developments in this area. The decision in *Port v Griffith* [1938] 1 All ER 295, concerning a landlord who let adjoining premises to the tenant's trade rival, was applied by Garland J in *Romulus Trading Co. Ltd v Comet Properties Ltd* [1996] 2 EGLR 70. The upshot of both these decisions has been that a landlord will not be in derogation from grant where, having let premises to the tenant for a particular purpose, he then lets adjoining property for a substantially similar purpose. The fact that this makes the tenant's business on the demised property more expensive (or less convenient) to carry on is irrelevant: *O'Cedar Ltd v Slough Trading Co.* [1927] 2 KB 123. The strict approach in the *Port* and *Romulus* line of cases has, however, been modified more recently in a number of cases involving shopping precincts. In *Chartered Trust v Davis* [1997] 2 EGLR 83, the Court of Appeal held that, where a landlord granted a lease of a shop in a shopping mall, over which he maintained control and recovered a service charge, and later let an adjoining unit for a different purpose (a pawnbroker) which created a nuisance, the landlord's failure to abate that nuisance constituted a derogation from grant. Crucially, however, what constituted the derogation in this case was not the mere fact of letting to a pawnbroker but the actual conduct of the pawnbroker's business. In *Petra Investments Ltd v Jeffrey Rogers plc* [2000] 3 EGLR 120, Hart

J. held that the covenant not to derogate carried with it an implied obligation on the part of the landlord not to alter or use the common parts of a retail centre in such a way as to cause it to lose its character as a retail shopping mall. In *Oceanic Village Ltd v Shirayama and Shokusan Ltd* [2001] L & TR 35, the scope of such liability was further extended beyond retail complexes so as to include lettings within a purpose-built building. In that case, the claimant was a tenant of a gift shop within the London Aquarium building who objected to the landlord's proposal to allow similar gift items to be sold from two kiosks to be erected on the walkway between the building and the river. In holding that this would constitute a derogation from grant, the court confined the earlier decisions in *Port* and *Romulus* to cases involving separate and independent retail units. See further: Levy, D., 'Competing Businesses — Derogation from Grant' (2001) 5 L & T Rev 72; Mowbray, J., 'Fishy Business' (2001) SJ 617 and Mowbray, J. and Juden, J., 'Derogation from Grant' (2000) SJ 1046. Another recent case, although not involving competing businesses, is also instructive in this area. In *Platt v London Underground Ltd* [2001] 2 EGLR 121, a confectionery kiosk was let near the exit to an underground station. The tenant complained that he was unable to trade successfully because the landlord had closed the exit thereby depriving the kiosk of much of its passing trade. Neuberger J. held that this amounted to a derogation from grant notwithstanding that the terms of the lease permitted the landlord to close the exit as and when it wished. The lease could not oust the doctrine of derogation from grant, especially where it was clear that both parties realised that the use of the exit was vital to the tenant's business. We have included a short question on this new line of cases: Question 5(b).

Another interesting development concerns the inter-relationship between the covenant for quiet enjoyment and a landlord's covenant to repair. In *Goldmile Properties Ltd v Lechouritis* [2003] 15 EG 143, the Court of Appeal concluded that these two (potentially conflicting) covenants coexisted on a basis of parity so that the tenant's entitlement to quiet enjoyment of the demised premises did not take priority over the landlord's obligation to keep the building in repair. Ultimately, there was a threshold for disturbance caused by such repairs based on the landlord taking all *reasonable* precautions to minimise damage to the tenant's enjoyment. We have also included a short question on this interesting topic: see Question 5(c).

You should, of course, also be aware of the House of Lords ruling in *Southwark London Borough Council v Mills* [2001] 1 AC 1, on the liability of a landlord for inadequate sound insulation. This is an important decision and one likely to feature in a landlord and tenant or housing law exam paper. It has recently been applied in the context of noise created by the use of a rubbish chute by tenants in a block of flats: *Long v Southwark London Borough Council* [2002] 47 EG 150. See further, Question 5(a). We have included an essay and problem type question on the *Mills* case: see Questions 2 and 4.

Most importantly, you should be familiar with the Housing Act 1988, s. 27(3), which imposes a statutory liability to pay damages on a landlord who personally, or through his agents, has committed acts which amount to the offences of unlawful eviction or harassment under the Protection from Eviction Act 1977, s. 1. This liability is incurred by acts occurring after 9 June 1988 and arises irrespective of whether or not there has actually been a conviction for the offence. Section 28(1) of the 1988 Act provides that the measure of damages for the purpose of s. 27(3) is the difference between the value of the landlord's interest subject to the residential occupier's right, and its value in the absence of the occupier's right (*Tagro* v *Cafane* [1991] 1 WLR 378). Note also that the tenant is entitled to damages under s. 27 of the 1988 Act or at common law for wrongful eviction, but not both (*Mason* v *Nwokorie* [1994] 05 EG 155). For a brief summary of these provisions, see de Havillande, J., 'Damage Limitation' [1998] EG 9837; Madge, N., 'Harassment and Eviction' (1993) 143 *New Law Journal*, pp. 844–46 and 880–82. See Question 1.

In the case of *Wandsworth London Borough Council* v *Osei-Bonsu* [1999] 1 All ER 265, the Court of Appeal held that a mistaken belief as to the law on the part of the landlord could be relevant as a defence under s. 27(8)(a) of the 1988 Act. However, if the landlord has no 'reasonable cause' for that mistaken belief, this defence will not succeed. The *Wandsworth* case also indicates that, when considering mitigation of damages on account of the occupier's conduct (under s. 27(7)(a)), it is necessary to look at that conduct in the light of all the surrounding facts. Thus, in *Wandsworth* itself, the reality was that the landlord's eviction was the culmination of an unbroken chain of events starting with the occupier's violence towards his wife. In the circumstances, the Court felt it appropriate to reduce damages by two-thirds. It seems also that a wilful withholding of rent amounts to conduct which the court can take into account in reducing damages (*Regalgrand Ltd* v *Dickerson* [1996] EGCS 182). As to the question of assessment of damages generally under s. 28(3)(a), the Court of Appeal also confirmed the generally held view that s. 28 requires valuation on a factual, as opposed to a notional, basis. In other words, the assessment must take account of the *actual* situation in the premises which are being valued. In *Melville* v *Bruton* [1997] 29 EG 319, for example, two tenants remained in occupation of the property after the eviction of a third tenant. As a result, no award under s. 28 could be made to the evicted tenant. Similarly, damages will be low in cases where the tenant has limited security of tenure regardless of the eviction. In *King* v *Jackson* [1998] 03 EG 138, only a small award was made because the tenant, who was holding under an assured shorthold tenancy, had given notice to quit effective just six days after the date of the unlawful eviction.

Apart from the tenant's civil remedies, you should also devote some time to studying the Protection from Eviction Act 1977, ss. 1, 2 and 3 (as amended by the Housing Act 1988). These provisions seek to protect by way of criminal sanction the rights of residential occupiers peaceably to enjoy their property. Notable cases in this area include *R* v *Yuthiwattana* (1984) 16 HLR 49 and *R* v *Phekoo* [1981] 1 WLR 1117. Remember also that the Criminal Law Act 1977 creates criminal offences that are of relevance to the law of unlawful eviction and harassment. Section 6(1) of the 1977 Act states that any person who, without lawful authority, uses or threatens violence to secure entry to premises commits an offence. Under s. 7, an offence is committed by a trespasser refusing to leave when required to do so by or on behalf of a displaced residential occupier. A 'displaced residential occupier' is defined as a lawful occupier who has been excluded from his residence by the trespasser

(s. 12(3)). While this provision is primarily intended against squatters, there is no reason why the trespasser should not be a landlord who refuses to leave the demised premises when required to do so by his tenant.

The subject of usual covenants is often omitted from landlord and tenant courses and so be guided by your lecturer as to how much time to devote to this relatively narrow topic. We have included it in this chapter together with a question on the tenant's denial of his landlord's title (see Question 3).

Q Question 1

Susan has been the weekly tenant of a furnished flat within a block of flats owned by Gerry since 1993. A few weeks ago, Gerry wrote to Susan seeking an increase in rent. Susan wrote back saying she would not pay anything over and above her current rent. Gerry was very irritated by this reply and wrote to Susan demanding that she vacate her flat by 10 a.m. the following morning. Susan did not comply with this demand and went to work as usual.

When she got back in the evening, Susan found that Gerry had changed the lock to her flat and thrown all her belongings out onto the landing. She could not get in and was forced to spend the night at a nearby hotel. Susan has been unable to gain access to the flat ever since.

Advise Susan as to her civil remedies against Gerry.

Commentary

This question covers a variety of legal issues on quiet enjoyment and unlawful eviction. Some reference to the Housing Act 1988 is also required.

Try to give your answer a logical structure. There is a lot to write down so be economical with the facts of the cases. Cite cases to support legal principle and do not dwell on one point to the detriment of others. If you follow this advice, you should be able to score a good mark without too much difficulty!

- Susan presumably an assured/assured shorthold tenant under the Housing Act 1988 and, hence, cannot be evicted without a court order

- Gerry's eviction constitutes a breach of the (express/implied) covenant for quiet enjoyment. Gerry's re-entry also amounts to a trespass and an offence under the Protection from Eviction Act 1977

- Consider civil remedies of injunction and damages. Apart from special damages, Susan entitled to general damages under various heads: (1) physical injury, discomfort and inconvenience for breach of covenant for quiet enjoyment (2) injured feelings and mental distress for tort of trespass/nuisance: *Branchett* v

Beaney (1992) (3) aggravated and exemplary damages for Gerry's tortious action: *Drane* v *Evangelou* (1978)

- Susan may also claim damages for statutory tort under s. 27 of the Housing Act 1988. Measure of damages under s. 28(1): *Tagro* v *Cafane* (1991)

⏻ Suggested answer

Presumably Susan's tenancy, unless an assured shorthold tenancy, will be assured and Susan will have security of tenure under the Housing Act 1988. Her tenancy is a weekly (periodic) tenancy and must be terminated by a written notice of proceedings for possession under s. 8 of the 1988 Act. In any event, the tenancy will continue until the landlord, Gerry, obtains a court order for possession by establishing one or more statutory grounds for possession.

Gerry has sought to increase Susan's rent. This he is entitled to do, provided he has served notice in the prescribed form after the applicable qualifying periods have elapsed under the Housing Act 1988, s. 13. The proposed rent will then take effect unless Susan refers the matter to a rent assessment committee. She is not, however, in breach of any terms of her tenancy by not agreeing to the increased rent; but if she fails to refer the matter to a rent assessment committee then after the requisite period the proposed rent would take effect (from the date of the landlord's notice) and she would be in breach of the tenancy if she simply carried on paying the old rent.

Clearly, however, Susan's apparent lack of cooperation with the landlord does not entitle him to re-enter the flat and change the lock. Even if Susan was in breach of her tenancy, Gerry would not be able to evict her save by proceedings in court because the premises comprise a dwelling (Protection from Eviction Act 1977, s. 2). If he had obtained a court order, his subsequent eviction would then have been lawful and not an interruption to Susan's quiet enjoyment: *Botu* v *Brent London Borough Council* (2001) 33 HLR 14.

Gerry's eviction of Susan constitutes a breach of her tenancy. Most tenancy agreements will contain an express covenant which provides that the tenant is entitled to quiet enjoyment of the premises demised. In the absence of an express covenant, however, an implied covenant by the landlord for quiet enjoyment will arise from the relationship of landlord and tenant. The implied covenant protects the tenant from acts which cause physical interference with the tenant's enjoyment of occupation (*Drane* v *Evangelou* [1978] 1 WLR 455).

Since Susan enjoys exclusive possession of the flat under her tenancy, Gerry's re-entry also amounts to a trespass.

By way of criminal sanction, the Protection from Eviction Act 1977 seeks to protect the rights of residential occupiers peacefully to enjoy their property. Susan clearly qualifies as a 'residential occupier' within the meaning of s. 1(1) of the Act since she occupies the flat as a residence under an assured tenancy under the Housing Act 1988. Section 1(2) provides that it is an offence for any person unlawfully to deprive a residential occupier of any premises of his occupation of the premises or of any part of them. In *R* v *Yuthiwattana* (1984) 16 HLR 49, the Court of Appeal held that an unlawful deprivation of occupation for this purpose must have the character of an eviction. Clearly, therefore, an offence has been committed by Gerry under s. 1(2) for unlawfully depriving Susan of her occupation of the flat. It may also be that Gerry's demands for an increase in rent (if written in aggressive terms), coupled with a demand that she vacate the flat within 24 hours, amounts to harassment and that an offence has been committed under s. 1(3) of the 1977 Act.

What civil remedies are available to Susan? Clearly, her immediate concern is to get back into her flat as quickly as possible. If the flat is now empty, she could use the remedy of self-help and break back into the flat. If Gerry was still physically in the property, she could use reasonable force to remove him without committing an offence under the displaced residential occupier provisions of the Criminal Law Act 1977, s. 6(3). However, it is likely that Susan would feel uneasy about taking physical action herself, and therefore she should apply to the court for a mandatory injunction ordering Gerry to give her possession of the flat. She should also seek a negative injunction restraining Gerry from further unlawful acts in the future. If Gerry should fail to comply with the terms of the injunction, he will be in contempt of court and liable to imprisonment.

The further remedy available to Susan is damages. Apart from claiming special damages representing any damage caused to her belongings and for the cost of alternative accommodation, she would be entitled to claim general damages for any physical injury, discomfort, inconvenience etc. caused as a result of the unlawful eviction, but not for injured feelings or mental distress for breach of the covenant for quiet enjoyment (*Branchett* v *Beaney/Branchett* v *Swale Borough Council* [1992] 3 All ER 910). Such damages may, however, be awarded in tort based on trespass or nuisance (*Rookes* v *Barnard* [1964] AC 1129 (HL)). Aggravated damages may also be awarded for claims brought in tort, and are appropriate where there has been especially severe suffering caused by the landlord's conduct. She would also be entitled to exemplary damages in tort (*Drane* v *Evangelou* [1978] 1 WLR 455). However, it is a necessary requirement for the award of such damages that the landlord's action was profit motivated in some way (*Ramdath* v *Oswald Daley* [1993] 20 EG 123, where the Court of Appeal held that an action for unlawful eviction could give rise to an award of exemplary damages under the *Drane* principle 'whenever necessary to teach the landlord a lesson'). If Gerry is prosecuted under the Protection from Eviction Act 1977 and receives a fine or is ordered to pay his victim compensation, then such sums may be taken into account when the court comes to award damages in the civil action (*Ashgar* v *Ahmed* (1984) 17 HLR 25 and *Smith* v *Jenkins* (1979) 129 NLJ 198).

Lastly, reference must be made to the Housing Act 1988, ss. 27 and 28, which provide a tenant with a statutory right to damages in cases of unlawful eviction or harassment. Section 27(3) imposes a statutory liability to pay damages on a landlord who personally (or through his agents) has committed acts which amount to the offences of unlawful eviction or harassment. (No claim for damages under the 1988 Act lies against the landlord's agent as a joint tortfeasor: *Sampson* v *Wilson* [1995] 3 WLR 455.) This liability is incurred by acts occurring after 9 June 1988 and arises irrespective of whether or not there has actually been a conviction for the offence. The liability is specifically stated to be in the nature of a tort and to be additional to any other liability in damages (i.e., breach of quiet enjoyment or trespass). By virtue of s. 27(6), the landlord has a complete defence either if the tenant is actually reinstated in the premises before the proceedings are finally disposed of, or if a court makes an order reinstating the tenant. In *Tagro* v *Cafane* [1991] 1 WLR 378, it was held that reinstatement did not consist of handing the tenant back a key to a lock which did not work and allowing her to resume occupation of a totally wrecked room.

Section 27(7) of the 1988 Act provides that any damages awarded against a landlord may be reduced where, prior to the events giving rise to the claim, the conduct of the tenant was such that it would be reasonable to reduce the damages payable, or where, before the proceedings were begun, the landlord offered to reinstate the tenant and the tenant unreasonably refused that offer. It seems that the court cannot award any damages under the 1988 Act where the tenant is reinstated before proceedings to enforce the landlord's liability are finally disposed of (*Murray* v *Aslam* (1995) 27 HLR 284).

It is apparent that Susan will be entitled to statutory damages unless, prior to the hearing, there is an offer of reinstatement by Gerry and it is unreasonable for her to refuse such an offer. This would not, however, preclude Susan from claiming damages at common law.

Section 28(1) of the 1988 Act provides that the measure of damages for the purpose of s. 27(3) is the difference between the value of the landlord's interest subject to the residential occupier's right and its value in the absence of the occupier's right (*Tagro* v *Cafane* [1991] 1 WLR 378). For these purposes, it is the landlord's interest in the building in which the premises are situated, not just his interest in the demised premises, which has to be valued. The valuation must reflect the true position of the actual tenant. If Susan's security of tenure is limited (for example, because she is an assured shorthold tenant), this will be reflected in the award of damages: *King* v *Jackson* [1998] 03 EG 138, where a nominal award was made under s. 28 because the tenant, under an assured shorthold tenancy, had given notice to quit effective just six days after the date of the illegal eviction. It should also be noted that damages cannot be awarded for the same loss (i.e., exemplary damages and s. 28 damages) (*Mason* v *Nwokorie* [1994] 05 EG 155).

Q Question 2

Critically assess the House of Lords ruling in *Southwark London Borough Council* v *Mills* [2001] 1 AC 1. Would the Law Commission's proposals for reform of the law of leasehold dilapidations redress the deficiencies in the law highlighted by the *Southwark* ruling?

Commentary

This is a relatively straightforward essay-type question requiring you to assess the legal impact of the *Southwark* decision. Apart from analysing the case itself, the question requires you to comment on the most recent Law Commission recommendations in this particular area: see the Law Commission's Report, 'The Law of Landlord and Tenant: Responsibility for State and Condition of Property' (Law Com. No. 238, 1996). (See also Question 5, **Chapter 7**.) You will obviously lose marks if you make no reference to the Law Commission's proposals.

Your answer should avoid a simple rehearsal of the facts and ruling in the case. Try to be analytical in your commentary of the judgments and be prepared to make reference to earlier case law which you consider requires re-examination in the light of the House of Lords ruling. In short, demonstrate to the examiner that you have a good understanding of the legal issues raised in the case and how they might be resolved by reform of the law. See further, Rook D., 'Excessive Noise can be a Breach of the Landlord's Covenant for Quiet Enjoyment' [2000] Conv. 161.

- Activities of neighbouring tenants in *Southwark* did not constitute a nuisance. Hence, landlord not liable in the absence of any express obligation to ensure adequate sound insulation between the flats. Obligation to repair did not cover this defect in the absence of disrepair: *Quick* v *Taff Ely Borough Council* (1986)

- Covenant for quiet enjoyment requires substantial interference with tenant's lawful possession which does not have to be direct or physical. But, like derogation from grant, it only operates prospectively and is confined to the subject-matter of the grant. Lack of sound-proofing already present when tenants took the premises

- Law Commission recommended extension of statutory implied condition as to fitness for human habitation (s. 8 of the Landlord and Tenant Act 1985) to every lease for less than seven years regardless of rental level. Also new criteria suggested for determining fitness for human habitation but these do not include sound insulation. Obvious gap needs to be re-examined

:Ọ: **Suggested answer**

The House of Lords in *Southwark* (the leading opinions were given by Lords Hoffmann and Millett) unanimously confirmed that a landlord cannot be liable in nuisance for authorising the activities of his tenant if those activities do not themselves constitute an actionable nuisance. Nuisance involves doing something on neighbouring land that constitutes unreasonable interference with the claimant's enjoyment of his land. In *Southwark*, the tenants complained of inadequate sound insulation between their flats and other flats in the same building, causing them to hear all of the everyday activities of neighbouring tenants. Those activities were not only reasonable but, in the words of Lord Millett, 'the necessary and inevitable incidents of the ordinary occupation of residential property'. They could not, therefore, as a matter of law, constitute an actionable nuisance.

Moreover, the tenants had taken their flats in the knowledge that the neighbouring flats were also occupied as residential flats; they could not, therefore, complain about the normal activities carried on by their neighbouring occupants which, of course, mirrored their own activities. Nor could they complain to the landlord for permitting such activities by letting the neighbouring flats. The tenancy agreements contained no express obligation on the landlord to ensure adequate sound insulation between the flats and no such obligation could be implied under the general law. The obligation to 'keep in repair the structure and exterior of the dwelling-house' (implied by s. 11 of the Landlord and Tenant Act 1985) has no application where the property is not actually in a state of disrepair (i.e., 'disrepair' means deterioration from a previous physical condition: *Quick* v *Taff Ely BC* [1986] QB 809). The statutorily implied condition as to fitness for human habitation (imposed by s. 8 of the 1985 Act) was equally unhelpful in so far as it is constrained by unrealistically low rental limits (unchanged since 1957) which render the provision redundant in virtually all (including the instant) cases. In the absence of any governing contractual or statutory provision, therefore, the principle that the tenant 'takes the property as he finds it' was held to prevail: see, e.g., *Kiddle* v *City Business Properties Ltd* [1942] 1 KB 269, at 274–275, *per* Lord Goddard.

By contrast, the covenant for quiet enjoyment requires a substantial interference with the tenant's lawful possession of the land which, according to their Lordships, did not have to be direct or physical. It could, therefore, cover regular excessive noise, despite contrary *dicta* in *Jenkins* v *Jackson* (1888) 40 ChD 71 and *Browne* v *Flower* [1911] 1 Ch 219. In the former case, Kekewich J pointed out that the word 'quietly' in the covenant 'does not mean undisturbed by noise', and in the latter, Parker J opined that 'a mere interference with the comfort of persons using the demised premises by the creation of a personal annoyance such as might arise from noise . . . is not enough'. Considerable doubt must now be cast on the correctness of these earlier judicial pronouncements. In Lord Millett's view, there was nothing in the wording of

the covenant to justify such a limitation. According to his Lordship, the covenant for quiet enjoyment is broken if the landlord does anything that substantially interferes with the tenant's title to or possession of the demised premises, or with his ordinary and lawful enjoyment of the property. The interference need not be direct or physical.

Moreover, the covenant for quiet enjoyment, in his Lordship's view, had two broadly similar features in common with the implied obligation not to derogate from grant. First, both operated prospectively (i.e., for the future) in the sense that the landlord undertook not to do anything *after* the date of the grant which would derogate from it or substantially interfere with the tenant's enjoyment of the demised property. Secondly, in both cases, the landlord's obligations were confined to the subject-matter of the grant, namely, the demised premises (including any incidental rights attached to it). In the *Southwark* case, the subject-matter of the grant was the flat having inadequate sound insulation. It was evident, therefore, that the landlord had covenanted not to interfere with the tenant's use and enjoyment of the flat having *that* built-in feature. To import into the covenant an obligation on the landlord to obtain possession of the adjoining flats (and not re-let them) or to install sound insulation would go beyond the operation of the grant. Lord Millett also emphasised the importance of looking at the location of the demised premises, and the use to which adjoining premises are put at the date of the tenancy and the use to which they may reasonably be put in the future. On this basis, it would have made no difference to the House of Lords ruling if the adjoining flats had been let subsequently to the tenants moving in.

Lord Hoffmann also viewed the covenant for quiet enjoyment as being only *prospective* in nature (i.e., it is a covenant that the tenant's lawful possession *will* not be interrupted by the landlord). Accordingly, it did not apply to things done before the grant of the tenancy (even though they may have continuing consequences for the tenant): *Anderson v Oppenheimer* (1880) 5 QBD 602. Here again, the principle is that the tenant takes the property as he finds it, in particular, subject to the uses which the parties contemplated would be made of the parts retained by the landlord: *Lyttleton Times Co. Ltd v Warners Ltd* [1970] AC 476. In *Southwark*, the tenants must reasonably have contemplated that there would be other tenants living normally in neighbouring flats, and so their sole complaint related to the structural defect (i.e., lack of sound proofing), which was present when they took the premises, and for which the landlord, applying the principle of *caveat lessee*, assumed no responsibility.

Interestingly, the Law Commission, in its Report, 'The Law of Landlord and Tenant: Responsibility for State and Condition of Property' (Law Com. No. 238), recommended that the statutory implied condition as to fitness for human habitation (contained in s. 8 of the 1985 Act) be extended to every lease for less than seven years regardless of rental level. The Commission also recommended that the criteria for determining whether a dwelling-house was fit for human habitation should be those listed in s. 604 of the Housing Act 1985 (as amended), including such matters as dampness, adequate provision for lighting, ventilation, etc. Significantly, however, there is no recommendation to extend the criteria so as to include sound insulation. This obvious gap in the proposed new legislative framework will need to be re-examined if the deficiencies in the law highlighted by the *Southwark* case are to be overcome. The difficulty facing most housing authorities, however, as indicated by Lord Millett, is the allocation of scarce financial resources to a variety of divergent housing needs. It is apparent that the installation of sound-proofing does not rank as a priority need with most councils, or indeed local residents' associations. As one academic commentator has observed, 'the boundary line between law reform and practical politics does become difficult to draw' (Bridge, S., 'Putting it Right? The Law Commission and the Condition of Tenanted Property' [1996] Conv 342, at 350).

Q Question 3

(a) What are the usual covenants? In what situation are they relevant?

(b) In what circumstances will a tenant be deemed to deny his landlord's title? What is the legal consequence of such a denial?

Commentary

This question is concerned with two specific areas, namely: (a) the law relating to the implication of usual covenants in agreements for leases; and (b) the implied condition on the part of the tenant not to deny or impugn his landlord's title.

For a summary of the law relating to the denial of a landlord's title, see Pawlowski, M., *The Forfeiture of Leases* London: Sweet & Maxwell, 1993, pp. 48–57.

- Common law will imply term into an agreement for a lease that it will, when executed, contain the usual covenants: *Propert* v *Parker* (1832)

- Usual covenants to be implied will vary according to prevailing custom and conveyancing practice: *Hampshire* v *Wickens* (1878), (indicating a list of usual covenants) and *Flexman* v *Corbett* (1930). Modern example: *Chester* v *Buckingham Travel Ltd* (1981)

- Denial of landlord's title categorised under three headings (1) denial by matter of record (2) denial by act *in pais* and (3) disclaimer by a yearly or other periodic tenant. The latter, however, does not give the landlord a right of forfeiture but merely operates to relieve him from serving notice to quit bringing the tenancy to an end

- Consider recent case law which treats a tenant's denial as an act of forfeiture and not a repudiatory breach: *Abidogun* v *Frolan Health Care Ltd* (2001)

☼ Suggested answer

(a) In some cases, the parties will precede an intended formal lease by an agreement for a lease (i.e., a contract whereby landlord and tenant agree that a legal lease will be granted and accepted on certain terms). If an agreement for a lease is silent as to the covenants to be included, the common law will imply a term into the agreement that the lease will, when executed, contain the 'usual covenants' (*Hampshire* v *Wickens* (1878) 7 Ch D 555 and *Propert* v *Parker* (1832) 3 My & K 280).

The usual covenants to be implied into the agreement will vary according to prevailing custom and conveyancing practice. However, in *Hampshire* v *Wickens* (above) Lord Jessel MR indicated that the following covenants and conditions are always 'usual': on the part of the landlord, a covenant for quiet enjoyment in the usual qualified form; and on the part of the tenant, a covenant to pay rent, a covenant to pay rates and taxes, a covenant to permit the landlord to enter and view the state and condition of the premises if the landlord has accepted a repairing obligation, and a condition of re-entry for non-payment of rent but not for breach of any other covenant (see *Re Anderton & Milner's Contract* [1890] Ch D 476 and *Re Lander and Bagley's Contract* [1892] 3 Ch 41). However, a covenant not to assign is not a usual covenant to be inferred in an agreement for a lease (*Hampshire* v *Wickens*, above).

The *Hampshire* case is a useful decision in so far as it provides an obvious list of the usual covenants to be implied into agreements for leases, but the list is by no means closed and, as stated earlier, much will depend on the established trade and conveyancing practice relevant to the proposed landlord and tenant relationship. In *Flexman* v *Corbett* [1930] 1 Ch 672, Maugham J indicated that the ultimate question was whether the form of the covenant was such as to constitute a defect in the subject-matter of the agreement. Thus, if it is established that the lease is in the form in which it would be anticipated as being in the great majority of cases, having regard to the nature of the property and to the place where it is situated, and to the purposes for which the premises are to be used, it would not be reasonable to say that there was a defect in the subject-matter of the agreement.

In *Flexman*, it was recognised that the question whether particular covenants are usual covenants is a question of fact, and that the decision of the court would depend on admissible evidence of conveyancers and others familiar with the practice in reference to leases and books of precedents. It is also permissible to obtain evidence with regard to the practice in the particular district in which the premises in question are situated. What is usual in Mayfair may not be usual at all in some other parts of London such as, for instance, Whitechapel.

In *Chester* v *Buckingham Travel Ltd* [1981] 1 WLR 96, an agreement was made in 1971 to grant a lease of a garage and workshop. Some years after the tenant had taken up occupation it was necessary to determine what covenants ought to be implied into the lease. Foster J, upon hearing evidence from conveyancers as to what covenants might be included as 'usual covenants' in such a letting, in the context of the subject-matter of the lease, recognised other covenants (outside the *Hampshire* list) as usual.

The word 'usual' means no more than 'occurring in ordinary use', so that if it is found that in nine out of 10 cases a covenant of a particular sort would be in a lease of premises of a given nature and in a given district, the covenant may be 'usual' for the particular premises in question (*Flexman* v *Corbett*, above).

(b) Implied into every lease is a condition that the tenant should not expressly or impliedly deny the landlord's title to the premises, or prejudice it by any acts which are inconsistent with the existence of the tenancy. Although it has been judicially suggested that a denial of title is analogous to the doctrine of repudiation of contract (*W.G. Clark (Properties) Ltd* v *Dupre Properties Ltd* [1992] 1 All ER 596), the Court of Appeal has held recently that a tenant's denial of his landlord's title is to be characterised as giving rise to a forfeiture action (not repudiation) and that, therefore, a s. 146 notice (under the Law of Property Act 1925) is an essential prerequisite to such an action: *Abidogun* v *Frolan Health Care Ltd* [2001] 45 EG 138 (CS). Such a forfeiture may be incurred (without recourse to a proviso for re-entry in the lease) in three distinct circumstances, namely: (i) denial by matter of record; (ii) denial by act *in pais*; and (iii) disclaimer by a yearly or other periodic tenant.

A denial by matter of record will arise when the tenant, in the course of his pleadings, expressly denies the landlord's title and is thereby estopped by the record from reasserting his lease or tenancy (*Warner* v *Sampson* [1959] 1 QB 297, where the Court of Appeal held that a general traverse in the tenant's pleadings did not involve the affirmative setting up by the tenant of a title adverse to that of the landlord as it merely put the landlord to proof of the allegations traversed). In *WG Clark (Properties) Ltd* v *Dupre Properties Ltd* [1991] 3 WLR 579, it was held that a partial disclaimer of the landlord's title is not sufficient to constitute a disclaimer of the whole since it does not show that the tenant has evinced the necessary intention no longer to be bound by his relationship with the landlord.

Once the landlord has commenced proceedings for possession based on disclaimer of his title in the tenant's pleading, the tenant cannot improve his position by amending his pleading to remove the disclaimer notwithstanding that the amendment of a pleading relates back to the date of the original pleading (*WG Clark (Properties) Ltd* v *Dupre Properties Ltd*, above). This is because the landlord's service of proceedings for possession is the equivalent to actual re-entry onto the demised premises which brings the landlord and tenant relationship to an end. The tenant may, however, avoid a forfeiture by retracting his denial of title *before* the landlord re-enters or takes effective proceedings for re-entry in reliance on the denial (*Warner* v *Sampson*, above).

A denial by act *in pais* will arise when the tenant deliberately attempts to set up an adverse (or hostile) title either in himself or in a stranger in the face of the landlord's title (*Doe d Ellenbrock* v *Flynn* (1834) 1 CM & R 137). The rule in *Ellenbrock* must, however, be cautiously applied where the tenant denies his landlord's title by mere words (*Wisbech St Mary Parish Council* v *Lilley* [1956] 1 WLR 121).

A disclaimer of the lease (whether by words or acts) by a yearly or other periodic tenant will operate as a waiver by the tenant of the usual notice to quit. The effect of such a disclaimer, therefore, is that the landlord may terminate the tenancy forthwith without serving the appropriate notice to quit on his tenant. The principle appears to be founded on the doctrine of estoppel, since the landlord is not obliged to determine the tenancy by notice to quit because the tenant has already asserted by words or conduct that it has no existence (*Doe d Calvert* v *Frowd* (1828) 4 Bing 557). Thus, strictly speaking, an act of disclaimer by a periodic tenant does not give the landlord a right of forfeiture but merely operates to relieve him from serving the appropriate notice to quit to bring the tenancy to an end.

Q Question 4

Bernard is the freehold owner of two adjacent houses, Nos 15 and 16, High Street, Barchester, Somerset.

In 1996, Bernard let No. 16 to Doris, a psychiatrist, on a monthly tenancy at a rent of £600 per month. She uses No. 16 as a private clinic where she offers therapy and assistance to victims of mental trauma.

Six months ago, Bernard let No. 15 to Tony on a monthly tenancy at a rent of £650 per month. Tony is a freelance concert pianist and uses the property occasionally for rehearsals.

The noise generated by Tony's rehearsals has upset Doris. She is concerned because her counselling sessions are being disrupted because of Tony's piano playing.

Doris has complained to the local authority about the noise level of Tony's rehearsals. The local authority, however, feel that the sound is not so high as to merit any action under the Environmental Protection Act 1990. Doris has also approached Bernard asking him to provide better sound insulation between the two properties, but Bernard has refused.

Advise Doris as to any legal claim she may have against Bernard. (You are not required to consider any potential legal claims against Tony.)

Commentary

This question requires consideration of several legal issues. A solid answer will consider the nature of the landlord's implied covenants of quiet enjoyment and non-derogation from grant. Your answer should also tackle Bernard's potential liability in nuisance following the House of Lords ruling in *Southwark LBC* v *Mills* [2001] 1 AC 1. See further, Rook, D.,

'Excessive Noise can be a Breach of the Landlord's Covenant for Quiet Enjoyment' [2000] Conv. 161.

- Tony's piano playing probably not an actionable nuisance and, hence, Bernard not liable applying the *Southwark* decision

- Moreover, Doris's tenancy agreement contains no obligation on Bernard to ensure adequate insulation. No state of disrepair so implied obligation under s. 11 of the Landlord and Tenant Act 1985 also inapplicable. Principle of *caveat lessee* will prevail

- Consider covenant for quiet enjoyment as interpreted in *Southwark* decision. Covenant operates prospectively only and confined to the subject-matter of the grant (i.e., demised property having inadequate sound insulation)

- In any event, Bernard not liable for Tony's activities unless he has positively authorised or ratified the same: *Malzy* v *Eicholz* (1916) and *Matania* v *National Provincial Bank Ltd* (1936)

☀ Suggested answer

Most leases will contain an express covenant on the part of the landlord that the tenant is entitled to quiet enjoyment of the demised premises. In the absence of an express provision, a covenant for quiet enjoyment will be automatically implied.

As its name suggests, this covenant is designed to ensure that the tenant may peacefully enjoy the demised property without interruption from the landlord or persons claiming under him (e.g., other tenants of the landlord). The interruption may be direct or indirect, physical or non-physical. Examples where the landlord has been held liable under the covenant include the illegal eviction of the tenant (*Drane* v *Evangelou* [1978] 1 WLR 455), physical interference with the tenant's business user by the erection of scaffolding outside the premises (*Owen* v *Gadd* [1956] 2 QB 99), a prolonged course of intimidation and harassment of the tenant (*Kenny* v *Preen* [1963] 1 QB 499), cutting off the tenant's gas and electricity supply (*Perera* v *Vandiyar* [1953] 1 WLR 672) and substantial disruption caused by the landlord's building works (*Guppy's (Bridport) Ltd* v *Brookling* (1984) 269 EG 846). It seems that an omission on the part of the landlord which is a breach of duty (e.g., to repair) may also constitute a breach of the covenant (*Hafton Properties Ltd* v *Camp* [1993] EGCS 101).

In *Jenkins* v *Jackson* (1888) 40 ChD 71, Kekewich J opined that the word 'quietly' in the covenant 'does not mean undisturbed by noise'. Similarly, in *Browne* v *Flower* [1911] 1 Ch 219, Parker J suggested that a 'mere interference with the comfort of persons using the demised premises by the creation of a personal annoyance such as might arise from noise . . . is not enough'. These observations, however, must now be read in the light of the recent House of Lords' decision in *Southwark London Borough*

Council v *Mills* [2001] 1 AC 1, in which Lord Millett concluded that there was nothing in the wording of the covenant to justify such a limitation. Accordingly, the covenant will be broken if the landlord does anything that substantially interferes with the tenant's title or possession of the demised premises, or with his ordinary and lawful enjoyment of the property. The interference need not be direct or physical.

In the *Southwark* case, tenants of flats complained of inadequate sound insulation between their flats and other flats in the same building, causing them to hear all the everyday activities of their neighbours. The House of Lords held unanimously that the covenant for quiet enjoyment (and non-derogation from grant) operated only prospectively (i.e., for the future) and thus it did not apply to things done before the grant of the tenancy even though they may have continuing consequences for the tenant. The landlord's obligation was confined to the subject-matter of the grant, namely, the demised property having inadequate sound insulation. He could not, therefore, be responsible for installing new insulation since that would go beyond the operation of the grant.

The basic principle is that the tenant takes the property as he finds it, in particular, subject to the uses which the parties contemplated would be made of the parts retained by the landlord. In *Southwark*, the tenants must have contemplated that there would be other tenants living in neighbouring flats, and so their sole complaint related to the structural defect (i.e., lack of sound proofing) which was present when they took the premises and for which the landlord, applying the principle *caveat lessee*, assumed no responsibility in the absence of express or implied obligation. In this connection, the tenancy contained no express covenant on the landlord as regards sound proofing. Moreover, the landlord's implied obligation to keep in repair the structure and exterior of a dwelling-house in respect of residential lettings for under seven years (see s. 11 of the Landlord and Tenant Act 1985) had no application in the absence of evidence of disrepair. In short, the House of Lords concluded that the covenant for quiet enjoyment (and non-derogation from grant) was not an appropriate mechanism for importing (through the back door) an improvement to the premises for which the landlord would not otherwise be liable under contract or statute.

The House of Lords also held that a landlord could not be liable in nuisance for authorising the activities of his tenants if those activities did not themselves constitute an actionable nuisance. In *Southwark*, the activities of the other tenants were not only reasonable but, in the words of Lord Millett, 'the necessary and inevitable incidents of the ordinary occupation of residential property'. They could not, therefore, as a matter of law, constitute an actionable nuisance. Interestingly, his Lordship concluded that it would have made no difference if the adjoining flats had been let *subsequently* to the tenants moving in since it must have been within the contemplation of the tenants that the adjoining flats would be let to residential tenants who would live normally in them.

In the present case, it is debatable whether Tony's piano playing constitutes an actionable nuisance. Nuisance involves doing something on neighbouring land that constitutes unreasonable interference with the claimant's enjoyment of his land. A person cannot increase the liabilities of his neighbour by applying his own property to special uses: *Robinson* v *Kilvert* (1889) 41 ChD 88 (ordinary heating damaging paper exceptionally susceptible to heat) and *Whycer* v *Urry* [1956] JPL 365 (practice of ophthalmic optician in a business area too specifically delicate for protection). In any event, it may be that Tony's activities can be characterised as no more than a necessary and inevitable incident of the ordinary occupation of the property, in which case Bernard will not be liable in nuisance in accordance with principles enunciated in the *Southwark* decision. Doris cannot complain about normal activities carried on by Bernard's neighbouring tenants. Nor can she complain to her landlord for permitting such activities by letting the adjoining property to Tony. Her tenancy agreement presumably contains no express obligation on Bernard to ensure adequate sound insulation between Nos 15 and 16 and such obligation, as we have seen, will not be implied under the general law. The implied obligation under s. 11 of the 1985 Act has no application where the property is not actually in a state of disrepair, and the statutorily implied condition as to fitness for human habitation (imposed by s. 8 of the 1985 Act) will not assist Doris in so far as the rent payable under her monthly tenancy is well above the rental limits imposed by that Act. In the absence, therefore, of any governing contractual or statutory provision, the principle that the tenant 'takes the property as [s]he finds it' will prevail (see, e.g., *Kiddle* v *City Business Properties Ltd* [1942] 1 KB 269, at 274–75, *per* Lord Goddard).

Similarly, there will be no liability under the covenant for quiet enjoyment (or non-derogation from grant) since the subject-matter of Doris's grant is the property (No. 16) having inadequate sound insulation. It is evident, therefore, that Bernard has covenanted not to interfere with Doris's use and enjoyment of the property having that built-in feature. Moreover, a landlord will not be liable to his tenant under a covenant for quiet enjoyment (or derogation from grant) for a nuisance caused by another of his tenants simply because he knows that the latter is causing the nuisance and does not himself take any steps to prevent what is being done; *Mowan* v *Wandsworth London Borough Council* (2001) 33 HLR 56. In order to render Bernard liable, therefore, there must be active participation on his part, or a sufficiently positive act, amounting to authorisation of the nuisance, so as to make him responsible for it (*Malzy* v *Eicholz* [1916] 2 KB 308 and *Matania* v *National Provincial Bank Ltd* [1936] 2 All ER 633). It seems, on the facts, that Bernard has not authorised or ratified Tony's activities in any way.

Q Question 5

(a) Linda is a secure tenant of a basement flat within a block of flats owned by the Drayfordshire County Council. There is a rubbish chute used by the tenants in the block for discarding rubbish into a large bin situated in the basement yard next to her flat. Linda has complained frequently to the Council about the considerable noise and unpleasant smell from the chute as well as the practice of tenants leaving their rubbish bags outside her flat. It appears the size of the chute is inadequate to cope with all the rubbish so tenants are forced to deposit their refuse next to the bin. Her tenancy agreement makes no mention of the Council's responsibility for the upkeep of the common parts or the facilities for the collection of refuse in the block.

Advise Linda on any legal claim she may have against the Council.

(b) Harry is the tenant of a fish and chip shop in a shopping precinct owned by a common landlord, Longcrest Properties Ltd. A few months ago, an adjoining unit was let by Longcrest to a fast-food outlet causing customers to queue outside awaiting their orders. This has caused Harry to lose a considerable amount of his passing trade. Longcrest now also threatens to reorganise the precinct by introducing a multiplex entertainment centre onto the site. The precinct has hitherto existed as a small shopping mall attracting mostly local residents.

Advise Harry of any legal action he may bring against Longcrest.

(c) Lionel is the tenant of a ground floor shop. His lease contains a tenant's covenant for quiet enjoyment as well as a landlord's obligation to repair the roof and external walls of the building. The landlord has recently engaged contractors to clean the external walls, which has required the erection of scaffolding outside Lionel's shop. As a result of the works, Lionel's trade has declined.

Advise Lionel whether he can claim against the landlord for lost profits and disruption to his business.

Commentary

In part (a), you are required to examine the potential liability of the Council under the covenant for quiet enjoyment and nuisance. This will involve an examination of the House of Lords' ruling in *Southwark London Borough Council v Mills* [2001] 1 AC 1 and the recent decision of the Court of Appeal in *Long v Southwark London Borough Council* [2002] 47 EG 150. If you are familiar with the principles in these two cases, the question should not pose any difficulty.

In part (b), you need to examine the recent case law on the covenant not to derogate from grant in the specific context of a landlord granting leases to competitors of the tenant's business in the same retail centre. The point to note here is that the earlier cases in *Port* v *Griffith* [1938] 1 All ER 295 and *Romulus Trading Co. Ltd* v *Comet Properties Ltd* [1996] 2 EGLR 70 now stand to be modified in circumstances where the carrying on of a rival business takes place in retail complexes.

In part (c), the question requires you to consider the recent Court of Appeal decision in *Goldmile Properties Ltd* v *Lechouritis* [2003] 15 EG 143 concerning the coexistence of the tenant's covenant for quiet enjoyment and the landlord's obligation to repair the property. Examiners have a tendency to set questions on recent case law, especially if the point has been covered either in lectures or seminars. One again, this is an easy question if you have covered the material.

Because this is a three-part question, you need to be careful not to spend too much time on any one part at the expense of the others. Spread your answers evenly in order to achieve the best posssible marks. Remember that the examiner will not expect a detailed response to each part in the limited time available. On the contrary, he is testing your ability to be clear and concise under pressure of exam conditions.

- No breach of covenant for quiet enjoyment since interference due to the existing condition of the chute and within the contemplation of parties when the flat was let: *Southwark London Borough Council* v *Mills* (1998). Covenant not a warranty by landlord as to fitness of the chute

- Private nuisance actionable since it has emanated from the Council's property (i.e., common parts) and it has failed to take reasonable steps to abate the nuisance: *Long* v *Southwark London Borough Council* (2002)

- Principle in *Port* v *Griffith* modified where derogation from grant takes place within the context of a retail centre or shopping mall: *Chartered Trust* v *Davies* (1997). Longcrest liable for causing nuisance and also for letting to a competitor: *Oceanic Village Ltd* v *Shirayama Shokusan Ltd* (2001) and *Platt* v *London Underground Ltd* (2001)

- Implied obligation on landlord not to alter or use common parts of a retail centre in such a way as to cause it to lose its character: *Petra Investments Ltd* v *Jeffrey Rogers plc* (2000) Possible breach here if Longcrest's actions have rendered Harry's tenancy less fit for the purpose for which it was granted

- Covenant for quiet enjoyment may be breached by landlord's execution of works which substantially interfere with tenant's ordinary enjoyment of the demised premises: *Owen* v *Gadd* (1956)

- But covenant for quiet enjoyment and landlord's repairing obligation must co-exist on a basis of parity (not priority): *Goldmile Properties Ltd* v *Lechouritis* (2003). Consider test of reasonableness for threshold for disturbance by repairs

:Q: **Suggested answer**

(a) The House of Lords in *Southwark* has held that a substantial interference with enjoyment of premises can amount to a breach of the covenant for quiet enjoyment. However, the case also shows that the covenant is prospective in nature and is not a warranty by the landlord as to the fitness of a building or its facilities. In that case, there was held to be no breach of the covenant since the interference was due to the condition of the property when let and the tenants took possession of their flats knowing that the walls were thin and that they would have to live with the noise from neighbouring occupants.

In Linda's case, I assume that the rubbish chute has formed part of the structure of the block for many years — in any event, before the grant of the tenancy to Linda. Accordingly, despite the inherent inadequacy of the chute, this will not amount to any breach of the covenant for quiet enjoyment. The noise from the use of the rubbish chute must have been contemplated by the parties at the start of her tenancy as, indeed, the noise emanating from the lack of adequate sound insulation in the *Southwark* case. Nor, for that matter, can there be any warranty as to the adequacy of this facility implicit in the covenant for quiet enjoyment itself. Indeed, in the absence of any express obligation to remedy the inherent design fault of the chute, no such liability (it seems) will be implied under the general law. Interestingly, the same point arose recently in the case of *Long* v *Southwark London Borough Council* [2002] 47 EG 150, also involving noise and nuisance from a rubbish chute, where the Court of Appeal emphatically rejected the notion that the landlord, in similar circumstances, was under any obligation to replace the inadequate chute or relocate the tenant to different premises.

Private nuisance consists of the wrongful interference with another's use of land, or of some right over or in connection with it. Assuming that the nuisance has emanated from the Council's property (i.e., the common parts of the building) and that it was put on notice that there was such a nuisance (by virtue of Linda's frequent complaints), the onus of proof will shift to the Council to show that it could not, by reasonable steps, have abated the nuisance: *Marcic* v *Thames Water Utilities Ltd* [2002] EWCA Civ 64. If that onus is not discharged, the appropriate remedy against the Council will be an order requiring it to abate the nuisance and pay damages. There is no doubt that, on the facts, there is an interference with Linda's convenient user of her flat caused by the accummulation of rubbish bags in the yard. It is also clear that the Council is in possession of the common parts (including the basement yard) and, hence, *prima facie* liable for that nuisance. The question, therefore, remains whether or not the Council has taken any reasonable steps to abate the nuisance so as to discharge its liability to Linda. In this connection, the cost to the alleged wrongdoer of taking any steps should be taken into account in determining what is reasonable: *Leakey* v *National Trust for Places of Historic Interest or Natural Beauty* [1980] QB 485.

Although designating some new area for the disposal of the rubbish would be unrealistic, it seems (from the *Long* case) that engaging a suitable contractor to regularly inspect the bin area and remove any accumulation of rubbish would be enough to satisfy the Council's duty to take reasonable steps. Since this does not appear to have been done, Linda may have a good claim against the Council for nuisance in respect of the rubbish accumulation. For the reasons already mentioned, however, she has no legal complaint in respect of the inadequate chute itself.

(b) Until recently, the answer to this question would have been fairly straight-forward. In *Port* v *Griffith* [1938] 1 All ER 295, Luxmore J held that, although the presence of a trade rival next door would of necessity be a detriment to the tenant, it did not render the premises on which the tenant was carrying on his business unfit for that purpose, although it might incidentally reduce the profit ratio to be earned from that business. In that case, the purpose of the letting could still be achieved, albeit with less convenience. The same conclusion was reached in *Romulus Trading Co. Ltd* v *Comet Properties Ltd* [1996] 2 EGLR 70, also involving the letting by a landlord of nearby premises for a similar use (i.e., the business of banking) as carried out by the claimant tenant. Basically, the principle was that, if premises are let for a particular trade, there is nothing to prevent the landlord from leasing an adjoining shop for the same purpose.

This principle, however, now stands to be modified in the light of more recent judicial pronouncements concerning lettings within purpose-built premises and retail complexes. In *Chartered Trust plc* v *Davies* [1977] 2 EGLR 83, the tenant was granted a lease of a shop in a shopping mall. Later, the landlord let the adjoining unit to a pawnbroker who (as in Harry's case) attracted customers outside the shop thereby adversely affecting the tenant's passing trade. The Court of Appeal held that the landlord had derogated from grant, not because it had let the shop to a pawnbroker, but because it had failed to control the nuisance which had rendered the tenant's premises less fit for the purpose for which they were let. Significantly, the tenant depended upon proper management of the shopping mall and the common parts by the landlord who had control and charged a service charge for such management. On this basis, Harry has a good cause of action against Longcrest for the nuisance affecting his premises. He may also have a legitimate complaint in respect of the letting to a potential rival, despite the principle in the *Port* and *Romulus* line of cases. This is because the principle appears to have been relaxed in the context of a rival letting within a purpose-built retail complex. In *Oceanic Village Ltd* v *Shirayama Shokusan Ltd* [2001] L & TR 35, the court declined to accept the view that there can never be implied into a lease a term that adjoining premises will not be let to a competitor. Much will depend on the purpose of the letting and what was within the reasonable contemplation of the parties at the time the lease was granted. If it would have been reasonably foreseeable to Longcrest that the operation of a fast-food outlet would make Harry's lease less fit for the commercial purpose for which it had been granted, Harry will have a good cause of action: see also, *Platt* v *London Underground Ltd* [2001] 2 EGLR 121, where the surrounding circumstances at the time of the grant indicated that it was contemplated by the parties that a station exit would remain open so as enable the tenant to trade from his nearby kiosk).

The threatened introduction of a multiplex entertainment centre into the precinct may also be the subject of a successful complaint. In *Petra Investments Ltd* v *Jeffrey Rogers plc* [2000] 3 EGLR 120, the tenant claimed a repudiatory breach of his lease because the landlord had created a new unit within the retail centre as a Virgin Megastore which resulted in the tenant losing trade. Hart J concluded that, in a purpose-built centre, there was an obligation on the landlord not to alter or use the common parts of the centre in such a way as to cause it to lose its character as a retail shopping mall. In relation to the letting of units within the centre, the landlord was required to take account of the expectations of its existing tenants by not doing or permitting something that it was reasonably foreseeable would render the premises already demised less fit for the purpose for which they had been let. On this reasoning, therefore, Longcrest's proposal may constitute a breach of Longcrest's covenant (express or implied) not to derogate from grant.

(c) There is no doubt that a covenant for quiet enjoyment may be breached by the landlord carrying out repairs which substantially interfere with the tenant's ordinary and lawful enjoyment of the demised property. The point was addressed in *Owen* v *Gadd* [1956] 2 QB 99, where (as in the problem) the landlord erected scaffolding on the pavement in front of the tenant's shop for the purpose of carrying out repairs to the landlord's upper premises. The scaffolding obstructed access to the tenant's shop window, although the landlord did what it could to minimise the damage and the repairs were completed (and the scaffolding removed) within two weeks. The Court of Appeal held that there could be a breach of the covenant without an actual physical interruption into or upon the demised premises by the landlord. On the facts, the erection of the scaffold poles was held to constitute a substantial interference and, accordingly, the landlord was held liable for damages to the tenant.

More recently, the Court of Appeal has held that the tenant's covenant for quiet enjoyment and the landlord's obligation to repair must co-exist on a basis of parity (not priority) so that one does not frustrate the operation of the other. In *Goldmile Properties Ltd* v *Lechouritis* [2003] 15 EG 143, Sedley LJ (giving the judgment of the court) concluded that the correct approach was to give proper effect, if possible, to both covenants. This meant that the threshold for disturbance by repairs was 'all reasonable' precautions rather than 'all possible' precautions. Significantly, in that case, the covenant for quiet enjoyment was qualified by the words 'except as herein provided' which, therefore, permitted the tenant's quiet enjoyment to be disturbed by the execution of external repair works carried out by the landlord. Since the landlord had taken all reasonable steps to avoid disruption to the tenant's premises, no breach of covenant for quiet enjoyment had taken place.

I assume that in Lionel's case (as in *Goldmile*), the repairing covenant is just as much for the tenant's benefit as well as for the landlord since it would be no advantage to Lionel to be running his shop in a dilapidated building. On the basis, therefore, the covenant for quiet enjoyment cannot be interpreted as being absolutely unqualified. In *Goldmile*, as mentioned earlier, the court adopted a threshold for disturbance by repairs based on a test of reasonableness—a test already applied in the law of nuisance. In this connection, the landlord (in *Goldmile*) had sent a copy of the estimate of the works to the claimant who replied that the proposed start date would interfere with his busiest trading period over Christmas. In response, the landlord postponed the commencement of the works until the following March and agreed to spread the first instalment of the claimant's service charge over a year. Most leases make no (or only limited) provision to compensate the tenant for disruption to the business during the execution of necessary works. In the absence of any such specific provision in Lionel's lease, the reasonableness (or otherwise) of the landlord's interference with Lionel's business activities will fall to be judged by all the circumstances of the case. At the end of the day, Lionel's case may not be as strong as appears at first glance.

Further reading

Clark, H., 'Recent Developments in Unlawful Eviction' (1999) 3 L & T Rev 140.

De Havillande, J., 'Damage Limitation' [1998] EG 158.

Levy, D., 'Competing Businesses — Derogation from Grant' (2001) 5 L & T Rev 72.

Mowbray, J., 'Fishy Business' (2001) SJ 617.

Pawlowski, M., 'Denial of Landlord's Title: Forfeiture or Repudiatory Breach?' [2002] Conv 399.

Saunders, P., 'Boundaries of the Doctrine of Quiet Enjoyment' (2000) SJ 348.

Assignment and sub-letting

Introduction

When can the tenant assign, sub-let, etc.? The answer to this question will depend essentially on the terms of the lease. There are five possible situations:

(a) If the lease contains no restriction, the tenant can freely assign or sub-let without obtaining consent from the landlord.

(b) The lease may contain an absolute covenant against assigning etc. A simple prohibition, unqualified by any words requiring the consent of the landlord, entitles the landlord to withhold his consent and to impose what conditions he likes. By way of statutory exception, a covenant purporting to restrict prospective assignees or sublessees on grounds of race, nationality or sex is deemed to be qualified (Race Relations Act 1976, s. 24, and Sex Discrimination Act 1975, s. 31).

(c) The lease may contain a qualified covenant. A covenant not to assign, sub-let etc. without obtaining the consent of the landlord brings into operation the Landlord and Tenant Act 1927, s. 19(1), which provides that, notwithstanding any provision to the contrary, such covenant shall be deemed to be subject to the proviso that such consent shall not be unreasonably withheld.

(d) The lease may contain an express proviso that consent shall not be unreasonably withheld, in which case the tenant is in the same position as in (c) above.

(e) The lease may contain a covenant by the tenant to offer a surrender to the landlord before assigning, sub-letting etc. Such a covenant is not invalidated by s. 19(1) of the 1927 Act (*Bocardo SA v S & M Hotels Ltd* [1980] 1 WLR 17). However, a clause requiring the tenant to offer a surrender of the lease before assignment will be void when contained in a business tenancy, since such a clause is contrary to the Landlord and Tenant Act 1954, s. 38(1) (*Allnatt London Properties Ltd v Newton* [1984] 1 All ER 423). If the lease is residential falling within the Landlord and Tenant Act 1954, Pt I (i.e., a long lease at a low rent), an obligation to offer the premises back to the landlord will not fall foul of s. 17 of the 1954 Act, which only makes void an actual agreement to surrender. The tenant's offer will only materialise into an agreement to surrender if the landlord accepts the tenant's offer. The offer itself, therefore, is not struck down by s. 17: *Tiffany Investments Ltd* v *Bircham & Co. Nominees (No. 2)* (2003) 12 EG 127 (CS).

Where the lease requires the landlord's consent to the assignment or sub-letting, a mass of case law has arisen as to whether the landlord's consent was reasonably or unreasonably withheld in the particular circumstances. In this connection, the Landlord and Tenant Act 1988 imposes a duty on the landlord to consent to a tenant's application to assign, sub-let etc. unless he has good reason for not doing so. For a summary of the provisions of the 1988 Act, see Austin, J., 'Landlord and Tenant Act 1988' [1989] EG 8912, 55. While the Act reverses the burden of proof so that it is now necessary for the landlord to prove that any refusal is reasonable and provides the tenant with an action for damages for breach of statutory duty, it does not alter the law in any other respect (*Air India* v *Balabel* [1993] 30 EG 90).

It is, in each case, a question of fact, depending upon all the circumstances, whether the landlord's consent to an assignment, sub-letting etc. is being unreasonably withheld. A leading case in this area is *International Drilling Fluids Ltd* v *Louisville Investments (Uxbridge) Ltd* [1986] Ch 513, where Balcombe LJ set out a number of guidelines for determining whether consent was being reasonably or unreasonably withheld, but these must now be read in conjunction with the statutory requirements of the 1988 Act. See further Williams, D., 'Assignment of Leases, Recent Developments' (1986) 279 EG 51; McLoughlin, P., 'To Consent or Not to Consent' [1990] EG 9011, 60 and 'Sureties in Commercial Leases' [1991] EG 9120, 86.

It seems that, in certain circumstances, a landlord's consent to a proposed assignment headed 'subject to licence' and qualified by the words 'in principle' may still be a valid consent: *Mount Eden Land* v *Prudential Assurance Co. Ltd* [1996] 74 P & CR 377 and *Next* v *National Farmers' Union Mutual Insurance Co.* [1977] EGCS 181. The point has arisen again most recently in *Aubergine Enterprises Ltd* v *Lakewood International Ltd* [2002] EWCA Civ 177, where the majority of the Court of Appeal confirmed that the words '[landlord's] prior written consent' in the lease did not require formal consent (in the form of a deed) or even necessarily unconditional consent, so long as there is a clear, unambiguous expression of consent in the landlord's correspondence. If the landlord does give consent subject to conditions, this can still be a valid consent if the conditions are such that the assignee could not validly object. So far as there may be conditions which remain unfulfilled, this is also not fatal because the landlord is entitled to insist on any reasonable conditions being satisfied. In the meantime, consent can be treated as having already been given. It is apparent, therefore, that 'written consent' does not necessarily mean execution and completion of a formal licence to assign, especially if the lease does not require this.

Not surprisingly, the decision in *Aubergine* has been criticised both by academics and practitioners, who argue that the Court of Appeal's approach will lead to uncertainty as to when precisely consent has been given. It also, of course, renders the phrases 'subject to licence' and 'in principle' (hitherto used confidently by conveyancers) largely meaningless. Of course, one simple way of avoiding the consequences of the *Aubergine* decision is for the landlord to incorporate a proviso in the alienation covenant to the effect that the landlord's consent will only be given upon completion (and delivery) of a formal deed of consent.

It is important that you are aware that the Landlord and Tenant (Covenants) Act 1995 has amended s. 19(1) of the 1927 Act in a number of significant respects. Under a lease granted after 1 January 1996, a former tenant will remain liable for the defaults of his immediate assignee if the landlord obtains an 'authorised guarantee agreement' (AGA) from him guaranteeing performance of the tenant's covenants by his immediate assignee. The landlord may require such an agreement from the former tenant either (i) automatically as one of the conditions for assignment set out in the covenant in the lease, or (ii) because it is reasonable to do so. In the latter case, the landlord may impose an AGA as a condition of granting consent where the lease contains an absolute prohibition against assignment, or where the lease contains a qualified covenant against assignment and it is reasonable, in all the circumstances of the case, for the landlord to require an AGA from the former tenant: see *Wallis Fashion Group Ltd* v *General Accident Life Assurance Ltd* (2001) 81 P & CR 28 in the context of a business tenancy renewal. (See further, Question 2(a), **Chapter 4**.)

You should also be aware of the remedies available to a landlord where the tenant has gone ahead and assigned, sub-let etc. in breach of covenant. Apart from damages, the landlord is entitled to forfeit the lease, or to seek an injunction where the tenant threatens to assign or sub-let. In *Hemingway Securities Ltd* v *Dunraven Ltd* [1995] 09 EG 322, the landlord obtained a mandatory injunction against the sub-tenant, requiring him to execute a deed delivering up the unlawful sub-lease to the tenant. (See Question 4.) The tenant's remedies include the seeking of a declaration under the Landlord and Tenant Act 1954, s. 53, that consent has been unreasonably withheld. Additionally, the tenant may bring a claim for damages alleging that the landlord is in breach of his statutory duty under the Landlord and Tenant Act 1988, s. 1 (see s. 4). Such a claim may be combined with a claim for an injunction requiring the landlord to comply with his statutory duty under the Act. In addition to seeking damages by way of compensation, the tenant may be entitled to exemplary damages if the landlord has unreasonably refused consent to an assignment in breach of his duty under s. 1: *Design Progression Ltd* v *Thurloe Properties Ltd* [2004] EWHC 324. In this case, the landlord had deliberately failed to respond within a reasonable time to the tenant's application for licence to assign. As a result, the proposed assignee took a lease of other premises causing the tenant to lose a premium of £75,000. See further, Gill, S., 'Time to Wake Up' [2004] EG 100.

This is a compact area of study and a favourite amongst examiners and examinees alike!

ⓠ Question 1

A & Co. Ltd is the tenant of a house on the Blackmore Estate owned by Lord Wealth. It wishes to assign its lease of the house to one of its directors for his personal use, but Lord Wealth has written to A & Co. Ltd refusing his consent to the assignment on the grounds that

(a) the house has been allowed to fall into disrepair,

(b) the proposed assignee would be entitled to claim the benefit of the Housing Act 1988, and

(c) the house has already been earmarked for occupation by a caretaker for the purposes of the more efficient management of the Estate. The lease, which expires in three months' time, contains a qualified covenant on the part of the tenant not to assign, sub-let or part with possession of the premises without the prior consent of the landlord.

Advise A & Co. Ltd of its legal position and the steps it may take to challenge the validity of the objections raised by Lord Wealth.

Commentary

The central issue in this question is whether Lord Wealth has unreasonably withheld his consent to the proposed assignment. It therefore requires a thorough discussion of the case law on this point. You will also need to examine the various remedies available to the tenant on the assumption that consent has been unreasonably withheld. If you have revised the cases, a question like this should enable you to score a good 2:1.

- Consider effect of Landlord and Tenant Act 1927, s. 19(1) and Landlord and Tenant Act 1988. Burden of proof on Lord Wealth to show consent reasonably withheld

- Mere disrepair does not justify refusal of consent: *Farr* v *Ginnings* (1928). Much will depend on nature and extent of disrepair: *Goldstein* v *Saunders* (1915) and *Orlando Investments Ltd* v *Grosvenor Estates Belgravia* (1989)

- Reasonable for landlord to refuse consent where proposed assignee would be entitled to statutory protection not enjoyed by the tenant: *Norfolk Capital Group Ltd* v *Kitway Ltd* (1977)

- Refusal of consent unreasonable if designed to obtain collateral advantage unconnected with terms of lease: *Bromley Park Garden Estates Ltd* v *Moss* (1982)

- Challenge validity of objections by applying for declaration that consent unreasonably withheld: Landlord and Tenant Act 1954, s. 53. Additionally, bring action for damages for breach of statutory duty under Landlord and Tenant Act 1988, s. 1(4)

:ϙ: Suggested answer

A covenant not to assign, sub-let etc. without first obtaining the consent of the landlord brings into operation the Landlord and Tenant Act 1927, s. 19(1), which provides, *inter alia*, that, notwithstanding any provision to the contrary, such covenant shall be deemed to be subject to the proviso that such consent shall not be unreasonably withheld. The section does not absolve the tenant from the formality of seeking consent, so that if A & Co. Ltd goes ahead without seeking consent it will commit a breach regardless of the reasonableness of the transaction (*Eastern Telegraph Co. Ltd* v *Dent* [1899] 1 QB 835).

The Landlord and Tenant Act 1988 imposes a duty on the landlord to consent to the tenant's application to assign, sub-let etc. unless he has good reason for not doing so. The burden of proof is, therefore, on Lord Wealth to show that his refusal of consent is reasonable. In this connection, three grounds have been put forward by Lord Wealth for refusing consent. First, the house is in a state of disrepair. The mere fact that A & Co. Ltd is committing a continuing breach of a covenant to repair does not necessarily entitle the landlord to refuse his consent to the proposed assignment (*Farr* v *Ginnings* (1928) 44 TLR 249; *Cosh* v *Fraser* (1964) 108 SJ 116). However, where the lack of repair is serious, the landlord's position will be much stronger (*Goldstein* v *Sanders* [1915] 1 Ch 549). In *Orlando Investments Ltd* v *Grosvenor Estate Belgravia* (1989) 59 P & CR 21, the Court of Appeal held that where there are extensive and longstanding breaches of a covenant to repair, it is not unreasonable for a landlord to refuse to consent to an assignment unless he can be reasonably satisfied that the proposed assignee will remedy the breaches. Thus, in the present case, much will depend on the nature and extent of the disrepair and whether the proposed assignee is prepared to remedy it.

The second ground for refusal is that the proposed assignee, being an individual, would be entitled to claim the benefit of the Housing Act 1988. It has been held to be reasonable for a landlord to refuse his consent where the proposed assignee would, unlike the assignor, be entitled to statutory protection (*Norfolk Capital Group Ltd* v *Kitway Ltd* [1977] QB 506 and *Bickel* v *Duke of Westminster* [1977] QB 517). In both these cases, the proposed assignee would have become entitled to purchase the freehold under the Leasehold Reform Act 1967. The fact that the proposed assignee would enjoy statutory protection not enjoyed by the current tenant may be a reasonable ground of refusal, particularly if the consent is sought shortly before the expiry of the term for the purpose of giving the assignee the benefit of such protection (*Lee* v *K Carter* [1949] 1 KB 85, where the landlord was held justified in refusing consent to an assignment by a company lessee of a flat to an individual director; similarly, in *Swanson* v *Forton* [1949] Ch 143, where the tenant, who was out of possession and so incapable of enjoying statutory protection under the Rent Acts, proposed to assign 12 days before the expiry of the term). See also *West Layton Ltd* v *Ford* [1979] 1 QB 593, where the effect of a proposed sub-letting would have been to confer statutory protection on the sub-tenant, and *Re Cooper's Lease* (1968) P & CR 541, where the proposed sub-tenant would have acquired statutory protection under the Landlord and Tenant Act 1954, Pt II. These decisions may be contrasted with *Thomas Bookman Ltd* v *Nathan* [1955] 1 WLR 815 (where seven and a half months remained unexpired and the object of the assignment had nothing to do with the Rent Acts) and *Deverall* v *Wyndham* [1989] 01 EG 70 (where the risk of the landlord being saddled with statutory tenants was outweighed by other considerations in favour of the tenant). It seems likely, therefore, bearing in mind that the lease has only three months left to run, that Lord Wealth's refusal of consent on this ground will be considered reasonable in all the circumstances.

Lord Wealth's third ground of refusal is that the house has been earmarked for occupation by a caretaker for the purposes of the more efficient management of the Estate. In *Bromley Park Garden Estates Ltd* v *Moss* [1982] 1 WLR 1019, the Court of Appeal held that a landlord's refusal to consent to an assignment will be unreasonable if it is designed to achieve a collateral result unconnected with the terms of the lease, even though the purpose is in accordance with good estate management. In that case, the landlords refused consent on the ground, *inter alia*, that, in the interests of the proper management of their estate, it was their policy not to permit multiple lettings in the same premises because it lowered their investment value. The court held that since the landlords' reason for refusing consent (namely, that a single lease of the whole building would enhance its investment value) was wholly extraneous to, and unconnected with, the bargain made by the parties to the lease when the covenant was granted and accepted, the landlords' refusal of consent was unreasonable: see also, *First Penthouse Ltd* v *Channel Hotels & Properties (UK) Ltd* [2004] 05 EG 148. Similar reasoning would apply in the present case, and accordingly Lord Wealth's refusal of consent on the ground that the house has been earmarked for a caretaker for the purpose of more efficient management of the Estate is not justified (as being extraneous to the bargain made between the parties).

By contrast, in *Moss Bros Group plc* v *CSC Properties Ltd* [1999] EGCS 47, the landlord was held to have reasonably withheld consent to an assignment of a lease of a men's fashion store in a major shopping mall to an electronic games retailer on the ground that the assignment and change of use would conflict with its policy of reserving that part of the mall for fashion-related stores. Given such a tenant-mix policy, it was not unreasonable to conclude that the games retailer would attract a clientele that was, for the most part, quite different from the shoppers who would seek out the fashion-related stores. The case is, therefore, authority for the proposition that the landlord's letting policy may be a relevant consideration in determining whether the landlord has acted reasonably.

It is, perhaps, also worth mentioning that a landlord cannot reasonably refuse his consent simply because he desires to obtain possession of the premises for himself (*Bates* v *Donaldson* [1896] 2 QB 241).

As to how A & Co. Ltd may challenge the validity of the objections raised by Lord Wealth, it is open to the tenant to go ahead with the transaction and simply wait for the landlord to sue, and then set up the unreasonable refusal by way of defence and counterclaim for a declaration that the landlord's refusal was unreasonable and that the tenant was entitled, notwithstanding the refusal, to assign. Alternatively, assuming A & Co. Ltd does not want to take the risk of going ahead and assigning without consent, it may apply to the county court for a declaration that the consent has been unreasonably withheld. This jurisdiction is given by the Landlord and Tenant Act 1954, s. 53. Additionally, A & Co. Ltd may bring an action for damages, alleging that Lord Wealth is in breach of his statutory duty under the Landlord and Tenant Act 1988, s. 1(4). Such a claim may be combined with a claim for an injunction requiring Lord Wealth to comply with his statutory duty to grant consent to the proposed assignment.

Q Question 2

Samuel Printers Ltd is the lessee of shop premises which it holds under a lease granted to it by Acrecrest Properties Ltd for a term of 21 years. A user covenant in the lease prohibits the lessee from using the premises 'for any purpose other than the trade or business of a printer without the lessors' written consent which shall not be unreasonably withheld'. By another clause in the lease, the lessee covenants 'not to assign, underlet or part with possession of the premises or any part thereof without the written consent of the landlords which shall not be unreasonably withheld'. Samuel Printers Ltd is desirous to assign the unexpired residue of the term to a company called London Lettings Ltd, which proposes to use the premises as offices.

The landlords, Acrecrest Properties Ltd, have raised written objections to the proposed assignment on the ground that it will necessarily result in a breach of the user covenant. Moreover, they have serious doubts as to the proposed assignee's ability to meet the obligations under the lease and have, therefore, required a surety as a condition of granting consent. They have also insisted that the proposed assignee pay a substantial rental deposit.

Advise Samuel Printers Ltd.

Commentary

This question has a similar format to Question 1 above, but the issues raised are obviously different. Here again, a good knowledge of the case law will pay dividends!

For an article on the requirement of a surety as a condition of granting consent, see McLoughlin, P., 'Sureties in Commercial Leases' [1991] EG 9120, 86.

- Landlord has statutory duty to give consent unless good reason for refusing it: Landlord and Tenant Act 1988, s. 1

- Usually reasonable for landlord to withhold consent where assignee proposes to use the premises in breach of user covenant, but there may be circumstances where refusal of consent on this ground would be unreasonable: *Ashworth Frazer Ltd* v *Gloucester City Council* (2001)

- Imposition of unreasonable conditions amounts to unreasonable refusal: *Premier Rinks* v *Amalgamated Cinematograph Theatres Ltd* (1912) and Landlord and Tenant Act 1988, s. 1(4). Open to landlord to consider financial standing of proposed assignee: *British Bakeries*, above. If financial standing in question, it would be reasonable to require a surety

- Rental deposit may be caught by Law of Property Act, s. 144. In any event, demand for rental deposit must satisfy test of reasonableness

:Q: Suggested answer

Since the lease contains a qualified covenant against assignment, sub-letting etc., the provisions of the Landlord and Tenant Act 1927, s. 19(1) will apply to render the covenant subject to the further proviso that the landlords' consent shall not be unreasonably withheld. Moreover, the landlords are under a statutory duty to give consent to the proposed assignment unless they have good reason for refusing it (Landlord and Tenant Act 1988, s. 1).

The objection based on the fact that the proposed assignment will necessarily result in a breach of the user covenant may be reasonable. The House of Lords in *Ashworth Frazer Ltd* v *Gloucester City Council* [2001] 1 WLR 2180 has held recently that there is no rule of law that the words 'unreasonably withheld' in an alienation clause had to be interpreted as meaning that a landlord could not withhold consent simply on the ground that the prospective assignee would breach the terms of a user covenant in the lease. The correct approach now in determining whether it was reasonable for the landlord to refuse consent to an assignment is to consider what the reasonable landlord would do when asked to consent in the particular circumstances. In the earlier case of *Killick* v *Second Covent Garden Property Co. Ltd* [1973] 1 WLR 658, the Court of Appeal held that even if, on its true construction, a user covenant precluded the assignee from using the premises, it was not a necessary consequence of the assignment that there would be a breach of covenant as, once the assignment had been made, the landlord would have the same rights to enforce the user covenant against the assignee as it had against the tenant. Thus, in *British Bakeries (Midlands) Ltd v Michael Testler & Co. Ltd* (1986) 277 EG 1245, the landlord refused consent on the ground, *inter alia*, of the proposed user of the premises. This ground was rejected by the court, in the light of the *Killick* decision, as being an expectation of a future breach of user covenant, which did not provide a good reason for a refusal of consent.

This approach has now been questioned by the House of Lords because, in reality, the reasonable landlord could well look at the matter more broadly and see that his position would be significantly altered by the proposed assignment, despite having exactly the same powers to prevent a breach of covenant by an assignee as by an existing tenant. The landlord may face the prospect of becoming involved in lengthy legal proceedings and a reasonable landlord would, therefore, be entitled to take that prospect into account when asked to give consent to an assignment. It is now, therefore, considered to be wholly unrealistic to suggest (as was done in *Killick*) that no reasonable landlord would withhold consent to an assignment simply because, technically, his legal position and his legal remedies would remain the same.

Because the central strand of the *Killick* decision has now been rejected by the House of Lords, the refusal of consent to the proposed assignment in the present case (involving potentially a breach of user covenant) will *prima facie* be considered reasonable. (The House of Lords did, however, intimate that there could be circumstances which would render the landlord's refusal unreasonable.)

As to the requirement of a surety as a condition of granting consent, the imposition of unreasonable conditions amounts to unreasonable refusal of consent. In particular, conditions designed to extort an advantage not otherwise obtainable are unreasonable (*Premier Rinks v Amalgamated Cinematograph Theatres Ltd* (1912) 56 Sol Jo 536). In *Orlando Investments Ltd v Grosvenor Estate Belgravia* (1989) 59 P & CR 21, the Court of Appeal held that it was not unreasonable, in the circumstances, for the landlord to require the proposed assignee to carry out essential works of repair to the premises and to provide security for the due execution of the work. This was required as evidence of the proposed assignee's willingness to do the repairs, not his financial ability to do them, and it was not unreasonable (given the past history of breaches) for the landlord to require proof of the proposed assignee's willingness to perform.

Under the Landlord and Tenant Act 1988, s. 1(4), the giving of consent subject to any condition which is not reasonable does not satisfy the statutory duty to give consent.

It is, of course, open to a landlord to consider the financial standing of the assignee in deciding whether or not to consent to the assignment. Apart from the usual references provided by banks, solicitors, accountants etc., the landlord may be entitled to ask for the trading profits of the proposed assignee with a view to satisfying himself of the latter's ability to meet his obligations under the lease (*British Bakeries (Midlands) Ltd v Michael Testler & Co. Ltd* (1986) 277 EG 1245, where it was held that the landlord was not acting unreasonably in refusing consent in view of his real doubts as to the proposed assignee's ability to meet the obligations under the lease; see also, *Venetian Glass Gallery Ltd* v *Next Properties Ltd* [1989] 30 EG 92). In *Warren* v *Marketing Exchange for Africa Ltd* [1988] 2 EGLR 247, HH Judge Finlay QC confirmed that a landlord need not be content with references of a qualified or superficial nature.

The trading accounts of the proposed assignee are likely to be a better guide to its financial ability than references. The accounts will show the capital adequacy of the assignee and the general level of profitability. The best indicator of whether the assignee will be able to pay the rent is the profit and loss account. In the *British Bakeries* case, evidence was given that a generally accepted test of the financial standing of any proposed assignee is that his accounts should show a pre-tax profit of not less than three times the amount payable under the lease. (The pre-tax profit is the relevant figure because it is that profit against which the rent will be charged.) This test, however, is only a guide. In the *Venetian Glass* case, the prospective assignee was a limited company whose recent trading profits were poor, but it was improving its trade and other factors (e.g., the availability of a strong guarantee) showed that the company was suitable despite its low profit margin. Another aspect of the accounts which may be relevant is the balance sheet since this will show the net asset value of the assignee, which may be relevant in so far as the landlord may have to sue for rent and rely on a suitable asset base from which to recover its debt. It has been held, however, that it may be artificial to look solely at the profit and loss account and balance sheet when the prospective assignee is a small one-man or two-person private company: *Old English Inns plc* v *Brightside Ltd*, May 18 2004, available on Lawtel, Master Moncaster, Ch D.

Generally speaking, a surety may be reasonably required by the landlord as a condition of granting consent if the proposed assignee is of insufficient financial standing, but ultimately much will depend on the particular circumstances of the case (*In re Greater London Properties Ltd's Lease* [1959] 1 WLR 503). In *London & Argyll Developments Ltd* v *Mount Cook Land Ltd* [2002] 50 EG 111 (CS), the landlord's insistence upon a surety was held to be unreasonable because the premises were ground-rented and there was no suggestion that the proposed assignee was unable to pay. Moreover, details regarding the assignee's financial position were supplied to which the landlord had raised no objection. (By contrast, if the requirement for a surety condition is contained in the assignment clause itself as a precondition to the right to assign and it is at the discretion of the landlord, he is not required to act reasonably: *Mount Eden Land Ltd* v *Towerstone Ltd* [2002] 31 EG 97 (CS).) Assuming, therefore, that the financial standing of London Lettings Ltd is not in question, it would be unreasonable for the landlords to require a surety.

As to the requirement of a rental deposit, under the Law of Property Act 1925, s. 144, every qualified covenant against assigning, sub-letting etc. without the landlord's consent is deemed, unless the contrary is expressed, to be subject to a proviso that no sum of money in the nature of a fine shall be payable for such consent. The landlord may, however, require the payment of a reasonable sum in respect of legal or other expenses incurred in granting consent. The question here is whether a rental deposit constitutes a 'fine' for the purpose of s. 144. It has been held, in a different context, that a large sum paid at the commencement of a lease and purporting to represent rent paid in advance was a fine for the purpose of deciding whether a lease was at a rent or a premium (*Hughes* v *Waite* [1957] 1 All ER 603). That decision is, however, distinguishable on the basis that the word 'fine' in *Hughes* was being used to describe a single capital payment as opposed to recurrent income payments by way of rent, whereas in s. 144 the word is used to denote a sum in the nature of a penalty. The decision in *Re Cosh's Contract* [1897] 1 Ch 9 also points to the conclusion that, for the purpose of s. 144, a deposit by way of security is not a fine.

Although a rental deposit may not be a fine prohibited by s. 144, it does not mean that a deposit may be demanded by the landlord as a matter of course. The demand must still, in the case of a qualified covenant, have to satisfy the requirement of reasonableness, and whether Acrecrest Properties Ltd are acting reasonably in the present case will again depend upon the financial strength of the proposed assignee. In *Straudley Investment Ltd* v *Mount Eden Land Ltd (No. 1)* (1996) 74 P & CR 306, for example, a request for a rent deposit was held to be unreasonable because the landlord would gain an additional security beyond its right under the lease.

Samuel Printers Ltd is advised to apply to the county court, under the Landlord and Tenant Act 1954, s. 53, for a declaration that consent has been unreasonably withheld. It should also seek damages, alleging that the landlords are in breach of their statutory duty under the Landlord and Tenant Act 1988, s. 1, and claim an injunction requiring them to comply with their statutory duty by granting consent.

Q Question 3

(a) How has the Landlord and Tenant Act 1988 altered the law in respect of the granting of consent to a proposed assignment of the demised premises? [20 marks]

(b) To what extent can a landlord give at the hearing other reasons for objections to the proposed assignment not given to the tenant at the time when the decision to refuse consent was made? [5 marks]

Commentary

The first part of this question should pose no difficulty to the well-prepared student who has revised this topic for the exam. Apart from referring to the 1988 Act itself, you should make reference to the pre-1998 position and draw appropriate comparisons. There have been several cases on the 1988 Act which should also be mentioned. For a brief outline of the workings of the 1988 Act, see Austin, J., 'The Landlord and Tenant Act 1988' [1989] EG 8912, 55.

The second part of this question is more problematic. It is quite specific, and unless you are familiar with the recent case law in point you will not know where to begin! Frankly, not a very fair question, but some examiners do like to throw one into the exam simply to test your detailed knowledge of one or two cases. For a summary of the relevant law, see Wilkinson, H. W., 'Reasons not put into Writing' (1999) 149 NLJ 1039.

- **The 1988 Act imposes duty on landlord to give consent (unless good reason for refusing it) within a reasonable time. Tenant has claim for damages if consent not forthcoming: s. 4**

- **Consider s. 1(6) in detail. Onus of proof on landlord that (1) he gave consent within a reasonable time (2) if subject to conditions, that conditions reasonable and (3) if no consent given, that it was reasonable to do so**

- **Effect of s. 2 requiring landlord to pass tenant's application for consent to third parties. Consider also s. 3 applicable to subleases**

- **Landlord can only rely on reasons which are stated in writing within a reasonable time of the tenant's application for consent. Consider effect of *Footwear Corporation Ltd* v *Amplight Properties Ltd* (1998)**

☼ Suggested answer

(a) Prior to the enactment of the Landlord and Tenant Act 1988, a restriction on dealings without the landlord's consent was primarily governed by the Landlord and Tenant Act 1927, s. 19(1), which implies a proviso that consent is not to be unreasonably withheld. Such a proviso is often expressly incorporated in a lease.

If a tenant considered that a landlord was unreasonably withholding consent, then the tenant could either seek a declaration, under the Landlord and Tenant Act 1954, s. 53, that consent was being unreasonably withheld, or alternatively assign without consent and use the unreasonableness as a defence to any subsequent action brought against him by the landlord. To seek a court declaration was time-consuming and costly, and at the end of the day the proposed assignee might not have been around by the time the declaration was made. On the other hand, to go ahead with the assignment without consent was risky for the tenant and, more particularly, for the potential assignee.

Moreover, the tenant did not previously have any right to damages from the landlord, even if the landlord was found to have withheld consent unreasonably (see *Rendall* v *Roberts and Stacey* (1959) 175 EG 265), except where there was an express covenant on the part of the landlord not to withhold consent unreasonably (see *dicta* in *Rose* v *Gossman* (1966) 201 EG 767). Furthermore, there was no obligation on the part of the landlord to give any reasons for his decision (except under the Housing Act 1985, s. 94 in the case of a secure tenancy) and the burden of proof was on the tenant to show that the landlord was acting unreasonably (*Pimms* v *Tallow Chandlers* [1964] 2 QB 547).

The 1988 Act imposes upon the landlord a duty to give consent (unless he has a good reason for withholding it) within a reasonable period, thus giving rise to a claim in damages (under s. 4) if consent is not forthcoming or is unreasonably withheld. It also imposes a duty on the landlord to serve on the tenant written notice of his decision whether or not to give consent, specifying any conditions and, if consent is withheld, the reasons for withholding consent. This must also be done within a reasonable time. Section 1(6) of the Act provides that it is for the landlord to show:

(a) if he gave consent, that he did so within a reasonable time (see *Midland Bank plc* v *Chart Enterprises Inc* [1990] 44 EG 68, where the landlords were held to have unreasonably delayed in the communication of their decision as to consent to the proposed assignment, and *Dong Bang Minerva (UK) Ltd* v *Davina Ltd* [1994] EGCS 104, where the landlords were held to have unreasonably delayed in granting consent to a proposed sub-tenancy);

(b) if he gave consent subject to any condition, that the condition was a reasonable condition; and

(c) if he did not give consent, that it was reasonable not to do so.

Although a landlord is entitled to make requests for information regarding the suitability of the proposed assignee or subtenant, this will not necessarily 'stop the clock' for making a decision whether or not to consent: *Norwich Union Life Insurance Society* v *Shopmoor Ltd* [1991] 1 WLR 531. In the *Dong Bang* case, for example, the landlord was held not entitled to delay giving consent merely because it had not received a full copy of the proposed sublease.

The recent Court of Appeal decision in *Go West Ltd* v *Spigarolo* [2003] EWCA Civ 17 has confirmed that the reasonable time under the 1988 Act, even in complicated cases, is to be measured in weeks rather than months. Moreover, as soon as the landlord gives written refusal of consent, this will necessarily end the reasonable period permitted for the landlord to deal with the tenant's application. In other words, the landlord is not allowed to reconsider the application during the remainder of what might otherwise have been a reasonable period. It is apparent, therefore, that the landlord may be faced with a difficult choice if information (pursuant to a reasonable request) is not forthcoming from the tenant. If he postpones his decision, there is a danger that any delay will constitute a breach of statutory duty if it later transpires that the request was unreasonable and consent should have been granted. If, on the other hand, the landlord goes ahead and refuses consent, the decision may turn out to be premature in the light of the subsequent information made available to the tenant. In this event, the landlord's refusal of consent will be unreasonable and, having already made a decision, he will not be afforded any further time to change his mind.

Section 2 of the 1988 Act places a further duty on the landlord to take reasonable steps to pass on the tenant's application for consent to anyone he believes may be required to consent to the transaction. Thus, for example, a landlord who receives an application from a tenant, which also requires the consent of the superior landlord, is under a duty to send a copy of the application to the superior landlord.

Although the intention of the Act is obviously to provide the tenant with a quick, safe remedy, it is still open to tenants to seek a declaration that the landlord is acting unreasonably where they do not want to take the risk of going ahead and assigning without consent. As an alternative, they may combine a claim for damages for breach of statutory duty with an application for an injunction requiring the landlord to comply with his statutory duty.

Section 3 of the 1988 Act deals with subleases. It applies in a situation where a tenancy includes a covenant on the part of the tenant not to consent to his sub-tenant's assigning, underletting, charging or parting with possession of the premises comprised in the sub-tenancy without the approval of the landlord, and the covenant is subject to the qualification that the approval is not to be unreasonably withheld. The section provides that the landlord owes a duty to the sub-tenant in terms comparable with the duty he owes to a tenant under the Act.

While the 1988 Act reverses the burden of proof so that it is now necessary for the landlord to prove that any refusal is reasonable, and while it provides the tenant with a claim for damages, it does not alter the law in any other respects. In particular, the Act does not require the landlord, when withholding consent to an assignment, to justify as a matter of fact the matters upon which it relies (*Air India* v *Balabel* [1993] 30 EG 90).

(b) Prior to the 1988 Act, it was open to a landlord to give at the hearing other reasons for objections to the proposed assignment not given to the tenant originally, provided that they were present in his mind when he made the decision to refuse consent (*Bromley Park Garden Estates Ltd* v *Moss* [1982] 1 WLR 1019, *per* Slade LJ). It is now clear that a landlord can only rely on reasons for withholding consent (or imposing conditions) which are stated in writing within a reasonable time of the tenant's application for consent: *London & Argyll Developments Ltd* v *Mount Cook Land Ltd* [2002] 50 EG 111 (C5). In *Footwear Corportion Ltd* v *Amplight Properties Ltd* [1998] 3 All ER 52, the tenant of retail premises wrote to the landlord seeking consent to a sub-letting. Three days later, the landlord's managing director telephoned the tenant's surveyor indicating that consent would not be granted for a variety of reasons. The Court held that the landlord was not entitled to rely on reasons justifying its refusal which had not been communicated to the tenant in *writing* within a reasonable time in compliance with s. 1(3) of the 1988 Act. The upshot of this decision, therefore, is that:

(a) if the landlord gives *no* reasons within a reasonable time of the tenant's application for consent, he cannot rely in court on any reasons which, in fact, brought about the refusal;

(b) if the landlord has given *written* reasons for refusal within a reasonable time, he cannot rely on unstated reasons which may also have affected his decision to refuse consent; and

(c) if the landlord has given *oral* reasons within a reasonable time, he cannot rely on these (or any other) reasons for justifying refusal of consent.

The rationale for the Court's ruling is that, even though there is a contractual duty not to withhold consent unreasonably, the 1988 Act imposes a distinct and separate *statutory* duty on the landlord, who is refusing consent, to respond in writing within a reasonable time giving his reasons for refusal. The Act therefore specifically requires consent or refusal of consent to be in writing, albeit that there may be no such contractual requirement under the terms of the covenant in the lease.

Although the landlord will not be entitled to rely on any further grounds not stated in its original notification in writing, this does not mean that, when seeking to show that it was reasonable for him to consent on the stated ground, he is confined to what he said in that notification. Section 1(6)(c) of the 1988 Act contains no such restriction. However, it has been decided recently that, if the landlord imposes conditions to consent to an assignment, his justification for imposing those conditions must be given at the time those conditions were imposed: *London and Argyll Developments Ltd* v *Mount Cook Land Ltd*, above. Whether or not the landlord's request(s) for information as to the proposed assignee's financial standing, suitability, etc. must also be in writing is still a moot question.

Q Question 4

Blackhorse Ltd holds the freehold title to a high-street property in Birmingham. Several years ago, it granted a 15-year lease to Dyers Ltd, a company which carries on a stationery business from the property. Under the terms of its lease, Dyers Ltd covenanted, *inter alia*, as follows:

> . . . not to assign, sub-let, charge or otherwise part with possession of the premises or any part thereof, or share occupation of the same or any part thereof, save with the landlord's prior written consent . . .

The lease also contains a forfeiture clause in the event of non-payment of rent or non-performance of other tenant covenants. The property comprises a shop with a flat above.

Herman is a managing director of Dyers Ltd. Three months ago, with the consent of the other directors of Dyers Ltd, but without the consent of Blackhorse Ltd, Herman took a sub-lease of the flat, paying Dyers Ltd a monthly rent of £300.

Blackhorse Ltd has recently discovered that Herman is living in the flat. It does not wish to bring forfeiture proceedings against Dyers Ltd, but is keen, nevertheless, to oblige Herman to vacate the flat.

Advise Blackhorse Ltd as to what legal action (other than forfeiture) it can take against Dyers Ltd and Herman.

Commentary

This is an interesting question, which raises a novel point of law. It is concerned with the remedies open to a landlord faced with an illegal sub-letting or sharing of occupation of the demised premises. A good answer will consider the important ruling in *Hemingway Securities Ltd* v *Dunraven Ltd* [1995] 09 EG 322. See further, Luxton, P. and Wilkie, M., 'Who Needs Section 146 Injunctive Relief for a Landlord' [1995] Conv 416.

- Difficulties associated with seeking forfeiture in cases involving unlawful assignments or sublettings. In majority of cases, relief against forfeiture will be granted: *Mount Cook Land Ltd* v *Hartley* (2000)

- Landlord cannot take direct action against illegal subtenant because no *locus standi* to sue in trespass: *Shelfer* v *City of London Electric Lighting Co* (1895)

- Open to landlord to seek mandatory injunction against subtenant requiring him to effect a surrender of the unlawful sublease: *Hemingway Securities Ltd* v *Dunraven Ltd* (1995). Tenant will be in breach of contract and subtenant will be liable for inducing a breach of contract (*Esso Petroleum Co. Ltd* v *Kingswood Motors (Addlestone) Ltd* (1974)) or for breaching covenant against subletting on the basis that latter binding on the subtenant under the rule in *Tulk* v *Moxhay* (1848)

- Injunctive relief may be refused if it would cause under hardship to subtenant. Consider then damages in lieu under Supreme Court Act 1981, s. 50

☼ Suggested answer

In a case of unauthorised assignment or sub-letting of the demised premises, a landlord will invariably opt to effect a forfeiture of the lease in order to recover the property from the unlawful assignee or sub-tenant. This, however, is usually a lengthy and expensive course of action involving the service of a s. 146 notice and the commencement of proceedings against both the tenant in breach of covenant and the unlawful occupier in possession. Although breach of a covenant against assigning, sub-letting and parting with possession is treated, as a matter of law, as an irremediable breach (see *Scala House & District Property Co. Ltd* v *Forbes* [1974] QB 575 and *Expert Clothing Service & Sales Ltd* v *Hillgate House Ltd* [1986] Ch 340), it is still open to the court to grant relief against forfeiture under s. 146(2) of the Law of Property Act 1925 in appropriate circumstances. An important factor in granting relief is the fact that it would have been unreasonable for the landlord to have withheld consent to the assignment (or sub-letting) of the lease had such consent been sought by the tenant. Thus, where it is clear that consent could not have been refused, it appears that relief against forfeiture will generally be granted (*Lam Kee Ying* v *Lam Shes Tong* [1975] AC 247 (PC)). Moreover, the general trend is for the courts to grant relief where there has been an assignment in breach of covenant, even where the breach is wilful and has resulted in the landlord being misled (*Southern Depot Co. Ltd* v *British Railways Board* [1990] 2 EGLR 39 and *Fuller* v *Judy Properties Ltd* [1992] 1 EGLR 75). In cases involving sub-letting in breach of covenant, the courts adopt the principle of pro-portionality, taking a number of factors into account in considering whether or not to grant relief, including whether consent would have been unreasonably withheld in any event, the value of the lease and the extent of any loss suffered by the landlord (*Mount Cook Land Ltd* v *Hartley* [2000] EGCS 26). In the majority of cases, therefore, relief will be granted and the landlord will not be in a position to forfeit the lease. In such circumstances, the landlord may seek to claim damages for breach of covenant or, alternatively, attempt to regularise the position by taking other steps to oust the unlawful occupier.

The landlord cannot, of course, take direct action against an illegal sub-tenant/ occupier of the premises, simply because he has no *locus standi* to sue in trespass during the subsistence of the lease. Because the landlord has divested himself of exclusive possession in favour of the tenant, he no longer retains any right to posses-sion in himself. A reversioner may sue for trespass only if it actually affects his rever-sionary interest. Accordingly, a mere trespass, unaccompanied by any permanent physical injury to the land, is not actionable by the landlord who must, therefore, wait until his interest falls into possession (*Jones* v *Llanrwst Urban Council* [1911] 1 Ch 393, at 404, and *Shelfer* v *City of London Electric Lighting Co.* [1895] 1 Ch 287, at 318). Thus, in *Moore Properties (Ilford) Ltd* v *McKeon* [1976] 1 WLR 1278, the tenancy had ended so that the landlord was able to bring summary possession proceedings against the defendants, who had taken up occupation by virtue of a sub-tenancy which had been granted in breach of an absolute prohibition against sub-letting and without the landlord's knowledge or consent.

Where, however, the head tenancy subsists, it may be open to a landlord to seek a mandatory injunction against the sub-tenant requiring him to effect a surrender of the unlawful sub-lease. In *Hemingway Securities Ltd* v *Dunraven Ltd* [1995] 09 EG 322 the lease contained a fully qualified covenant against sub-letting and required, as a condition precedent to the landlord's consent, that the prospective sub-tenant enter into a direct covenant with the landlord to observe all the tenant's covenants contained in the head lease. The tenant, without the landlord's consent (and apparently without its knowledge), sub-let the premises to four individuals in partnership, who duly entered into possession of the premises. The landlord sought a mandatory injunction against the tenant alleging a breach of contract, and against the sub-tenants either for inducing a breach of contract, or for breaching the covenant against sub-letting on the basis that it was binding on the sub-tenants under the rule in *Tulk* v *Moxhay* (1848) 2 Ph 774. Jacob J held that the landlord was entitled to a mandatory injunction on both grounds, requiring the sub-tenants to execute a deed delivering up their unlawful sub-lease to the tenant.

In cases such as this, if the landlord acts promptly, he may be able to obtain a prohibitory injunction against the tenant, preventing the latter from assigning or sub-letting, etc. in breach of covenant (*Williams* v *Earle* (1868) LR 3 QB 739). The landlord may also seek such an injunction where the tenant is himself an assignee of the lease (*McEacham* v *Colton* [1902] 2 AC 104 (PC)). However, an unlawful sub-letting or assignment, which has already been executed, will create a valid title which will vest in the unlawful sub-tenant or assignee. The sub-letting or assignment is not void but voidable at the option of the landlord. In other words, the sub-tenant (or assignee) will take a defeasible title (i.e., subject to the landlord's right of forfeiture) (*Old Grovebury Manor Farm Ltd* v *W. Seymour Plant Sales & Hire Ltd (No. 2)* [1979] 1 WLR 1397). The significance of the decision in *Hemingway*, therefore, is that it gives the landlord a means of actually *undoing* the transaction without recourse to expensive forfeiture proceedings culminating in the potential determination of the lease.

The point was also addressed in *Esso Petroleum Co. Ltd* v *Kingswood Motors (Addlestone) Ltd* [1974] QB 142, where a collusive conveyance was executed to allow the vendors to avoid a solus agreement by which they were bound to buy petroleum only from Esso. The court held that the purchaser's conduct amounted to a deliberate inducement of a breach of the vendor's contract. On this basis, a mandatory injunction was granted against the purchaser requiring it to reconvey the legal estate. The *Esso* case establishes the principle that a party to a contract may obtain an injunction against a third party who induces (or who threatens to induce) the other contracting party to breach the contract. In the *Hemingway* case, Jacob J similarly found that the sub-tenants had intentionally induced a breach of the tenant's contract with the landlord not to sub-let without consent, and so was able to award a mandatory injunction against the sub-tenants to surrender the sub-lease. In so doing, he clearly treated the lease as a species of contract — an approach much in keeping with contemporary judicial trends: see, e.g., *Hussein* v *Mehlman* [1992] 32 EG 59, involving a repudiatory breach of a contract of letting.

The alternative ground relied upon by Jacob J in the *Hemingway* case was based on the application of the rule in *Tulk* v *Moxhay*. Jacob J concluded that a qualified covenant against sub-letting was, in essence, a restrictive covenant enforceable in equity as against the sub-tenants by means of a mandatory injunction. This aspect of the case has, however, been criticised by academic writers on the ground that the breach of covenant against sub-letting was a 'once and for all' breach committed, not by the sub-tenant, but by the tenant: see Luxton, P. and Wilkie, M. [1995] Conv 416.

It is apparent from the foregoing that Blackhorse Ltd should be advised to pursue injunctive relief against Dyers Ltd (alleging breach of contract) and Herman (based on the tort of interference with contract). The jurisdiction to grant an injunction against Herman for inducing a breach of contract will be available if Herman had knowledge that the grant of the sub-lease was a breach of a covenant in the head lease. In this connection, it is more than likely that Herman had notice of the terms of the head lease (in particular, the qualified covenant against assignment) by virtue of his position as a director of Dyers Ltd.

An order should be sought against Dyers Ltd restraining any like breaches in future. The order against Herman should require him to execute a deed of surrender delivering up his unlawful sub-lease to Dyers Ltd. Herman may seek to argue that injunctive relief will operate harshly against him because it will deny him the right to seek relief, which would otherwise be open to him as a sub-tenant if the landlord had invoked forfeiture proceedings against Dyers Ltd. However, the injunction, being a creature of equity, is a discretionary remedy and undue hardship to the defendant, or unreasonable delay or lack of 'clean hands' on the part of the claimant, are grounds upon which the remedy may be refused. In the present case, it would seem that injunctive relief would cause little hardship to Herman. He did not pay a premium on the grant of the sub-lease which, in any event, is only periodic in nature. It seems also that a mandatory injunction can be granted even if the claimant has suffered no serious damage or inconvenience (*Kelson* v *Imperial Tobacco Co. Ltd* [1957] 2 QB 334). In *Hemingway*, Jacob J also thought it wrong in principle that an unlawful sub-tenant should be allowed to stay on at the premises and thereby benefit from his wrong-doing. Similar reasoning would, no doubt, apply in the present case. If the court, however, was minded to exercise its discretion *against* granting an injunction, Blackhorse Ltd would still be entitled to an award of equitable damages in lieu of an injunction (under the Chancery Amendment Act 1858, now s. 50 of the Supreme Court Act 1981), and presumably also damages in tort for inducing a breach of contract. It would also have a claim in damages against Dyers Ltd for breach of covenant.

Further reading

Draper, M., 'Subject to Licence' (2002) SJ 678.

Goldberg, J., 'It Stands to Reason' [2002] EG 149.

Haley, M., 'Business Tenancies: Renewal and Authorised Guarantee Agreements' [2000] Conv 566.

Luxton, P., and Wilkie, M., 'Who Needs Section 146? Injunctive relief for a Landlord' [1995] Conv 416.

Miller, K., 'A Licence to Print Money' [2003] EG 132.

Norris, D., 'Store Wars' (2003) SJ 198.

Pawlowski, M., 'Consent to Assign or Sublet — Case Law Update' (2002) PLJ 7.

Leasehold dilapidations

Introduction

The subject of leasehold dilapidations is vast, and the student may be asked to answer questions on any one or more of the following topics:

(a) the meaning of repair;

(b) the standard of repair;

(c) the rule that a landlord is liable only on notice in respect of defects arising on the demised premises;

(d) implied obligations to repair; and

(e) remedies for breach of a repairing obligation.

Questions in this area tend to take the form of lengthy problems, the student usually being asked to advise a party to the lease as to its legal liability (if any) in respect of a number of alleged defects on the demised premises. You should be aware that liability for defects on the property may arise either in contract or in tort or by virtue of statutory provision.

In relation to express covenants, the question will invariably require you to consider the case law contrasting a work of repair with renewal and improvement (see, e.g., *Ravenseft Properties Ltd* v *Davstone (Holdings) Ltd* [1980] QB 12). This may be linked with a secondary issue as to what standard of repair should apply.

Invariably, it is a matter of construction of the relevant covenant(s) to determine whether the proposed works fall within the definition of repair. A recent case has raised the interesting point whether a covenant to repair carries with it a duty not to modify or destroy the subject premises. In *British Glass Manufacturers Confederation and NHE (Northumberland) Ltd* v *The University of Sheffield* [2003] EWHC 3108 (Ch), Lewison J held that the issue of whether a tenant is entitled to alter or demolish all or part of the demised premises will depend upon a true construction of the terms of the lease in the light of the overall commercial context. There is no absolute rule that alteration or demolition constitutes a breach of covenant. If the proposed user is not forbidden by the lease, a right to adapt the property for that user will readily be implied, provided that the lease contains no restriction on alterations (*Hannon* v *169 Queen's Gate Ltd* [2000] 1 EGLR 40) or the covenant against alterations does not extend to or prohibit the contemplated works of alienation (*Rose* v *Spicer* [1911] 2 KB 234. See further, Pawlowski, M., 'Covenant to Repair — Do Not Disturb?' (2004) PLJ 14.

Sometimes, the question will focus on the landlord's implied obligations to repair in the absence of any express covenant to maintain the premises. Here, the student may be required to consider liability at common law (i.e., fitness for human habitation and main-tenance of essential means of access) and under statute (i.e., the Landlord and Tenant 1985, ss. 8 and 11, as amended by the Housing Act 1988, s. 116). This may be contrasted with the tenant's implied obligation to use the premises in a tenant-like manner (*Warren* v *Keen* [1954] 1 QB 15).

With regard to liability in tort, the question may involve an examination of the landlord's liability:

(a) in negligence (e.g., *Rimmer* v *Liverpool City Council* [1985] QB 1; *McNerny* v *Lambeth London Borough Council* [1989] 19 EG 77);

(b) under the Defective Premises Act 1972, s. 4 (e.g., *McAuley* v *Bristol City Council* [1992] 1 All ER 749); and

(c) under the Environmental Protection Act 1990, ss. 79–82 (e.g., *Dover District Council* v *Farrar* (1980) 2 HLR 35 and *GLC* v *London Borough of Tower Hamlets* (1983) 15 HLR 54).

So far as the tenant is concerned, liability may arise under the torts of waste (see *Dayani* v *Bromley London Borough Council* [1999] 3 EGLR 144) or nuisance, or under the Occupiers' Liability Act 1957.

The rule that the landlord's liability to repair the demised premises arises only after he has been given sufficient notice of the defects has been the subject of considerable case law, in particular, the Court of Appeal decision in *British Telecommunications plc* v *Sun Life Assurance Society plc* [1995] 4 All ER 44, where a number of earlier authorities were reviewed. We have included an essay-type question on this topic: see Question 6.

It is very common now for commercial leases to contain a service charge provision. The service charge clause will place the burden of repair, maintenance of common parts, insurance, service staff, etc., on the landlord. Normally, the landlord will expressly covenant with the tenant to perform these services. In some clauses, however, performance by the landlord is merely a condition precedent of the tenant's obligation to pay the service charge. In other words, if the landlord does not perform the services, the tenant's obligation to pay does not arise. In the absence of an express covenant, the tenant may find it difficult to compel the landlord to provide the various services.

The primary aim of the service charge from the landlord's standpoint is, of course, to provide him with complete reimbursement for all his expenditure in maintaining and servicing the premises. It is important, therefore, that the service charge covers exactly all the expenditure which the landlord has undertaken to perform. Obviously, not all expenditure will be recoverable under a service charge provision since some works will fall outside the definition of 'repair' or 'maintenance' and constitute an improvement to the property. For example, in *Mullaney v Maybourne Grange (Croydon) Management Co. Ltd* [1986] 1 EGLR 70, the landlord was held not entitled to recover expenditure on replacing windows since the work went beyond repair and the new windows could not be regarded as an 'additional amenity' within the service charge clause: see further, **Chapter 8**, question 5.

In the context of residential leases, the Landlord and Tenant Act 1985 provides a comprehensive scheme for the recovery of service charges entitling the landlord to recover only such sums as are reasonably incurred and which relate to the provision of services or carrying out of works to a reasonable standard: s. 19(1). Disputes relating to service charges are referred to a leasehold valuation tribunal in order to determine the reasonableness of the charge. See further, Ward, V.C., 'Service Record', [2001] EG 156. Under s. 81 of the Housing Act 1988, a landlord is not entitled, in relation to residential premises, to exercise a right of forfeiture for failure to pay a service charge unless the amount of the charge is agreed by the tenant or has been the subject of determination by the court or an arbitral tribunal. This provision has now been extended to cover non-payment of administration charges: s. 170 of the Commonhold and Leasehold Reform Act 2002. The remedy of forfeiture is altogether excluded if the amount of rent, service charge or administration charges unpaid is less than an amount prescribed by Regulations, which cannot be more than £500: s. 167 of the 2002 Act.

The subject of remedies for disrepair is also a complex one. The student may be asked to advise on the landlord's remedies of forfeiture of the lease and/or damages for breach of covenant. Both these remedies are limited by statute and you will need to possess a good understanding of the workings of the Law of Property Act 1925, s. 146, the Leasehold Property (Repairs) Act 1938, and the Landlord and Tenant Act 1927, s. 18. So far as the tenant's remedies are concerned, these will include damages, specific performance, set off against rent, the appointment of a receiver or manager and the ability to acquire and exercise management of a block of flats under the Landlord and Tenant Act 1987 and the Commonhold and Leasehold Reform Act 2002.

Although a complex area of study, questions on dilapidations tend to be popular with both examiners and students. Most landlord and tenant courses focus on this subject in some depth, and the well-prepared student should have little difficulty in scoring a good mark.

Lastly, it is worth mentioning that the whole topic of leasehold dilapidations has been the subject of consideration by the Law Commission: see Law Commission Report (Law Com. No. 238, 1996), 'Landlord and Tenant: Responsibility for State and Condition of Property', and Bridge, S., 'Putting in Right? The Law Commission and the Condition of Tenanted Property' [1996] Conv 342. It is possible that your examiner may wish to set a question on the Law Commission's proposals, and this will undoubtedly take the form of an essay question. Essay questions give you the chance to show that you have read beyond the basic texts and have understood some of the broader issues affecting your topic of study: See Question 5.

Q Question 1

By a lease, dated 1 March 1990, the Earl of London demised Flatacre Hall to Albert Smith for a term of 99 years. By clause 2 of the lease, Albert covenanted 'to keep the demised premises and all additions thereto at all times during the said term in good and tenantable repair'. The Earl has now presented Albert with a formidable schedule of dilapidations, the items of which may be summarised under the following headings:

(a) Renew roof of stable block. Estimated cost: £15,000. The wood has rotted and the entire roof structure needs to be replaced;

(b) Eradicate rising damp in basement of main building. Estimated cost: £35,000. There is no damp-course as the building dates from 1850;

(c) Re-build side wall of kitchen. Estimated cost: £12,000. The wall is unsafe due to old age. The work will involve compliance with modern building standards;

(d) Redecorate throughout the main building. Estimated cost: £8,000. The wallpaper is badly stained and worn. The paintwork has faded and turned yellow. Much of the external woodwork has rotted.

Advise Albert as to his legal liability (if any) in respect of each of the alleged defects set out above.

Commentary

This is an example of a multi-part question, where you are asked to advise the tenant as to his liability in respect of a number of alleged defects. Essentially, the question seeks to test your understanding of the meaning of 'repair' and requires you to contrast works of repair with renewal and improvement. Try to avoid giving the examiner a 'mini-lecture' on the subject, and instead concentrate on being selective in your information and actually answering the question as set. Each part of the question revolves around a specific cluster of cases and so a thorough knowledge of the case law will pay dividends!

The fourth part of the question calls for an examination of cases on decorative repairs, in particular, *Proudfoot* v *Hart* (1890) 25 QBD 42.

- **Criteria for determining whether remedial works are repair or improvement:** *McDougall* v *Easington District Council* (1989)

- Renewal of roof not giving back to the landlord a wholly different thing from that demised: *Ravenseft Properties Ltd v Davstone (Holdings) Ltd* (1980). Simply a building with a new roof: *Elite Investments Ltd v TI Bainbridge Silencers Ltd* (1986).

- No liability to eradicate rising damp: Compare *Pembery v Lamdin* (1940) with *Elmcroft Developments Ltd v Tankersley-Sawyer* (1984)

- Rebuilding of wall simply a replacement of subsidiary parts: *Lurcott v Wakeley and Wheeler* (1911)

- Redecoration outside scope of repairing covenant, unless necessary to prevent rot: *Crayford v Newton* (1886), but consider also 'reasonably-minded tenant' test in *Proudfoot v Hart* (1890)

☼ Suggested answer

A tenant who has covenanted to *keep* in repair the demised premises during the term must have them in repair at all times during the term, and so if they are at any time out of repair he commits a breach of the covenant. It has been held that a covenant which requires the landlord to keep the building in 'good and tenantable condition' is wide enough to require him to put the building in that condition which, given the property's age, character and locality, would make it reasonably fit for the occupation of a reasonably-minded tenant of the class likely to take it (*Credit Suisse v Beegas Nominees Ltd* [1994] 4 All ER 803). Consequently, the covenant in the present case obliges Albert to *put* the premises in repair (if they are not in repair when the lease begins) and to *leave* them in repair during the currency of the term.

The essential issue is whether, having regard to all the circumstances of the case, the proposed remedial works can fairly be regarded as 'repair' in the context of this particular lease (*Holding & Management Ltd v Property Holding & Investment Trust plc* [1990] 05 EG 75). Three criteria have been established over the years for determining whether a work constitutes repair, namely:

(a) whether the works go to the whole or substantially the whole of the structure, or only to a subsidiary part;

(b) whether the effect is to produce a building of a wholly different character from that which had been let; and

(c) what is the cost of the works in relation to the previous value of the building and what is the effect on the value and life of the building (*McDougall v Easington District Council* [1989] 25 EG 104).

(a) 'Renew roof of stable-block'. As mentioned above, one test to be applied in deciding whether particular works can properly be described as 'repair', as opposed to works of renewal or improvement, is whether they involve giving back to the landlord a wholly different thing from that demised under the lease. This was the test put forward in *Ravenseft Properties Ltd* v *Davstone (Holdings) Ltd* [1980] QB 12, following the observations of Lord Esher MR in *Lister* v *Lane* [1893] 2 QB 212. In deciding the question whether the works would involve giving back to the landlord a wholly different thing, regard may be had, as a guide, to the proportion which the cost of the disputed works bear to the value or cost of the whole building.

In *Elite Investments Ltd* v *TI Bainbridge Silencers Ltd* (1986) 280 EG 1001, a case involving a dilapidated roof of an industrial unit, the evidence was that the replacement of the roof would cost around £84,000. In its dilapidated condition, the unit had virtually no value for lettings, but its value as repaired would be about £140,000–£150,000. It is noteworthy that the roof was beyond patching and had come to the end of its useful life and needed to be entirely replaced. The court held, rejecting the tenant's argument based on giving back to the landlord an entirely different thing, that this was not a different thing but merely an industrial building with a new roof. It was also suggested in this case that in a situation where the value of the demised building when repaired (£140,000–£150,000) is very much less than the cost of putting up a new building altogether (£1m), it is the cost of putting up the new building, not the value of the old building when repaired, which should be compared with the cost of the works required to repair the old building (£84,000).

In *New England Properties plc* v *Portsmouth New Shops Ltd* [1993] 23 EG 130, the original design of the roof was inadequate and it was necessary to replace the entire roof at a cost in excess of £200,000. It was held that the lease imposed an obligation on the landlord not simply to repair but also to renew or replace where necessary. It was also suggested *obiter* that, although it was a borderline case, the replacement of the roof fell to be regarded in any event as a work of repair.

In the present case, the information given is that the estimated cost of repairs amounts to £15,000. There is no mention of the value of the stable-block when repaired, or indeed of the cost of erecting a new stable-block altogether. Nevertheless, despite the extensive nature of the remedial works, it seems almost certain that the courts would treat the same as works of repair thereby rendering Albert liable under his covenant.

(b) 'Eradicate damp in basement'. Prior to the decision in *Ravenseft* (above), it had been thought that 'repair' did not include the remedying of an inherent defect in the design or construction of the demised premises. This view has now been exploded and the question, in all cases, is one of degree (*Brew Brothers Ltd* v *Snax (Ross) Ltd* [1969] 1 WLR 657).

The facts here show that there is no damp-course in the basement as the building dates back to 1850. In *Pembery* v *Lamdin* [1940] 2 All ER 434, a case involving a cellar built without a damp-course, it was held that the landlord was not liable under his repairing covenant to carry out remedial works to prevent damp penetrating into the cellar because this would involve ordering him to give the tenant a different thing from that which was demised. Similarly, in *Yanover v Romford Finance & Development Co. Ltd* (1983), unreported, Park J held that the proposed remedial work of the installation of a damp-course in a ground-floor flat at a cost of £8,000 was a major building operation which was not within the landlord's covenant relating to external repairs. More recently, it had been held that the installation of a damp-course where none had previously existed constituted an improvement: *Eyre* v *McCrackin* (2000) 80 P&CR 220.

These cases may be contrasted with *Elmcroft Developments Ltd* v *Tankersley-Sawyer* (1984) 270 EG 140, where there was evidence of penetrating damp in flats due to the existing damp-course having been positioned below ground level, with consequent 'bridging' causing rising damp in the walls. The remedial work required included insertion of a damp-course by silicone injection. The Court of Appeal held that the landlords were in breach of their covenant to repair since the remedial work did not go beyond repair and did not involve the provision of a wholly different thing from that which was demised. It is to be observed that the *Pembery* case involved premises built in 1840, whereas the more recent decision in *Elmcroft* concerned a modern letting of flats in a high class residential area of Central London.

In the present case, the estimated cost of the remedial work is £35,000. Looking at the matter as one of degree, therefore, Albert should be advised that he is not liable to eradicate the rising damp in the basement.

(c) 'Re-build side wall'. The word 'repair' has been defined as meaning the restoration by renewal or replacement of *subsidiary* parts of the whole, as opposed to the reconstruction of the whole or substantially the whole. In *Lurcott* v *Wakeley and Wheeler* [1911] KB 905, the front wall of a house had to be pulled down due to its dangerous condition. The house was very old and the condition of the wall was caused by old age. The Court of Appeal held that the tenant was liable under his covenant to repair and to replace worn out parts of a house. Essentially, where the remedial works would produce premises of a wholly different character from those which had been let, the works fall to be classified as improvements (as opposed to repair) to the premises. In the words of Cozens-Hardy MR in *Lurcott*, 'is it something which goes to the whole, or substantially the whole, or is it simply an injury to a portion, a subsidiary portion, of the demised property?'

In the present case, Albert should be advised that the side wall of the kitchen is merely a subsidiary portion of the main building, the rebuilding of which would not change the character or nature of the building as a whole. The fact that the work will involve compliance with modern building standards does not, it is submitted, change the position. Albert is obliged to repair the wall in the only sense in which it can be repaired, namely, by rebuilding it according to current building regulations etc. (*Ravenseft Properties Ltd* v *Davstone (Holdings) Ltd* [1980] QB 12, per Forbes J., at p. 22). The fact that the repairs will inevitably incorporate some improvement in design and construction does not mean that they cease to be works of repair: *Creska*

Ltd v *Hammersmith and Fulham London Borough Council* [1998] 37 EG 165 (repair of an under-floor heating system) and *Minja Properties Ltd* v *Cussins Property Group plc* [1998] 30 EG 114 (replacement of existing rusted single-glazed window frames with double-glazed units). Ultimately, in deciding whether the remedial works constitute repair, the court should consider, *inter alia*, the nature, extent and cost of the proposed remedial works, the value of the building and its expected lifespan: *Ultraworth Ltd* v *General Accident Fire and Life Assurance Corporation plc* [2000] 2 EGLR 115.

(d) 'Redecoration throughout main building'. As a general rule, a repairing covenant does not carry with it the obligation to carry out decorative repairs, except painting necessary for the prevention of decay as opposed to mere ornamentation. In *Crayford* v *Newton* (1886) 36 WN 54, the Court of Appeal held that a tenant who agreed to keep the inside of the premises in tenantable repair and who occupied them for 17 years without having painted or papered was only bound to paint and paper so as to prevent the house from going into decay. There seems little doubt, therefore, that Albert is obliged to paint the external woodwork to prevent rot.

In *Proudfoot* v *Hart* (1890) 25 QBD 42, however, the Court of Appeal, while laying down the general rule that the tenant is not bound by a general repairing covenant to do repairs which are merely decorative, also concluded that he is bound to repaper, paint and whitewash walls and ceilings if the condition of the house in those respects is such that it would not be taken by a reasonably minded tenant of the class likely to take it. The court also held that, in determining the standard of repair, regard is to be had to the age, character and prospective life of the premises and the locality in which it is situated. Applying the test of the reasonably minded tenant, it seems that Albert may be liable to repaper and paint the interior of the main building, although it is possible that he may be able to avail himself of the special form of relief available to a tenant in respect of internal decorative repairs under the Law of Property Act 1925, s. 147. This section provides that the court may relieve the tenant from liability for such repairs if, having regard to all the circumstances of the case (including in particular the length of the tenant's term or interest remaining unexpired), the court is satisfied that the landlord's notice is unreasonable.

Q Question 2

Compare and contrast the remedies available to:

(a) a landlord; and

(b) a tenant

for breach of a covenant to repair.

To what extent are the landlord's remedies limited by statute and the tenant's remedies extended by statute?

Commentary

This is a relatively straightforward question on remedies for disrepair. However, there is a lot of ground to cover and there is a real danger that the student will spend too much time on one particular remedy at the expense of others. Essentially, the question requires a broad outline of the various remedies, but with particular emphasis on statutory intervention. For a good summary of the relevant law, see Williams, D., 'Landlord's Remedies for Disrepair' [1989] EG 8938, 24, and Williams, D., 'Tenant's Remedies for Disrepair' (1984) *Law Society Gazette*, 9 May, p. 1269. See also, Madge, N., 'Damages for Breach of Repairing Obligations' (1999) 149 NLJ 1643.

- Landlord must comply with Law of Property Act, s. 146 and Leasehold Property (Repairs) Act 1938: *Associated British Ports CH Bailey plc* (1990). Landlord may avoid these procedural requirements by use of self-help remedy: *Jervis* v *Harris* (1996). Section 146 notice cannot validly be served under a long lease of a dwelling unless the fact that there is a breach has been determined by an appropriate court order or tribunal or admitted by the tenant

- Tenant's ability to claim relief against forfeiture: s. 146(2). Also, landlord's damages limited by Landlord and Tenant Act 1927, s. 18(1). But landlord may seek specific performance in exceptional circumstances: *Rainbow Estates Ltd* v *Tokenhold Ltd* (1998)

- Tenant's claim for damages under various heads: *Calabar Properties Ltd* v *Stitcher* (1984) and *McGreal* v *Wake* (1984). In addition, tenant may seek specific performance under Landlord and Tenant Act, s. 17 and at common law: *Jeune* v *Queens Cross Properties Ltd* (1974)

- Consider also tenant's remedy of set-off and right of deduction against rent: *British Anzani (Felixstowe) Ltd* v *International Marine Management (UK) Ltd* (1980) and *Lee-Parker* v *Izzet* (1971). Also appointment of receiver/manager: Supreme Court Act 1981, s. 37. Powers of management and acquisition under Landlord and Tenant Act 1987 and Commonhold and Leasehold Reform Act 2002

⚙ Suggested answer

(a) Landlord's remedies. A landlord faced with a tenant who is in breach of his covenant to repair may elect to forfeit the lease and claim damages for any loss suffered to his reversion. In all cases (other than non-payment of rent), a prerequisite to forfeiture is the service by the landlord of a notice under the Law of Property Act 1925, s. 146(1). He must, in the notice, specify the particular breach complained of and, if the breach is capable of remedy, require the tenant to remedy the same within a reasonable time. In addition, where appropriate, the notice must refer to the land-lord's claim for compensation. A landlord under a long lease of a dwelling may not, however, serve a s. 146 notice in respect of a breach by a tenant of any covenant or condition in the lease unless the breach has been admitted by the tenant or proved in proceedings before the court or a Leasehold Valuation Tribunal: s. 168 of the Commonhold and Leasehold Reform Act 2002.

Where the lease in question was granted for seven or more years and three years or more remain unexpired at the date of the s. 146 notice, the landlord's remedy of forfeiture (and damages) is further limited by the Leasehold Property (Repairs) Act 1938. Where the Act applies, the landlord cannot proceed without first serving a s. 146 notice, which must also inform the tenant of his right to serve a counternotice claiming the benefit of the Act. If the tenant does serve such a counternotice within 28 days, no further proceedings by action or otherwise can be taken by the landlord without leave of the court establishing a case, on the balance of probabilities, that one or more of the five grounds set out in s. 1(5) of the Act have been fulfilled (*Associated British Ports* v *C.H. Bailey plc* [1990] 2 AC 703). The relevant date upon which the landlord has to prove one or more of the s. 1(5) grounds is the date of his application for leave to bring proceedings: *Landmaster Properties Ltd* v *Thackeray Property Services* [2003] 35 EG 83.

Under s. 146(2) of the 1925 Act, the tenant is also entitled to apply to the court for relief against forfeiture. The court may grant or refuse relief on terms as it thinks fit, and in the case of a breach of a repairing covenant the court will usually require the tenant to remedy the disrepair and make compensation to the landlord for any damage to the reversion before it grants such relief. A special form of relief is given to the tenant under s. 147 of the 1925 Act in respect of internal decorative repairs. Upon the tenant's application for relief, the court may relieve the tenant from liability for such repairs if, having regard to all the circumstances of the case (including, in par-ticular, the length of the term unexpired), the court is satisfied that the landlord's notice is unreasonable.

Apart from claiming forfeiture, the landlord will invariably seek to claim damages. Where the landlord's claim is brought during the currency of the lease, damages will represent the amount by which the landlord's reversion has depreciated in marketable value by the premises being out of repair. Practically, this is the amount by which the saleable value of the premises is reduced by the neglect bearing in mind the length of the unexpired term. However, by the Landlord and Tenant Act 1927, s. 18(1), damages for breach of a repairing covenant during the currency of a lease are not to exceed the amount (if any) by which the value of the premises is reduced. This, in effect, provides an upper limit to the amount of damages recoverable. At the end of the term, the landlord may bring a claim on the covenant to yield up the premises in repair. The measure of damages is the cost of repair (*Foyner* v *Weeks* [1891] 2 QB 31) plus loss of rental while the repair is being done (*Woods* v *Pope* (1895) 6 C & P 732).

Here again, the common law measure is subject to s. 18 of the 1927 Act (*Hansom v Newman* [1934] Ch 298 and *Shortlands Investments Ltd v Cargill plc* [1995] 08 EG 163).

Section 18(1) of the 1927 Act also provides that no damages are recoverable by the landlord for failure to leave or put premises in repair at the end of a lease if it is shown that they, in whatever condition, would, at or shortly after the end, have been pulled down or such alterations made as to render the tenant's repairs valueless.

It is possible for a landlord to avoid the procedural requirements of the 1938 Act if he has the benefit of a covenant in the lease enabling him to inspect the state of repair of the demised premises and serve notice on the tenant requiring him to execute the necessary repairs. If he fails to do so, the landlord may carry out the work himself and recover the cost from the tenant. In these circumstances, a claim by the landlord to recover the cost of the repairs is, by reason of the express terms of the covenant, either a claim for a *debt* or *rent* due under the lease rather than a claim for damages for breach of covenant within the 1938 Act. Accordingly, the landlord does not require leave under the Act to bring the claim against the tenant (*Colchester Estates (Cardiff) v Carlton Industries plc* [1986] Ch 80 and *Jervis v Harris* [1996] 1 EGLR 78 (CA)). This self-help remedy, however, may not be available to the landlord if the carrying out of the repairs would be highly disruptive to the tenant's business (*Hammersmith and Fulham London Borough Council v Creska Ltd* (1999) 78 P & CR D46).

In exceptional cases, it may be open to the landlord to seek specific performance of his tenant's repairing obligations: *Rainbow Estates Ltd v Tokenhold Ltd* [1998] 3 WLR 980, where specific performance was granted because the lease contained no forfeiture clause nor any right entitling the landlord access to the premises to carry out the repairs with a view to claiming the cost from the tenants as a debt or rent arrears. Moreover, there was evidence of serious disrepair and deterioration to the property.

(b) Tenant's remedies. Where the landlord is in breach of his repairing covenant, the tenant has basically four remedies, namely:

(a)   damages;

(b)   specific performance;

(c)   set off against rent; and

(d)   appointment of a receiver/manager.

In addition, the tenant may be able to invoke action by the local authority in extreme cases of disrepair.

Damages may be awarded under the various heads of claim set out in *Calabar Properties Ltd v Stitcher* [1984] 1 WLR 287, a decision of the Court of Appeal applied in *McGreal v Wake* (1984) 269 EG 1254. In the latter case, the tenant was held to have a valid claim against the landlord for having to live in an unrepaired house for several months, and was entitled to recover costs of redecoration, storing furniture and for alternative accommodation. Substantial damages may also be awarded for distress, discomfort and inconvenience (*Choidi* v *DeMarney* (1989) 21 HLR 6). Usually, such damages are assessed by means of a notional reduction in rent: *English Churches Housing Group* v *Avrom Shine* [2004] EWCA Civ 434. If the tenant does not remain in occupation because of the disrepair but is forced to sell, he may recover the diminution of the price occasioned by the landlord's failure to repair (*Wallace* v *Manchester City Council* (1998) 30 HLR 1111 (CA)). It appears, however, that damages for diminution in capital value will not be recoverable unless the tenant had acquired the premises with the intention of re-selling (*Calabar Properties* above).

In addition to damages, the tenant may seek to enforce a landlord's repairing obligation by means of a decree of specific performance under the Landlord and Tenant Act 1985, s. 17(1). Section 17(1) provides that in any proceedings in which a tenant of a dwelling alleges a breach on the part of his landlord of a repairing covenant relating to any part of the premises in which the dwelling is comprised, the court may, in its discretion, order specific performance of the covenant whether or not the breach relates to a part of the premises let to the tenant and notwithstanding any equitable rule restricting the scope of that remedy. Apart from this statutory right, the tenant may invoke the court's inherent equitable jurisdiction to make an order where the landlord is in possession of the land where the defect exists (*Jeune* v *Queens Cross Properties Ltd* [1974] Ch 97).

By way of 'self-help', the tenant may also opt to do the repairs himself and deduct the expense from current or future rent. Upon being sued for unpaid rent by his landlord, the tenant will be able to rely upon his own counterclaim against the landlord for breach of the landlord's repairing covenant as effecting a complete defence by way of an equitable set off to the claim for rent (*British Anzani (Felixstowe) Ltd* v *International Marine Management (UK) Ltd* [1980] QB 137). In addition, the tenant has a common law right to deduct the repairing cost from the rent where, having given notice to the landlord, the tenant carries out the repairs which are the landlord's responsibility (*Lee-Parker* v *Izzet* [1971] 1 WLR 1688 and *Asco Developments Ltd* v *Gordon* (1978) 248 EG 683). Reference may also be made to the Housing Act 1985, s. 96 (as substituted by the Leasehold Reform, Housing and Urban Development Act 1993, s. 121), under which secure tenants whose landlords are local housing authorities are entitled to have qualifying repairs carried out, at their landlords' expense, to the dwelling-houses of which they are such tenants.

Lastly, the tenant may seek to rely upon the court's power, either as an interim measure or as part of a final order, to order the appointment of a receiver and manager of the premises. Under the Supreme Court Act 1981, s. 37, the High Court has power to appoint a receiver in all cases where it appears just and convenient to do so. A receiver has, accordingly, been appointed in cases where the landlord was in serious breach of his covenant to repair (*Hart* v *Emelkirk Ltd* [1983] 1 WLR 1289). The function of a receiver in such cases is to receive the rents and service charges from the tenants and to repair and manage the premises (usually a block of flats) during his appointment. In addition to this general jurisdiction, the Landlord and Tenant Act 1987, Pt II provides for the appointment of managers by the county court to assume responsibility for the management of premises containing flats (*Howard* v *Midrome Ltd* [1991] 03 EG 135). A more extensive power of management is now also given to leaseholders of flats under the Commonhold and Leasehold Reform Act 2002. This includes the ability to take over the management of a block even though the landlord is complying with its obligations. Under the 2002 Act, a private company limited by guarantee and formed for the purpose, is given the right, if certain statutory tests are met, to acquire and exercise management of the block. The 1987 Act also introduced a limited right of compulsory acquisition of the landlord's interest by qualifying tenants, but this was restricted to cases where there was mismanagement by the landlord.

Q Question 3

North London Properties (NLP) are the freehold owners of Stanley Estate, a tower block, comprising 26 self-contained flats let on weekly tenancies. During the past year, NLP have received various complaints from Arthur, one of the tenants of the block, alleging:

(a) severe condensation dampness in his flat resulting from poor ventilation, inadequate heating and insulation. In particular, Arthur has drawn attention to the single-glazed metal framed windows which he insists should be replaced. The condensation has caused furniture and fabrics to become rotten, but there is no evidence of physical damage to the property itself. He has also complained of frequent colds and bronchial infections which he attributes to the condensation problem; and

(b) inadequate water supply attributable to a faulty boiler situated in the basement of the block. The boiler is not functioning properly because the landlord had replaced (some years ago) the water pipework with pipes of a smaller bore which are now inadequate to supply water to the various flats due to an increased demand for water within the block.

NLP have denied liability for any of these defects, pointing to the absence of any express covenants on the part of the landlord to repair or maintain the block.
Advise Arthur:

(a) whether NLP are liable to remedy the condensation dampness; [20 marks]

AND

(b) whether NLP are liable to repair the faulty boiler and pipework. [5 marks]

Commentary

This is a difficult problem concerning a landlord's implied obligations to repair, both at common law and under statute. In addition, the question requires some discussion of a landlord's liability in negligence for inherent defects in the design and construction of the property (*Rimmer* v *Liverpool City Council* [1985] QB 1 and *McNerny* v *Lambeth London Borough Council* [1989] 19 EG 77).

Condensation dampness continues to be a serious problem for tenants of blocks of flats built in the 1960s and 1970s. It is generally thought that the law is quite inadequate in this area. See further, Pawlowski, M., 'Tenant's Remedies for Condensation Dampness' [1993] EG 9335, 108 and (Mainly for Students) 'The Curse of the Black Spot: Condensation and the Law' [1995] EG 9513, 128 and [1995] EG 9515, 103.

- Consider implied condition at common law relating to fitness for human habitation. Alternatively, examine Landlord and Tenant Act 1985, s. 8

- Landlord's implied covenant to repair structure and exterior of dwelling-house inapplicable as no disrepair to fabric of premises: Landlord and Tenant Act 1985, s. 11(1)(a) and *Quick* v *Taff-Ely Borough Council* (1986)

- Landlord's liability in negligence: *Rimmer v. Liverpool City Council* (1985) and *McNerny* v *Lambeth London Borough Council* (1989). Also statutory nuisance liability under Environmental Protection Act 1980, ss. 79–82

- Liability for faulty boiler will depend on when Arthur's tenancy granted: *Campden Hill Towers Ltd* v *Gardner* (1977) and Housing Act 1988, s. 116. Consider also *O'Connor* v *Old Etonian Housing Association Ltd* (2002) in relation to the pipework

:Q: Suggested answer

(a) A number of causes of action may be open to Arthur despite the absence of any express covenant to repair on the part of NLP. In furnished lettings, there is at common law (under the rule in *Smith* v *Marrable* (1843) 11 M & W 5) an implied condition on the part of the landlord that the demised premises will be fit for human habitation at the commencement of the tenancy. If this condition is not fulfilled on the day the tenancy commences, the tenant is entitled to treat the letting as discharged, quit the premises and sue for damages. However, because the condition relates to fitness only at the *commencement* of the tenancy, it will not protect a tenant if the premises later become unfit during the currency of the term (*Sarson* v *Roberts* [1895] 2 QB 395). Assuming the flats are rented furnished and that the condensation was present at the commencement of the letting, NLP would appear to be in breach of this implied condition.

Alternatively, the Landlord and Tenant Act 1985, s. 8 (formerly the Housing Act 1957, s. 6), implies a condition on the part of the landlord that premises are fit for human habitation at the commencement of the tenancy, and an undertaking that the landlord will *keep* the premises in that condition during the term of the tenancy. The standard of fitness is measured having regard to the condition of the premises in respect of a variety of matters including ventilation and freedom from damp (s. 10). Although s. 8 applies to both furnished and unfurnished lettings, s. 8(3) stipulates that it takes effect only in relation to lettings below certain rent limits (e.g., if the letting was made on or after 6 July 1957, the rent limit is £80 p.a. in London and £52 p.a. elsewhere). These very low limits are far below normal market rents, and therefore it is more than likely that Arthur's letting falls outside the ambit of the section.

The Landlord and Tenant Act 1985, s. 11(1)(a), implies a covenant on the part of the landlord to keep in repair the structure and exterior of a dwelling-house. The section applies in general to any tenancy of a dwelling-house granted on or after 24 October 1961 for a term of less than seven years (s. 13) and includes periodic tenancies. In *Quick v Taff Ely Borough Council* [1986] QB 809, the claimant was the tenant of a house which suffered from severe condensation caused by lack of insulation, single-glazed metal frame windows and inadequate heating. The Court of Appeal held that the liability under the implied covenant did not arise because of lack of amenity or efficiency, but only where there existed a physical condition which called for repair to the structure or exterior of the dwelling-house. As there was no evidence to indicate physical damage to the windows or any other part of the structure and exterior, the landlord was not liable to carry out work to alleviate the condensation (see also, *Southwark London Borough Council, McIntosh* [2002] 08 EG 164; *Post Office* v *Aquarius Properties Ltd* [1987] 1 All ER 1055 and *Stent* v *Monmouth District Council* (1987) 282 EG 705, where this same principle was applied). These decisions may be contrasted with *Staves* v *Leeds City Council* [1992] 29 EG 119, where plasterwork in the flat was so saturated that it required complete renewal. The position will also be different if the landlord has expressly covenanted to keep the premises 'in good condition' as well as in repair: *Welsh* v *Greenwich London Borough Council* (2001) 33 HLR 40, where it was held that excessive condensation due to lack of insulation rendered the flat's condition not 'good' and, therefore, the landlord was in breach.

The upshot of this analysis is that NLP will be liable under s. 11 of the 1985 Act only if Arthur can point to some disrepair to the physical condition of the structure and/or exterior of his flat (e.g., the walls, plaster, windows). Mere damage to furniture and fabrics will not be sufficient to render NLP liable.

Apart from liability under statute, it is possible that NLP may be liable in negligence. At common law, a 'bare' landlord is under no duty of care to ensure that the premises are reasonably safe at the time of the letting (*Cavalier* v *Pope* [1906] AC 428). But a landlord who has designed and/or constructed the premises remains liable for faults of construction and design despite having disposed of the property by selling or letting it (*Rimmer* v *Liverpool City Council* [1985] QB 1). In *McNerny* v *Lambeth London Borough Council* [1989] 19 EG 77, the tenant sought to apply the *Rimmer* principle to premises suffering from condensation dampness. Unfortunately, on the facts, the landlord council, being a bare landlord (i.e., a mere owner as opposed to an owner-builder), was held to owe no duty of care, and accordingly the tenant's claim for damages based on negligence failed. The same principles would govern NLP's liability.

Lastly, it is possible that Arthur may have recourse under the Environmental Protection Act 1990, ss. 79–82 (replacing the provisions of the Public Health Act 1936, Pt III). Section 79(1)(a) includes in the definition of a statutory nuisance 'any premises in such state as to be prejudicial to health or a nuisance'. Section 82 empowers a magistrates' court to make an order requiring the defendant, *inter alia*, to abate the nuisance within a specified time and to execute any works necessary for that purpose. The provisions have been applied successfully in the context of premises suffering from condensation dampness (*Greater London Council* v *London Borough of Tower Hamlets* (1984) 15 HLR 54, but contrast *Dover District Council* v *Farrar* (1980) 2 HLR 32). Moreover, in *Herbert* v *Lambeth London Borough Council* (1993) 90 LGR 310, a case involving damp and mouldy accommodation, it was held that the magistrates' court has jurisdiction to make a compensation order under the Powers of Criminal Courts Act 1973, s. 35, on the making of a nuisance order under s. 82 of the 1990 Act. Accordingly, Arthur may have a strong claim based on statutory nuisance. The court, however, will take into account only the loss or damage caused by the continuation of the nuisance from the date when the period stated in the complainant's notice expired to the date of the hearing (*R* v *Crown Court at Liverpool, ex parte Cooke* [1996] 4 All ER 589). It seems also that the relevant provisions of the 1990 Act do not give rise to a *civil* cause of action entitling Arthur to damages for any loss suffered as a result of the condensation dampness (*Issa* v *Hackney London Borough Council* [1997] 1 All ER 999).

(b) In *Campden Hill Towers Ltd* v *Gardner* [1977] QB 823, the phrase 'structure and exterior' of a dwelling-house in the context of the Landlord and Tenant Act 1985, s. 11, when applied to a flat separately occupied within a block of flats, was held to mean not the exterior of the whole building but anything which would be regarded as part of the structure or exterior of the particular flat in question. Similarly, a central heating boiler situated in the common parts of the block was held not to be an installation *in the dwelling-house* within the meaning of the section. The amendments to s. 11 introduced by the Housing Act 1988, s. 116, overturn the effect of this decision, but only in respect of tenancies entered into after 15 January 1989. Section 116 (which adds s. 11(1A)(a) to the Landlord and Tenant Act 1985, s. 11) provides, *inter alia*, that a landlord is obliged to keep in repair and proper working order an installation which, directly or indirectly, serves the dwelling-house and which either

(i) forms part of any part of a building in which the landlord has an estate or interest, or (ii) is owned by the landlord or is under his control. Failure to repair or maintain in working order must also affect the tenant's enjoyment of the dwelling-house (or any common parts which he is entitled to use).

In *Niazi Services Ltd* v *Van der Loo* [2004] EWCA Civ 53, the Court of Appeal held that a tenant of a flat was not liable to his subtenant for breach of s. 11 because the tenant had no interest in that part of the building in which the defect was situated (a faulty boiler in the basement of the building). Equally, he did not own or control the relevant part of the pipework which formed the subject-matter of the claim. Accordingly, the tenant was not responsible for the faulty boiler. This is in contrast, of course, to Arthur's case because he holds a tenancy directly from his landlord (NLP) so that the latter is *prima facie* liable for the defect even though the problem is not in Arthur's flat itself but elsewhere in the block owned or controlled by NLP: s. 11(1A)(b)(ii).

In *O'Connor* v *Old Etonian Housing Association Ltd* [2002] 09 EG 221, the Court of Appeal held that the duty imposed on a landlord under s. 11(1A)(a) 'to keep in proper working order' carried with it an obligation to remedy any defect in design or construction. Moreover, the court also concluded that an installation must be able to function under such conditions of supply as can reasonably be anticipated by the parties. In our case, it seems that the change in supply was not forced upon the landlord by wholly unforeseen events (for example, a drought or collapsed reservoir) but by an increased demand for water within the block — something which is likely to persist for the foreseeable future. In these circumstances, it would not be considered unreasonable for the landlord to be required to modify the boiler and pipework so as to function properly.

Q Question 4

Albert and Jane Smith are the joint tenants of a terraced house which is let to them by John Jones under an assured tenancy agreement for a fixed term of 10 years. The written tenancy agreement obliges the tenants to repair the interior of the demised premises but places no obligation on the landlord to repair the exterior. Clause 3 of the agreement provides as follows:

> The Tenants shall give the Landlord's agents and workmen access to the demised premises for any purpose which may from time to time be required by the Landlord.

Albert and Jane are in dispute with John Jones over the following matters:

(a) The gutters are in poor condition and allow rainwater to penetrate into the premises. As a result, damage has occurred to the internal plaster and timbers in the upper parts of the house.

(b) A few weeks ago, Albert fell and fractured his arm when an unstable concrete step, sunk in earth at the top of the garden of the demised premises, moved under his weight causing him to lose his footing.

Advise Albert and Jane as to the liability (if any) of John Jones in respect of the above matters of complaint.

Commentary

This question raises a number of specific issues requiring a good understanding of the workings of the Defective Premises Act 1972, s. 4.

As to part (a), because the Landlord and Tenant Act 1985, s. 11, does not apply on the facts (the tenancy is for over seven years), you should consider the principle that an obligation to repair may be implied on the landlord in order to match a *correlative obligation* on the part of the tenant (*Barrett* v *Lounova (1982) Ltd* [1990] 1 QB 348).

The facts of part (b), on the other hand, should trigger a discussion of the Defective Premises Act 1972, s. 4, and the Court of Appeal decision in *McAuley* v *Bristol City Council* [1992] 1 All ER 749. For a good summary of the case, see Murdoch, S., 'Landlord's Liability Under the Defective Premises Act' [1991] EG 9143, 133.

This is a difficult problem and the danger is that the poor student will simply enter into a discussion of the Landlord and Tenant Act 1985, s. 11, without realising that it is irrelevant to the question.

*   Landlord subject to implied (correlative) obligation to repair the guttering: *Barrett* v *Lounova* (1990). Alternatively, liability arises under the Defective Premises Act 1972, s. 4

*   Liability for the concrete step not caught by Environmental Protection Act 1980 as dangerous premises *per se* not capable of being a statutory nuisance: *R* v *Bristol City Council, ex parte Everett* (1998)

*   Consider landlord's liability under Defective Premises Act 1972, s. 4(4): *McAuley* v *Bristol City Council* (1992) and *Smith* v *Bradford Metropolitan Council* (1982)

*   Significance of express provision requiring tenant to give landlord access to the premises. Although no specific right of entry to repair steps in garden, this may be implied: *McAuley*, above

·Ọ́· Suggested answer

(a) Guttering. Although the Landlord and Tenant Act 1985, s. 11 (formerly the Housing Act 1961, s. 32), imposes on a landlord an implied covenant, *inter alia*, to keep in repair the structure and exterior of the dwelling-house (including specifically drains, gutters and external pipes), this section applies only to short, residential lettings granted for *less* than seven years. Accordingly, s. 11 has no application to the present case.

A similar problem arose in the case of *Barrett* v *Lounova* [1990] 1 QB 348, where s. 11 did not apply because the tenancy was created before 24 October 1961. In that case as well, the drains and gutters were in poor condition causing extensive water penetration and damage to the internal plaster and timbers. The tenancy obliged the tenant to repair the interior but placed no obligations on the landlords to repair the exterior. The Court of Appeal held that the ordinary rules for implying terms into contracts also applied to leases, and that there was an implied covenant on the landlords to repair the exterior. In that case, the tenant had repairing obligations in respect of the interior and there would come a time when these could not be performed if the exterior were in disrepair. That raised the question as to who had the correlative obligation to repair the exterior. As the tenant's repairing obligation was enforceable throughout the term, an implied covenant was necessary to give business efficacy to the tenancy agreement. The obligation to repair the exterior could not be upon the tenant as it would be unrealistic to expect the tenant to do such work. A covenant upon both parties would be unworkable and so that left an implied covenant upon the landlord as the only solution that made business sense. It is submitted that a similar argument could be put forward on behalf of Jane and Albert.

The later decision in *Adami* v *Lincoln Grange Management Ltd* [1998] 17 EG 148, in which the *Barrett* case was not applied, may be distinguished on the basis that it concerned a long lease at a nominal rent, which dealt expressly with the repair of the subject premises and imposed an insurance obligation to cover catastrophic damage to the building. In these circumstances, there was no basis on which to presume any intention that the landlord should be obliged to repair the structure. It seems, therefore, that where the lease provides a comprehensive code for the carrying out of repairs and payment for them, the courts will be disinclined to imply correlative obligations on the parties: *Hafton Properties Ltd* v *Camp* [1994] 1 EGLR 67.

Since John Jones is in breach of his implied covenant to repair the exterior, he will be liable for the consequential damage caused to the internal plaster and timber. In *Barrett* v *Lounova*, this was agreed at £1,250. In addition, Albert and Jane are entitled to claim damages for distress, discomfort and inconvenience (*Choidi* v *DeMarney* (1989) 21 HLR 6). They may also seek specific performance of the covenant under s.17, Landlord and Tenant Act, 1985.

Alternatively, it may be that Albert and Jane could make a claim under the Defective Premises Act 1972, s. 4(1), and seek an injunction compelling John Jones to carry out remedial works to the defective gutters. Had it been necessary to decide this alternative claim in the *Barrett* case, the court would have been prepared to grant the injunction sought.

(b) Concrete step. Here again, it seems that the Landlord and Tenant Act 1985, s. 11, has no application since (apart from the tenancy being for 10 years) this provision does not extend to the repair of a backyard or garden (*Hopwood* v *Rugeley Urban District Council* [1975] 1 WLR 373). Equally, it has been held that premises which are in a state such as to give rise to a danger of accident or physical injury are not capable of being a statutory nuisance within the meaning of s. 79(1)(a) of the Environmental Protection Act 1990 (*R* v *Bristol City Council, ex parte Everett* [1998] 3 All ER 603, involving a steep staircase). Equally, mere layout or lack of facility do not render premises prejudicial to health: *Birmingham City Council* v *Oakley* [2001] AC 617. Moreover, a physical accident cannot be described as an injury to health in the context of this legislation, which is directed at premises that create a risk of disease and illness. The question, therefore, is whether Albert and Jane can successfully argue that John Jones is in breach of his duty of care under the Defective Premises Act 1972, s. 4.

The effect of s. 4 is to impose on a landlord who has covenanted to repair, an obligation to the tenant (and third parties) to keep them 'reasonably safe from personal injury or from damage to their property' caused by defects in the state of the property: *Sykes* v *Harry* [2001] 17 EG 221, involving a faulty gas fire appliance. Although s. 4(1) is concerned with a landlord who is in breach of his own repairing covenant, s. 4(4) also operates to impose liability on a landlord despite the fact that, under the terms of the tenancy, it is the tenant who is obliged to repair. Moreover, where personal injury or damage to property is caused by a defect which is outside the express repairing obligations of *both* the landlord and tenant, the case of *McAuley* v *Bristol City Council* [1992] 1 All ER 749 demonstrates that the landlord can become liable to the tenant under s. 4(4).

In *McAuley*, the Court of Appeal held that s. 4(4) of the 1972 Act imposes a duty of care on a landlord towards his tenant where premises are let under a tenancy which expressly or impliedly gives the landlord the right to enter the premises to carry out repairs. In *Smith* v *Bradford Metropolitan Council* (1982) 44 P & CR 171, the Court of Appeal held that a provision in the tenancy agreement to the effect that the tenant should give the landlord's agents reasonable facilities for inspecting the premises and their state of repair and for carrying out repairs, gave the landlord an *express* right of re-entry to carry out repairs to the back yard of the house. Accordingly, the landlord was held liable under s. 4(4) for injuries caused to the tenant when he fell because of the condition of the yard.

In *McAuley*, the tenant fell and broke her ankle on a loose step in the garden of the property. There was no express right on the part of the landlord to enter to repair the garden steps, but instead (as in the question set) there was an express provision which required the tenant to give the landlord's agents reasonable facilities for entering upon the premises for any purpose which may be required by the landlord. In the absence, therefore, of any express right of re-entry to repair the garden step, the central issue was whether such a right should be *implied*. The Court of Appeal came to the conclusion that a right to re-enter to carry out any repair necessary to remove the risk of injury should be implied, and accordingly held the landlord liable.

On this basis, Albert should be advised that he has a good claim against John Jones under s. 4(4) of the 1972 Act.

Q Question 5

What proposals have been put forward for reform of the current law on leasehold dilapidations? Do you agree that the law should be changed in this area?

Commentary

This is a straightforward essay question which seeks to test your knowledge of the broader issues governing the law of dilapidations. Apart from referring to the Law Commission's proposals for reform (i.e., Law Commission Report (Law Com. No. 238, 1996), 'Landlord and Tenant: Responsibility for State and Condition of Property'), you should also try and use some examples of current defects in the law and explain how these would be rectified under the new regime. Remember that the question specifically asks you to comment on whether a change in the law is desirable. For a good analysis of the Law Commission's proposals, see Bridge, S., 'Putting it Right? The Law Commission and the Condition of Tenanted Property' [1996] Conv 342.

- Outline criticisms of the current law: (1) concept of repair precludes remedy of inherent defects in design (2) distinction between repair and improvement problematic (3) standard of repair judged at date of letting (4) landlord's remedy of specific performance limited and (5) existing law too complex

- Law Commission's proposal to extend scope of Landlord and Tenant Act 1985, s. 8. But Law Commission's original proposal (to introduce implied duty on landlord to maintain premises in a condition suitable for intended use) abandoned

- Proposal for default repair provision and enhancement of enforcement remedies (i.e., specific performance) to ensure premises are actually repaired. Also suggestion to abolish common law doctrine of waste and tenant-like user

- Criticisms of Commission's proposals — no comprehensive review of tenant's remedies and negative practical implications (i.e., landlord's passing expense of repairs onto tenants by means of higher rents and pursuing retaliatory eviction)

☼ Suggested answer

In 1996, the Law Commission published its Report, 'Landlord and Tenant: Responsibility for State and Condition of Property' (Law Com. No. 238, 1996). The aim of the

Report was to examine the scope of the current obligations to repair and to consider their deficiencies.

One of the main criticisms of the existing law is that it is based on the concept of 'repair', which involves looking at the physical state of the property as opposed to its lack of efficiency or amenity. In particular, it has been held that 'repair' denotes deterioration from a previous physical condition (*Quick* v *Taff Ely Borough Council* [1986] QB 809, a case involving condensation dampness). The consequence is that inherent defects which result in a building being unfit for its intended purpose (e.g., the metal window frames in *Quick*, above), but which do not give rise to a physical deterioration, fall outside the ambit of 'repair'. Thus, a tenant has been held not liable to repair a concrete basement, which had in the past suffered from an ingress of water, because there was at the time of the hearing no physical damage to the concrete walls or floor (*Post Office* v *Aquarius Properties Ltd* [1987] 1 All ER 1055).

Another problem lies in the current distinction between works of repair and improvement which can lead to difficulties in practice. Thus, the insertion of a damp-proof course in a building which was constructed without one is treated as an improvement (*Pembery* v *Lamdin* [1940] 2 All ER 434), but replacing an old two-pipe drainage system with a modern one-pipe system is classified as a repair (*Morcom* v *Campbell-Johnson* [1956] 1 QB 106).

Thirdly, the standard to which property is to be repaired is judged by reference to its age, character and locality at the date of the letting (*Proudfoot* v *Hart* (1890) 25 QBD 42 and *Calthorpe* v *McOscar* [1924] 1 KB 716). Thus, changes in the neighbourhood during the currency of the lease can make the legal standard inappropriate.

Fourthly, there is considerable scope for improving the rules governing the enforcement of repairing obligations. For example, the remedy of specific per-formance is currently available to a landlord against a defaulting tenant only in exceptional circumstances (*Rainbow Estates Ltd* v *Tokenhold Ltd* [1998] 3 WLR 980).

Lastly, it is generally thought that the existing law is too complicated, in so far as it is full of overlapping obligations and derives from a wide variety of different statutes.

For all these reasons, it is apparent that this area of law is ripe for reform. The Law Commission considers that one of the primary objectives should be to ensure that residential premises are reasonably fit to live in. In addition, it feels that greater emphasis should be placed on the *enforcement* of repairing obligations, given the nation's interest in the quality of its housing stock. Accordingly, greater emphasis should be placed on remedies which ensure that remedial works are actually carried out, and this may mean giving local authorities greater powers of enforcement.

At present, s. 8 of the Landlord and Tenant Act 1985 implies into residential leases let for a term of less than seven years a condition that the dwelling-house be fit for human habitation both at commencement and during the term of the lease. The difficulty with this provision is that it is severely curtailed in its operation by very low rental limits (which have remained unchanged since 1957). The Law Commission proposes to abandon these rental limits and thereby extend s. 8 to all residential leases for less than seven years. This new statutory covenant would stand alongside the existing implied obligations (as to structure and exterior) under s. 11 of the 1985 Act. The definition of 'fitness for human habitation' would also be harmonised with the criteria set out in s. 604 of the Housing Act 1985. Although this recommendation is to be welcomed, it is not what the Law Commission originally proposed in its Consultation Paper (No. 123, 1992). The Commission originally advocated the idea of an implied duty to maintain premises (both commercial and residential) in a condition suitable for their intended use. It was suggested that this new duty would be imposed on the landlord and that it would not be limited to defects of which he had notice. Unfortunately, the proposal has been resisted by the commercial sector and, hence, it has not been adopted in the Commission's Report.

The 1992 Consultation Paper also advocated a new definition of 'repair' so as to include some works of improvement (e.g., those necessary to cure any defect which rendered the premises unfit for their purpose). The Commission has now abandoned this proposal (largely on the basis that it would lead to uncertainty and promote litigation) in favour of a 'default provision' (imposed in all cases where the parties had failed to make express provision for repairs) whereby the landlord would be obliged to put the premises in repair at the commencement of the term, and keep them in repair for its duration. The standard of repair would be that which was appropriate having regard to the age, character, and prospective life of the demised property and to its locality. Essentially, this default covenant would apply principally to commercial leases.

As mentioned earlier, the Commission is anxious that enforcement of repairing obligations is shifted away from compensation towards ensuring that premises are actually repaired. Accordingly, specific performance is seen as the major remedy in this field. Although the case of *Rainbow Estates Ltd* v *Tokenhold Ltd* [1998] 3 WLR 980 has acknowledged that a landlord may seek specific performance of his tenant's repairing obligations, it is unlikely that the remedy will be invoked in the majority of cases involving disrepair. The *Rainbow* case had a number of unusual features which favoured the grant of specific performance against the tenants. First, the lease in question contained no forfeiture clause so that a breach of the tenant's repairing covenant did not entitle the landlord to forfeit the lease. Nor did the lease contain a clause entitling the landlord access to the premises to carry out the repairs with a view to claiming the cost from the tenants as a debt or rent arrears. This all pointed to the fact that there was no adequate alternative remedy other than specific performance against the tenants. The recommendation by the Law Commission that the remedy of specific performance be made generally available as a discretionary remedy to enforce repairing obligations in all leases to landlords and tenants alike remains, therefore, a fundamental reform of leasehold law.

The Commission also recommended the abolition of the common law doctrine of waste and the implied covenant of tenant-like user. In their place, the Commission suggests a new covenant to be implied in all leases whereby the tenant would undertake to take proper care of the premises and make good any damage wilfully done or caused to the premises by him (or any other person lawfully in occupation or visiting the premises), and not to carry out any alterations which would result in the destruction or alteration of the character of the premises to the detriment of the landlord's interest.

Although the Commission's proposals are to be welcomed, they have been criticised for failing to provide a comprehensive review of tenant's remedies for the landlord's default, in particular, the tenant's ability to terminate the tenancy at common law (see *Hussein* v *Mehlman* [1992] 32 EG 59) and to set-off the cost of repairs against rent (*British Anzani (Felixstowe) Ltd* v *International Marine Management (UK) Ltd* [1979] 2 All ER 1063). It has also been suggested by one academic commentator that landlords in the private sector will seek to pass on the expense of repairs to their tenants by means of substantial rent increases: see Bridge, S. [1996] Conv 342, at 350. Moreover, if a tenant is minded to initiate proceedings for specific performance in order to compel his landlord to repair the demised property, the likely response from the landlord will be to seek to recover possession from the tenant. As Bridge points out, security of tenure in the private sector is precarious under the assured shorthold tenancy regime and the danger of the landlord pursuing such 'retaliatory eviction' cannot be underestimated. Ultimately, as Bridge explains, little purpose may be served in giving residential tenants rights if they have no security, as any attempt to exercise those rights can be met by the landlord bringing proceedings for the recovery of possession. On this analysis, the Law Commission's recommendations may prove disappointing.

Q Question 6

> . . . a covenant to keep premises in repair obliges the covenantor to keep them in repair at all times, so that there is a breach of the obligation immediately a defect occurs. (*British Telecommunications plc* v *Sun Life Assurance Society plc* [1995] 4 All ER 44 (CA), *per* Nourse LJ).

To what extent does this statement apply to a landlord's obligation to repair defects in the demised premises or outside the landlord's control? (Illustrate your answer by reference to decided cases.)

Commentary

This is a straightforward question on the rule that a landlord is only liable for defects occurring in the demised premises if he has sufficient notice of their existence. The reference to defects outside the landlord's control is more tricky. The point was canvassed in the *Sun Life* case itself and also several earlier authorities, notably, *Bishop* v *Consolidated London Properties Ltd* (1933) 102 LJ KB 257 and *Melles & Co.* v *Holme* [1918] 2 KB 100. The law is unclear as to the landlord's position in the absence of any direct ruling. See further, Smith, P. F. 'Something of a Surprise' [1997] Conv 59.

You should note that the question requires you to illustrate your answer by reference to case law. This means that you must make reference to the decided cases in order to score a good mark. Most of the relevant cases were reviewed in the *Sun Life* decision, so if you have read the judgment of Nourse LJ carefully, this should not pose any problem.

- Basic rule that covenant to keep in repair requires landlord to keep in repair at all times so that landlord in breach immediately a defect occurs: *British Telecommunications plc* v *Sun Life Assurance Society plc* (1995)

- Exception where defect occurs in the demised premises where landlord only liable if put on notice or has knowledge of defect: *O'Brien* v *Robinson* (1973)

- Cases on what constitutes sufficient notice: *Al Hassani* v *Merrigan* (1988) and *Sheldon* v *West Bromwich Corporation* (1973). Knowledge can be imputed through agent: *Dinefwr Borough Council* v *Jones* (1987). Notice rule requires landlord to execute works within a reasonable time: *McGreal* v *Wake* (1984)

- Further possible exception where defect caused by an occurrence wholly outside landlord's control: *Sun Life*, above

·Ọ· **Suggested answer**

In *British Telecommunications plc* v *Sun Life Assurance Society plc* [1995] 4 All ER 44, the claimant was the tenant of the sixth and seventh floors of a building under a lease which required the defendant landlord to keep the building in repair. The question in issue was whether the landlord became liable to repair immediately any defect which appeared in the building (as contended by the tenant), or only on the expiration of a reasonable period for doing the repairs following the appearance of the defect (as argued by the landlord). The Court of Appeal, accepting the tenant's argument, reiterated the general rule that a covenant to *keep* in repair obliged the landlord to keep the property in repair at all times so that a breach occurs immediately a defect appears.

This basic proposition may be illustrated by a number of authorities. In *Melles & Co.* v *Holme* [1918] 2 KB 100, for example, the landlord was held liable for exterior guttering which had become blocked, even though he had no express notice of the defect from the tenant. The Divisional Court held that the notice rule had no application where the landlord demised only part of the premises and retained in his own control the portion the defective condition of which caused the damage. More recently, in *Loria* v *Hammer* [1989] 2 EGLR 249, a case involving the intrusion of rainwater into the tenant's flat caused by a defective flat roof, the Court held that the landlord's liability to keep his retained premises in repair was not dependent on his receiving notification of the defect. Thus, the moment there was a disrepair, the landlord's duty to keep in repair had been broken.

In the course of his judgment in *Sun Life*, Nourse LJ recognised that there were a number of exceptions to the general rule referred to above. One important exception is where the defect occurs in the demised premises, in which case the landlord is in breach of his obligation only when he has information about the existence of the defect such as would put a reasonable landlord on inquiry as to whether works of repair were needed and he had failed to carry out the necessary works within a reasonable time thereafter.

There are a number of cases which clearly support this exception, although it has not been without its judicial critics: see, for example, *McGreal* v *Wake* (1984) 269 EG 1254, where Sir John Donaldson MR remarked that the rule was 'unfortunate' because it 'penalised the conscientious landlord and rewarded the absentee'. The leading authority is *O'Brien* v *Robinson* [1973] AC 912, where the tenant complained of the noise above his flat and warned the landlord that, if something was not done, the ceiling would collapse. No defects in the ceiling were or became visible and, shortly afterwards, those responsible for the noise moved out. Three years later, the ceiling fell and caused injury to the tenant and his wife. The House of Lords held that liability for breach of the implied covenant to repair under (what is now) s. 11 of the Landlord and Tenant Act 1985 arose only when the landlord had notice of the defect. In the instant case, the landlord was held not to have notice of the defect by reason of the incidents of nuisance and annoyance some three years earlier.

The notice rule has been applied in a number of cases: *Hugall* v *M'Lean* (1885) 53 LT 94 (defective condition of drains); *Broggi* v *Robbins* (1899) 15 TLR 224 (unsafe condition of wooden flooring); *Torrens* v *Walker* [1906] 2 Ch 166 (dangerous outside walls of demised premises); and *McGreal* v *Wake* (1984) 269 EG 1254 (rising damp, wet rot, decayed brickwork and cracked/sagging ceilings). It is well-established that the notice rule applies even though the landlord has expressly reserved a right to inspect the demised premises for disrepair.

As to what constitutes sufficient notice, it is evident that the tenant is not obliged to identify the precise nature or degree of disrepair. For example, in *Griffin* v *Pillet* [1926] 1 KB 17, the tenant's letter to the landlord, stating merely that 'the steps to the front door want attention', was held good notice. In *Al Hassani* v *Merrigan* (1988) 20 HLR 238, however, the tenant's notice was held bad since it stated that the tenant would be ascertaining what was necessary to put matters right and submit estimates. Since the notice told the landlord that he would be informed what was necessary in due course and that he could then either do the remedial work or have the cost deducted from the rent, it was held insufficient to bring into effect the landlord's implied obligations. Actual knowledge, or information about the existence of a defect such as would put a reasonable man on inquiry as to whether works of repair were needed, is sufficient to trigger the landlord's obligation to repair, in the absence of express notice (*Sheldon* v *West Bromwich Corporation* (1973) 25 P & CR 360, where an inspection by the landlord's plumber of an old water tank was sufficient to give the landlord actual knowledge of the need for repair).

It is sufficient if the landlord is given notification of the defect through its agent, for example, a rent collector, officer or employee (*Dinefwr Borough Council* v *Jones* (1987) 284 EG 58, where it was held that knowledge of defects obtained by an official of the landlord's health department constituted notice for the purpose of s. 11 of the 1985 Act). The fact that knowledge was acquired for a different purpose (e.g., in connection with the tenant's right to buy the property) did not prevent it from fixing the landlord with notice of the disrepair. (See also, *Hall* v *Howard* [1988] 44 EG 83, where a valuation report, obtained by the tenant in connection with his possible bid for the reversion, specifying items of disrepair, was held sufficient notice.)

The notice rule requires the landlord to execute the remedial works within a reasonable period of time from being given notice of the defect. What is a reasonable time is, of course, a question of fact depending on the urgency of the required repairs: see *McGreal* v *Wake*, above, where two months from the date of notice was considered reasonable on the facts.

In *Sun Life*, Nourse LJ intimated, but without reaching a concluded view on the point, that a further exception to the general rule might arise where a defect is caused by an occurrence wholly outside the landlord's control. He postulated a case where the roof of a house had been damaged by a branch from a tree standing on neighbouring land not in the possession or control of the landlord and rainwater had found its way down into the tenant's rooms by that means. Provisionally, he accepted that such a case could be made the subject of a further exception. It is interesting to observe, however, that in *Bishop* v *Consolidated London Properties Ltd* (1933) 102 LJ KB 257, Du Parq J held that the landlords were nonetheless liable for breach of covenant though they could show that the cause of the defect (a dead pigeon causing an obstruction in a downfall overflow pipe) was fortuitous and occurred through no fault on their part. Similarly, in *Melles & Co.* v *Holme* [1918] 2 KB 100, referred to earlier, there was evidence suggesting that the blockage in the downpipe was caused mainly by refuse which had been thrown into the gutter by another tenant. It is difficult to see how these cases differ from Nourse LJ's example. Interestingly, in *Passley* v *London Borough of Wandsworth* (1998) 30 HLR 165, Hobhouse LJ was sceptical about the possible validity of this exception. If the cause of the defect can be attributed to neither party, one comes back to the meaning of the covenant, as established by the decisions.

A further possible exception to the general rule identified by Nourse LJ is where the covenant is not to keep in repair but simply to repair. Being somewhat of a rarity in modern leases and tenancy agreements, his Lordship expressed no concluded view as to whether such a covenant merited different analysis.

Q Question 7

(a) Melanie is the tenant of commercial premises under a lease, which obliges her 'to the satisfaction of the landlord's surveyor well and substantially maintain, amend, repair and keep in good condition the demised premises'.

The landlord has recently brought a claim for terminal dilapidations stating that Melanie's obligation as tenant extends beyond matters of repair so as to require the replacement of various equipment forming part of the demised premises. The equipment is admittedly old but still functions normally at the present time.

Advise Melanie whether she is liable to replace the equipment. Explain also how Melanie's obligation is affected (if at all) by the requirement that works to comply with the repairing covenant must be to the satisfaction of the landlord's surveyor. Assuming there are breaches of repairing covenant in other respects, how will the quantum of damages be affected by s. 18(1) of the Landlord and Tenant Act 1927?   [15 marks]

(b) Does a tenant have an implied licence at common law to enter upon his landlord's premises in order to carry out repairs which are the landlord's responsibility?   [10 marks]

Commentary

(a) Although this is ostensibly a two-part question, there are, in fact, four separate components which will require your attention. You will need to be familiar with some of the recent case law, as well as demonstrate a general understanding of how damages for disrepair are assessed at the end of the term. The question also gives you the opportunity to make some mention of the dilapidations protocol endorsed by the RICS.

(b) This refers to a short point which has been the subject of recent case law. If you are able to refer to this and provide the reader with a statement of principle, you will score good marks.

- Covenant to repair presupposes some defect or malfunction: *Fluor Daniel Properties Ltd* v *Shortlands Investments Ltd* (2001). It does not cover purely anticipatory or preventative works: *Mason* v *TotalFinaElf* (2003)

- Reference in covenant to works being 'to satisfaction of landlord's surveyor' entitles surveyor to prescribe what works should be done: *Mason*, above. But, works have to be to make good a want of repair and, in any event, surveyor must act honestly and come to a decision that a reasonable surveyor would make

- Action by landlord on the covenant to yield up in repair. Common law measure of damages: *Proudfoot v Hart* (1890). Assessment of damages under s. 18(1). Cost of remedial works or actual valuation? Relevance of Dilapidations Protocol

- Consider recent decision in *Metropolitan Properties Co. Ltd v Wilson* (2002) which suggests that tenant may have implied licence to enter and carry out repairs in appropriate circumstances

☼ Suggested answer

(a) The obligations contained in Melanie's repairing covenant presuppose that the item in question (i.e., the equipment) suffers from some defect (i.e., some physical damage, deterioration or malfunction) such that repair, amendment or renewal is reasonably necessary.

The point arose in *Fluor Daniel Properties Ltd* v *Shortlands Investments Ltd* [2001] 2 EGLR 103, which involved a modern commercial block with an extensive air-conditioning system. Under the lease, the landlord was obliged to keep the structure of the building and all apparatus, equipment, plant and machinery in good repair. This included the air-conditioning. The tenants, in turn, were obliged to pay a service charge to cover the expenses incurred by the landlord. The landlord wrote to the tenants informing them that he was about to spend £2m on works to the air-conditioning and some structural repairs. The tenants challenged this on the ground that the works were unnecessary. Significantly, the court held that, although the landlord's obligations went beyond mere repair, those obligations only arose if some malfunction occurred so that repair, amendment or renewal became reasonably necessary, having regard to what was reasonably acceptable to an office tenant in that kind of building. In that case, the air-conditioning was working properly (despite having exceeded its recognised life span) and was capable of rendering the relevant service to the standard required under the lease. The service charge demanded by the landlord was, accordingly, held not to be recoverable.

The upshot of the *Fluor* decision is that purely anticipatory or preventative work (where no damage or deterioration in the condition of the subject-matter has yet occurred) cannot be required under a repairing covenant. The mere fact that a piece of equipment is old and will inevitably have to be replaced in time does not mean that preventative works can be demanded to prevent the consequences of the equipment failing where, in the meantime, it continues to perform its function.

The point has been addressed more recently by Blackburne J. in *Mason v TotalFina-ELF* [2003] 30 EG 145 (CS) involving a lease of a petrol-filling station, garage and shop premises. The tenant's repairing covenant imposed an obligation on the tenant similar to that contained in Melanie's lease with an additional obligation to deliver up the premises so repaired at the end of the lease. His Lordship concluded that, although the covenant extended to the doing of works that went beyond repair, strictly so called, this did not permit the landlord to require purely preventative works (i.e., works undertaken by way of *anticipation* to avoid the occurrence of damage from a future, albeit reasonably anticipated, disrepair). Equally, such works could not be regarded as works necessary to keep the relevant item in 'good condition' under the covenant. It seems apparent, therefore, that Melanie's obligation under her lease does not extend to replacing old equipment which shows no signs of deterioration or malfunction at the present time.

The reference in the covenant to works being 'to the satisfaction of the landlord's surveyor' entitles the surveyor to prescribe what works should be done (i.e., it is not limited to determining purely the *manner* in which work is to be performed). Significantly, the phrase in Melanie's lease qualifies the whole of the content of the tenant's obligation, not just a part of it. Moreover, as was stressed in *Mason*, it may not always be easy to distinguish the manner in which work is to be done from what the work is that is to be done. However, this does not mean that the surveyor has a free-hand over what to require. As mentioned earlier, the works have to be to make good a want of repair or absence of good condition. Although free to exercise his own judgment in this regard, he must act honestly and come to a decision that a reasonable surveyor could reach. It is irrelevant, however, that Melanie's surveyor may favour a cheaper, but not less reasonable, option: *Mason*, above.

The decision in *Mason* also shows that there is a continuing obligation on the part of the tenant both to repair to the satisfaction of the landlord's surveyor and to deliver up the premises so repaired. From a practical view, therefore, the onus is on the tenant (i.e., Melanie) to identify what work should satisfy the landlord's surveyor and, if necessary, consult the latter to find out what might be required before vacating the premises at the end of the lease. If no response is received and the tenant proceeds to carry out works which, in its view, are appropriate to comply with the covenant, it is likely that the landlord would be in no position later, through his surveyor, to require some other method of compliance provided that what the tenant had done was fairly to be regarded as compliance with the covenant.

At the end of the term, the landlord is entitled to bring an action on the covenant to yield up the premises in repair. Although not mentioned in the problem, I assume that Melanie's lease contains such a covenant in terms similar to the obligations imposed upon her during the currency of the lease. The measure of damages is the amount necessary to put the demised premises into the condition in which they should have been left in accordance with the covenant, bearing in mind the class of property and its age: *Proudfoot* v *Hart* (1890) 25 QBD 42. This common law measure is, however, subject to s. 18(1) of the 1927 Act which states that the damages recoverable by a landlord cannot exceed the diminution in the value of his freehold reversion resulting from the breaches of the repairing covenant. Diminution is assessed as at the lease expiry date and involves two valuations of the landlord's interest. The first is on the assumption that the premises were then in the state that they would have been in if the tenant had performed its covenants. The second is of the premises in their actual state and condition at that date. The purpose of this exercise is to isolate the effect on value of the tenant's failure to do the relevant works.

Diminution is calculated in one of two ways. First, if the landlord has carried out the remedial works or intends to do so, the cost of the works is *prima facie* evidence of the diminution in value. Alternatively, if he has not carried them out and does not intend to, then diminution is determined by actual valuation evidence given at the hearing. Assuming, therefore, that Melanie's landlord does not propose to remedy the (other) defects himself, it will be incumbent on the parties to exchange expert valuation reports with a view (hopefully) to agreeing a figure representing diminution in value prior to any court hearing. The voluntary dilapidations protocol (drafted by the Property Litigation Association but not yet in force under the Civil Procedure Rules) will be relevant here because it relates to claims for damages for breach by tenants of repairing obligations at the expiry of the lease. This requires that the landlord serves on the tenant his claim and a schedule of dilapidations, together with a s. 18(1) valuation if he does not intend to do the remedial works. The Protocol encourages the parties to hold a without prejudice meeting on site in order to resolve any items in dispute. It also requires the tenant to serve a response to the landlord's claim and to provide his (or her) own valuation if the tenant is intending to rely on s. 18(1).

(b) By way of a self-help remedy, it is open to a tenant to do repairs which are the landlord's responsibility and deduct the cost from current or future rent. In addition to having an equitable set-off, the tenant can rely on a common law right to deduct the repairing cost from the rent: *Lee-Parker* v *Izzet* [1971] 1 W.L.R. 1688. There will be no problem where the defect is situated in the demised property, but what if it involves the carrying out of remedial works on the landlord's retained premises?

In *Granada Theatres Ltd* v *Freehold Investment (Leytonstone) Ltd* [1959] 1 Ch 592, Jenkins LJ stated that a *landlord* has an implied licence to enter upon the demised premises for the purpose of performing his covenant to repair. Clearly, if such a licence can be implied in the landlord's favour, there seems no reason why a corresponding right should not, in an appropriate case, be implied in favour of the tenant when the entry is to do the necessary works under the landlord's obligation to repair. This was recognised, albeit at first instance, in *Loria* v *Hammer* [1989] 2 EGLR 249. In that case, the court alluded to the action of the tenant in carrying out the remedial works herself as probably not amounting to a trespass but an entry under an implied licence onto the landlord's premises. The point has arisen more recently in *Metropolitan Properties Co. Ltd* v *Wilson* [2003] L & TR 15, where the landlord sought various interim injunctions restraining the tenants from, *inter alia*, trespassing on the landlord's premises by permitting scaffolding to remain on the exterior of the building.

The tenants argued, by way of defence, that there was a long history of the landlord failing to carry out repairs in accordance with its obligations under the lease and that they had engaged their own contractors to carry out the required works, who had erected scaffolding on the building. As such, there was no trespass because the tenants were simply availing themselves of their right of self-help.

Significantly, Etherton J held that the remedy of self-help might, in appropriate circumstances, entitle a tenant to the benefit of an implied licence to enter onto his landlord's premises in order to effect repairs which were the landlord's responsibility. On the facts, however, the judge concluded that the tenants had no prospect of establishing at trial that they had been acting under any such licence. Significantly, the scaffolding had been erected without warning or any prior notice to the landlord. Moreover, the scaffolding had gone up at a time when the tenants had not entered into any contract for the carrying out of the external works, nor had they even entered into negotiations or tenders for the work. Indeed, there had been no consultation between residents of the building as to the selection of any contractors. By contrast, the landlord's proposed scheme for the external works had already been largely agreed and instructions to the landlord's builders already given to proceed with the works. In view of the fact that (both in relation to internal and external works) a proper tendering process had been completed by the landlord, as well as the requisite notification and consultation procedures pursuant to the Landlord and Tenant Act 1985, the tenant's action in proceeding to erect their own scaffolding was high-handed and inappropriate. Moreover, it was relevant that the tenants had not pursued any of their remedies apart from self-help (for example, the appointment of a receiver or manager of the building, an order for specific performance, a challenge to the reasonableness of past service charges, or enfranchisement of the building).

It seems from the *Wilson* decision that the courts will be prepared to uphold a tenant's right to enter upon the landlord's premises to carry out repairs within the landlord's repairing covenant provided that the landlord is given adequate notice of the tenant's works. It will be incumbent on the tenant to disclose the contract or specification for the repairs so as to give the landlord the opportunity for consultation and approval. If the landlord is already engaged in a tendering process himself and has initiated the statutory framework laid down under the 1985 Act, it may prove very difficult for the tenant to argue that his entry on the landlord's property was justified. This may be so regardless of whether there has been a previous history of neglect and failure to repair. Moreover, the tenant should first consider whether other legal remedies are open to him to ensure compliance with the landlord's obligations. Ultimately, whether or not the court will be persuaded to hold that the tenant acted under an implied licence from the landlord will depend on a wide range of factors. The mere fact that the premises are in urgent need of repair will not entitle the tenant to 'steal a march' on the landlord and oblige him to accept an unwarranted instrusion onto his property.

Further reading

Blake, L., 'Foundations of Housing' [2000] EG 130.

Driscoll, J., 'New Right to Manage' (2002) SJ 588.

Haler, P., 'The Right to Manage — Commonhold and Leasehold Reform Act 2002' (2003) 7 L & T Rev 106.

Hanbury, W., 'Safe as Houses?' (2001) SJ 768.

Hindle, A., 'Human Rights and Schemes of Management under the Leasehold Reform Acts — Pt I and II (2001) 5 L & T Rev 119 and (2002) 6 L & T Rev 6.

Hull, M., and McIntosh, M., 'What about My Rent?' [1999] EG 84.

Joyce, J., 'Dilapidations Protocol' (2002) SJ 784.

Madge, N., 'Damages for Breach of Repairing Obligations' (1999) NLJ 1643.

Pawlowski, M., and Brown, J., 'Specific Performance of Repairing Obligations' [1998] 62 Conv 495.

Pawlowski, M., 'When Does the Landlord's Liability to Repair Arise?' (1996) 1 L & T Rev 5.

Pawlowski, M., 'A Few Home Truths' [2001] EG 136.

Pawlowski, M., 'Covenant to Repair — Do Not Disturb?' (2004) PLJ 14.

Pawlowski, M., and Brown J., 'Liability of Landlords for Condensation Dampness' [2001] Conv 184.

Smith, P.F., 'Dampness Again' [2001] Conv 102.

Spencer-Silver, J., 'Manage to Feel at Home' [2001] EG 130.

Spencer-Silver, J., 'Management Power' [2002] EG 128.

Ward, V.C., 'Service Record' [2001] EG 156.

Wilkinson, H.W., 'Omission, Omission, All Fall Down' (2001) NLJ 916.

Wilkinson, H.W., 'Ageing and Defective Parts — Whose Duty to Repair?' (2000) NLJ 892.

Express covenants

Introduction

In this chapter, we have set out five questions on express covenants, namely, rent review, alteration and user, option to renew, and insurance and service charges. Questions on covenants against assignment, sub-letting etc. and repair will be found in **Chapters 6** and **7**, respectively.

The law relating to the construction and operation of rent review clauses has become a highly specialised subject in its own right. The amount of time you should devote to this topic will depend very much on the emphasis given to it by your lecturer. The aim of rent review clauses has been commented upon judicially (see, e.g., the judgment of Lord Diplock in *United Scientific Holdings Ltd* v *Burnley Borough Council* [1978] AC 904) and it is commonly accepted that the object of such a clause is to provide the landlord with a safeguard against the devaluing effects of inflation on his rental income. A review clause may provide for the rent to be reviewed upwards or downwards, although it is generally more common to find upwards only clauses. Exam questions in this area will usually require the student to analyse the review clause and assess whether the landlord, in seeking to review the rent, has complied with the necessary review machinery. Of particular relevance in this regard is the law relating to the 'timing' and 'notice' requirements which govern the operation of the rent review clause.

Questions on alteration and user of the demised premises tend also to be of the problem variety. Covenants against alteration may take the form of a total prohibition on the tenant's ability to effect structural changes to the property, or may be qualified so that only such alterations as are authorised by the landlord may be effected. In the latter case, the tenant must seek the landlord's formal approval prior to carrying out any work. A qualified covenant may state that the landlord will not unreasonably refuse his consent to the proposed alteration (i.e., a fully qualified covenant). In the absence, however, of any such express requirement of reasonableness, the Landlord and Tenant Act 1927, s. 19(2), provides that a qualified covenant against alterations is subject to the proviso that the landlord's consent to the making of 'improvements' is not to be unreasonably withheld. The term 'improvement' refers to a type of alteration which, from the tenant's perspective, enhances and improves his beneficial user of the demised premises (*FW Woolworth & Co. Ltd* v *Lambert* [1937] Ch 37 and *Lambert* v *FW Woolworth & Co. Ltd (No. 2)* [1938] Ch 883).

The landlord, however, is not prevented from seeking a reasonable sum in relation to any damage or diminution in value of his reversionary interest in the property. Moreover, such a sum may take the form of a condition for the granting of consent, and the onus is on the tenant to prove that such conditional consent (or refusal) is unreasonable (*FW Woolworth & Co. Ltd* v *Lambert* [1937] Ch 37 and *Haines* v *Florensa* [1990] 09 EG 70).

Covenants which restrict the tenant's ability to alter the user of the demised premises also provide a fruitful area for examination questions. In the absence of any covenant restricting user, a tenant is free to use the property for whatever purpose he likes, provided no acts of waste are committed and any requisite planning permission has been obtained for a change of use. A well drafted lease, however, will almost certainly contain an express covenant restricting the tenant's ability to change the way in which he uses the demised premises. Such a covenant may take the form of an absolute prohibition on any change of user, or, alternatively, provide that the landlord's consent is required before the tenant may effect any change (i.e., a qualified covenant). The covenant may also expressly declare that the landlord will not withhold consent unreasonably (i.e., a fully qualified covenant). In the case of qualified covenants, the landlord has an unfettered veto over the proposed change of user (*Guardian Assurance Co. Ltd* v *Gants Hill Holdings Ltd* (1983) 267 EG 678) unless the tenant can show that the landlord has waived any breach of the covenant (*Chelsea Estates Ltd* v *Kadri* [1970] EGD 1356). Note also that a qualified covenant against change of user is subject to a proviso that no fine is payable by the tenant for the landlord's consent if no structural alteration of the premises is involved (Landlord and Tenant Act 1927, s. 19(3)). This, however, does not preclude the landlord from requiring payment of a reasonable sum in respect of any damage to, or diminution in the value of, the premises (or any neighbouring premises) belonging to him, and of any legal or other expenses incurred in connection with such consent.

For a review of the case law in this area, see Williams, D., 'User Covenants and Breaches' [1991] EG 9149, 63. For a summary of the Law Commission's recommendations, see Smith, P. F., 'The Law Commission Report on Covenants Restricting Dispositions, Alterations and Changes of User' (1985) 135 NLJ 991 and 1015.

Questions on options to renew/purchase also frequently crop up in the examinations. Here again, much will depend on the emphasis given to the subject by your lecturer. In formally drafted leases, it is not unusual to find that a landlord has granted the tenant either the right to purchase the freehold, or the right to extend the lease for a further term. These rights will exist independently of any statutory rights of enfranchisement. It will invariably be a condition precedent to the exercise of the option to renew that the tenant has abided by all the tenant's covenants in the lease, and even the most minor breach may act as a bar to the right of renewal (*West Country Cleaners (Falmouth) Ltd* v *Saly* [1966] 3 All ER 210). In order to be enforceable, such an option must also be sufficiently certain (*King's Motors (Oxford) Ltd* v *Lax* [1969] 3 All ER 665), but the courts will strive to give a workable interpretation to the wording where this is possible (*Brown* v *Gould* [1972] Ch 53).

It is also noteworthy that options to renew leases and options to purchase are proprietary in their nature, being 'estate contracts', and, if registered correctly, in the context of registered or unregistered land, will bind third party purchasers.

For the sake of completeness, we have also included a question on the topics of insurance and service charges in this chapter.

Lastly, a word of caution! Although you will find, in the various law reports, a plethora of cases concerned with the interpretation of leasehold covenants, you should be aware that many of these will simply turn on their own facts and on the particular wording of the covenant in question. Such cases are time-absorbing and, at the end of the day, may provide little by way of precedent. Our advice is to stick to the leading cases which establish general principles.

∎ Question 1

(a) How can a tenant ensure that 'time is made of the essence' in relation to the operation of a rent review clause?

(b) By a lease, dated 1 June 1999, Property (UK) Ltd demised office space to Doubledoor Ltd for a term of 10 years at an initial rent of £20,000 per annum. The rent review clause in the lease provided that the rent was liable to an 'upwards only' review as from the first day in the fifth year calculable as from 1 June 1999, and that during the year preceding the fifth year, the landlord should, within the final calendar month of the said year, serve on the tenant a 'notice of rental increase'.

The increased rental sum was expressed in the review clause to be either one-half of the sum total of the rack rent for the demised premises (as at the time of notice), or £50,000, whichever is the greater.

On 15 July 2004, Property (UK) Ltd served on Doubledoor Ltd a notice of rental increase, which stated that, as from 1 June 2004, Doubledoor Ltd was liable to pay an annual rent of £60,000, this figure representing half of the rack rent for the demised premises.

The notice was headed 'subject to contract'. Doubledoor Ltd maintains that it is not obliged to pay the higher rent.

Advise Property (UK) Ltd as to whether it can demand the higher rent.

Commentary

This question is divided into two parts, but both parts require you to examine the principles governing the timing and operation of rent review clauses. The only real difference between the two parts is that part (a) is in the form of a mini-essay, whereas part (b) is a problem question, designed to test the student's practical application of his or her knowledge of the law.

In answering both parts of the question, you should make reference to case law — a good knowledge of the cases will impress the examiner! Always structure your answer by identifying the key issues and applying the relevant law clearly and concisely. A student who adopts a structured answer is best equipped to score a healthy mark!

On the subject of trigger notices which are headed 'subject to contract' or 'without prejudice', see Brown, J., and Pawlowski, M., 'Without Prejudice Communications' (1993) 13/4 RRLR, 284.

- Time may be made of the essence of a review clause by a number of means: (1) review clause may expressly provide that time of the essence (2) wording of clause may evidence an intention to make time of the essence (3) lease may contain a break clause or (4) tenant may serve formal notice on landlord making time of the essence

- Property (UK) Ltd's notice served seven months late in July 2004. Notice valid, despite lateness, in view of presumption that time not of the essence: *United Scientific Holdings Ltd v Burnley Borough Council* (1978). Nothing in lease to displace this presumption. Mere delay will not, therefore, invalidate the notice: *Amherst v James Walker Goldsmith and Silversmith Ltd* (1983)

- No justification for reading into lease any implied term that landlord has to serve notice within a reasonable time: *London & Manchester Assurance Co. Ltd v GA Dunn & Co.* (1983). No estoppel or waiver on the facts

- Subject to contract rubric will not necessarily invalidate the notice: Compare *Shirclar Properties Ltd v Heinitz* (1983) and *Royal Life Insurance v Phillips* (1990)

⚲ Suggested answer

(a) A number of courses of action are open to a tenant who wishes to ensure that time is 'made of the essence' in relation to the operation of a rent review clause.

First, he can insist that the review clause expressly provides that all stipulations as to time in the rent provisions of the lease are to be of the essence of the contract and incapable of extension save by agreement between the parties (*Weller v Akehurst* [1981] 3 All ER 411). Clear words, however, are needed to make time of the essence (*Thorn EMI Pension Trust Ltd v Quinton Hazell plc* (1984) 269 EG 414). For example, where the lease provides for a landlord to serve a trigger notice invoking the rent review process within a certain time 'but not otherwise', a failure to serve the notice within the time-limit will disentitle the landlord from serving the review notice (*Drebbond Ltd v Horsham District Council* (1979) 37 P & CR 237).

Secondly, the tenant may insist that the wording of the review clause is such as to evidence a clear intention to make time of the essence. This could be done by setting out a clear timetable for review with provision for what is to happen in the event of non-compliance (see, e.g., *Henry Smith's Charity Trustees* v *AWADA Trading and Promotion Services Ltd* (1984) 269 EG 279). In *Starmark Enterprises Ltd* v *CPL Distribution Ltd* [2002] 4 All ER 264, the rent review clause provided that the tenant 'shall be deemed' to have agreed to pay the increased rent specified in the landlord's rent notice if it failed to serve a counternotice within one month of receipt of the rent notice. The Court of Appeal held that an express deeming provision in a rent review clause was sufficient to rebut what otherwise would be the presumption that time was not of the essence. Such a provision was not mere administrative machinery (the decision in *Mecca Leisure Ltd* v *Renown Investments (Holdings) Ltd* (1984) 49 P & CR 12 was expressly disapproved on this point). In *First Property Growth Partnership LP* v *Royal & Sun Alliance Property Services Ltd* [2002] EWHC 305, the lease provided for the landlord to serve a trigger notice at any time not more than 12 months before the review date 'but not at any other time'. The concluding phrase was held to make time of the essence of the rent notice. By contrast, in *McDonald's Property Co. Ltd* v *HSBC Bank plc* [2001] 36 EG 181, although the review clause provided a detailed timetable for the determination of the review rent, the court held that there were no compelling contra-indications in the lease so as to make time of the essence.

Thirdly, a tenant may be able to insist that the lease contains a break clause entitling the tenant to determine the lease, within a certain period after the reviewed rent has been determined, if he is not minded to accept the reviewed rent. In relation to such a break clause, time may be held to be of the essence, in which case it would be arguable that, by necessary implication, time was also of the essence in relation to the operation of the rent review clause itself. Thus, in *Al Saloom* v *Shirley James Travel Service Ltd* (1981) 259 EG 420, the presumption that time was not of the essence was rebutted because of the interrelation of the rent review provisions and a break clause in the lease. See also, *Legal and General Assurance (Pensions Management) Ltd* v *Cheshire County Council* (1984) 269 EG 40.

Many review clauses incorporate a provision for the service of a counter-notice by the tenant after such time as a trigger notice has been served on him by the landlord. A counter-notice gives the tenant the opportunity to challenge the proposed new rent, and often encourages the landlord and tenant to come to an agreement as to the proposed rent increase. Even if served late, the counter-notice will operate so as to challenge the proposed new rental because the presumption that time is not of the essence will apply equally to this form of notice, save where there exists a contrary indication. It is open, however, to either party to make time of the essence (of a trigger or counternotice) by giving formal notice to that effect: *Amherst* v *James Walker Goldsmith & Silversmith Ltd* [1983] 1 Ch. 305. In that case, the review clause contained a time limit for the service of a landlord's trigger notice and it was suggested that the tenant could, if it so wished, have made time of the essence by serving a formal 'warning' notice on the landlord: see also *Iceland Foods plc* v *Dangoor* [2002] 21 EG 146. A time limit can, it seems, also be implied so as to enable the tenant to serve formal notice making time of the essence. In *Barclays Bank plc* v *Savile Estates Ltd* [2002] 24 EG 152, the rent review provision did not impose any time limit on the landlord to apply for the appointment of an independent expert. The Court of Appeal, however, held that an obligation to apply within a reasonable time could be implied into the review clause so as to enable the tenant to formally make time of the essence. Any such warning notice (making time of the essence) can be given once the reasonable time period for the making of an appointment had expired: *Northern and Midland Holdings Ltd* v *Magnet Ltd* [2004] EWHC 120 (Ch). The use of such formal notices is likely to become more common given that modern rent review clauses tend not to include time limits.

(b) The review clause provides for a unilateral 'upwards only' review, so that only the landlord has the power to increase the rent provided he complies with the requisite procedure for triggering the review.

The review clause provides that the existing rent (of £20,000) may be increased either by £30,000 to £50,000 per year, or to a sum representing half of the rack rental for the property, if this sum is greater than £50,000. The clause also provides that, in order to so increase the rent, the landlord must serve a notice of rental increase within the twelfth month of the year preceding the fifth year of the term. In order, therefore, to comply with the review machinery, Property (UK) Ltd was obliged to serve its notice in December 2003. In this case, however, the notice was actually served some seven months late in July 2004.

In view of the lateness in triggering the review, is the rental increase valid? Since the House of Lords decision in *United Scientific Holdings Ltd* v *Burnley Borough Council* [1978] AC 904, the position is that, save where there exists a contrary indication in the lease, time will not be of the essence in relation to the issue and service of a landlord's notice triggering a rent review. In the present case, there appears to be nothing in the wording of the rent review clause to displace the presumption that time is not of the essence, and accordingly Property (UK) Ltd should be advised that their notice is not invalid despite being late. In this connection, the courts are generally loathe to prevent a landlord from exercising his contractually agreed right to review the rent, even in circumstances where the landlord has delayed unreasonably in serving the relevant trigger notice. (In *Amherst* v *James Walker Goldsmith and Silversmith Ltd* [1983] 1 Ch 305, the Court of Appeal held that, time not being of the essence of the review clause, mere delay, however lengthy, could not preclude the landlord from exercising his contractual right to invoke the rent review provisions of the lease. Moreover, there was no justification for reading into the lease any implied term that the landlord had to serve his notice within a reasonable time. In *Amhherst* (as in our case), a time limit for the landlord's trigger notice was provided for in the review clause. In these circumstances, it would have been open to the tenant, had it chosen to do so, to serve a formal 'warning' notice on the landlord making time of the essence. In the absence, however, of any such formal notice, the presumption that time was not of the essence prevailed. Similar reasoning would, in my view, apply in our problem. (The recent decision in *Barclays Bank plc* v *Savile Estates Ltd* [2002] 24 EG 152 is distinguishable because, in that case, the issue was whether a time limit should be implied in the absence of any express timetable.) See also, *London & Manchester Assurance Co. Ltd* v *GA Dunn & Co.* (1983) 265 EG 39 and *Acuba* v *Allied Shoe Repairs* [1975] 3 All ER 782. An estoppel or waiver may, however, preclude the right to a review (see, e.g., *Esso Petroleum Ltd* v *Anthony Gibbs Financial Services Ltd* (1983) 267 EG 351), but this does not arise on the facts of the present case.

Of greater difficulty is the fact that Property (UK) Ltd's notice was expressly headed 'subject to contract'. In order to be valid, a landlord's trigger notice must be unequivocal and certain in its terms of reference. In *Shirclar Properties Ltd* v *Heinitz* (1983) 268 EG 362, Davies J held that the landlord's notice, which contained the rubric 'subject to contract', did not constitute an unequivocal notice because it appeared to contemplate discussion and the possibility of ultimate agreement. However, in *Royal Life Insurance* v *Phillips* [1990] 43 EG 70, the landlord's letter triggering the review was headed 'subject to contract' and 'without prejudice'. Nolan J held that these rubrics made no sense in the context of a document clearly intended to have legal effect. A reasonably-minded tenant receiving such a letter by recorded delivery four days prior to the expiry of the time-limit would have understood it as a notice pursuant to the review clause. Accordingly, the notice was held to constitute a valid notice initiating the review procedure. The upshot of the foregoing is that a notice qualified by the use of the words 'subject to contract' may still be an effective notice if it is clear from the context that the document is a review notice, but if the notice is itself couched in ambiguous language it will be held to be a mere negotiating document and not a formal notice. In the present case, it is submitted that the notice is unambiguous and that, accordingly, Property (UK) Ltd can claim the higher rent.

Q Question 2

In 1998, Big Estate Ltd granted Sheila a 25-year lease of a small, single-storey retail unit. The lease contains, *inter alia*, the following covenants:

> The LESSEE for herself and her assigns hereby covenants:
>
> (i) not to alter the demised premises in any way whatsoever save with the consent of the Lessor
>
> (ii) at all times during the said term to use the demised premises only as a florist shop and not to effect any change of user save with the consent of the Lessor.

In 2004, Sheila's florist business began to run into financial difficulties. She now wishes to turn the premises into a wool and hosiery shop. The change of user would require Sheila to demolish an internal wall in the shop, thus converting two rooms into one.

In 2004, she wrote to Big Estate Ltd seeking its consent to the change of user and structural alteration. Big Estate Ltd has replied, stating that it will only agree to the proposed changes if Sheila pays compensation in the sum of £1,000 in relation to the change of user and £5,000 in relation to the alteration.

Advise Sheila.

Commentary

This is a straightforward question on covenants against change of user and alteration of the demised premises. Essentially, you are asked to identify the nature of the two covenants, state the relevant law and apply the same to the particular facts. The question does not require you to draw heavily on any particular cases but seeks to test the understanding of general principles in this area. A good working knowledge of the Landlord and Tenant Act 1927, s. 19(2) and (3) is, however, essential.

An easy question for the well-prepared student!

- Sheila's covenant not to alter the premises is qualified and her proposed demolition constitutes an improvement. Hence, Landlord and Tenant Act 1927, s. 19(2) will apply: *FW Woolworth & Co. Ltd v Lambert* (1937) and *Lambert v FW Woolworth & Co. Ltd (No. 2)* (1938)

- Effect of s. 19(2) is to impose on the landlord a requirement of reasonableness in relation to any refusal of consent or conditional consent. The sum of £5,000 may be lawfully required if it is a reasonable reflection of the diminution in the landlord's reversionary interest. Sheila may challenge this by seeking a declaration under Landlord and Tenant Act 1954, s. 53(1)(b)

- Sheila's user covenant also qualified, but no requirement of reasonableness imposed by general law: *Guardian Assurance Co. Ltd v Gants Hill Holdings Ltd* (1983)

- But consider also Landlord and Tenant Act 1927, s. 19(3). Sheila's proposed change of user involves a structural change so, in principle, sum of £1,000 is legitimate if it reasonably represents compensation for diminution in value of the premises

:Ϙ: **Suggested answer**

By virtue of covenant (i), it is a term of the lease that Sheila will not alter the demised premises save with the landlord's consent. Covenants such as this are commonly found in well-drafted leases.

An alteration may be defined as a change in the constitution, fabric or form of a building (e.g., the conversion of houses into flats: *Duke of Westminster* v *Swinton* [1948] 1 KB 524). But a change in the constitution or form of the building must necessarily involve something more than just a cosmetic change or a change to the appearance of a building (*Joseph* v *LCC* (1914) 111 LT 276 and *Bickmore* v *Dimmer* [1903] 1 Ch 158). Clear examples of alterations include the conversion of two rooms into one, the subdivision of rooms, the creation and moving of existing doorways and windows, or the demolition of attached outhouses etc. It seems evident, therefore, that Sheila's proposed works would amount to an alteration of the demised premises (*Haines* v *Florensa* [1990] 09 EG 70, where the works involved the conversion of a loft).

Covenants which restrict alterations may come in three forms: first, the covenant may amount to an absolute prohibition against the carrying out of alterations to the property; secondly, the covenant may be qualified in its nature, that is, prohibit alterations save those to which the landlord has consented; and, thirdly, the covenant may be fully qualified in that it prohibits alterations save those in relation to which the landlord has consented, but such consent is not to be unreasonably withheld: *Iqbal* v *Thakrar* [2004] EWCA Civ 592, where the landlord expressed concerns that the alterations would cause structural damage to the rest of the building. In Sheila's lease, the covenant falls into the second category (i.e., it is qualified).

An alteration will be deemed to be in the nature of an 'improvement' if, from the tenant's standpoint, it enhances the tenant's beneficial user of the demised premises even where it diminishes the letting value of the premises (*FW Woolworth & Co. Ltd* v *Lambert* [1937] Ch 37 and *Lambert* v *FW Woolworth & Co. Ltd (No. 2)* [1938] Ch 883). In our case, Sheila's proposed alteration may be termed an improvement since it will clearly assist her to obtain a better user of the premises.

Since the covenant is qualified and her proposed user constitutes an improvement, the provisions of the Landlord and Tenant Act 1927, s. 19(2), will come into play. This subsection, despite any express provision to the contrary, converts a qualified covenant against alterations into a fully qualified one (i.e., subject to a proviso that the landlord's consent to the making of improvements is not to be unreasonably withheld). This proviso, however, does not preclude the landlord from requiring, as a condition of consent, the payment of a reasonable sum in respect of any damage to or diminution in the value of the demised premises or any neighbouring premises belonging to the landlord. The landlord will not, however, be confined to seeking financial compensation if the tenant's proposed alterations would have a detrimental effect on the landlord's business interests (i.e., loss of profitability as opposed to diminution of the value of the landlord's retained land). In these circumstances, the landlord can legitimately refuse consent to the proposed works or impose appropriate conditions *Sargeant* v *Macepark (Whittlebury) Ltd* [2004] EWHC 1333 (Ch). Moreover, the landlord is free to claim any legal (or other) expenses properly incurred in connection with such consent. In the case of an improvement which does not add to the letting value of the premises, the landlord may also require, as a condition of consent, where such a requirement would be reasonable, an undertaking from the tenant to reinstate the premises in the condition in which they were before the improvement was executed (s. 19(2)).

The effect of s. 19(2), therefore, is that there is imposed on Big Estate Ltd the requirement of reasonableness in relation to any refusal of consent, or conditional consent, to Sheila's proposed alteration. If the landlord's refusal (albeit in the form of a conditional consent) is reasonable, then Sheila cannot alter the premises except in compliance with the condition. If, however, its refusal of consent (or refusal by way of imposing the condition) is unreasonable, then she may go ahead and carry out the proposed alteration.

If Sheila wishes to challenge the landlord's refusal, two courses are open to her. She may either ignore the landlord's decision, treat it as unreasonable and effect the alteration work, or she may apply to the county court for a declaration (pursuant to the Landlord and Tenant Act 1954, s. 53(1)(b)) that (i) the landlord's refusal is unlawful because the condition stated is unreasonable, and (ii) she be permitted to carry out the alteration despite the refusal (see, e.g., *Haines* v *Florensa* [1990] 09 EG 70). The second course of action is clearly more sensible since it does not expose Sheila to a possible action for forfeiture of her lease and damages for breach of covenant if the landlord's refusal is held to be reasonable. It would also preclude the landlord from seeking a mandatory injunction requiring the tenant to reinstate the premises as they were originally prior to the alteration (*Mosley* v *Cooper* [1990] 1 EGLR 124).

It is for the court to determine whether the condition imposed by Big Estate Ltd is reasonable, but (as mentioned earlier) s. 19(2) dictates that a sum may be lawfully required by a landlord for such consent if it is a reasonable reflection of the amount by which (if at all) the landlord's reversionary interest has diminished, and/or represents any properly incurred expenses in relation to the consent. In our case, it would be necessary to examine, with the assistance of a surveyor, the basis upon which the landlord arrived at the sum of £5,000 before any firm view could be given as to whether this condition is lawful. If Sheila decided to challenge the landlord's refusal of consent by way of declaration, the burden of proof would lie on her to establish the unreasonableness of the sum sought by Big Estate Ltd (*FW Woolworth* v *Lambert* above).

In relation to the covenant which seeks to restrict Sheila's ability to change the user of the premises, such covenants are commonly known as 'restrictive user covenants' and also come in three forms:

(a) the covenant may be absolute (i.e., imposing a total prohibition);

(b) the covenant may be qualified; or

(c) it may be fully qualified.

If fully qualified, the covenant will expressly state that the landlord's consent for any proposed changes of user will not be unreasonably withheld. If qualified (but not fully qualified), however, the covenant makes no reference to reasonableness and the landlord has an absolute veto over the tenant's proposed change of user. Moreover, unlike qualified covenants against alterations which constitute the making of improvements, no requirement of reasonableness is imposed by law (*Guardian Assurance Co. Ltd v Gants Hill Holdings Ltd* (1983) 267 EG 678). In the present case, the covenant against change of user is qualified (as opposed to fully qualified).

However, the Landlord and Tenant Act 1927, s. 19(3), does state that where the change of user does not involve a structural alteration to the premises, no fine or premium can be demanded by the landlord save for sums which reasonably represent compensation for the diminution in value of the premises, or legal or other expenses. In this case, however, Sheila's proposed change of user would involve a structural change and, therefore, in principle, the sum of £1,000 seems to be legitimately demanded, if reasonable. Nevertheless, it is for the court to determine this in the light of expert evidence.

Lastly, it may be mentioned that, since Sheila is a business tenant, she may be entitled to compensation for the improvement under the Landlord and Tenant Act 1927, Pt I, if (before making the improvement) she notifies the landlord of the proposed work. Should Big Estate Ltd then serve a notice of objection, she may apply to the court to have the proposed improvement certified as a proper improvement. Section 9 of the 1927 Act states that Pt I of the Act applies notwithstanding any contract to the contrary.

Q Question 3

In 1985, the Earl of Dover granted Michelle a 20-year lease of a fishmonger's shop. The lease provides that Michelle should 'maintain and keep the demised premises in good and tenantable repair'. Also included in the lease is an option which confers on Michelle the right:

> after the expiration of 19 years from the date of the demise herein, by notice, to renew the lease of the demised premises for a further term of 20 years as from the expiry date of this demise, on the same terms as this lease, save that the rent for any renewed term shall be fixed having regard to the market value of the demised premises at the time of exercising this option and any renewed lease shall not contain this option to renew but, in any event, this option being conditional on the observance by the tenant of the tenant's covenants in the lease.

The option is expressed as personal to Michelle and incapable of assignment, and that it would cease to have effect on assignment of the lease.

The lease further provides that if Michelle desires to renew the lease, she should serve on the landlord a notice of intention so to do.

In 1997, the Earl of Dover sold his reversionary interest to Buzby Property Ltd. Last year, Michelle contracted to sell her leasehold interest in the shop to Malcolm. Although a formal assignment has been executed, Michelle remains the registered proprietor of the property. In 2004, Michelle served on Buzby Property Ltd a notice of intention to renew, as required under the terms of her lease. Her new landlords, however, have refused to renew the lease on the ground that Michelle, by failing to repair a cracked brick wall at the side of the shop, has breached the tenant's repairing covenant in the lease and is, therefore, barred from exercising the option. They also claim that the option is void for uncertainty and unenforceable as against them for non-registration, and that because Michelle assigned the property the option is no longer exercisable by her under the terms of the lease. Michelle admits to failing to repair the wall but contends that the cracking is *de minimis*.

Advise Michelle.

Commentary

This question is concerned with an option to renew a lease. It is relatively straightforward provided you are familiar with the issues being raised.

Nowadays, statute (in the form of the Leasehold Reform Acts 1967–1982 and the Leasehold Reform, Housing and Urban Development Act 1993) has conferred on many residential tenants the right (either individually or collectively) compulsorily to acquire from their landlords either the freehold or an extension to their existing leases.

Despite the growing availability of statutory enfranchisement, a lease may confer on the tenant a *contractual* right either to purchase the freehold reversion or to acquire some form of leasehold extension. Such privately conferred rights take the form of options to purchase or options to renew, respectively. For a good summary of the law in this area, see Smith, P.F., 'Renewal of Leases by Covenant' (1994) 14/3 RRLR, 31.

One tricky point relates to Michelle's assignment of her leasehold estate to Malcolm. Does she still have the right to exercise the option to renew? See *Brown & Root Technology Ltd* v *Sun Alliance & London Assurance Co. Ltd* [1997] 18 EG 123 (CA).

- Option sufficiently certain as to title and relevant procedural mechanisms. So far as rent is concerned, in the absence of agreed machinery, court would resolve dispute as to rent payable by applying the formula laid down in the option clause: *Brown* v *Gould* (1972)

- Michelle cannot excuse herself by saying that want or repair is trivial where compliance with repairing obligations is a condition precedent to exercise of option: *West Country Cleaners (Falmouth) Ltd* v *Saly* (1966) and *Bairstow Eves (Securities) Ltd* v *Ripley* (1992)

- But Michelle has until expiry of lease (not date of notice exercising option) to remedy the breach: *King's Motors (Oxford) Ltd v Lax* (1970) and *Trane (UK) Ltd v Provident Mutual Life Assurance* (1995)

- If premises comprise registered land, option will bind any assignees of the Earl as an unregistered interest which overrides the registered disposition: Land Registration Act 2002, para. 2, sch. 3. If unregistered land, the option will be void if not registered as a class C(iv) land charge. Option still exerciseable by Michelle, despite having assigned her lease to Malcom, because she is still the registered proprietor of the shop: *Brown & Root Technology Ltd v Sun Alliance & London Assurance Co. Ltd* (1997)

:Q: Suggested answer

Michelle has been granted a personal option to renew her lease for a further 20 years at a market rent. To be valid, such options must be certain and unequivocal in their terms (*King's Motors (Oxford) Ltd v Lax* [1970] 1 WLR 426, where the option was held void on the ground that it provided for the new rent to be agreed between the parties without any reference to arbitration, or some supplementary agreement fixing the rent to be paid). A vaguely worded option to renew will be upheld, however, if it is capable of having some workable meaning. In *Brown v Gould* [1972] Ch 53, the option clause provided for the new rent to be fixed having regard to the market value of the premises at the time of exercising the option, taking into account any increased value of the premises attributable to structural improvements made by the tenant during the currency of his lease. Although the clause provided no machinery for fixing the rent, the court held that it was not void for uncertainty since it was not devoid of any meaning; nor could it be said that there was a wide variety of meanings which could fairly be put on the clause so that it was impossible to say which of them was intended.

In our case, the option would seem sufficiently certain in its terms of reference, namely, as to the title to be acquired and relevant procedural mechanisms. So far as the rent is concerned, applying *Brown v Gould*, it is submitted that, in the absence of machinery agreed on by the parties, the court would not be precluded from resolving any dispute as to the rent payable, if the parties disagreed as to the quantum, applying the formula laid down in the option clause. The courts are reluctant to hold void for uncertainty any provision that was intended to have legal effect, and in the present case it cannot be doubted that the option was intended to have business efficacy.

However, the wording of the option clearly prevents Michelle from being able potentially to convert the lease into a 2,000-year term as a perpetually renewable lease under the Law of Property Act 1922, sch. 15 (see e.g., *Caerphilly Concrete Products Ltd v Owen* [1972] 1 WLR 372).

Whether existing as an integral part of the lease, or as collateral to it, an option to renew is a conditional estate contract (*Spiro* v *Glencrown Properties Ltd* [1990] 1 All ER 600). If the landlord refuses to complete the transaction by renewing the lease as agreed, then prima facie he will be in breach of contract and can be compelled to renew the lease by a decree of specific performance. However, being a contract for the sale of land, the option must comply with the necessary legal formalities and either be evidenced in writing (or partly performed) if entered into before 27 September 1989 (see Law of Property Act 1925, s. 40), or, if entered into on or after this date, actually be reduced to writing with all the terms contained therein and signed by both parties (see Law of Property (Miscellaneous Provisions) Act 1989, s. 2). As the option, in the present case, is contained in the lease (seemingly created in or around 1985), the relevant formalities (s. 40 of the 1925 Act) have been complied with and the option is valid.

Buzby Property Ltd also contend that Michelle is unable to rely on the option because she has breached her repairing covenant and that the option does not bind them as assignees of the reversion because of lack of registration.

As to the first point, the option states that it is only exercisable if Michelle has complied with all the tenant's covenants in the lease. Buzby Property Ltd contend that she has not complied with the repairing covenant by failing to repair the cracked brick wall. It is a question of evidence as to the nature of this breach, and only an expert building surveyor can really determine the extent of the cracking and whether or not the defect is *de minimis*. If a breach has occurred, it would seem that this would be a bar to Michelle being able to exercise the option to renew. In *West Country Cleaners (Falmouth) Ltd* v *Saly* [1966] 3 All ER 210, the tenants were held to be disqualified from exercising their option to renew the lease for an extended term by reason of their breaches of a painting covenant (albeit that the breaches were only trivial). Similarly, in *Bairstow Eves (Securities) Ltd* v *Ripley* [1992] 2 EGLR 47, the Court of Appeal confirmed the proposition that a tenant seeking to enforce an option to renew in a lease, where compliance with repairing obligations was a condition precedent to the exercise of the option, could not excuse himself by saying that the want of repair was trivial or merely a technical breach. The general principle is that where an option is conditional upon the performance by the grantee of some act in a stated manner (or at a stated time), the act must be performed strictly in order to entitle the grantee to exercise the right (*Greville* v *Parker* [1910] AC 335). However, the position will be different where the tenant is under an obligation to 'reasonably perform and observe' the tenant's covenants in the lease as a condition of renewal (*Basset* v *Whiteley* (1982) P & CR 87 and *Reed Personnel Services plc* v *American Express Ltd* [1997] 1 EGLR 229). In such a case, the tenant will be entitled to renew if he has behaved as a reasonable tenant.

The material date for determining whether the tenant has complied with the condition(s) upon which the option to renew is granted is the date of the expiry of the original term and not the date when the tenant gives notice purporting to exercise the option (*King's Motors (Oxford) Ltd* v *Lax* [1970] 1 WLR 426). Thus, even though she may technically be in breach of the repairing covenant, Michelle may still validly enforce the option provided she remedies the breach prior to the expiry of her lease in 2005 (see *Trane (UK) Ltd* v *Provident Mutual Life Assurance* [1995] 1 EGLR 33 and *Bass Holdings Ltd* v *Morton Music Ltd* [1987] 3 WLR 543 (CA)).

As to the registration point, if the premises comprise registered land, then despite the fact that Michelle should have registered the option by way of notice or caution so as to bind any assignees of the Earl of Dover, such an option can, in any event, bind assignees as an unregistered interest which will override a registered disposition under the Land Registration Act 2002, sch. 3 para. 2, being a proprietary right (see *Re Button's Lease* [1964] 1 Ch 263, 271) belonging to the tenant in actual occupation of the demised premises (*Webb* v *Pollmount Ltd* [1966] 1 All ER 481, involving an option to purchase). If, however, the demised premises comprise unregistered land, Michelle should have registered the option as a Class C(iv) (estate contract) land charge against the Earl of Dover, pursuant to the Land Charges Act 1972, in order to ensure that Buzby Property Ltd (as assignee purchasers) were bound by the same (*Kitney* v *MEPC Ltd* [1977] 1 WLR 981). Thus, it would seem that in the context of unregistered land the option would be void (for lack of registration) as against her current landlords. In this connection, it makes no difference that Buzby Property Ltd may have, in fact, known of the existence of the unregistered option. It may be that Michelle could claim that Buzby were estopped (e.g., by acquiescence) from asserting the invalidity of the option (*Taylor Fashions* v *Liverpool Victoria Trustees* [1982] QB 133), but there is nothing on the facts to suggest this.

Lastly, the landlords contend that the option is no longer exercisable by Michelle because she assigned her leasehold estate to Malcolm last year. Although, undoubtedly, the option is personal to Michelle and ceases to have effect upon assignment under the terms of the lease, we are told that Malcolm has not (to date) been registered as the new proprietor of the property. The point arose in *Brown & Root Technology Ltd* v *Sun Alliance & London Assurance Co. Ltd* [1997] 18 EG 123, where the Court of Appeal held that, in relation to the operation of a tenant's break clause, the assignment of the legal estate in the lease was not effective as the assignee was never registered as the proprietor. The assignment in the break clause meant assignment of the legal estate, which remained with the tenant. On the same reasoning, Michelle is not debarred from exercising the option on this ground because she remains the registered proprietor of the shop.

Q Question 4

'The separate interest of landlord and tenant in leased buildings present problems which are at their most acute in the considerations relating to insurance, reinstatement of damaged property and the division of insurance moneys if the buildings are destroyed.'

Discuss this proposition and illustrate your answer from the decided cases.

Commentary

There have been several important cases concerning the interpretation and application of covenants to insure. Invariably, the courts will determine such disputes with reference to the wording of the lease and the construction of the particular covenant in question.

Landlord and tenant courses differ as to the amount of time devoted to the topic of insurance. If your lecturer makes only passing reference to the subject, this is a good indication that it is unlikely to feature in the examination.

For a good summary of the case law, see Williams, D., 'The Covenant to Insure' (1985) 274 EG 577.

- If landlord obliged to insure under terms of the lease, no implied obligation that he should place insurance with insurer with lowest quotation: *Bandar Property (Holdings) Ltd* v *SJ Darwen (Successors) Ltd* (1968) and *Havenridge Ltd* v *Boston Dyers Ltd* (1994)

- Application of insurance moneys can give rise to problems between landlord and tenant: Compare *Re King (Deceased) Robinson* v *Gray* (1963) with *Beacon Carpets Ltd* v *Kirby* (1984). If obligation to insure satisfied at tenant's expense, it will enure for the benefit of both landlord and tenant so that former obliged to use money towards reinstatement: *Mumford Hotels Ltd* v *Wheler* (1964)

- Consider effect of Fires Prevention (Metropolis) Act 1774, s. 83: *Reynolds* v *Phoenix Assurance Co. Ltd* (1978). If no notice served by tenant under the 1774 Act, tenant in precarious position in the absence of express provision to reinstate: *Leeds* v *Cheetham* (1827)

·Q· Suggested answer

A well-drafted lease will provide for either the landlord or the tenant to execute a policy of insurance for the premises against risks such as fire, vandalism, flooding etc. Often, it will be the landlord who covenants to insure, but it is the tenant who will bear the burden of meeting the cost of the insurance premiums which are often made payable as additional rent. In such cases, the courts will not imply a term to the effect that the landlord should safeguard the tenant's financial interests by placing the insurance with the insurer who provides the lowest quotation. See *Bandar Property Holdings Ltd* v *JS Darwen (Successors) Ltd* [1968] 2 All ER 305, where Roskill J held that a term that the landlord should place the insurance so as not to impose an unnecessarily heavy burden on the tenant would not be implied. The decision was followed in *Havenridge Ltd* v *Boston Dyers Ltd* [1994] EGCS 53, where the Court of Appeal reiterated the principle that it was sufficient for the landlord to prove that the premium paid was no greater than the going rate for that insurer in the normal course of his business at the time (see also, *Berrycroft Management Co. Ltd* v *Sinclair Gardens Investments (Kensington) Ltd* [1997] 22 EG 141 (CA)).

On occasion, where the tenant has undertaken to effect the necessary insurance cover for the property, the landlord reserves in his own favour a power of veto as to the appropriateness of the insurer in question. In such cases, the landlord's power of veto is valid and the landlord's consent is a condition precedent to the insurance being effected; and in the absence of any express provision to the contrary, the landlord is not under any implied obligation to act reasonably in the withholding of consent (*Tredegar* v *Harwood* [1929] AC 72).

If the premises are destroyed or damaged, for example, by fire, the question of the application of the insurance moneys can often pose difficult problems as between landlord and tenant. In *Re King (Deceased) Robinson* v *Gray* [1963] Ch 459, the tenant had covenanted to keep the premises in repair; at her own expense, to insure the premises against fire in the joint names of the landlord and tenant; and to apply the insurance moneys in rebuilding. When the premises were destroyed by fire, the insurance moneys were paid in the joint names of the parties, but reinstatement was not possible owing to a local authority's compulsory acquisition of the property. The Court of Appeal held that the tenant was entitled to the whole of the insurance moneys since the landlord's only interest therein was as security for the performance by the tenant of her obligations to repair and reinstate and that, as the premiums had been paid by the tenant to meet her obligations, the moneys belonged to her.

In *Beacon Carpets Ltd* v *Kirby* [1984] 3 WLR 489, the insurance moneys under a policy effected by the landlord in the joint names of the parties for their 'respective rights and interests' proved insufficient to pay for full reinstatement after a fire destroyed the building. The Court of Appeal held that the basic right of the parties was to have the insurance moneys applied in rebuilding for their respective benefit. However, because the parties had by their own acts released that right without agreeing how the moneys were to be dealt with, it could only be inferred that, in default of agreement, they were treating the insurance moneys as standing in the place of the building which would otherwise have been replaced. It followed that the insurance moneys belonged to the parties in shares proportionate to their respective interests in the property insured. *Re King*, above, was distinguished since that case dealt only with rights in the insurance moneys once the prime purpose of rebuilding had been frustrated by the actions of a third party, and did not affect the case (as in *Beacon*) where the parties were treating the insurance moneys as standing in the place of the building.

Where the landlord's obligation to insure is satisfied at the tenant's expense, it will enure for the benefit of *both* the landlord and the tenant, and accordingly the landlord will be obliged to use the insurance moneys, if called upon to do so, towards the reinstatement of the demised premises (*Mumford Hotels Ltd* v *Wheler* [1964] Ch 117). In this case, the lease did not contain an express covenant to reinstate. When the premises were destroyed by fire, the insurance moneys were paid to the landlord, who refused to reinstate the property. The court held that the issue was not whether a covenant to reinstate should be implied, but whether the true inference was that the landlord should be treated as insuring on her own behalf or for the joint benefit of herself and the tenant. In the circumstances, the landlord's obligation to insure, at the tenant's expense, was intended to be for the benefit of both the landlord and the tenant, so that the landlord was obliged to use the insurance moneys to reinstate the premises if called upon to do so.

The Fires Prevention (Metropolis) Act 1774, s. 83, provides that where the demised premises are burnt down, demolished or damaged by fire, the party who has not expressly covenanted to insure the property (e.g., the tenant) may require the insurance moneys paid to the insuring party (e.g., the landlord) to be spent on the reinstatement of the premises. In *Reynolds* v *Phoenix Assurance Co. Ltd* (1978) 247 EG 995, the claimants had written to request that the defendant insurers lay out and expend moneys towards reinstating the fire-damaged premises. They made this request in order to bring into effect the provisions of the 1774 Act. The court, however, held that the Act was intended to deal with a different situation, namely, to prevent the insurance moneys being paid to an insured (e.g., the landlord) who might make away with them. It was not intended to apply to a case where the insured and the person serving the notice were one and the same person.

In the event that property has been demised to the tenant on a full-repairing lease and the premises have been destroyed by fire with no notice having been served under the 1774 Act, it seems that the tenant, in the absence of express provision, has no equity to compel his landlord to expend the insurance moneys on the demised premises (*Leeds* v *Cheetham* (1827) 1 Sim 146). Such a tenant also remains bound, despite the fire, to abide by his own repairing and rental obligations. However, today, developments in the doctrine of frustration may offer the tenant a remedy in this regard (*National Carriers Ltd* v *Panalpina (Northern) Ltd* [1981] AC 675). From the standpoint of the tenant, it would seem sensible to include a covenant for insurance moneys to be applied towards reinstatement in the lease which would cover such an eventuality.

Q Question 5

Foxgrove Estates plc holds the registered freehold title to a block of 20 flats in central London. Each flat has been demised on identical 125-year leases, with all leaseholders belonging to a tenants' association recognised by the freeholder.

In the past few months, it has come to the attention of the surveyors acting for the freeholder that certain maintenance works are required to the block. In a report prepared by the surveyors, these works have been detailed as:

(i) replacement of all wooden windows (all being rotten) with double-glazed units;

(ii) replacement of ten broken tiles to the roof of the building.

The landlord's surveyors estimate the total cost of this work to be £25,000 and take the view that each tenant should contribute equally to the costs, partly raised from the existing service charge fund with the balance being made up in this year's annual service charge.

Each long lease provides that the landlord is liable, *inter alia*, for 'the repair and maintenance of the property and keeping the same in good condition'. Each lease also makes provision for the landlord to be able to recoup the costs of 'these works' through levying a 'fair proportion' of the same from each leaseholder by way of an annual service charge and, in the event of disagreement, the dispute to be settled by arbitration.

In the light of the advice given by its surveyors, Foxgrove Estates plc now wishes to carry out the proposed works, but is concerned that the tenants' association is minded to object to some or all of the works and the costs involved. Foxgrove Estates plc is also desirous of replacing the roof tiles immediately as this is considered urgent by its surveyors.

Advise Foxgroves Estates plc.

Commentary

This question concerns the law relating to the levying of service charges for maintenance works in the context of long leases. In particular, the question requires you to demonstrate knowledge of the following matters:

(1) the general nature and operation of service charges in the context of long leases;

(2) the recent changes to the law on consultation requirements as brought into effect by s. 20ZA of the Landlord and Tenant Act 1985 (as amended by the Commonhold and

Leasehold Reform Act 2002) and the Service Charges (Consultation Requirements) (England) Regulations 2003;

(3) the law relating to the calculation of the tenant's proportion of the costs;

(4) the law relating to the resolution of service charge disputes.

• **Outline the relevant legislation, as amended by the Commonhold and Leasehold Reform Act 2002**

• **Consider whether the proposed works are permitted under the lease:** *Sutton (Hastoe) Housing Association* v *Williams* **(1988)**

• **How should the service charge be calculated in respect of each tenant's share? Consider again the** *Sutton* **case, above**

• **Consider whether the arbitration clause prevents the LVT having jurisdiction to determine any dispute: s. 27(A) of the 2002 Act**

• **How will the statutory consultation requirements apply? Examine the procedures relating to (1) notice of intention (2) obtaining estimates (3) notice of estimates and (4) notice after entering into a contract. No exception for urgent works, so Foxgrove must apply to LVT for a consultation dispensation: s. 20Z(1) of the Landlord and Tenant Act 1985, as substituted by s. 151 of the 2002 Act**

ːϙ̈ː Suggested answer

Most long residential leases will invariably contain provision for the landlord to repair and maintain the property and/or offer services to leaseholders, with provision in the lease for the landlord to recoup the costs through an annual service charge levied from the leaseholders. The Landlord and Tenant Act 1985 (as amended by the Landlord and Tenant Act 1987) was the first statute passed to give long residential leaseholders a degree of protection in relation to the levying of service charges. In particular, the 1985 Act introduced various detailed requirements which were designed to ensure that landlords consult long lessees of dwellings in relation to proposed service charges.

Further substantial changes to the 1985 Act have been introduced recently by the Commonhold and Leasehold Reform Act 2002, which came into force on October 31 2003. In particular, a fresh consultation regime has been brought into effect by virtue of a new s. 20ZA (replacing s. 20 of the 1985 Act), with detailed consultation requirements set out in the Service Charges (Consultation Requirements) (England) Regulations 2003, which also came into force on October 31 2003.

Section 18(1) of the 1985 Act defines a service charge as, *inter alia*, '. . . an amount payable by a tenant of a dwelling as part of or in addition to the rent . . . which is payable directly or indirectly for services, repairs, maintenance, or insurance or the landlord's costs of management . . .'. Interestingly, the 2002 Act amends this definition to include 'improvements'. The 1985 Act also provides that only those service charges 'reasonably incurred' are payable by a leaseholder to a landlord: s. 19(1).

Many service charge disputes relating to the 'reasonableness' of the sums sought by landlords are dealt with by the Leasehold Valuation Tribunal (LVT). In this connection, changes introduced by the 2002 Act have generally broadened the jurisdiction of such tribunals in relation to service charge disputes. A new s. 27A to the 1985 Act (introduced by the 2002 Act) provides that an application may be made to an LVT for a determination whether a service charge is payable and, if it is, as to the person by whom it is payable, the person to whom it is payable, the amount which is payable, the date at or by which it is payable, and the manner in which it is payable: s. 27A(1). By s. 27A(2), equivalent provision is made for future or proposed service charge costs. Following the amendments introduced by the 2002 Act, it will now normally be the LVT (and not the court) that has jurisdiction to decide whether to waive s. 20ZA consultation requirements.

In relation to the works proposed by Foxgrove, certain specific matters need to be considered: (1) whether the works proposed are works permitted by the lease; (2) the impact of the service charge clause on the calculation of each tenant's share; (3) whether the arbitration clause prevents the LVT from having jurisdiction over any dispute; and (4) the applicability and operation of any statutory consultation requirements.

(1) Whether the works are permitted by the lease

If the proposed works are outside of the landlord's repairing obligations as defined in the lease, Foxgrove will not be entitled to seek reimbursement of these costs as service charges. In each case, it is a question of construing the wording of the landlord's obligations and seeing whether the works fall within the relevant covenant. The covenant here states that the landlord is liable, *inter alia*, 'for the repair and maintenance of the property and keeping the same in good condition', which will cover the renewal of existing defective parts of the whole: see, *Lurcott* v *Wakely* [1911] 1 KB 905 and *Calthorpe* v *McOscar* [1924] 1 KB 716. In particular, it has been held that replacing singled-glazed windows with double-glazing is a genuine repair where the existing windows are rusted, because repair included the replacement of worn out parts: *Minja Properties Ltdr* v *Cussins Property Group Ltd* [1998] 2 EGLR 52. By contrast, however, in *Mullaney* v *Maybourne Grange (Croydon) Management Co.* (1986) 277 EGLR 70, where a landlord sought to recover a proportion of the cost of replacing wood-framed windows with double glazed and maintenance free windows throughout a block of flats, the cost was held irrecoverable because the new windows were treated as long term improvements. More relevant to our case, however, is the decision in *Sutton (Hastoe) Housing Association* v *Williams* (1988) HLR 321, where the Court of Appeal held recoverable from the tenants the cost of replacing rotten wooden windows with double glazed ones by way of service charge on the basis that the service charge provision in the lease allowed recovery of costs of improvements. In particular, the relevant clause allowed the landlord to recover by way of service charge the costs of 'maintaining, repairing, renewing and in all ways keeping in good condition the block . . .'. The requirement of 'keeping in good condition' is similarly to be found in the instant lease thereby entitling Foxgrove to recover the cost of improvement works. I would advise, therefore, that all the works proposed by Foxgrove are works within the ambit of the repairing covenant.

(2) The impact of the service charge clause on the calculation of each tenant's share

The proportion of the costs payable by an individual tenant will usually be specified in the lease, often in percentage terms. Sometimes, it will be expressed by reference to the proportion that the floor area (or rateable value) bears to that of the building as a whole. Alternatively, as in our case, it will be expressed simply as a 'fair proportion' of the cost of the works. In *Sutton (Hastoe) Housing Association* v *Williams* [1988] 1 EGLR 70, the lease required the tenant to pay a reasonable part of the costs of works to a block of flats, where the landlord had replaced all the windows. It was held that the tenant's share was a reasonable part of the total costs of repair even though each tenant was, in effect, paying the whole of the cost of replacing the windows to his own flat: see also, *Rapid Results College* v *Angell* (1986) 277 EG 856 and *Pole Properties* v *Feinberg* (1981) 43 P & CR 121. This suggests that, instead of each tenant paying an equal share of the cost of the works (i.e., £1,250), each will be responsible (by way of fair proportion) for the cost attributable to his (or her) own flat. So, if tenant A has more wooden windows than tenant B, the former will pay more by way of service charge.

(3) Whether the arbitration clause prevents the LVT having jurisdiction over any dispute over the proposed service charge

Jurisdiction to decide liability to pay service charges is now conferred upon the LVT by virtue of s. 27A(1)(3) of the 1985 Act. This is not an exclusive jurisdiction but runs parallel to that of the county court: s. 27(A)(7) and s. 19(4)(5). The county court has power, however, to transfer proceedings within the LVT jurisdiction and give effect to the LVT determination as an order of the court: sch. 12, para. 3 to the 2002 Act.

The jurisdiction of the LVT in relation to service charge disputes has been clarified in specific respects by the 2002 Act: s. 27(A). Prior to the 2002 Act, the LVT's remit was restricted to determining whether service charges were reasonably incurred and/or works carried out were of a reasonable standard. Now, the LVT has jurisdiction to decide any issue as to the liability to pay service charges whether 'alleged to be payable' (under the former s. 19(2A) of the 1985 Act) or already paid. (On this point, the decision in *Dajean Properties Ltd* v *London LVT* [2002] L & TR 5 has been effectively reversed by the 2002 Act). The new s. 27A(2) now provides that applications may be made to the LVT to determine whether a service charge is payable 'whether or not any payment has been made', and s. 27A(4) states that 'the tenant is not to be taken to have agreed or admitted any matter by reason only of having made any payment.'

Prior to the 2002 Act, LVT's could not adjudicate in relation to a service charge dispute over any matter which 'under an arbitration agreement to which the tenant is a party is to be referred to arbitration': see, the old s. 19(2)(c) of the 1985 Act. Under the 2002 Act, however, applications to the LVT are now only precluded where the tenant has actually agreed to go to arbitration after a service charge dispute has arisen: s. 27(A)(4). Apart from this situation, the existence of an arbitration clause does not now, by itself, bar the LVT having jurisdiction to determine a service charge dispute. I would advise, therefore, that the existence of an arbitration clause in our case will not prevent either party from seeking a determination from the LVT on the level of service charge claimed.

(4) The applicability and operation of any statutory consultation requirements

The changes introduced by the 2002 Act (and the Regulations thereunder) strengthen the requirement of landlords to 'consult' tenants in relation to service charge matters. The consultation requirements now apply where any one tenant's contribution exceeds the prescribed threshold of £250; this means that Foxgrove will need to calculate each tenant's contribution in order to know whether consultation is required. In our case, the proposed cost to each tenant clearly exceeds this figure, so the new consultation procedures (as set out in Pt 2 of the Regulations) must be followed. In summary, this means that Foxgrove must comply with four basic procedural steps:

Notice of intention

Notice must be given (in writing) to each tenant and any recognised tenants' association of the landlord's intention to carry out 'qualifying works' (i.e., works to the building or any other premises) and the notice must include: (i) a general description of the proposed works or details of the time and place when a description can be inspected, (ii) the landlord's reasons for considering it necessary to carry out the works, (iii) a statement inviting observation in relation to the proposed works, (iv) the address to which any observations should be sent, a statement that they should be delivered within 30 days of the notice and the date when the 30 day period expires, and (v) a statement inviting proposals within the 30 day period of the persons from whom the landlord should try to obtain an estimate. Foxgrove must also supply facilities to the tenants to inspect the description of the proposed works, free of charge. Whilst it is obliged to have regard to the observations received, it is not bound to accept them.

Obtaining estimates

If Foxgrove, having complied with step 1 (above), receive more than one nomination as to whom it should approach for an estimate, it should try to obtain an estimate from at least one person nominated by a tenant and at least one person nominated by an association. In short, it must approach the most popular nominee. (If there is a dead heat, the choice of who to approach is the landlords).

Notice of estimates

Foxgrove must supply the tenants with a statement containing at least two estimates, a summary of the observations received in step 1 (above), and the its response as landlord. The estimates must also be made available to the tenants for inspection. At least one of the estimates must be from a wholly unconnected person. Where an estimate has been obtained from a person nominated by the tenants, that estimate must be included. The notice of estimates to be served on the tenants by the landlord must, as in step 1, include the following: (i) the hours and place where estimates can be inspected, (ii) an invitation to make observations, (iii) the address where observations should be sent, a statement that they should be sent within 30 days of the notice and the date when the 30 day notice period expires, and (iv) where the observations have been made by tenants in response to step 1, a summary of those observations and the landlord's response to them. Again, in this connection, Foxgrove must have regard to any observations received.

Notice after entering into a contract

Finally, once the above procedural steps have been taken, Foxgrove must give a further notice, within 21 days of entering into a contract to carry out the works, unless the estimate chosen was made by a nominated person, or was the lowest. Where a further notice is required, the landlord must include in its notice: (i) its reasons for awarding the contract, or a place and time when reasons can be inspected, and (ii) a summary of any observations and the landlord's response to them.

Foxgrove must comply with these consultation procedures. Significantly, (as regard the tiles), there is no exception for urgent works, and thus if this work is carried out without consultation, Foxgrove will need to apply to the LVT for a dispensation in this regard, either before or after the works have been effected. If the replacement of the tiles is really so urgent that it must be undertaken before any application to the LVT (for a consultation dispensation) can take place, Foxgrove will have to take the chance that the LVT will not find the carrying out of this emergency work unreasonable in the circumstances and thus waive the consultation requirements in this regard: see, s. 20Z(1) of the 1985 Act, as substituted by s. 151 of the 2002 Act.

If Foxgrove does not follow the new consultation procedures (assuming no waiver of the consultation requirements is upheld by the LVT), it will be prevented from recovering anything above the £250 threshold from each tenant: *Martin* v *Maryland Estates* [1999] 26 EG 151.

Further reading

Ackland, M., 'Insurance — The Stuff of Nightmares' (2001) EG 134.

Garton J., 'Uninsured Risks — Are these in Your Cover?' [2000] EG 132.

Holbrook J., 'Unfair Terms in Leases and Mortgages' (2000) L & T Rev 38.

Ross, J., 'Lack of Notice: Problems on Rent Review' (2002) NLJ 581.

9 Q&A

Termination of leases

Introduction

In this chapter, you will find questions on forfeiture of leases, the doctrine of frustration, repudiation, surrender, tenant's right to fixtures and tenant's break notices.

Questions on forfeiture are quite popular with examiners. The forfeiture of the lease is, of course, the primary remedy of a landlord faced with a tenant who has defaulted in the payment of his rent or other obligations in the lease. At the same time, the lease will invariably be a valuable asset which the tenant will seek to preserve in most cases by seeking relief from forfeiture. There is a vast body of case law on the subject as well as important statutory provisions. See, generally, Pawlowski, M., *The Forfeiture of Leases*, London: Sweet & Maxwell Ltd, 1993. Note that s. 81 of the Housing Act 1996 precludes a landlord, in relation to premises let as a dwelling, from exercising a right of forfeiture for failure to pay a service charge unless the amount of the service charge is admitted by the tenant or has been the subject of determination by a court or arbitral tribunal: *Mohammadi* v *Anston Investments Ltd* [2003] EWCA Civ 981. This provision has been extended to cover non-payment of administration charges: s. 170 of the Commonhold and Leasehold Reform Act 2002. The 2002 Act also provides that a s. 146 notice cannot validly be served in respect of a long lease of a dwelling unless the fact that there is a breach has been determined by an appropriate court or tribunal or admitted by the tenant: s. 168. Moreover, forfeiture may not be used at all if the amount of rent, service charge or administration charges unpaid is less than an amount prescribed by Regulations, which cannot be more than £500: s. 167.

In 1985, the Law Commission, as part of its programme for the codification of the law of landlord and tenant, published a report entitled 'Forfeiture of Tenancies' (Law Com. No. 142, 1985), which examined various defects in the current law and recommended the replacement of the present structure with an entirely new system. In 1994, the Commission published a further Report ('Landlord and Tenant Law: Termination of Tenancies Bill', Law Com. No. 221, 1994) which contained a draft bill implementing the Commission's proposals. In 1998, the Law Commission produced a Consultative Document relating specifically to the landlord's current right to forfeit by actual physical re-entry onto the demised premises. It recommended, contrary to the previously held view, that a right of physical re-entry should be retained under the proposed termination order scheme and should be placed on a statutory footing which would integrate it properly with the rest of the scheme: Pawlowski, M., 'Termination of Tenancies by Physical Re-entry', (1998) 2 L & T Review, pp. 24–27. Since this is an important topic of study, we have included an essay question on the latest Law Commission's proposals: Law Comm CP No. 174 and Pawlowski, M., 'New Consultation on Termination of Tenancies for Tenant Default' (2004) 8 L & T Rev 31. See Question 3.

It was once thought that the doctrine of repudiatory breach (to be found in the law of contract) had no application to leases (*Total Oil Great Britain Ltd* v *Thompson Garages (Biggin Hill) Ltd* [1972] 1 QB 318, *per* Lord Denning MR, at p. 324). This view no longer represents the law (*Hussein* v *Mehlman* [1992] 32 EG 59). However, the extent to which the doctrine may be applied universally to leases has not yet been fully worked out. We have, therefore, included a question on this interesting topic for those students wishing to explore some of the less charted waters of landlord and tenant law! For further reading, see Pawlowski, M., 'Repudiatory Breach in Leases' [1994] Lit. Vol. 14/1, pp. 7–14; 'Repudiatory Breach in the Leasehold Context' [1999] Conv 150; 'The Application of the Doctrine of Mitigation of Damages to Leases' [1995] *Liverpool Law Review*, vol. XVII(2), pp. 173–88; 'Contractual Termination of leases: Unresolved Issues' (1998) 13 JPL 4.

Although the House of Lords has held that the doctrine of frustration applies to leases (*National Carriers Ltd* v *Panalpina Northern Ltd* [1981] AC 675), the actual circumstances in which a lease can be frustrated will be rare. Once again, an interesting topic which we have coupled with a question on repudiatory breach: see Question 4 (and Question 3, **Chapter 16**).

For the sake of completeness, we have also included a problem question on surrender and tenant's fixtures: see Questions 5 and 6. There is also a question on tenant's break notices: Question 7.

Q Question 1

In 1990, Lillian acquired the freehold of a shop in a shopping parade. The shop had been let on a 30-year lease in January 1989. The rent under the lease was payable quarterly in advance. The lease contained, *inter alia*, covenants against assignment or sub-letting without consent, with a right of re-entry exercisable on breach of any tenant's covenant. Michael was the original tenant of the shop which he ran as a pizza takeaway.

In 2002, Michael had asked Lillian for consent to assign the lease, but Lillian took so long over the matter that the potential assignee withdrew. In January 2004, he found another assignee, Norma, who had satisfactory references. Not wishing to risk any delay, Michael assigned the lease to Norma without asking Lillian. The following month, Lillian found out about this. Her agent demanded rent by mistake for the March 2004 quarter. The rent was again demanded for the June 2004 quarter but this time qualified by the words 'without prejudice'.

In July 2004, Lillian served notice on Norma under the Law of Property Act 1925, s. 146. One day later, she repossessed the property while it was unoccupied and changed the locks.

Advise Norma as to her rights, if any, in relation to the property.

Commentary

This is a fairly typical question on the forfeiture of leases. It raises a number of issues, each requiring discussion and illustration through statute and case law. If you miss the key point on waiver, your marks will be very low!

Ideally, in a question of this sort, you need to tackle the various issues as they arise chronologically on the facts. It is important that you structure your answer carefully so that it deals with each issue in a logical sequence. The tendency, under exam conditions, is simply to write down the first relevant thing that comes into your head. If you spend a few minutes *planning your answer*, this will undoubtedly pay dividends and earn you higher marks.

- Although Michael in breach of covenant in assigning without consent, consider whether Lillian has waived the breach. Distinction between 'continuing breach' and 'once and for all breach': *Scala House & District Property Co. Ltd v Forbes* (1974)

- Unambiguous demand for rent constitutes a waiver: *Welch v Birrane* (1975). Consider waiver by agents: *Central Estates (Belgravia) Ltd v Woolgar (No. 2)* (1972). Demand for rent qualified by words such as 'without prejudice' still a waiver: *Segal Securities Ltd v Thoseby* (1963)

- Breach of covenant against assignment incapable of remedy: *Expert Clothing Service & Sales Ltd v Hillgate House Ltd* (1986). But Lillian's re-entry too early: *Fuller v Judy Properties Ltd* (1992)

- Norma may also safeguard her position by seeking relief against forfeiture: Law of Property Act 1925, s. 146(2) and *Billson v Residential Apartments Ltd* (1992)

:Q: Suggested answer

The central issue is whether Lillian's physical re-entry onto the premises in July 2004 was lawful. If not, Norma will be able to seek a declaration that the lease has not become forfeited and that Lillian's purported re-entry was a trespass.

It is important to stress from the outset that the assignment, despite being made without Lillian's consent, is not void but *voidable* at the option of the landlord.

Accordingly, Norma will take a defeasible title (i.e., subject to Lillian's right of forfeiture) (*Williams* v *Earle* (1868) LR 3 QB 739).

The lease contains a qualified covenant against assignment and sub-letting. Such a covenant is subject to the further proviso that the landlord's consent shall not be unreasonably withheld (Landlord and Tenant Act 1927, s. 19(1)). The section, however, does not absolve the tenant from the formality of seeking consent, so that if he goes ahead without seeking consent (as Michael has done in the present case) he commits a breach of the covenant regardless of the reasonableness of the transaction (*Eastern Telegraph Co. Ltd* v *Dent* [1899] 1 QB 835).

Although Michael was clearly in breach of covenant in assigning the lease to Norma without seeking Lillian's consent, the question arises whether Lillian can be said to have waived the breach so as to disentitle her from relying on it as a ground of forfeiture. We are told that Lillian, having actual knowledge of the breach, demanded rent (through her agent) for the March 2004 quarter. The effect of a waiver depends on the nature of the breach giving rise to the landlord's election to forfeit. In this connection, the tenant's breach will be classified either as a 'continuing' breach, or as a 'once and for all breach'. If the breach is of a continuing nature, there is a continually recurring cause of forfeiture and the waiver will operate only in relation to past breaches (i.e., breaches committed in the period prior to the landlord's act which constitutes the waiver). Thus, a landlord who has waived a continuing breach for a period of time will not be precluded from subsequently ending his waiver and enforcing the covenant in the lease. Where, on the other hand, the breach is classified as a 'once and for all breach', the right to forfeit for that breach will be lost upon waiver. A covenant against assigning or sub-letting has been held to be a once and for all breach (*Walrond* v *Hawkins* (1875) LR 10 CP 342 and *Scala House & District Property Co. Ltd* v *Forbes* [1974] 1 QB 575).

Moreover, an unambiguous demand for rent due after the breach constitutes an act of waiver. Thus, in *Welch* v *Birrane* (1975) 29 P & CR 102, the landlords refused the tenant permission to assign his lease to sitting sub-tenants in the demised premises on the ground that the proposed assignee might become entitled to enfranchisement under the Leasehold Reform Act 1967. The tenant, nevertheless, assigned the lease as originally intended. The landlords continued to demand rent from the tenant despite the breach of covenant and claimed forfeiture. Lawson J, following the decision of Swanwick J in *David Blackstone Ltd* v *Burnetts (West End) Ltd* [1973] 1 WLR 1487, held that the landlords, by demanding rent accruing due *after* the breach of covenant, had effectively waived the forfeiture. See also *Van Haarlam* v *Kasner Charitable Trust* [1992] 36 EG 135.

The fact that the March quarter rent was demanded by Lillian's agent by mistake will not affect the position. Whether a particular act, coupled with the requisite knowledge of the breach, constitutes a waiver is a question of law to be considered objectively without regard to the intention of the landlord, or the belief or understanding of the tenant (*Matthews* v *Smallwood* [1910] 1 Ch 777). Thus, since it is irrelevant *quo animo* an act of waiver was made, knowledge of the breach by the landlord's agent will be sufficient even where the act of acknowledgement of the lease is that of another agent who is unaware of the breach (*Central Estates (Belgravia) Ltd* v *Woolgar (No. 2)* [1972] 1 WLR 1048). In this case, the landlords' managing agents instructed their staff to refuse all rent from the tenant. The instructions failed to reach one of the clerks who sent out a routine demand for the quarter's rent and a subsequent receipt. The Court of Appeal held that the landlord's demand for the rent through their agents, with knowledge of the breach, effected a waiver of the forfeiture. Accordingly, the fact that Lillian's agent did not intend to waive the forfeiture by demanding rent for the March quarter will make no difference to the result.

As to the demand of rent for the June quarter, there is little doubt that a demand for rent qualified by such words as 'without prejudice' or 'under protest' will operate as an effective waiver (*Segal Securities Ltd* v *Thoseby* [1963] 1 QB 887). In order, however, to constitute a waiver, the demand must have been communicated to the tenant. Thus, there will be no waiver if the demand has been prepared and sent by the landlord but never received by the tenant (*Trustees of Henry Smith's Charity* v *Willson* [1983] QB 316 and *David Blackstone Ltd* v *Burnetts (West End) Ltd* [1973] 1 WLR 1487, *per* Swanwick J, at p. 1499). In these circumstances, the uncommunicated rent demand can be withdrawn by the landlord at any time before it is received by the tenant. In the present case, it is assumed that both demands were actually received by Michael.

Quite apart from the waiver of the breach, we are told that Lillian repossessed the property a day after service of the s. 146 notice. Since the breach of a covenant against assignment is technically incapable of remedy as a matter of law (see *Expert Clothing Service & Sales Ltd* v *Hillgate House Ltd* [1986] Ch 340 and contrast *Savva* v *Houssein* [1996] 47 EG 138, involving a breach of a negative covenant not to display signs or alter the premises without the landlord's consent, which was held to be capable of remedy), the s. 146 notice need not require the tenant to remedy it and the landlord may proceed with his action or physical re-entry with little delay provided he gives the tenant enough time to consider his legal position: *Courtney Lodge Management Ltd* v *Blake* [2004] civ 975. EWCA. In such circumstances, it has been held that 14 days is a sufficient time to elapse between the service of the notice and the date of re-entry (*Scala House & District Property Co. Ltd* v *Forbes* [1974] QB 575). In *Fuller* v *Judy Properties Ltd* [1992] 14 EG 106, involving a breach of covenant against assignment, seven days was held a reasonable time. In the present case, Lillian has re-entered just one day after the service of her s. 146 notice. This may be held an insufficient time and provide Norma with another basis for invalidating the forfeiture.

In addition to Norma bringing an action alleging trespass, she should be urged to safeguard her position by claiming, in the alternative, relief from forfeiture under s. 146(2) of the 1925 Act. This she can do despite Lillian's physical re-entry onto the premises (*Billson* v *Residential Apartments Ltd* [1992] 2 WLR 15). As assignee of the lease, she is the 'lessee' for the purposes of s. 146 of the 1925 Act (*Old Grovebury Manor Farm Ltd* v *Seymour Plant Sales & Hire Ltd (No. 2)* [1979] 1 WLR 1397) and so she will be concerned to avoid the forfeiture, and not the original tenant, Michael.

◾ Question 2

(a) What are the principles governing relief from forfeiture in the case of failure by a tenant to comply with a covenant other than the payment of rent?

(b) Mary lets commercial premises to Tim at a rent of £35,000 per year. There is a forfeiture clause in the lease. Tim falls into arrears with the rent and Mary brings proceedings in the High Court for forfeiture of the lease.

Advise Tim as to whether he can seek relief from forfeiture.

What would be the position if the proceedings were brought in the county court?

Commentary

This is a question dealing specifically with relief from forfeiture for non-payment of rent and other breaches of covenant. The statutory provisions governing relief, particularly for non-payment of rent, are highly complex and you should attempt this question only if you are reasonably familiar with the relevant principles. The subject of relief from forfeiture is quite popular with examiners, so be warned!

For a brief summary, see Pawlowski, M., *The Forfeiture of Leases*, London: Sweet & Maxwell Ltd, 1993, pp. 10–16.

- Consider statutory power of relief for breaches of covenant (other than non-payment of rent) under Law of Property Act 1925, s. 146(2)

- Court has wide discretion to grant or refuse relief which will depend on a number of factors: *Hyman* v *Rose* (1912). Consider also special form of relief in respect of internal decorative repairs: Law of Property Act 1925, s. 147

- Consider effect of Common Law Procedure Act 1852, ss. 210–212 and Supreme Court Act 1981, s. 38(1): *Standard Pattern Co. Ltd* v *Ivey* (1962)

- Relief in the county court based upon the making of a suspended order for possession: County Courts Act 1984, s. 138(3) and *Di Palma* v *Victoria Square Property Ltd* (1986)

:Q: Suggested answer

(a) The court's inherent equitable jurisdiction to relieve against forfeiture of leases for wilful breaches of covenant (other than non-payment of rent), which was retrospectively resurrected by the House of Lords in *Shiloh Spinners Ltd* v *Harding* [1973] AC 691, is implicitly removed by the Law of Property Act 1925, s. 146, conferring statutory powers of relief in the landlord and tenant context (*Billson* v *Residential Apartments Ltd* [1991] 3 WLR 264). Thus, for example, if a tenant cannot obtain relief under s. 146(2) he has no recourse to any underlying equitable jurisdiction to be relieved against a wilful breach of covenant in order to preserve his lease.

The general statutory provisions relevant to relief against forfeiture for breaches of covenant (other than non-payment of rent) are contained in s. 146(2) of the 1925 Act. Under s. 146(2), the tenant is entitled to apply to the court (in the landlord's action or in an action brought by himself) for relief against forfeiture of his lease. The court may grant or refuse relief on terms as it thinks fit, and in the case of a breach of a repairing covenant the court will usually require the tenant to remedy the disrepair and make compensation to the landlord for any damage to the reversion before it grants such relief.

Section 146(2) provides that the court may grant or refuse relief, having regard to the proceedings and conduct of the parties and to all other circumstances, as it thinks fit. Moreover, in the case of relief, the court may grant it on such terms, if any, as to costs, expense damages, compensation, penalty, or otherwise, including the granting of an injunction to restrain any like breach in the future as, in the circumstances of each case, it thinks fit. The court's discretion to grant or refuse relief is very wide and will usually depend on any one or more of the following factors:

(a) whether the tenant is able and willing to remedy and/or recompense the landlord for the breach (*Duke of Westminster* v *Swinton* [1948] 1 KB 524);

(b) whether the breach was wilful (*Shiloh Spinners Ltd* v *Harding* [1973] AC 691);

(c) the gravity of the breach;

(d) the extent of the diminution in the value of the landlord's reversionary interest as compared to the value of the leasehold interest threatened with forfeiture (*Southern Depot Co. Ltd* v *British Railways Board* (1990) 2 EGLR 39);

(e) the conduct of the landlord (*Segal Securities Ltd* v *Thoseby* [1963] 1 QB 887);

(f) the personal qualifications of the tenant (*Bathurst* v *Fine* [1974] 1 WLR 905);

(g) the financial position of the tenant; and

(h) whether the breach involves an immoral/illegal user (*Egerton* v *Esplanade Hotels, London Ltd* [1947] 2 All ER 88).

While there is no doubt that the court's discretion to grant relief under s. 146(2) is very wide, it is equally clear that it must be exercised judicially, having regard to the circumstances of each individual case and to the specific matters referred to in s. 146(2), and with the object of ensuring that the landlord is not substantially prejudiced or damaged by the revival of the tenant's lease (*Hyman* v *Rose* [1912] AC 623).

A special form of relief is available to the tenant in respect of internal decorative repairs under s. 147 of the 1925 Act, which provides that the court may relieve the tenant from liability for such repairs if 'having regard to all the circumstances of the case (including in particular the length of the lessee's term or interest remaining unexpired), the court is satisfied that the landlord's notice is unreasonable'. The court's power under s. 147 is to grant relief not merely from forfeiture but from the need to do the decorative repairs at all.

If relief is granted by the court, the tenant will retain his lease as if it had never been forfeited.

(b) Tim can seek relief in the High Court under the Common Law Procedure Act 1852, ss. 210–212, and the Supreme Court Act 1981, s. 38(1) and (2).

Under s. 212 of the 1852 Act, Tim is entitled to be relieved in equity if at least six months' rent is in arrears and, at any time before the trial of Mary's action, he pays or tenders all the arrears and costs to Mary or into court. The relief under s. 212 will take the form of a stay of Mary's action and Tim will continue to hold the demised premises under his original lease without any new lease. In *Standard Pattern Co. Ltd* v *Ivey* [1962] Ch 432, it was held that relief under s. 212 only applied where six months' rent was in arrears, and accordingly a tenant could not, by payment of the sums necessary to meet the landlord's claim, compel a stay of proceedings under the section where only one quarter's rent was unpaid. Thus, if less than six months' rent is in arrears in the present case, Tim should be advised to invoke the court's jurisdiction to grant relief under s. 38(1) of the Supreme Court Act 1981 which is of more general application.

Under s. 210 of the 1852 Act, Tim will also be entitled to relief in equity at or after the trial of the landlord's action, if he pays all the arrears of rent and costs within six months of the execution of the order for possession.

In the county court, relief is based upon the making of a suspended order for possession. Under the County Courts Act 1984, s. 138(3), where the tenant seeks relief at the trial of the landlord's action, the court is obliged to order possession of the land to be given to the landlord at the expiration of such period, not being less than four weeks from the date of the order, as the court thinks fit, unless within that period the tenant pays into court all the rent in arrears and the costs of the action. The court has power, under s. 138(4), to extend the period for payment at any time before possession of the land is recovered by the landlord. If the tenant pays the rent due and costs within the time fixed under the order (or any extension thereof), he will continue to hold under the lease, but if he fails to pay within the time limit the order for possession will be enforced and the tenant will be barred from all relief (including relief in the High Court — see, *Di Palma* v *Victoria Square Property Ltd* [1986] Ch 150) except that afforded by s. 138(4) and (9A) of the 1984 Act.

Under s. 9A of the 1984 Act (inserted by the Administration of Justice Act 1985, s. 55(5)), the tenant has the right to apply for relief at any time within six months from the date on which the landlord recovers possession of the demised premises.

Q Question 3

'The Law Commission's proposals for termination proceedings are so obviously such an improvement on the present arrangements for forfeiture and the grant of relief that one is amazed that it has taken so long for this solution to the mess to be put forward'.

To what extent are the present arrangements a 'mess'? Do you agree with the comment that the proposals are an obvious improvement on the present arrangements?

Commentary

This is an essay question which is intended to test the student's knowledge of the broader issues surrounding the law of forfeiture of leases. The usual principles apply in tackling such questions in exam conditions — prepare a rough plan, structure your answer, do not waffle, make a series of points, write a conclusion.

For a survey of the Law Commission's proposals, see Peet, C., 'The Termination of Tenancies Bill' [1994] EG 9426, 133. See also Smith, P. F., 'Reform of the Law of Forfeiture' [1986] Conv 165, Pawlowski, M., *The Forfeiture of Leases*, London: Sweet & Maxwell, 1993, Ch. 12, Hutchinson, L., 'Law on Your Side' [1998] EG 9808, 149 and Pawlowski, M., 'Termination of Tenancies by Physical Re-entry' (1998) 2 L & T Review, pp. 24–27. The most recent proposals of the Law Commission were published in a Consultation Paper entitled 'Termination of Tenancies for Tenant Default' in January 2004: Law Comm CP No. 174. Your answer should reflect the most recent revisions to the Commission's general scheme: see further, Pawlowski, M., 'New Consultation on Termination of Tenancies for Tenant Default' (2004) 8 L & T Rev 31.

- Three major sources of difficulty: (1) doctrine of re-entry (2) doctrine of waiver and (3) separate regimes for forfeiture for non-payment of rent and all other breaches of covenant

- Doctrine of re-entry to be retained and placed on a statutory footing. Replacement of doctrine of waiver with simplified proposal. Removal of two regimes for forfeiture in favour of a unified structure

- Consider latest Law Commission proposals regarding peaceable re-entry, waiver and pre-action notice requirement

- Tenant's right to terminate under original scheme abandoned as being too innovative and unlikely to receive universal support

:Q: Suggested answer

The Law Commission in its report entitled 'Forfeiture of Tenancies' (Law Com. No. 142, 1985) noted three major sources of difficulty under the present law, namely:

(a)   the doctrine of re-entry;

(b)   the doctrine of waiver; and

(c)   the separate regimes for forfeiture for non-payment of rent and all other breaches of covenant.

Essentially, its report recommended abolition of the first two defects and assimilation of the rule of forfeiture for non-payment of rent and other breaches of covenant into a single, comprehensive code. The justification for such a radical change was that the present law is unnecessarily complicated, incoherent and may give rise to injustice.

Under the doctrine of re-entry, a landlord forfeits a lease by re-entry upon the demised premises and the lease terminates on the date on which the re-entry takes place. In cases where the landlord forfeits by bringing court proceedings for possession, a notional re-entry is deemed to take place from the date when the proceedings are served on the tenant (*Canas Property Co. Ltd* v *KL Television Services Ltd* [1970] 2 QB 433). This gives rise to the anomaly that, although the lease is notionally forfeited from that date, nevertheless the tenant remains in possession of the premises for an indefinite period until the final outcome of the landlord's proceedings. Accordingly, the date of the service of the proceedings has no real significance and there is no reason why it should mark the ending of the lease.

Because the lease is deemed to end at the time of re-entry, there is the further difficulty that all the obligations which it imposes upon the tenant terminate also at that time. The tenant will remain in possession for an indefinite period after forfeiture (pending his application for relief), and during this period he will be under no obligation to pay rent or to perform any of his other covenants in the lease unless he is subsequently granted relief from forfeiture. During this 'twilight period' (see *Meadows* v *Clerical, Medical and General Life Assurance Society* [1981] Ch 70, *per* Sir Robert Megarry V-C, at p. 78), the status of the lease is somewhat obscure, the landlord is deprived of his right to claim rent or to seek any equitable remedy (e.g., an injunction) to enforce the tenant's covenants, and any damages payable for breaches by a tenant of his covenant to repair are assessable only down to the service of the proceedings.

The anomalies surrounding the doctrine of re-entry can be illustrated by reference to the case of *Hynes* v *Twinsectra Ltd* [1995] 35 EG 136, where the Court of Appeal held that, despite a forfeiture, there was an existing tenancy sufficient for the purposes of allowing the tenant to make an application to acquire the freehold under the

Leasehold Reform Act 1967. The Court reached this decision largely on the basis of a subsisting claim for relief from forfeiture made by the tenant's predecessor in title. Although the landlord is effectively estopped from denying the continued existence of the forfeited lease, the lease remains in existence so far as the tenant is concerned at least until the final outcome of his application for relief: see *GS Fashions Ltd v B & Q plc* [1995] 09 EG 324, where it was held that the landlord, who by service of the writ had unequivocally elected to forfeit, was thereby prevented from subsequently disputing the validity of the forfeiture.

In view of these difficulties, the Commission initially recommended the abolition of the doctrine of re-entry and its replacement by a scheme under which (apart from termination by agreement) court proceedings and a termination order would always be necessary to end a lease, and until that time it would simply continue in full force. In its 1998 Consultative Document, however, the Commission recommended, contrary to its previously held view, that a right of physical re-entry should be retained and placed on a statutory footing which would integrate it properly with the rest of the termination order scheme. This change of view was prompted largely by concerns expressed by the commercial property industry that the landlord's right of physical re-entry should not be abolished on the ground that it provides an 'effective management tool' and is commonly used as a means of bringing a tenancy to an end quickly and in a cost-effective way in cases where there is no prospect of the tenant remedying the particular breach complained of. The most recent Commission's Consultation Paper (CP No. 174) suggests the introduction of a unilateral recovery of possession procedure to replace the current common law right of peaceable re-entry as an alternative means of terminating a tenancy other than by court order. The landlord would be obliged to serve a pre-action notice on the tenant as a preliminary to recovering possession in this way. This would be in-line with the Civil Procedure Rules and the impact of the Human Rights Act 1988.

The Commission viewed the doctrine of waiver of forfeiture as equally artificial. At present, the landlord may lose his right of forfeiture for a particular breach by the mere act of a demand or acceptance of rent irrespective of his intention. With the introduction of the scheme of termination orders, the lease would remain in existence until the court decided whether or not, in its discretion, to terminate it and rent would continue to be payable until that time. Accordingly, there would no longer be any justification for inferring a waiver from the mere demand or acceptance of rent, or, moreover, from any conduct by the landlord amounting merely to a recognition of the continued existence of the lease. Under its earlier proposals, the Commission recommended that the doctrine of waiver should be abolished and replaced with a new rule that the landlord would lose his right to seek a termination order only if his conduct was such that a reasonable tenant would believe and the actual tenant did in fact believe, that he (the landlord) would not seek a termination order. Not surprisingly, this cumbersome formulation has now been abandoned and it is proposed to replace the doctrine of waiver with a simple requirement that the landlord serve his pre-action notice on the tenant within a six-month period of becoming aware of the tenant default. However, a further proposal is that, in deciding whether to make an absolute termination order, the court should be required to have regard to the conduct of both the landlord and tenant before and during the proceedings. Thus, where the landlord's conduct had led the tenant to reasonably believe that he (the landlord) would not seek to terminate the tenancy in response to a particular default, then the court would be unlikely to grant a termination order.

The Commission also noted that the present distinction, in relation to relief against forfeiture, between cases involving non-payment of rent and other breaches of covenant, gave rise to unnecessary complexity in the law. The distinction has an historical basis in so far as, from early times, equity granted relief against non-payment of rent upon payment of the arrears and costs of the action, viewing the landlord's right to forfeit on this ground as no more than security for the payment of a specific sum of money. On the other hand, so far as other breaches of covenant were concerned, the old Court of Chancery considered that the forfeiture clause should be fully enforced (even if the default could be put right) unless there was some element of fraud, accident, mistake or surprise which rendered it inequitable to grant relief. Coupled with this attitude lay equity's inherent inability to compensate the landlord for any loss occasioned by a breach other than non-payment of rent by means of an appropriate award of damages.

While the jurisdiction to grant relief in non-rent cases was considerably extended by legislation during the 19th century, equity's inherent power to relieve in cases of non-payment of rent was also embodied in separate legislative provisions during this period, with the result that there now exist two parallel systems of relief, each operating to produce very similar results. Moreover, unnecessary differences exist between the granting of relief in the High Court and county court in cases involving non-payment of rent.

The Law Commission, accordingly, proposed the removal of these two regimes and their replacement by a much simplified, unified structure. There is no doubt that such a reform is long overdue, particularly because, as can be seen, the reason for having two separate systems for relief is largely historical. The upshot, therefore, is the proposed introduction of a streamlined statutory framework, which would require the landlord (with one exception) to always apply to the court for a termination order against a tenant who is in breach of covenant (including a failure to pay rent) or in breach of certain conditions of the tenancy. The one exception, as mentioned earlier, relates to the landlord's unilateral right to recover possession (upon service of a pre-action notice) in relation to any commercial premises, or residential premises (falling within the scheme) which are no longer occupied. Interestingly, the new code will apply only to residential tenancies granted for a term of at least 21 years. Other residential tenancies (in the private and public sector) will be subject to a different set of termination procedures currently proposed in the Commission's *Renting Homes* Report (Law Com. No. 284). No doubt, this will give rise to some complexity but it seems that separate codes for the two regimes cannot be avoided.

The most recent innovation (since the Commission's last proposals in 1998) is the pre-action notice requirement which is intended to apply in all cases where the landlord intends to terminate the tenancy for tenant default. The requirement of such a notice stems inevitably from the wider notion that the court process is to be viewed as very much a measure of last resort. Giving the tenant the opportunity to take action to put right the breach(es) within a specified period and providing due warning of the landlord's intentions is seen as not only safeguarding the rights of tenants but also the rights of those holding derivative interests (e.g., subtenants and mortgagees).

At present, where the landlord is in breach of his obligations under the lease, the tenant may have no means of bringing the relationship of landlord and tenant to an end, because his lease is unlikely to contain a right to terminate on the part of the tenant. The Commission, therefore, proposed originally the inclusion of a *tenant's* right to terminate in the new scheme. However, in its 1994 report ('Landlord and Tenant Law: Termination of Tenancies Bill', Law Com. No. 221, 1994), the Commission decided not to pursue its 1985 proposal for a new scheme of termination of tenancies by tenants, largely because this would be too innovative and unlikely to receive universal support. This is a pity, because the original structure would have vastly simplified the law by providing a system of termination orders under which either the landlord or the tenant would have been entitled to terminate the tenancy upon the fault of the other.

Q Question 4

In April 2002, Betty granted Jane a five-year tenancy of a hairdressing salon in Greenwich, London, at an annual rent of £15,000. The lease provided, *inter alia*, that Betty would 'keep and maintain the demised premises in good repair'. The property is approached from a small alleyway which leads to the main Greenwich High Street.

In May 2004, the ceiling to the property collapsed through old age. Jane immediately wrote to Betty and told her of the state of disrepair. To date, Betty has failed to acknowledge Jane's correspondence.

Two weeks ago, the local authority began major construction works to the Greenwich High Street which adjoins the alleyway. Jane has received a letter from the local authority stating that that alleyway will be blocked off for six months to allow the works to be carried out. As a result of the closure of the alleyway, Jane has suffered a 70 per cent reduction in her business.

Two days ago, Jane posted the keys to the premises back to Betty, after packing up her equipment and moving out of the property to a new location.

Advise Jane as to whether she is still liable for the rent to Betty for the remainder of the contractual term of the lease.

Commentary

This question requires you to consider in detail the House of Lords decision in *National Carriers Ltd v Panalpina (Northern) Ltd* [1981] AC 675 and the decision in *Hussein v Mehlman* [1992] 32 EG 59.

Since Jane's lease is presumably a business tenancy within Pt II of the Landlord and Tenant Act 1954, you will also need to consider briefly the effect (if any) of contractual termination under the Act. This is by no means an easy task since there is no case law (to date) on the interaction of these common law methods of termination and the workings of Pt II. See however, Pawlowski, M., 'Contractual Termination of Leases — Unresolved Issues' (1998) 13 JPL, pp.4–6.

The temptation is simply to regurgitate the facts and ruling in the two main cases without getting to grips with the various issues raised by the current case law. This is clearly an area of leasehold law where the courts have yet to give authoritative guidance: see, however, the further reading listed in the Introduction to this chapter. See also Question 3, **Chapter 16**.

- Has the lease become frustrated due to local authority works? Consider *National Carriers Ltd v Panalpina (Northern) Ltd* (1981). Jane's business will suffer only six months' disruption and her lease will still have over two years' left to run after works completed. Unlikely that lease has become frustrated: *Cricklewood Property and Investment Trust Ltd v Leighton's Investment Trust Ltd* (1945)

- Consider doctrine of repudiatory breach: *Hussein v Mehlman* (1992) and *Chartered Trust plc v Davies* (1997). Does the breach deprive Jane of substantially the whole of her bargain?: *Nynehead Developments Ltd v RH Firbreboard Containers Ltd* (1999)

- Does a repudiatory breach determine the leasehold estate? Consider 'independent' and 'integrated' approaches

- Interrelation of contractual termination and the provisions for termination contained in the Landlord and Tenant Act 1954, Pt II. Consider s. 24(2) which expressly preserves surrender as a means of ending a business tenancy: *Wood Factory Property Ltd v Kiritos Property Ltd* (1985)

:Q: Suggested answer

Recent cases have seen growing judicial acceptance that the contractual doctrines of frustration and repudiatory breach are, as a matter of legal theory, applicable to leasehold law.

In *National Carriers Ltd* v *Panalpina (Northern) Ltd* [1981] AC 675, the House of Lords held that a lease was capable of being discharged by the occurrence of a frustrating event. In this case, a warehouse was demised to the tenants for a term of 10 years from 1 January 1974. The only vehicular access to the warehouse was by a street which the local authority closed on 16 May 1979 because of the dangerous condition of a derelict warehouse nearby. The road was closed for 20 months, during which the tenant's warehouse was rendered useless. In an action by the landlords for the recovery of unpaid rent, the tenants claimed that the lease had been frustrated. The House of Lords, although recognising that the doctrine was, in principle, applicable to leases, held on the facts that the lease had not become discharged. The tenants had lost less than two years of use of the premises out of a total of 10 years. Moreover, the lease would still have nearly three years left to run after the interruption had ceased. Similar reasoning would apply in the instant case, where Jane's business would suffer only six months' of disruption and her lease would still have over two years (i.e., about half the term) left to run after the works were completed. As against this, we are told that Jane has suffered a 70 per cent reduction in her business as a result of the closure of the alleyway. Although this may have been the primary reason for her relocating elsewhere, it is doubtful whether the blocking of the alleyway would be considered so serious that it goes to the whole foundation of the lease, rendering the leasehold estate worthless or useless (*Cricklewood Property and Investment Trust Ltd* v *Leighton's Investment Trust Ltd* [1945] AC 221 (HL). Accordingly, Jane's lease is unlikely to have been discharged by a frustrating event.

It seems more likely that Jane will be able to rely upon the doctrine of repudiatory breach as determining her lease. In *Hussein* v *Mehlman* [1992] 32 EG 59, it was held that a lease may be terminated by the acceptance of a repudiatory breach of its terms. Here, the landlord granted the tenants an assured shorthold tenancy of a dwelling-house subject to the repairing covenants implied by the landlord under the Landlord and Tenant Act 1985, s. 11. From the commencement of the term, the tenants complained to the landlord about the state of disrepair of the premises; in particular, one of the bedrooms had been made uninhabitable by a ceiling collapse. The landlord refused to carry out this and other repairs. Eventually, the tenants returned the keys and vacated the premises. The court held that the landlord was in repudiatory breach of the contract of letting, and by returning the keys and giving up possession the tenants had accepted the breach and the tenancy was therefore at an end.

The decision in *Hussein* (albeit only at county court level) was treated as apparently correct, without argument, by the Court of Appeal in *Chartered Trust plc* v *Davies* [1997] 2 EGLR 83. The most recent case in point, namely, *Nynehead Developments Ltd* v *RH Fibreboard Containers Ltd* [1999] 02 EG 139, suggests that the actual circumstances in which a lease will be effectively brought to an end by acceptance of a landlord's repudiatory breach are likely to be exceptional. Before a breach can be characterised as repudiatory, it must deprive the tenant of substantially the whole of his bargain, just as a supervening event must substantially deprive the tenant of the whole benefit of the contract before it can frustrate the lease. In both the *Hussein* and *Chartered Trust* cases, the tenant was deprived of substantially the whole of his bargain because, in the former, the tenant could not live in the house for the remainder of the term, and in the latter, her business had been effectively destroyed. By contrast, in *Nynehead*, although the breaches were serious, the consequences for the tenant were not such as to deprive the tenant of the essence of his bargain. Interestingly, in *Hussein*, the tenancy was granted for a three-year term commencing in December 1989, and the ceiling collapse and water penetration (which rendered the premises uninhabitable) occurred in March 1991. It was evident that there was no likelihood that the condition of the house would improve before the end of the term and, hence, the landlord's breach was sufficient to vitiate 'the central purpose of the contract of letting'. In *Chartered Trust*, although the lease had still about 20 years left to run, the landlord's conduct in derogating from grant resulted in substantial interference with the tenant's business driving her to bankruptcy. This, in itself, was considered sufficient to deprive the tenant of the whole benefit of her contract and constituted a repudiation of the lease regardless of the unexpired term of the lease.

In the present case, Jane's lease still has over two years left to run. In these circumstances, she may find it difficult to argue that she has been substantially deprived of the whole of her bargain. Applying *Chartered Trust*, however, if the ceiling collapse has seriously disrupted her business, such consequence may be enough substantially to deprive Jane of the benefit of her contract.

Even if Jane is able to rely on the doctrine of repudiatory breach so as to discharge her *contractual* tenancy, this may not be sufficient to determine the actual (leasehold) estate. In *Hussein*, the court allowed the tenants to make use of the doctrine to put an end to the tenancy independently of any proprietary mechanism for termination (e.g., surrender, notice to quit, etc.). The difficulty with using this 'independent' approach is that a lease is both an executory contract and an executed demise. In other words, it may be artificial to regard the parties' rights as governed solely by executory promises where those rights are also properly viewed by reference to their character as an estate in land. It may be, therefore, that an *integrated* approach is required whereby the repudiation is effected by some proprietary measure. For example, it may be possible to employ the fiction of an implied surrender on Jane's behalf in order to give a proprietary basis to the operation of the contractual repudiation. Although the judgments in *National Carriers* and *Hussein* appear to favour an independent approach to the question of contractual termination, any conclusions based on these authorities must remain speculative in the absence of any authoritative guidance on this point.

A further difficulty relates to the interrelation of contractual termination and the provisions for termination contained in Pt II of the Landlord and Tenant Act 1954. Presumably, Jane's lease is a business tenancy falling within Pt II of the 1954 Act. In this connection, s. 24(2) of the Act expressly preserves surrender as a means by which a business tenancy may validly be brought to an end. It may be possible, therefore, to argue that a tenant who accepts his (or her) landlord's repudiatory conduct by vacating the premises and returning the keys to the landlord should be categorised as having effected a common law surrender of the property and thus fall within the ambit of s. 24(2). In *Wood Factory Property Ltd* v *Kiritos Property Ltd* [1985] 2 NSWLR 105, the Supreme Court of New South Wales suggested that it may be possible to classify the acceptance by a *landlord* of a tenant's repudiatory breach as a new species of surrender by operation of law. Unfortunately, the English courts have not yet had the opportunity to consider this issue, so the question whether the 1954 Act would limit Jane's ability to apply contractual principles of repudiation in the context of her business tenancy remains an open one.

Q Question 5

Barry is the tenant of a house under a lease for seven years which is about to expire. Advise Barry whether he can lawfully remove the following articles before the end of the term, all of which have been fitted and erected by him:

 (a) Bookshelves in a recess in the sitting-room.

 (b) A small safe cemented into a cavity in the wall of his study and which is used for storing personal possessions.

 (c) A stone sundial and statue resting on their own weight in the garden.

Commentary

This is a straightforward question concerning a tenant's right to remove fixtures on the expiry of the lease. In answering the question, you should refer to the two tests (i.e., degree of annexation and purpose of annexation) for determining whether a particular item constitutes a fixture or not. You will also score higher marks if you are able to refer to the cases in point.

You should assume that the lease provides no guidance as to whether the objects are fixtures or not, or in relation to rights of removal. It may also be assumed that Barry and the landlord have not entered into any agreement in relation to the objects.

For further reading, see Haley, M., 'The Law and Fixtures: When is a Chattel not a Chattel?' (1985) 135 NLJ 539 and 588; Williams, D., 'To Have and Have Not' [1994] EG 9738, 143; and Pawlowski, M., 'House: Chattel or Realty' (1997) 1/2 JHL, pp. 23–26.

• Two tests: (1) degree of annexation and (2) purpose of the annexation. Ultimately a question of fact whether an object a fixture or chattel: *Elitestone Ltd* v *Morris* (1997)

- Three exceptions where a tenant may remove fixtures: (1) domestic and ornamental fixtures (2) trade fixtures and (3) agricultural fixtures. These classified as 'tenant's fixtures'

- If bookshelves free-standing (as opposed to built into the wall), presumption that they are chattels. If fixtures, they may still rank as tenant's fixtures if installed for business reasons or of an ornamental nature

- Strong presumption that safe forms part of the land since it is cemented into the wall. Stone sundial and statue not physically secured to the land so probably chattels. Consider purpose of annexation test: *Hamp* v *Bygrave* (1983)

⌀ Suggested answer

The term 'fixture' is applied to anything which has become so attached to the land as to form part of it in law. In determining whether an object has become a fixture or not, the two main factors a court will consider are:

(a)   the degree of annexation; and

(b)   the purpose of the annexation.

It has been said that the second of these two tests is likely to be more decisive than the first (see *Berkeley* v *Poulett* (1976) 241 EG 911 and *Hamp* v *Bygrave* (1983) 266 EG 720), but ultimately it is always a question of fact in each case whether an object is a fixture (and therefore attached to the land) or a chattel.

The degree of annexation test dictates that if an article is attached to the land in a substantial way, or secured in such a way that any removal would be likely to damage the land, then it will probably be a fixture; whereas if the object merely rests on the land under its own weight, it remains a chattel (*Holland* v *Hodgson* (1872) LR 7 CP 328). Thus, a fireplace and an ornamental chimney piece have been held to be fixtures on the basis that they could not be removed without injuring the land. See also, *Buckland* v *Butterfield* (1802) 2 Brod & Bing 54.

By contrast, articles which are capable of removal without damage to the land, such as a 'Dutch barn' (*Elwes* v *Maw* (1802) 3 East 38), or a greenhouse bolted to a concrete plinth lying on the ground under its own weight (*Deen* v *Andrews* (1986) 52 P & CR 17) have been held to be chattels.

Under the purpose of annexation test, if a chattel substantially attached to the land is only physically so annexed with the purpose of putting it to better use (rather than enhancing the land), then despite appearing to be a fixture it will nonetheless remain a chattel and will thus be capable of removal, if removal is practical and feasible (see, e.g., *Leigh* v *Taylor* [1902] AC 157, concerning a wall tapestry). In relation to this more subjective test, the authorities show no clear line of reasoning, and therefore much will depend on the facts of each individual case.

In *Elitestone Ltd* v *Morris* [1997] 1 WLR 687, the House of Lords confirmed that the answer to the question whether a structure (in that case a wooden bungalow resting on concrete pillars attached to the ground) became part and parcel of the land itself depended on the degree and the object of annexation to the land. In that case, the bungalow could be removed only by being demolished and, accordingly, it was held to form part of the realty.

If an article is classified, as a matter of law, as a chattel, it may be removed by the person bringing it onto the land or his successors in title. This principle applies to tenants of demised land. If, however, the object is deemed a fixture, prima facie it cannot be removed and must be left for the landlord on the basis that it has become part of the freehold land. There are, however, three significant exceptions to this rule where a tenant may remove certain fixtures, namely:

(a)   domestic and ornamental fixtures;

(b)   trade fixtures; and

(c)   agricultural fixtures.

These are known as 'tenant's fixtures'. It has been held, however, that a tenant is not entitled to remove tenant's fixtures following forfeiture of the lease by peaceable re-entry (*Re Palmiero: debtor 3666 of 1999* [1999] 38 EG 195).

Domestic and ornamental fixtures may be removed in their entirety by the tenant provided the injury to the land is no more than decorative (*Spyer* v *Phillipson* [1931] 2 Ch 183). Fixtures which permanently improve the premises cannot be removed (e.g., a fitted kitchen). Trade fixtures may be removed by the tenant if they have been installed by him for the purpose of his business or trade. Thus, engine machinery has been held to be removable (*Climie* v *Wood* (1869) LR 4 Ex 328) and so have shrubs planted by a commercial gardener (*Wardell* v *Usher* (1841) 3 Scott NR 508). In relation to agricultural fixtures, agricultural tenants have certain statutory rights to remove fixtures added by them to the demised land, under the Agricultural Holdings Act 1986, s. 10.

The upshot of the foregoing is that Barry may only remove such objects as are classified in law as chattels or amount to tenant's fixtures.

(a) The bookshelves. It would be useful to discover whether the bookshelves are free-standing or built into the wall of the sitting-room. If they are free-standing, applying the degree of annexation test, it may be presumed that the shelves are mere chattels. If the shelves are secured to the recess, it seems that they would be deemed fixtures and would belong to the landlord. However, this presumption could be rebutted. Applying the purpose of annexation test, Barry may be able to show that the securing of the shelves merely enhanced them in their own right. Alternatively, if classified as fixtures, he may be able to demonstrate that the shelves were installed for purely business reasons or were of an ornamental nature. As such, they would rank as tenant's fixtures, entitling Barry to remove them if removal is possible without damaging the recess.

(b) The small safe. Due to the manner in which the safe has been secured (i.e., cemented into a cavity in the wall of the study), there is a strong prima facie presumption that the safe forms part of the land (i.e., it is a fixture). It may be possible for Barry to argue that the safe was cemented simply for purposes of storage, in which case this could rebut the presumption that the safe is a fixture due to its cementation. This would be a question of fact for the trial judge. It is unlikely, however, that this argument would succeed because it would be extremely difficult to remove the safe without severely damaging the cavity in the wall.

If the safe falls to be classified as a fixture, it is unlikely to constitute a tenant's fixture. We are told that Barry uses the safe for storing his personal possessions and not for any business user. Moreover, it is difficult to envisage the safe as being ornamental. It is submitted, therefore, that the safe is a fixture which passes to the landlord.

(c) The stone sundial and statue. These, we are told, rest on their own weight in the garden. Not being physically secured to the land, these objects would prima facie, applying the degree of annexation test, be regarded as chattels, and hence be removeable by Barry. Under the purpose of annexation test, however, it is also relevant to examine the intention with which he placed these objects in the garden (*Hamp* v *Bygrave*, above). If they were placed to improve the land in a permanent way, they will be regarded as fixtures, but if placed to enhance the objects themselves they will be regarded as chattels. This is a question for the trial judge to determine on the hearing of evidence. The courts have, however, in the light of the *Elwes* and *Holland* cases (above), shown a tendency to treat objects placed on land under their own weight as mere chattels. In the unlikely event that it was held that these items were fixtures, it would still be open to Barry to argue that he has the right to remove them, being tenant's ornamental and domestic fixtures.

Q Question 6

Discuss the ways in which a tenant may terminate his lease by surrender and consider the possible legal consequences which may flow from a surrender of a lease. (Illustrate your answer by reference to decided cases.)

Commentary

This is a standard type of essay question concerned with the topic of surrender. Students should be familiar with the various forms of surrender (express and implied) and the effects of a surrender on the parties to the lease and any sub-tenants. A structured answer, demonstrating a good knowledge of case law, will contribute to the attainment of a 2:1 mark.

- Consider formalities required for express surrender: Law of Property Act 1925, s. 52(1). Also agreement to surrender: 1925 Act, s. 40 and Law of Property (Miscellaneous Provisions) Act 1989, s. 2

- Examples of implied surrender (i.e., by operation of law). Abandonment of premises by tenant: *R. v London Borough of Croydon, ex parte Toth* (1986). Replacement of existing lease with new lease on different terms: *Bush Transport Ltd v Nelson* (1987)

- Effect of surrender on subtenancy: 1925 Act, s. 139 and s. 150(1)

- Liability of tenant after surrender for past breaches of covenant and rent arrears. Consider also tenant's right to remove tenant's fixtures

☀ Suggested answer

A surrender of a lease is the process by which a tenant gives up his (leasehold) estate in the land to his immediate landlord. The lease is essentially destroyed by mutual agreement. The effect of a surrender is to terminate the tenant's liability under his covenants as from the date of the surrender. A surrender may arise expressly or by implication (i.e., by operation of law).

An express surrender must be made by deed (Law of Property Act 1925, s. 52(1)). An express surrender must operate immediately and will be invalid if it is expressed to operate at some future date (*Doe d Murrell v Milward* (1838) 3 M & W 328). A future surrender may, however, take the form of an agreement to surrender, in which case it will be valid if made in compliance with the relevant legal formalities necessary for contracts for the disposition of interests in land (i.e., s. 40 of the 1925 Act or the Law of Property (Miscellaneous Provisions) Act 1989, s. 2, depending on whether the contract was made before or on or after 27 September 1989). To be effective, the surrender must be to the immediate landlord. Thus, a transfer of a sub-tenancy not to the mesne tenant but to the head landlord will not operate as a surrender, but rather as an assignment of the benefit of the sub-tenancy to the head lessor.

An implied surrender (i.e., by operation of law) is expressly exempted from the requirement of a deed by virtue of the Law of Property Act 1925, s. 52(2)(c). Such a surrender may arise from any unequivocal conduct of the parties which is inconsistent with the continuation of the lease in circumstances where it would be inequitable for them to rely on the fact that there has been no surrender by deed: *Unicomp Inc v Eurodis Electron plc* [2004] EWHC 979 (Ch). A common example of such a surrender is where the tenant abandons the premises and the landlord accepts his implied offer of a surrender by changing the locks and re-letting the premises to a third party (*R v London Borough of Croydon, ex parte Toth* (1986) 18 HLR 493). The abandonment must, however, be of a permanent, and not a temporary, nature. A mere temporary abandonment is too equivocal unless the tenant is absent for a long time with large rent arrears owing (*Preston Borough Council* v *Fairclough* (1982) 8 HLR 70). Moreover, although the taking of keys (coupled with other acts) may evidence the taking of possession of the premises by the landlord, this will not be the case where there is no intention to accept a surrender until after the grant of a new lease (*Proudreed Ltd* v *Microgen Holdings plc* [1996] 12 EG 127 (CA)).

Another example of a surrender by operation of law will arise where the tenant agrees with the landlord to replace his existing lease with a new lease on different terms, or with substantially different premises (see, e.g., *Bush Transport Ltd* v *Nelson* (1987) 1 EGLR 71 and *Foster* v *Robinson* [1951] 1 KB 149). In the latter case, a protected tenant accepted a rent-free licence to occupy the same premises to replace his existing tenancy. By contrast, a mere variation in the rent payable will not give rise to a surrender by implication (*Jenkin R. Lewis & Son Ltd* v *Kerman* [1971] Ch 477), nor where there is a replacement of an old rent book with a new one which contains substantially the same terms with only slight variations (*Smirk* v *Lyndale Developments Ltd* [1975] Ch 317).

No surrender of the lease will be implied where the tenant accepts a new lease from the landlord which is void or voidable (*Barclays Bank* v *Stasek* [1957] Ch 28). This is because a surrender by operation of law is subject to an implied condition that the new lease is valid; if it is not, the current lease remains in force.

In surrendering his lease, a tenant cannot prejudice the rights of other parties affected by it. For example, the Law of Property Act 1925, s. 139, provides that, in the event of a surrender of the head lease by a mesne tenant, the head landlord automatically becomes the landlord in relation to the sub-tenant so as to preserve the validity of the sub-lease. By s. 150(1) of the 1925 Act, a lease may be surrendered with a view to the acceptance of a new lease, without any surrender of any sub-lease.

Following a surrender, a tenant may remain liable for past breaches of covenant occurring during the term of his lease (*Richmond* v *Savill* [1926] 2 KB 530). It is possible, however, for the parties to agree that all past (as well as future) liability of the tenant should cease upon surrender.

Prima facie, a surrender includes the right to remove tenant's fixtures in the absence of express contrary agreement. Where there is a surrender by operation of law and the tenant remains in possession under a new lease (see earlier), the right to remove such fixtures continues throughout the tenant's possession (*New Zealand Government Property Corporation* v *HM and S Ltd* [1982] 1 All ER 624).

As regards rent, the tenant is not entitled to recover any part of any rent paid in advance, but rent accruing before the surrender (but not yet due) may be the subject of apportionment under the Apportionment Act 1870, s. 3. The tenant remains liable for any arrears due before the surrender under any personal covenant, if any. If not, the landlord will be able to maintain an action for use and occupation (*Shaw* v *Lomas* (1888) 59 LT 477).

Q Question 7

In February 1999, Mountbatten Ltd granted to Tolkein Ltd a lease of an office suite in central London for a term of 10 years from and including 19 January 1999. The lease contained, *inter alia*, the following clause:

> . . . the tenant may, by serving not less than six months' notice in writing on the landlord, or its solicitors, such notice to expire on the *fifth* anniversary of the term commencement date, determine this lease and upon expiry of such notice this lease shall cease and determine and have no further effect . . .

By a letter, dated 21 May 2003, Tolkein Ltd gave notice to Mountbatten Ltd to determine the lease on 17 January 2004.

Shortly after the notice was served, Tolkein Ltd vacated the demised premises. It has not paid any rent since the expiry date of its notice, and the property remains vacant and unoccupied.

Mountbatten Ltd is of the view that the notice of determination served on it by Tolkein Limited is invalid and of no effect. Despite several demands for rent, Tolkein Ltd has refused to make any further payments.

Advise Mountbatten Ltd as to its legal position.

Commentary

This is an interesting question concerning the law relating to break clauses in leases; in particular, the rules governing the validity of a notice where an incorrect break-date has been specified. A good answer will give consideration to the House of Lords ruling in *Mannai Investment Co. Ltd* v *Eagle Star Life Assurance Co. Ltd* [1997] 2 WLR 945 and subsequent cases in point.

For further reading, see: Williams, P., 'When Time Runs Out' [1997] EG 9724, 112–14, Wilkinson, H.W., 'Construing Break Notices' (1997) 147 NLJ 1187 and Blaker, G., 'Reasonable Notice' (2003) SJ 1070.

- If notice invalid, premature abandonment by tenant will constitute a repudiatory breach. Landlord may accept repudiation so as to bring about a surrender of the lease. Alternatively, open to landlord to elect to continue with lease and claim rent when falling due

- If notice valid (despite incorrect break-date), lease effectively determined on January 19 2004 and tenant's liability to pay rent extinguished

- Is error fatal to validity of notice? Consider *Mannai Investment Co. Ltd* v *Eagle Star Life Assurance Co. Ltd* (1997) and *Carradine Properties* v *Aslam* (1976). Examine also subsequent case law

- Apply 'reasonable recipient' test. Minor error in notice not fatal. Contrast *Lemmerbell Ltd* v *Britannia LAS Direct Ltd* (1998) where defect more substantial

☼ Suggested answer

If the notice served by Tolkein Limited is invalid (as having been served two days early) then the lease will remain alive and the premature abandonment by Tolkein Limited and its refusal to pay rent will constitute a repudiatory breach of contract.

It would then be open to Mountbatten Limited to accept the repudiation as terminating the tenancy — effectively bringing about a surrender of the lease by operation of law. Such a surrender is exempt from any legal formality by virtue of s. 52(2) of the Law of Property Act 1925. A surrender by operation of law can be inferred from the parties' conduct where, for example, the tenant abandons the property and the landlord changes the locks and re-lets the premises to a third party (see *R* v *London Borough of Croydon, ex parte Toth* (1986) 18 HLR 493 and *Re AGB Research plc, Re* [1994] EGCS 73). Alternatively, it may be open to Mountbatten Ltd to elect to continue with the lease if there are genuine economic reasons for so doing (see *White and Carter (Councils) Ltd* v *McGregor* [1963] AC 413).

On the other hand, if Tolkein Ltd's notice is valid (despite the incorrect break-date), the lease will have been effectively determined (on 19 January 2004) and Tolkein Ltd's liability to pay rent extinguished from that date.

On the face of it, the notice is clearly incorrect in so far as it specifies 17 January 2004 as the termination date of the lease, whereas the actual termination date (as required under the break clause) is 19 January 2004. Is this error fatal to the validity of the notice? At one time, the rules as to the validity of contractual break notices were very strict. Any error could easily invalidate the notice: see, for example, *Hankey* v *Clavering* [1942] 2 KB 326. However, the House of Lords in *Mannai Investment Co. Ltd* v *Eagle Star Life Assurance Co. Ltd* [1997] 2 WLR 945 has now adopted the more flexible approach to determining the validity of break notices enunciated in the earlier case of *Carradine Properties* v *Aslam* [1976] 1 WLR 442. The question in each case is whether it was obvious to the 'reasonable recipient' of the notice, with knowledge of the terms of the lease (in particular, the relevant anniversary dates), that the tenant wished to determine the lease on that anniversary and not an earlier time. A minor error in the notice will not, therefore, normally detract from the validity of the notice. In *Mannai* itself, applying this objective test, a contractual break notice in a lease, which was one day short of the appropriate anniversary date, was held to be valid.

In *Carradine*, the landlord served a break notice on 6 September 1974, purporting to break the lease on 27 September 1973, instead of 27 September 1975. The court held that this was an obvious slip as the specified date had already passed. The notice was, therefore, held valid. Similarly, in *Micrografix Ltd* v *Woking 8 Ltd* [1995] 37 EG 179, the tenant's break notice specified 23 March 1994 instead of 23 June 1995. This notice was also held valid. Again, in *Garston v Scottish Widow's Fund and Life Assurance Society* [1998] 3 All ER 596, a lease, dated 10 July 1985, was granted for a term of 20 years from 24 June 1985. Under a break clause, the tenant had the right to end the lease at the end of the tenth year (i.e., on 24 June 1995). By an error, the tenant's notice purported to end the lease on 9 July 1995. A moment's reflection would have indicated to the landlord (as a reasonable recipient of the notice) that the tenant intended to end the lease at the end of the tenth year but had confused the date of the lease with the date for the commencement of the term. The notice was, therefore, held to be valid. (See also, *Havant International Holdings Ltd v Lionsgate (H) Investment Ltd* [2000] L&TR 297) and *Trafford Metropolitan Borough Council v Total Fitness (UK) Ltd* [2002] 44 EG 169. In *Trafford*, the landlord's break notice gave 17 days' notice of determination of the lease stating that the premises (a car park) would be closed 'as at and from midnight on 24 October 2001'. The tenant argued that the notice was invalid as it was not clear when the lease was supposed to expire. According to the first part of the notice, the lease expired at the last moment of 25 October (excluding the date of service). The second part of the notice, on the other hand, stated that the lease expired at the last moment of 24 October, thus providing for only 16 days' notice. The Court of Appeal, however, applying *Mannai*, concluded that no reasonable recipient would have been confused by the notice. The statement as to the expiry date in the notice made it clear that the date of service was being included and this was entirely consistent with the given period of notice. In all these cases, the intended purpose and effect of the notice were quite clear to the recipient and it would have been unjust if such a technicality were to render it ineffective. The standard of reference was that of the reasonable man exercising common sense in the context of the particular circumstances of the case.

By contrast to the foregoing, in *Lemmerbell Ltd v Britannia LAS Direct Ltd* [1998] 48 EG 188, the Court of Appeal, applying the *Mannai* test, held that the tenant's break notice was defective. Here, the defects in the notices were more substantial and could not, therefore, be cured by the application of the *Mannai* ruling. On an objective analysis, the reasonable landlord recipient of the notice could not know, in the absence of evidence of an assignment of the lease, whether the notice was given by the tenant (as stated in the notice) or not. It was, accordingly, impossible to cure the defect: See also, *Proctor & Gamble Technical Centres Ltd v Brixton* Estates plc [2003] 31 EG 69, where the notice wrongly identified the tenant.

It is evident from the decision in *Lemmerbell* that the *Mannai* test will not avail every party who has served a defective break notice. In *Lemmerbell*, it was by no means obvious that there was an error in the name of the tenant in the notice, nor who the actual tenant was, nor whether the sender of the notice was an authorised agent of the tenant. The obvious conclusion to be drawn from this case is that, while minor errors may be excused, substantive defects remain incurable. It is apparent also that the *Mannai* principle has no application where the notice itself is not defective but has been sent to the wrong address. If the lease provides a mandatory (as opposed to permissive) requirement that the notice should be delivered to a particular place, the 'reasonable recipient' test will not save it: *Claire's Accessories UK Ltd* v *Kensington High Street Associates LLC*, unreported, (2001).

In the present case, the notice served by Tolkein Ltd is two days short of the relevant anniversary date. However, in my view, a reasonable landlord recipient of this notice (who must be taken to be aware of the provisions in the lease) would not be misled by it, since it must have realised that the tenant was seeking to determine the lease in accordance with the relevant break clause in the lease. On this analysis, therefore, the notice was effective to bring the lease to an end on 19 January 2004. If that is right then Tolkein Limited is released from any further obligations in the lease as from that date, in particular, its obligation to pay rent. Mountbatten Limited is, therefore, best advised to endeavour to find another tenant for the property as soon as possible.

Further reading

Blaker, G., 'Reasonable Notice' (2003) SJ 1070.

Joyce, J., 'The End of the Line for Forfeiture' [2004] EG 123.

Lovitt, A., and Martin, J., 'A Closer Look at *Mannai*' [2000] EG 170.

Marks, S., 'Take a Break' (2002) SJ 826.

Pawlowski, M., and Brown, J., 'Repudiatory Breach in the Leasehold Context' [1999] Conv 150.

Shorrock, K., 'Notice to Quit by One Joint Periodic Lessee of Residential Property — Time for Statutory Intervention?' [1995] Conv 424.

Ward, V.C., 'There are Two Ways to Leave Your Tenant' [2000] EG 94.

Wilkinson, H.W., 'Relief Against Forfeiture — Parts I and II' (2001) NLJ 27 and 140.

10 Q&A

Rent Act tenancies

Introduction

A tenancy of residential premises will usually be a protected tenancy under the Rent Act 1977 if it is granted before 15 January 1989. A residential tenancy granted on or after this date is generally subject to the Housing Act 1988, Pt I, and will be either an assured or an assured shorthold tenancy (see **Chapter 10**).

To qualify as a protected tenancy, the premises must comprise a dwelling-house and the purpose of the letting must be residential use as one dwelling. The tenancy may be of part of a house, being a part let as a separate dwelling. There are also a number of excluded tenancies which do not qualify for Rent Act protection. For example, a tenancy is not protected if under the tenancy the dwelling-house is bona fide let at a rent which includes any payments in respect of board or any substantial payments in respect of attendance (s. 7(2); *Otter* v *Norman* [1989] AC 129 and *Nelson Developments Ltd* v *Taboada* [1992] 34 EG 72). Other notable exclusions include holiday lettings, company lettings, and tenancies granted by resident landlords.

After the termination of a protected tenancy, the protected tenant is entitled to be the statutory tenant of the dwelling-house provided he continues to occupy it as his residence (s. 2(1)(a)). The requirement of continuing residence has been the subject of numerous cases, and of particular interest is the tenant who is a genuine 'two-homes' occupant who may claim statutory protection under the Rent Act 1977 despite residing in *both* properties (see, e.g., *Langford Property Co. Ltd* v *Tureman* [1949] 1 KB 29; contrast *Walker* v *Ogilvy* (1974) 28 P & CR 288). You should remember that a tenant's forced absence from the property while, for example, in prison, or in hospital or on military service, does not necessarily destroy a statutory tenancy (*Tickner* v *Hearn* [1960] 1 WLR 1406). However, a long absence from the premises raises an inference of cesser of residence requiring the tenant to show an *animus revertendi* (an intention to return) *and* a *corpus possessionis* (i.e., some symbol of occupation) such as leaving the premises furnished or occupied by someone on the tenant's behalf (*Brown* v *Brash* [1948] 2 KB 247). You may well be asked to answer a question on any of these topics which may also include some discussion of succession rights.

If you decide to revise the Rent Act 1977, make sure you cover the landlord's grounds for possession in some depth. It is almost certain that a problem question on the 1977 Act will require you to consider one or more of the mandatory and/or discretionary grounds listed in sch. 15 to the 1977 Act. For example, since the last edition of this book, the House of Lords have ruled that, where a protected tenancy provides for re-entry in the event of the tenant's bankruptcy and the tenant is made bankrupt after becoming a statutory tenant, the bankruptcy constitutes a breach of an obligation of the previous protected tenancy within the meaning of Case 1 of sch. 15 and, therefore, provides grounds for possession, even though the tenant is paid up with his rent: *Cadogan Estates Ltd* v *McMahon* [2001] AC 378. Be aware also that a landlord who claims possession against a protected or statutory tenant must establish:

(a) the effective termination of the contractual tenancy (e.g., by expiry of time, notice to quit, forfeiture etc.); and

(b) that one or more of the statutory grounds for possession apply.

Thus, a common law forfeiture of the tenancy will only destroy the protected (contractual) tenancy and the tenant will remain a statutory tenant of the premises (*Wolmer Securities Ltd* v *Corne* [1966] 2 QB 243).

The discretionary grounds for possession are contained in sch. 15, Pts I, III and IV of the 1977 Act. A landlord relying on any of these grounds must additionally prove that it is reasonable to make an order for possession (s. 98(1)). The mandatory grounds, on the other hand (which are contained in sch. 15, Pt II of the 1977 Act as amended by the Housing Act 1988, s. 66 and sch. 7), are not subject to any overriding consideration of reasonableness. A landlord who establishes any of the mandatory grounds can claim possession as of right, provided that:

(a) the dwelling-house is let on a protected tenancy; and

(b) not later than 'the relevant date' the landlord gave the tenant written notice that possession might be recovered under the ground in question.

For most tenancies the relevant date is the commencement of the tenancy.

A brief word also about restricted contracts. A restricted contract is defined in s. 19 of the 1977 Act and may exist where the resident landlord exclusion applies, or where the rent includes payment for the use of furniture or services, provided that, in the latter case, the payments are for board or substantial attendance. A furnished contractual licence may also come within this category (*Luganda* v *Service Hotels* [1969] 2 Ch 209). A restricted contract occupier has no security of tenure other than:

(a) protection from harassment and unlawful eviction under the Protection from Eviction Act 1977 (as amended by the Housing Act 1988, s. 29);

(b) the right to apply to a rent tribunal for deferment of a notice to quit for up to six months at a time in respect of a periodic tenancy granted before 28 November 1980, or, alternatively, to apply to the court for deferment of the order for possession for up to three months subject to the imposition of conditions with regard to payment by the tenant of arrears of rent (if any) and rent or mesne profits, in respect of periodic or fixed-term contracts created on or after 28 November 1980 (see Housing Act 1980, s. 69, inserting a new s. 106A into the Rent Act 1977).

As from 15 January 1989, however, no tenancy or other contract is capable of being a restricted contract (Housing Act 1988, s. 36(1)).

The impact of the Human Rights Act 1998 (which came into force in October 2000) on residential leasehold law has been the subject of several important cases in the last few years. We have, therefore, included a new question on this topical area, which requires you to survey the case law and give a critique as to how far the human rights dimension has affected residential tenants in both the private and public sectors. See Question 5.

There are five questions in this chapter which are intended to give you the opportunity to test your broad knowledge of the area. The usual principles apply in tackling such questions in exam conditions — draw up a plan in rough, make a series of points, and list the relevant cases (before you forget them!).

Q Question 1

Fred is the weekly tenant of a room at 2 Bedsit Lane, owned by Bertram. He has been Bertram's tenant since 1988. He pays a weekly rent of £75 which entitles him to a 'continental breakfast' seven days a week which is served in his room. In addition, the rent includes an amount (£12) in respect of daily cleaning of the room and change of bed linen each week.

Bertram's wife resides on the premises three nights a week in order to fulfil these duties as caretaker. The rest of the time she spends living with her husband in Brighton.

Fred's tenancy agreement is described as a 'holiday let' although it has periodically been renewed.

Bertram now wishes to evict Fred and sell the house with vacant possession.

Advise Bertram.

Commentary

This problem question deals with a number of the well-known exclusions to a protected tenancy. Do not waste time dealing with points which do not cause problems. There is no need, for example, to write at length about the distinction between a tenancy and a licence.

You are actually told in the question that Fred is the weekly tenant of the room in question. Instead, begin by considering whether Fred has a tenancy of a *separate dwelling*, which is more to the point (*Curl v Angelo* [1948] 2 All ER 189 and *Uratemp Ventures Ltd v Collins* [2001] 3 WLR 806). The issue regarding the continental breakfast is covered by House of Lords authority (*Otter v Norman* [1989] AC 129) and your answer should consider the principles emerging from this case in some depth.

The point regarding attendance is more difficult since, unlike board, it must be substantial in the terms of s. 7(2) to avoid statutory protection (*Nelson Developments Ltd v Taboada* [1992] 34 EG 72). For a good article, see Rogers, C.P., 'Making a Meal out of the Rent Acts: Board, Attendance and the 'Protected Tenancy' (1988) 51 MLR 642.

The residence of Bertram's wife may also give some students a problem. The key lies in the fact that the test as to what constitutes residence for the purposes of the resident landlord exclusion is the same as that for statutory tenants under the 1977 Act (sch. 2, para. 5; *Jackson v Pekic* [1989] 47 EG 141). For a discussion of this point, see Pawlowski, M., 'Residence and the Resident Landlord' [1991] EG 9111/9112, 78 and 52. In the statutory tenant context, a tenant can maintain statutory tenant status by virtue of his wife's occupation (*Brown v Draper* [1944] KB 309). Moreover, a statutory tenant has been held to reside in premises where he spends only two nights a week (*Langford Property Co. Ltd v Tureman* [1949] 1 KB 29). It may be possible to combine these propositions and apply them in the context of a resident landlord.

As to holiday lets, your answer should refer to some of the cases in this area (*Buchmann v May* [1978] 2 All ER 993; *R v Rent Officer for London Borough of Camden, ex parte Plant* (1980) 257 EG 713 and *McHale v Daneham* (1979) 249 EG 969). For further reading, see Waite, A., 'Dodging the Rent Acts' (1981) 131 NLJ 460, and Lyons, T.J., 'The Meaning of "Holiday" under the Rent Acts' [1984] Conv 286. This exclusion will take Fred's tenancy wholly outside the Rent Act 1977. The other exclusions, on the other hand, will deny Fred protected status but will still give him limited protection as a restricted contract tenant.

As with most problem questions of this kind, you are not expected to give a definitive answer to all the issues raised — it is enough that you state the general principles, refer to the relevant cases and apply the law to the particular problem giving a reasoned view. Although there is a lot of ground to cover, this is the sort of question where you could score a high 2:1.

- Fred's room must be let as a separate dwelling in order to qualify for Rent Act protection: *Uratemp Ventures Ltd v Collins* (2001)

- If breakfast prepared and served by Bertram at the premises, board exclusion will apply: Rent Act 1977, s. 7 and *Otter v Norman* (1989). Also Fred's rent includes substantial payment (£12) in respect of attendance: *Nelson Developments Ltd v Taboada* (1992)

- Bertram may qualify as a resident landlord in view of his wife's residence on the premises. Test of residence same as that for statutory tenants: *Jackson* v *Pekic* (1989); *Brown* v *Draper* (1944) and *Langford Property Co. Ltd* v *Tureman* (1949)

- Holiday letting a sham because of continued renewal since 1988: *Buchmann* v *May* (1978). Thus, in view of exclusions above, Fred probably a restricted contract tenant: 1977 Act, s. 19

:Q: Suggested answer

Fred has been the weekly tenant of the room since 1988, and accordingly the central issue is whether Fred qualifies as a protected tenant under the Rent Act 1977. Part I of the Housing Act 1988 has no application since the tenancy was granted before 15 January 1989.

We are not told what facilities are available in the room. This may be relevant in determining whether or not Fred has a separate dwelling in order to qualify for full Rent Act protection. In *Uratemp Ventures Ltd* v *Collins* [2001] 3 WLR 806, the House of Lords held that the expression 'dwelling' in s. 1(1) of the Housing Act 1988 (which is also contained in the Rent Act 1977) meant a place where the occupier lived and treated as his (or her) home. In that case, the accommodation had no cooking facilities but this was held not to be fatal to establishing Housing Act security. Although a dwelling was characterised as being the place where the occupier lives and to which he returns and which forms the centre of his existence, the actual use made of it when living there was largely a matter for the occupier and his particular mode of life. According to Lord Millett, therefore, a home will still remain a home even if the occupier decides not to cook there but prefers to eat out or bring in ready-cooked meals. It seems, therefore, that a single room need not have any particular or 'essential' facilities available in order to be a dwelling.

We are told that Fred pays a weekly rent of £75 which entitles him to a continental breakfast seven days a week which is served in his room. It has been held that any amount of board which is not *de minimis* is sufficient to exclude statutory protection under s. 7 of the Rent Act 1977 (*Otter* v *Norman* [1989] AC 129, applying the majority view in *Wilkes* v *Goodwin* [1923] 2 KB 86). In *Otter*, the House of Lords concluded that the provision of breakfast by itself, with the implicit inclusion of the ancillary services involved in preparing it and the provision of crockery and cutlery with which to eat it, amounted to board for the purposes of the Rent Act 1977. In that case, the landlord let a room to the tenant at a rent which included payment for the provision daily by the landlord of a continental breakfast served in the communal dining room of the building in which the tenant's room was situated. The House of Lords stressed that a *bona fide* obligation to provide board entailed not only the cost of the food and drink provided but also all the housekeeping chores which had to be undertaken in shopping for provisions, preparation and service of meals on the premises, and clearing and washing up after meals. See also *Holiday Flat Co.* v *Kuczera* (1978) SLT 47, a Scottish case.

Assuming, therefore, that the breakfast is prepared and served by Bertram at the premises (albeit in Fred's room), the board exclusion would prima facie apply rendering Fred's tenancy unprotected under the 1977 Act.

In addition, we are told that Fred's rent includes an amount (£12) in respect of daily cleaning and a change of bed linen each week. In this connection, a tenancy will not be protected under the 1977 Act if the rent includes substantial payments in respect of attendance (s. 7(2)). Attendance has been held to include services in the form of daily room cleaning and weekly laundry (*Nelson Developments Ltd* v *Taboada* [1992] 34 EG 72 and *Palser* v *Grinling* [1948] AC 291). In *Nelson*, the initial rent was £55, of which no less than £11 was treated as being attributable to services. Having regard to the county court practice of taking 10 per cent as the lower end of the bracket and 20 per cent as the upper end, the Court of Appeal concluded that the attendance exclusion applied. In Fred's case, the amount of rent attributable to the services is £12, and hence well above the 10 per cent watershed applied in the *Nelson* case.

The next point to consider is that Bertram's wife resides on the premises three nights a week in order to carry out her duties as caretaker. Section 12 of the Rent Act 1977 (as amended by the Housing Act 1980) sets out four preconditions for the operation of the resident landlord exclusion. First, the tenancy (whether furnished or unfurnished) must have been granted on or after 14 August 1974. Secondly, the tenancy must be of a dwelling-house forming part of a building or flat which, in the former case, is not a purpose built block of flats. These pre-conditions appear to be met in the present case. Thirdly, the tenancy was granted by a person who, at the time when he granted it, occupied as his residence another dwelling-house which forms part of the flat or building. We are not told whether Bertram resided at the premises when he granted the tenancy to Fred in 1988. Fourthly, at all times *since* the tenancy was granted, the interest of the landlord under the tenancy has belonged to a person who, at the time he owned that interest, occupied as his residence another dwelling-house which also formed part of the flat or building. The test of residence for a resident landlord is basically the same as that for a statutory tenant under the 1977 Act (*Jackson* v *Pekic* [1989] 47 EG 141), thus it is possible for a landlord to have two homes on the analogy of the position of a statutory tenant (*Wolff* v *Waddington* [1989] 47 EG 148). Moreover, it is clear that a tenant can maintain statutory tenant status by virtue of his wife's occupation (*Brown* v *Draper* [1944] KB 309) and where he resides on the premises for a minimum of two nights a week (*Langford Property Co. Ltd* v *Tureman* [1949] 1 KB 29). It is arguable, therefore, that Bertram will qualify as a resident land-lord on the basis of his wife's limited occupation of the premises, provided the other preconditions are satisfied.

We are told that the agreement is described as a holiday let. Holiday lettings fall outside the protection of the Rent Act 1977 altogether. Since the tenancy agreement expressly states the purpose for which it was made (i.e., a holiday), that statement will stand as evidence of the purpose of the parties unless Fred can establish that it does not correspond with the true purpose (*Buchmann* v *May* [1978] 2 All ER 993, involving a holiday let for three months). In the present case, the court would undoubtedly view the letting as a sham in so far as the tenancy has been periodically renewed. However, in *McHale* v *Daneham* (1979) 249 EG 969, the county court judge held that persons from abroad who signed a six-month holiday letting agreement and then renewed it, first for one month, then for a further two months, had a genuine holiday letting. The tenants were working in this country but the landlord understood that they were on holiday. The case is clearly distinguishable on the ground that Fred has been a weekly tenant of the room since 1988 and is, presumably, working in this country (see *R* v *Rent Officer for London Borough of Camden, ex parte Plant* (1980) 257 EG 713). It is highly unlikely, therefore, that Bertram will be able to avail himself of the holiday let exclusion.

Assuming, however, that one or more of the other exclusions apply, this will mean that Fred will not have protected tenancy status but will still be entitled to the limited protection afforded to a restricted contract tenant under the 1977 Act (s. 19). As such, Fred will have no security of tenure other than:

(a) protection from harassment and unlawful eviction under the Protection from Eviction Act 1977; and

(b) since his tenancy was granted after 28 November 1980, the right to apply to the court for deferment of the order for possession for up to three months subject to the imposition of conditions with regard to the payment of arrears of rent (if any) and rent or mesne profits (Housing Act 1980, s. 69, inserting a new s. 106A into the Rent Act 1977).

Q Question 2

In August 1998, Susan bought from Mark the freehold of a house in London divided into three flats.

(a) The first floor flat had been let by Mark in January 1986 to James on a monthly tenancy. It appears that Mark gave James a notice to quit in 1988, but that James stayed on, along with his wife, Cinzia, and son, David.

(b) Mark had let the ground floor flat to Sarah in July 1987 for a fixed term of one year. Sarah wanted the flat as it was near to her office, but she has spent most weekends in her cottage in Wales.

(c) The basement flat was let by Mark to a company called Acrecrest Ltd in December 1988. It appears that Mark was approached by George, who was looking for a place to rent. After taking legal advice, Mark insisted that George acquire Acrecrest Ltd, an 'off the shelf company', and Mark let the basement flat to Acrecrest Ltd for a fixed term of six months. George moved in and has been paying the monthly rent ever since with his own cheque.

James died last month, leaving his widow and son (aged 30) residing in the first floor flat.

Advise Susan as to the likelihood of her being able to recover possession of the three flats.

Commentary

This is a fairly typical problem question on the Rent Act 1977 which requires you to demonstrate an understanding of a number of different issues. Be careful not to linger too much on any one particular point — plan your answer and remember that your task is to advise Susan in relation to all three flats.

The subject of company lets is a favourite amongst examiners, and is likely to arise also in the context of the Housing Act 1988 since the 1988 Act specifically provides that an assured tenancy must be one granted to an 'individual'. Accordingly, a letting to a company will have the attraction of being completely outside the statutory provisions of the 1988 Act from the beginning of the tenancy. By way of contrast, a letting of residential premises to a company as a separate dwelling ranks as a protected tenancy under the Rent Act 1977, and consequently it will be entitled to the benefit of the fair rent provisions (*Carter v SU Carburreter Co.* [1942] 2 KB 288). It will not, however, rank as a statutory tenancy since a company cannot (by its very nature) reside personally in the premises. For a good discussion of the company let device, see Radevsky, T., 'Sham Company Lets' (1990) 140 NLJ 620; Murdoch, S., 'Company Lets' [1989] EG 8907, 85; Waite, A., 'Dodging the Rent Acts' (1981) 131 NLJ 460, and Martin, J.E., 'Nominal Tenants and the Rent Act 1977' [1982] Conv 151.

Here again, the well prepared student should score very heavily!

- Notice to quit in 1988 terminated James' tenancy at common law. Thus, James became a statutory tenant under Rent Act 1977. Cinzia entitled to succeed to the tenancy on his death: Rent Act 1977, sch. 1 and Housing Act 1988, s. 39 and sch. 4. Consider also position of David as family member

- Sarah's protected tenancy ended in July 1988. Does she qualify as a statutory tenant? Mere temporary absence at weekends will not affect her statutory tenancy status: *Langford Property Co. Ltd v Tureman* (1949)

- Since company incapable of occupying the premises personally, it cannot claim a statutory tenancy after end of contractual term: *Hiller v United Dairies (London) Ltd* (1934) and *Carter v SU Carburreter Co* (1942)

- But consider whether letting to Acrecrest Ltd is a sham: *Hilton* v *Plustitle* (1989) and *Estavest Investments Ltd* v *Commercial Express Travel Ltd* (1988). If so, George is the statutory tenant. Conclusion is that all three flats are currently occupied by statutory tenants, who cannot be evicted without proof of grounds for possession

·Ọ́· Suggested answer

(a) First floor flat. The effect of serving a notice to quit on James in January 1988 was to terminate the contractual tenancy at common law. However, assuming James was a protected tenant of the flat immediately before termination, he would have remained in occupation as a statutory tenant of it (Rent Act 1977, s. 2(1)). James has now died, and the question arises whether his widow, who continues to reside in the flat, is entitled to the statutory tenancy by succession. The relevant provisions are contained in sch. 1 to the Rent Act 1977, as amended by the Housing Act 1988, s. 76. The schedule is further amended where the original tenant died on or after 15 January 1989 by virtue of the Housing Act 1988, s. 39 and sch. 4. Under these provisions, Cinzia is entitled to succeed as the widow of the original tenant if she resided in the flat immediately before James's death, provided that she occupied the flat as her residence. These preconditions appear to be met in the present case.

Moreover, as a spouse, her succession will remain a statutory tenancy under the 1977 Act. Accordingly, it is unlikely that Susan will be entitled to possession of this flat unless she is able to establish grounds for possession (under sch. 15 to the 1977 Act) or Cinzia ceases to reside (in which case she will lose her statutory tenant status).

As to James's son, David, the position is that a member of the family of the deceased statutory tenant cannot take the tenancy by succession if there is a surviving spouse. Subject to this, the family member claimant cannot obtain a succession unless he or she has resided in the dwelling-house immediately before the original tenant's death and for a minimum period of two years immediately before then. In these circumstances, the family member obtains an assured tenancy by succession under the Housing Act 1988.

(b) Ground floor flat. Sarah's tenancy expired by effluxion of time in July 1988. Assuming she was a protected tenant under the 1977 Act, the question arises whether she qualifies as a statutory tenant under the Act. A statutory tenancy depends on continuing residence. But the courts have accepted that a tenant may have two homes. In *Langford Property Co. Ltd* v *Tureman* [1949] 1 KB 29, the owner of a cottage in the country resided there with his wife and family. His work was in London and he took the tenancy of a London flat where he slept, on average, for two nights a week. The Court of Appeal held that the tenant was in personal occupation of the flat as his home. See also, *Blanway Investments Ltd* v *Lynch* [1993] EGCS 8, where the tenant lived in Essex but was held to have retained his statutory tenancy of a London maisonette to assist in his business activities. By contrast, in *Walker* v *Ogilvy* (1974) 28 P & CR 288, the flat in question was used only occasionally at weekends and for holidays, and consequently was not held on a statutory tenancy. Thus, occupation merely as a convenience for occasional visits (e.g., for a holiday or as a temporary retreat) will not be classified as residence so as to entitle the tenant to protection under the 1977 Act (*Beck* v *Scholz* [1953] 1 QB 570).

We are told that Sarah wanted the flat as it was near to her office, but that she spends most weekends in her cottage in Wales. It seems evident that Sarah treats her London flat as her home and mere temporary absence at weekends will not deprive her of statutory tenant status (*Roland House Gardens* v *Cravitz* (1975) 29 P & CR 432).

(c) Basement flat. If a company is made the tenant of residential premises, since it is inherently incapable of occupying the premises personally, it cannot claim a statutory tenancy and so has no security of tenure after the contractual tenancy has expired (*Hiller* v *United Dairies (London) Ltd* [1934] 1 KB 57 and *Carter* v *SU Carburreter Co.* [1942] 2 KB 288). Hence the legal advice to Mark that the tenancy should be placed in the name of Acrecrest Ltd. However, it is possible that a letting to a company may be viewed by the courts as a sham device to avoid the protection of the 1977 Act.

In *Hilton* v *Plustitle* [1989] 1 WLR 149, the landlord let a flat to a limited company for a six-month term with a view to enabling the defendant, who was a shareholder and director of the company, to occupy the flat without the right of becoming its statutory tenant. The Court of Appeal held that, although the purpose of the letting was to prevent the creation of a statutory tenancy, the letting was not a sham since it was the intention of both parties (knowing all that was involved) that the flat was to be let to the company. Although the defendant paid the rent with a personal cheque, the letting was clearly intended to be to the company. The same result was reached in *Estavest Investments Ltd* v *Commercial Express Travel Ltd* [1988] 49 EG 73 and *Kaye* v *Massbetter Ltd* [1991] 39 EG 129. In *Estavest*, the rents were paid by the tenant companies and there was no evidence that the amounts came out of the occupier's pocket. Where, however, there is a letting in which the company does not perform genuinely the obligations under the lease and in which a company has been put in as tenant solely as a cloak to avoid statutory protection, the argument that the letting is a sham becomes more persuasive. Ultimately, the issue is one of the genuineness of the transaction: see, most recently, *Eaton Square Properties Ltd* v *O'Higgins* (2001) 33 HLR 68. The fact that George has been paying the rent with his own cheque points to the fact that he was intended to be the real tenant. If that is the case, George is now the statutory tenant of the flat who cannot be evicted without proof of Rent Act grounds.

The conclusion must be that all three flats are currently occupied by statutory tenants and that Susan is unable to recover possession without establishing grounds for possession.

Q Question 3

Martha is an elderly residential tenant who holds a statutory tenancy under the Rent Act 1977. The landlords have indicated that they require possession of the accommodation for redevelopment purposes and have offered Martha alternative premises in a neighbouring area.

Martha, however, is unhappy with this offer because the new property is in a busy street with no garden or park nearby. Moreover, she is worried that she will lose most of her friends in her current locality and will be unable to attend her local church and bridge club.

Can Martha object to the new premises on these grounds? (Illustrate your answer by reference to decided cases.)

Commentary

This question requires a discussion of cases on the meaning of suitable alternative accommodation as a ground for possession under the Rent Act 1977, sch. 15, Pt IV. For further reading, see Wilkinson, H.W., 'Suitable Alternative Accommodation and the Environment' (1983) 266 EG 1166, and Williams, D.W., 'How Suitable is Suitable?' (1983) 268 EG 882.

Try to plan a structure before you start writing your answer — the examiner will be impressed by a well-structured answer which draws on cases to illustrate points of principle.

If you have revised this topic well, it should be plain sailing all the way!

- Provision of suitable alternative accommodation is a ground for possession under the Rent Act 1977. But accommodation must fulfil various criteria: sch. 15, Pt IV

- Consider case law on the relevance of environmental factors: *Redspring* v *Francis* (1973); *Hill* v *Rochard* (1983); *Roberts* v *Macilwraith-Christie* (1987) and *Battlespring Ltd* v *Gates* (1983)

- Consider whether society of friends and cultural interests fall within the meaning of 'character' in sch. 15, para. 5(1)(b): *Siddiqui* v *Rashid* (1980). Relevance to court's discretion to make an order for possession only where it would be reasonable to do so

☼ Suggested answer

The provision of suitable alternative accommodation is a ground for possession contained in the Rent Act 1977, sch. 15, Pt IV. In the absence of a certificate of the local housing authority that it will provide suitable alternative accommodation, the accommodation must fulfil various criteria. In particular, the accommodation must be either:

(a) similar as regards rental and extent to local housing authority dwellings provided for persons having similar needs as regards space to the tenant and his family; or

(b) reasonably suited to the means of the tenant and to the needs of the tenant and his family as regards extent and character.

In *Redspring* v *Francis* [1973] 1 WLR 134, it was held that the court is obliged to have regard to environmental factors where these render the alternative accommodation unsuitable as regards 'character'. In that case, the tenant occupied a flat under a protected tenancy. The flat was situated in a quiet residential road and the tenant had the use of a garden. The alternative accommodation offered was nearby and more spacious, but it had no garden and was in a busy traffic thoroughfare. The Court of Appeal concluded that what a tenant 'needed' was somewhere where he or she could live in reasonably comfortable conditions suitable to the type of life which he or she led. In so far as environmental factors affected the suitability of the proposed accommodation, it was proper to take them into account either as affecting the suitability of the accommodation as regards character, or as affecting the question whether it was reasonable to make an order for possession. In *Redspring*, the trial judge had failed to take the environmental factors into account, and accordingly had misdirected himself in making an order for possession.

The decision in *Redspring* may be contrasted with *Hill* v *Rochard* [1983] 1 WLR 478, in which an elderly couple held a statutory tenancy of a period country house in which they had resided for many years. The premises contained many spacious rooms, outbuildings, a stable, and one and a half acres of land, including a paddock, where the tenants kept a pony. The landlords offered the tenants a modern, detached, four-bedroomed house as alternative accommodation. The house was situated in a cul-de-sac on a housing estate in a nearby country village. The garden covered one-eighth of an acre and there was no stable or paddock. The Court of Appeal held that, in determining whether alternative accommodation was reasonably suitable to the needs of a tenant as regards extent and character, a court should have regard to the particular tenant's *housing need* and not to other ancillary advantages enjoyed by a tenant in his or her present accommodation. In the present case, the trial judge's finding that the new environment would permit the tenants to live reasonably comfortably in the style of life which they liked to lead was a crucial finding directed to the particular tenants which could not be faulted. Accordingly, the order for possession was upheld.

Similarly, in *Roberts* v *Macilwraith-Christie* [1987] 1 EGLR 224, the tenant had lived in the basement of a large, early 19th century house and the alternative accommodation offered was in a modernised ground floor flat, smaller but in better condition than the basement, on a very low rent. The disadvantages were exchanging access to the public garden in Kensington Square for access to Shepherd's Bush Green, lack of room for the large amount of furniture which the tenant possessed, and lack of accommodation for a subtenant. Despite these disadvantages, the Court of Appeal upheld the trial judge's order for possession. By contrast, in *Battlespring Ltd* v *Gates* (1983) 268 EG 355, an elderly widow was offered alternative accommodation in a flat similar in many respects to her maisonette, in the same road, at a slightly smaller rent, the alternative flat being at the more pleasant end of the road and, when renovated, probably more comfortable than her present accommodation. However, after 35 years, having brought up her family there, she was attracted to her present maisonette, with the memories it had for her, and did not want to move. The Court of Appeal held that it would not be reasonable to make an order for possession in all the circumstances. Again, in *Dawncar Investments Ltd* v *Plews* (1993) 25 HLR 639, the flat in question was in a quiet road in Hampstead and the alternative accommodation was on a busy commercial road in Kilburn. Not surprisingly, this was held to be unsuitable.

Also of direct relevance in the present context is the case of *Siddiqui* v *Rashid* [1980] 1 WLR 1018, in which the tenant, a Muslim, was the protected tenant of a flat in London where he had friends and attended a mosque and cultural centre. His place of work, however, was in Luton. The landlords offered him alternative accommodation in Luton near to his place of work. The Court of Appeal held that the word 'character' in sch. 15, para. 5(1)(b), was confined to the character of the property, and although that might be affected by environmental factors (such as noise and smell) which would directly affect the tenant in the enjoyment of the property, it did not extend to the society of friends or cultural interests of the tenant. Accordingly, it was not possible to say that the accommodation offered in Luton was not such that the tenant could not live there in reasonably comfortable conditions suitable to the style of life he had been leading in London.

It is apparent from the foregoing that, in considering Martha's housing needs as regards character, it is permissible to compare the environment to which she has become accustomed with that offered by the alternative accommodation. The upshot of the *Hill* case, however, is that it is not necessary that the character of the alternative accommodation should be similar to that of the existing premises. The real question is whether the alternative accommodation is reasonably suitable to Martha's 'housing need' as regards its character. Since I assume that Martha has had the benefit of a garden or park near her existing accommodation, she is entitled, as part of her housing need, to something which is broadly equivalent in terms of amenity. In *Redspring*, as mentioned earlier, it was stressed that what a tenant 'needed' was somewhere where he (or she) could live in reasonably comfortable conditions. Accordingly, her need for a garden or park close to her home should be taken into account as either affecting the suitability of the accommodation as regards character or, more generally, as a factor governing the reasonableness of making an order for possession against her: *Battlespring*, above.

It seems, however, that factors not directly associated with the property itself (e.g., loss of friends or social interests in the area) have no relevance in determining whether the new premises are reasonably suited to Martha as regards character: *Siddiqui*, above. Such factors, however, may be relevant in determining the broader issue of whether it would be reasonable, in all the circumstances, to make an order for possession. On this basis, Martha can legitimately oppose an order for possession based on the personal disruption this will inevitably cause her in terms of loss of friends and social activities.

Q Question 4

Martin purchased a block of three flats in April 1987.

(a) Flat 1 was unoccupied and Martin lived there for six weeks. He then let it on a weekly tenancy to David, giving notice under the Rent Act 1977, sch. 15, case 11, that he might wish to regain possession. During his six weeks in the flat, Martin spent two or three nights each week in his girlfriend's house where he kept most of his belongings.

(b) When he was staying in Flat 1, Martin granted a weekly tenancy of Flat 2, which was unoccupied, to Michelle, a single mother with two small children. Martin has recently found out that Michelle works as a prostitute, advertising her services and the flat's telephone number in the windows of local newsagents. He has also discovered that she has been convicted recently of possessing cannabis on the premises.

(c) When Martin purchased the block, Flat 3 was occupied by Doris as a statutory tenant under the Rent Act 1977. When she fell ill in January 1990, her daughter Ellen, who had her own house nearby, moved in to look after her mother. Ellen has spent most nights at the flat, returning to her house every few days to make sure that everything was in order. Doris has just died.

Advise Martin, who wishes to obtain possession of the three flats with a view to a sale of the block.

Commentary

This is another fairly typical problem question raising a number of issues on the Rent Act 1977. Remember that there are, essentially, three parts to the question so you should not spend an undue amount of time on one part at the expense of the other parts. Here again, a good knowledge of the case law will pay dividends!

- Consider whether Martin can rely on Case 11 in order to obtain possession of Flat 1. Quality of Martin's residence prior to letting to David: *Mistry v Isidore* (1990) and *Naishe v Curzon* (1984). Martin must also show that he genuinely intends to occupy the flat as a residence for himself: *Kennealy v Dunne* (1977); *Whitworth v Lipton* (1993) and *Rowe v Truelove* (1977)

- Martin not a resident landlord in relation to Flat 2, but may have a ground for possession against Michelle under Case 2. Is she guilty of conduct amounting to a nuisance or annoyance to adjoining occupiers, or has she been convicted of 'using' the premises for immoral or illegal purposes?: *Frederick Platts Co. Ltd v Grigor* (1950) and *Abrahams v Wilson* (1971)

- Can Ellen succeed to her mother's statutory tenancy? Has she been 'residing with' her mother for the requisite period of two years? Requirement that she made her home with her mother and had the intention of forming a family unit: *Foreman v Beagley* (1969) and *Swanbrae Ltd v Elliott* (1987)

:Q: Suggested answer

(a) Flat 1. The question here is whether Martin can rely on case 11 in order successfully to obtain possession of the flat. Martin must show:

(i)   he let the flat on a regulated tenancy;

(ii) before the letting, he occupied it as his residence;

(iii) at the commencement of the tenancy, he gave notice in writing to David that possession might be recovered under case 11; and

(iv) the flat is now required by Martin as a residence for himself.

As to the requirement of residence prior to the letting, occupation by the landlord immediately before the letting is no longer necessary (Rent (Amendment) Act 1985 reversing the decision in *Pocock v Steel* [1985] 1 WLR 229). A more obvious problem relates to the quality of Martin's residence prior to the letting to David. For the purposes of case 11, it is not necessary for the landlord to show that he has occupied the premises as a home but merely for the purposes of residence, which may be temporary or intermittent. In *Mistry v Isidore* [1990] 31 EG 43, the landlord slept in the flat five or six nights each week, spending the other night(s) in his brother's home where he kept most of his belongings. The landlord kept at the flat such clothes as he needed for work and such things as he required for daily living. There were no facilities for washing or cooking in the flat. He remained at the flat on this basis for some eight to nine weeks until he let the flat to the tenant. On these facts, the Court of Appeal held that the landlord had occupied the flat as his residence within the meaing of case 11. Similarly, in *Naishe v Curzon* (1984) 273 EG 1221, where the landlord had used the place as his home on only an intermittent basis prior to letting it out, the Court of Appeal held that whether or not a dwelling-house is occupied as a residence is a question of fact and that temporary or occasional residence can be sufficient.

Although very much a borderline case, given the courts' generous attitude to residence, it is submitted that Martin has occupied the flat as his residence for the purpose of case 11. In order to succeed, however, he must also show that he requires the flat as a residence for himself. In this connection, it has been held that a landlord seeking possession of a dwelling-house under case 11 need not show that he reasonably requires to occupy the house, but merely that he genuinely wants and intends to do so as a residence for himself (or for members of his family) (*Kennealy* v *Dunne* [1977] QB 837). Thus, Martin must establish a genuine desire and a genuine immediate intention to use the flat as his residence. An intention on his part to live in the flat until it can be sold would be consistent with occupying it as a residence under case 11 (*Whitworth* v *Lipton* [1993] EGCS 172). However, if all that he established was an intention to realise his interest in the premises as soon as possible and live in the flat temporarily until he was able to do so, then he would not be entitled to succeed (*Rowe* v *Truelove* (1977) 241 EG 533).

(b) Flat 2. There is no question of Martin relying on the resident landlord exclusion since, even though he may have been technically resident in the block at the time he granted the tenancy to Michelle, the requirement of continuing residence is not satisfied (Rent Act 1977, s. 12). It is likely, however, that Martin may have a ground for possession of the flat under sch. 15, case 2, to the 1977 Act. This case applies where the tenant, *inter alia*, has been guilty of conduct which is a nuisance or an annoyance to adjoining occupiers, or has been convicted of using or allowing the dwelling-house to be used for immoral or illegal purposes.

It is not necessary to show that the tenant has committed the tort of nuisance (see, e.g., *Shine* v *Freedman* [1926] EGD 376, where the tenant had persistently turned the landlord's customers away instead of directing them to the landlord's premises on the first floor). More to the point, it was suggested in *Frederick Platts Co. Ltd* v *Grigor* [1950] WN 194, that a tenant prostitute could be evicted on this ground without proof that adjoining occupiers were annoyed by her activities.

As to the conviction for possession of cannabis in the flat, the mere fact that drugs were on the premises and the tenant was there and had them in her immediate custody will not involve a 'using' of the premises in connection with the offence for the purpose of case 2. The premises must actually be employed as a storage or hiding place for the drugs for a conviction for being in possession of them to come within case 2 (*Abrahams* v *Wilson* [1971] 2 QB 88). See also *S. Schneiders and Sons Ltd* v *Abrahams* [1925] 1 KB 301 (conviction of receiving stolen goods at the demised premises).

The first step will be for Martin to serve Michelle with four weeks' notice to quit the flat, complying with the Protection from Eviction Act 1977, s. 5, thereby terminating her contractual tenancy. Since case 2 is a discretionary ground of possession, Martin must additionally prove that it would be reasonable to make an order for possession (s. 98). In considering reasonableness, the court may take into account the widest range of circumstances. Thus, the fact that Michelle is a single mother with two small children may be relevant. However, it has been held that the statutory protection given to residential tenants under the Rent Act 1977 was not intended to apply where the premises were being used for immoral purposes and, in such cases, therefore, an immediate order for possession is appropriate (*Yates* v *Morris* [1950] 2 All ER 577).

(c) Flat 3. The problem here is that Ellen may wish to claim that she is entitled to succeed to her mother's statutory tenancy. Since her mother died after 15 January 1989, the relevant provisions are to be found in the Rent Act 1977, sch. 1, as amended by the Housing Act 1988, s. 76 and sch. 4. In the absence of a surviving spouse, a family member of the deceased may succeed if he or she resided with the deceased tenant immediately before his death and for a minimum of two years immediately before then.

Since there is no doubt that she qualifies as a member of the family, the central issue is whether Ellen has been 'residing with' her mother for the requisite period of time. The phrase 'residing with' in the statutory succession provisions requires some factual community of family living and companionship. In *Foreman* v *Beagley* [1969] 1 WLR 1387, the tenant was in hospital for the last three years of her life, and her son came to the flat to air the premises and eventually lived there for the last year of her life. The Court of Appeal held that he had not been 'residing with' her as he only moved in as a caretaker without any intention of establishing a joint household. Similarly, in *Swanbrae Ltd* v *Elliott* (1987) 281 EG 916, a daughter who moved in with her sick mother, sleeping three or four nights a week at the premises and spending the other nights in her own house where her son continued to live, was held not to be residing with her mother as she was only a regular visitor. The test, therefore, is whether the claimant had made his or her home with the deceased and had the intention of forming a family unit (*Morgan* v *Murch* [1970] 1 WLR 778; *Hildebrand* v *Moon* (1989) 37 EG 123 and *Hedgedale Ltd* v *Hards* (1991) 15 EG 107).

On the facts of the present case, it is debatable whether Ellen will be able to satisfy this test of residence. However, if she does qualify as successor, she will obtain an assured periodic tenancy of the flat under the Housing Act 1988 (see s. 39(5) and (6)).

Q Question 5

What impact (if any) has the Human Rights Act 1998 made on the private residential rented-sector? Has the public rented-sector faired any better?

Commentary

This is a highly topical question given that the Human Rights Act 1998 was enacted only a few years ago (2000) and a significant line of case law is already emerging both in the private and public-rented sector. You must, of course, refer to the House of Lords' ruling in *Harrow London Borough Council* v *Qazi* [2003] 3 WLR 792, as well as some of the more prominent Court of Appeal decisions in recent years. Show the examiner that you have a good understanding of the issues raised in the case law and, most importantly, develop a theme in your answer which should point towards a useful conclusion. The general consensus amongst academic writers is that the human rights dimension has had only a limited impact on landlord and tenant law. Try and bring this out in your answer and concluding thoughts. We have included a considerable amount of literature on this subject in the **Further Reading** section to be found at the end of this Chapter.

The human rights case law is, undoubtedly, increasing and provides a good source of debate in seminars. Most exam papers will now contain some aspect of human rights law. Your lecturer will, no doubt, indicate what specific aspects are covered in the syllabus.

- Examine the relevance of Arts 1, 6, 8, and 14 of the European Convention. Consider overall impact of House of Lords' decision in *Harrow London Borough Council* v *Qazi* (2003)

- Consider impact of 1988 Act on private-rented sector. Meaning of 'home': *Qazi*, above. Impact on assured shorthold regime: *Poplar HARCA* v *Donoghue* (2001). Existing legislation in respect of protected and assured tenants already provides adequate safeguards: *Castle Vale HAT* v *Gallagher* (2001) and *Lambeth LBC* v *Howard* (2001)

- Consider public sector tenants: *R. (McLellan)* v *Bracknell Forest DC* (2001). Article 14 discrimination claims: *Wandsworth LBC* v *Michalak* (2002) and *Ghaidan* v *Godin-Mendoza* (2002). Article 8 claims: *Newham LBC* v *Kibata* (2004) and *Kensington and Chelsea RLBC* v *O'Sullivan* (2003)

- Overall impact not significant as balance of interests arising under Art 8(2) already adequately struck by existing legislation. Courts reluctant to interfere with statutory schemes

:Ọ́: Suggested answer

The Human Rights Act 1998 came into force on 2 October 2000. It brought much of the European Convention on Human Rights into our domestic (UK) law and allows claimants to use the Convention directly in proceedings in the UK courts.

At first glance, it might seem that the likely impact of the new legislation on landlord and tenant law would be significant given that Art 1 of the First Protocol of the

European Convention (which gives a right to protection from interference with possessions) undoubtedly extends to the various rights inherent in the possession of leasehold property. Other Articles also appear of immediate relevance, in particular Art 8 (right to respect for the home), Art 6 (right to fair procedures) and Art 14 (prohibiting discrimination). However, as we shall see, the reality is that there has been little change from the way in which these Articles had already been interpreted by the European Commission in the specific context of landlord and tenant relations. Art 8 is, perhaps, the most important Convention right applicable in the leasehold context. An individual can rely on Art 8 in any legal proceedings brought against him: s. 7(1)(b) of the 1998 Act. An individual occupier, therefore, in possession proceedings has the potential for arguing Art 8 in any private sector possession claim. The court itself in possession proceedings must act in compliance with Art 8 since it is a 'public authority' within the meaning of s. 6(3)(a).

Article 8 is restricted to premises comprising the claimant's home. This concept is not strictly concerned with the legal basis on which a person occupies particular property, but with the existence of sufficient and continuous links with it. In *Harrow London Borough Council* v *Qazi* [2003] 3 WLR 792, the House of Lords held that the house in question was to be regarded as the defendant's 'home' for the purposes of Art 8 even though he had no legal equitable right to occupy it. However, the majority of their Lordships also concluded that contractual and proprietary rights to possession available to the landlord could not be defeated by a defence based on Art 8. In other words, the relevant statutory scheme would provide the necessary objective justification for the decision whether or not to seek possession. If, therefore, the landlord has an unqualified right to possession, it is apparent that Art 8 will not avail the tenant.

A similar judicial reluctance can be seen in cases prior to the enactment of the 1998 Act. In *Di Palma* v *UK* (1988) 10 EHRR 149, a claim that a landlord's exercise of his right of forfeiture of a lease constituted a breach of Art 1 was emphatically rejected by the European Commission. The fact that the forfeiture clause was effected by means of a court order for possession did not qualify it as a state activity. Moreover, the consensual nature of the forfeiture clause (common to virtually all fixed-term leases and tenancy agreements) was held to preclude a successful claim under Art 1. Interestingly, a claim based on Art 8 also failed on the ground that a right to forfeit was necessary in a democratic society for the protection of the rights and freedoms of others: Art 8(2). Again, in *Kilbourne* v *UK* (1986) 8 EHRR 81, the Commission concluded that rent control was a 'legitimate aim of social policy' and within the state's margin of appreciation.

In the domestic context, recent attempts to strike down the landlord's automatic right to possession of an assured shorthold tenancy upon serving the requisite notice under the Housing Act 1988 have also failed: *Poplar Housing & Regeneration Community Association Ltd* v *Donoghue* [2001] 3 WLR 183 and *R. (McLellan)* v *Bracknell Forest*

District Council (2001) 33 HLR 989. In such cases, it is apparent that Art 8 has no effective role to play in the protection of the tenant's home. Where, however, the claim for possession is against a protected tenant (under the Rent Act 1977) or an assured tenant (under the Housing Act 1988), the tenant can now additionally rely on Art 8 and require the court to 'respect' his home. In *Portsmouth County Council v Bryant* (2000) 33 HLRT 906, the Court of Appeal intimated that the 'nuisance' grounds relating to protected and assured tenants (under which an innocent tenant may be held vicariously liable for the acts of other household members) may have to be reconsidered in the light of the human rights dimension. However, although a possession action will clearly 'engage' Art 8, the various statutory requirements relating to the service of a notice by the landlord and the obtaining of a court order for possession will readily satisfy (in most cases) the conditions in Art 8(2) for legitimate interference with the right to respect for a home. Indeed, the residential statutory codes go further by requiring the landlord to establish one or more of the recognised grounds for possession and, in the case of the discretionary grounds, to show additionally that it would be reasonable to grant possession in all the circumstances. There is no doubt that the requirement of reasonableness covers much of the same ground as the considerations of 'necessity' and 'proportionality' in Art 8(2). Even more importantly, the courts may stay or suspend orders for possession in the exercise of further discretionary powers. Here again, the courts already consider the outcome of the proceedings from the individual tenant's standpoint of what is essentially necessary and proportional having regard to the tenant's right to respect for his (or her) home. It is evident, therefore, that the terms of Art 8 have made little difference to the way in which the English courts have approached the issue of reasonableness and the appropriate order to make in any given case: *Castle Vale Housing Association Trust* v *Gallagher* (2001) 33 HLR 810. In this connection, Art 8 merely reinforces the importance of making a court order depriving a tenant of his/her home only where a clear case for so doing has been made out. In *Lambeth London Borough Council* v *Howard* (2001) 33 HLR 636, for example, the Court of Appeal intimated that there was nothing in Art 8 which would lead county courts to act materially differently in determining whether it is reasonable to make outright, suspended or no possession orders.

In the public sector, the landlord itself may be a 'public authority' for the purposes of s. 6 of the 1998 Act and thus independently subject to the obligation to avoid transgressing the tenant's rights under the Act. However, in the *Poplar Housing* case, referred to above, the Court of Appeal rejected the notion that all housing associations were automatically 'public authorities' within the meaning of the Act. The facts relating to a particular association needed to be looked at to determine whether its relevant functions were of a sufficiently public nature.

Much, however, of what has already been said in relation to protected and assured/ assured shorthold tenants in the private sector, applies equally to secure tenants in

the public sector. Although a possession action will engage Art 8, the various requirements under the Housing Act 1988, Pt I (in relation to secure tenants) means that
there is already considerable overlap between the court's statutory functions and
the obligation to meet the requirements of Art 8. Interestingly, in the *McLellan* case,
mentioned earlier, the Court of Appeal dismissed the tenant's argument that the
whole statutory scheme for introductory tenancies (introduced by the Housing Act
1996, Pt V) was incompatible with the European Convention. In *Lee* v *Leeds City
Council* [2002] 1 WLR 1488, the Court of Appeal held that there was no general and
unqualified obligation on local authority landlords to ensure that the condition
of their housing stock did not infringe their tenants' Convention rights in respect
of their home and family life. Only in extreme cases could public housing that was
unfit for human habitation give rise to a breach of the 1988 Act. In *Wandsworth
London Borough Council* v *Michalak* [2002] 4 All ER 1136, a relative of the deceased
secure tenant argued that the succession provisions in the Housing Act 1985 were
discriminatory in that they only applied to a narrowly defined group of family
members: see, s. 113 of the 1985 Act. The Court of Appeal, however, dismissed this
argument on the basis that the legislation had provided a legitimate rationale for
allocating public resources. In *Ghaidan* v *Godin-Mendoza* [2002] 4 All ER 1162, on the
other hand, the Court of Appeal held that a same-sex partner could succeed to a Rent
Act-protected tenancy under para. 2 of sch. 1 to the Rent Act 1977, which allowed a
person living with the tenant as 'his or her wife or husband' to succeed. The decision
has been upheld recently on appeal to the House of Lords: [2004] UKHL 30. To construe para. 2 other than to include same-sex partners was incompatible with the
Convention: see, *Fitzpatrick* v *Sterling Housing Association Ltd* [2001] 1 AC 27, where
the House of Lords held that a same-sex partner could only succeed if he (or she) was a
member of the original tenant's family.

Most recently, in *Newham London Borough Council* v *Kibata* [2004] 15 EG 106, the
Court of Appeal held that Art 8 was unavailable to the husband of a secure tenant
once the latter had given notice to the Council terminating her tenancy of the flat.
The tenant had complained of domestic violence by the husband and sought to be
rehoused. It was the Council's policy to require the tenant to give notice terminating
her tenancy so that she could be considered for rehousing. The Court held that
the Council's policy was not unlawful and that it had a right to possession of the
flat against the husband. Article 8 had not been infringed. Moreover, the act of
the Council in obtaining from the tenant a notice to quit did not amount to a determination of the husband's civil rights within meaning of Art 6. In another recent
case, the Court of Appeal has held that it is not discriminatory (under Art 14) for
a local authority to have a policy granting a tenancy to a husband alone when providing accommodation for couples: *Kensington and Chelsea Royal London Borough
Council* v *O'Sullivan* [2003] EWCA Civ 371 and *Sheffield City Council* v *Smart* [2002]
EWCA Civ 04. It has also been held that the county court procedure for issuing

possession warrants against secure tenants does not infringe either Art 6 or 8 of the Convention: *St. Brice v. Southwark London Borough Council* [2001] All ER (D) 209.

What emerges from this overview? It is apparent that legislation that has a legitimate social purpose is difficult to challenge, particularly if the deprivation of the individual's rights is already subject to adequate safeguards and limitations. In most cases, the courts have been reluctant to interfere with domestic housing legislation concluding that housing law is largely a matter for the allocation of resources in accordance with government welfare and economic policies. Invariably, the balance of interests arising under Art 8(2) has already been struck adequately by the legislature so the courts are naturally reluctant to interfere with the various statutory schemes. Thus far, therefore, the overall impact of the 1988 Act on the private and public sector has been only marginal.

Further reading

Berry, C., 'Expediency Rules OK' (2000) SJ 128.

Bruce, A., 'Barring Peaceable Re-entry' (2000) NLJ 462.

Davies, L., 'New Rights for Unlawful Occupants' (2002) SJ 214.

Driscoll, J., 'What is a Dwelling?' (2001) NLJ 1634.

Heppinstall, A., and Walker, A., 'End of the Line?' (2003) SJ 798.

Iles, A., 'Issuing Possession Warrants' (2001) NLJ 1546.

Murdoch, S., 'Unlawful Occupiers' [2004] EG 127.

Preston, D., 'A Modern Day Dwelling' (2001) SJ 1064.

Price, G., 'A Conservative Take on Housing Law' [2003] EG 60.

Price, G., 'A Conventional View on Housing and Human Rights' [2003] EG 138.

Probert, R., 'Tenancies and Same-sex Partners' (2002) NLJ 1801.

Redpath-Stevens, A., '*Qazi* and the Right to a Home' (2003) SJ 1011.

11 Q&A

Assured and assured shorthold tenancies

Introduction

This chapter contains questions on the Housing Act 1988, Pt I (i.e., the assured and assured shorthold tenancy), which came into force on 15 January 1989. The assured tenancies scheme replaces that of the Rent Act 1977 in respect of tenancies created on or after 15 January 1989.

One of the basic aims of the new scheme was to enable landlords to grant tenancies to residential tenants at a market rent, with the ability more easily to regain possession of the premises at the expiry of the lease than was possible in the case of a Rent Act protected or statutory tenant.

Prior to the enactment of the Housing Act 1996, an assured shorthold tenancy had to be for a fixed term with a minimum duration of at least six months and the landlord must have served a notice on the proposed tenant before the tenancy began, informing the tenant that the tenancy was to be a shorthold. The court had no power to waive this requirement. Thus, if the requisite notice was not served, the tenancy would be an assured tenancy enjoying the full benefit of security under Pt I. The 1996 Act changed the law by providing (in s. 96) that an assured tenancy post-dating the commencement date of the section (i.e., 28 February 1997) is to be automatically treated as an assured shorthold, unless it falls within any of the stated exceptions. The exceptions are narrowly defined to maximise the scope of shortholds and contain obvious exclusions such as, for example, where it is explicitly stated (either before or during the assured tenancy) that it is not to be an assured shorthold.

The upshot of these amendments is that a landlord is no longer required to serve any preliminary notice on the tenant, neither is there any requirement that the tenancy is of a fixed term. However, the landlord is not entitled to an order for possession until at least six months have elapsed from the grant of the tenancy (s. 99). A number of recent cases have, however, emerged regarding the validity of s. 20 notices in respect of pre–1996 assured shorthold tenancies. The trend of these cases is difficult to discern and it is still unclear to what extent the test of the 'reasonable recipient' enunciated in *Mannai Investment Co. Ltd* v *Eagle Star Life Assurance Co. Ltd* [1997] AC 749 is applicable in this context: see Question 4.

You will find that most of the questions on Pt I of the Housing Act 1988 will require you to delve into Rent Act case law since the provisions of the two Acts are similar (but not necessarily identical) in many respects. We would urge you, therefore, to look also at the questions featured in the preceding chapter on the Rent Act 1977.

Q Question 1

Maud has just inherited a house converted into flats, with part vacant possession. She intends to use the house as a source of rental income rather than to sell it or grant long leases. Advise her to what extent she may ensure that future occupants do not enjoy security of tenure.

Commentary

This is a straightforward essay question on the exclusions to an assured tenancy and the mechanics of the assured shorthold tenancy. The sch. 1 exclusions (in the 1988 Act) bear a close resemblance to those of the Rent Act 1977, ss. 4–16, but they are not identical. In particular, a letting which includes payments in respect of board or attendance, exempt from protected status under the 1977 Act (see s. 7), is not prevented from being an assured tenancy on that ground. It should also be noted that, with the repeal of the restricted contract provisions (see s. 19 of the 1977 Act), there is no residual security of tenure for tenancies which are excluded from assured status by sch. 1 to the 1988 Act.

- Maud should consider creating assured shorthold tenancies under the Housing Act 1988, Pt I. Examine current requirements under Housing Act 1996. What will be the effect of granting assured shorthold status?

- Alternatively, she may be able to bring her tenancies within several of the exclusions contained in sch. 1 to the Housing Act 1988. Thereby avoiding assured status altogether. Consider holiday lets: *Buchmann* v *May* (1978)

- Consider also resident landlord status: sch. 1, para. 10. Alternatively, grant licences instead of tenancies: *Street* v *Mountford* (1985). But courts astute to detect sham devices: *AG Securities* v *Vaughan/Antoniades* v *Villiers* (1988)

- Also consider use of company let — a tenancy is only assured if and so long as the tenant is an individual: s. 1(1)(a). Also, tenant must occupy the dwelling-house as his home: *Hiller* v *United Dairies (London) Ltd* (1934). Similar schemes have proved successful in the Rent Act context: *Hilton* v *Plustitle Ltd* (1988)

☼ Suggested answer

An obvious way in which Maud can ensure that her future occupants do not enjoy security of tenure is to grant assured shorthold tenancies of the flats under Pt I of the

Housing Act 1988. Section 96 of the Housing Act 1996 (which came into force on 28 February 1997) has amended the 1988 Act by abolishing the requirement for a preliminary notice as a precondition for the grant of an assured shorthold tenancy. Moreover, the requirement of a minimum fixed term of at least six months has also been removed so that a shorthold tenancy can now be granted for any term (fixed or periodic), although the landlord will not be entitled to obtain a court order for possession until at least six months have elapsed from the grant of the tenancy (s. 99). If the tenancy is made orally (i.e., if it is periodic or for a term not exceeding three years: s. 54(2) of the Law of Property Act 1925), the landlord is obliged to provide written terms of the tenancy (rent, duration, etc.) only if requested by notice in writing served by the tenant.

The effect of granting an assured shorthold tenancy is that once the fixed term has expired by effluxion of time (subject to s. 99), Maud can obtain possession of the flat without establishing any grounds for possession. She must, however, give the tenant two month's written notice, but this may be given before the fixed term has expired (s. 21(1) and (2)). By the time the action comes to court, the tenant may be holding over as a statutory periodic tenant (see s. 5(2)) but this will not prejudice Maud's right to possession. In fact, the court, on being satisfied of the above conditions, must order possession.

Instead of granting assured shorthold tenancies of the flats, Maud may be in a position to bring her tenancies within one or more of the exclusions contained in sch. 1 to the Housing Act 1988 and thereby avoid assured status altogether. One possibility is that she grants holiday lettings of the flats. A tenancy cannot be an assured tenancy (and, hence, an assured shorthold tenancy) if its purpose is to confer on the tenant the right to occupy the dwelling-house for the purpose of a holiday (sch. 1, para. 9). The word 'holiday' is not defined in the statute but, in the context of the Rent Act 1977, it has been judicially interpreted as 'a period of cessation of work or a period of recreation' (*Buchmann* v *May* [1978] 2 All ER 993). Although the onus is on the tenant to displace the prima facie evidence of the parties' true purpose which the written agreement provides, the courts are astute to detect shams, whose only object is to avoid statutory protection such as the Housing Act 1988.

Another possibility is for Maud actually to live in the house and thereby qualify as a resident landlord (sch. 1, para. 10). The first precondition for resident landlord status is that the flat let to the tenant forms part of a building which is not a purpose-built block of flats. The phrase 'purpose-built block of flats' is defined in sch. 1, para. 22. It must *as constructed* contain two or more flats. The date of construction is the relevant time to consider, and a distinction is drawn between conversions of existing buildings (which will not, generally speaking, constitute 'purpose-built blocks of flats') and constructions of new buildings which, if they consist of two or more flats, will be within the definition (see *Bardrick* v *Haycock* (1976) 31 P & CR 420 and *Barnes* v

Gorsuch (1981) 43 P & CR 294). Assuming the house is *not* a purpose-built block of flats, then several further preconditions must be satisfied, namely:

(a) the flats let to the tenants must form part only of the building;

(b) Maud (being the person who granted the tenancies) must have been an individual and she must have occupied another dwelling-house in the same building as her only or principal home; and

(c) she must continue to occupy part of the building as her only or principal home from the date of the tenancies to the date possession is claimed.

A further exclusion which Maud may wish to consider relates to the granting of licences (as opposed to tenancies) of the flats. An assured/assured shorthold tenancy under the 1988 Act must be a tenancy. The classic definition of a tenancy is to be found in *Street* v *Mountford* [1985] AC 809 (i.e., there must be a grant of exclusive possession for a term at a rent). It has been the common practice of landlords to grant 'non-exclusive occupation agreements', whereby a landlord issues joint occupiers with identical licence agreements under which each occupier agrees that he or she will share the dwelling-house with the other(s) or, in some cases, with whomsoever the landlord may nominate. The argument for upholding such agreements is that they do not confer on the occupants exclusive possession of the premises and therefore fall outside statutory protection. However, such agreements have been successfully attacked on the basis that they are shams or pretences in so far as the landlord does not genuinely intend them to be a true statement of the nature of the possession to be enjoyed by the occupiers (see, e.g., *AG Securities* v *Vaughan/Antoniades* v *Villiers* [1988] 3 WLR 1205). If the true effect of the agreement is to confer on the occupiers a *joint* right of exclusive possession, then they will be joint tenants.

It may also be possible for Maud to utilise the company let device for avoiding security of tenure under the Housing Act 1988. A tenancy is assured only if and so long as the tenant is an individual (s. 1(1)(a)). Moreover, the tenant must occupy the dwelling-house as his home (*Hiller* v *United Dairies (London) Ltd* [1934] 1 KB 57). These provisions are intended to prevent companies from claiming the benefits of the legislation. In its simplest form, the company let involves the landlord letting the property to a limited company (which undertakes to pay the rent and comply with the tenant's covenants), and the company then allows a person into occupation as licensee. The company cannot be an assured tenant, as it is not an individual, and the occupier is not an assured tenant either (i.e., he may not be a tenant at all, or he may be paying no rent). Similar schemes have succeeded in avoiding Rent Act protection (*Hilton* v *Plustitle Ltd* [1988] 3 All ER 1051).

A less well-known device for avoiding security of tenure involves a provision in the tenancy agreement permitting the landlord unilaterally to increase (or reduce) the rent to a level at which Housing Act 1988 protection is removed. The Court of Appeal ruling in *Bankway Properties Ltd* v *Dunsford* [2001] 1 WLR 1369 suggests that such artificial devices are unlikely to find favour with the courts. In that case, the assured tenancy agreement provided that the reviewed rent should be the sum of £25,000 per year (thereby bringing the tenancy outside the 1988 statutory code). Such a sham device, however, was outlawed by the Court as being an attempt to contract out of the scheme of the 1988 Act.

Lastly, it should be mentioned that a letting which includes payment in respect of board or attendance, exempt from protected status under the Rent Act 1977, is not prevented from being an assured tenancy on that ground.

Q Question 2

Greenleaves and Brownleaves are two detached freehold properties in the ownership of Mr Wright.

In October 1989, Mr Wright granted an assured monthly tenancy of Flat 1 at Greenleaves to Tom, who is currently four months in arrears with his rent. Tom has had a history of late payment of rent over the past few years.

In January 1990, Mr Wright granted an assured tenancy for a fixed term of three years of Flat 1 at Brownleaves to Dick, who has recently separated from his wife and no longer lives at the premises with her.

In May 1993, Mr Wright granted an assured shorthold tenancy of Flat 2 at Brownleaves to Harriet. Since the expiry of this tenancy, Harriet has remained in occupation paying a weekly rent.

In order to run both properties efficiently, Mr Wright has (since acquiring both properties in 1985) spent three nights a week at Flat 2, Greenleaves, and four nights a week (including weekends) at Flat 3, Brownleaves. He has now decided to retire from the business and wishes to sell both properties with vacant possession. He seeks your advice as to whether he can successfully bring proceedings to evict Tom, Dick, and Harriet prior to the sale of the properties.

Advise Mr Wright.

Commentary

This is a factually complicated question and certainly not one for the faint-hearted! Although there are numerous issues to cover, be consoled by the fact that you cannot be expected to deal with all the issues in any great detail.

Before you start, draw up a rough plan showing which flats are situated in the two buildings, details of each tenancy and key issues arising. Our suggestion is to deal with each tenancy in turn and then consider the general point regarding the resident landlord exclusion.

Greenleaves	Brownleaves
Flat 1: assured monthly tenancy to Tom	**Flat 1**: assured fixed-term tenancy to Dick
Flat 2: Mr Wright (three nights a week)	**Flat 2**: assured shorthold tenancy to Harriet. Now, a weekly tenant.
	Flat 3: Mr Wright (four nights a week)

- Serve s. 8 notice on Tom seeking possession on grounds 8, 10 and 11 — all relating to non-payment of rent. Proceedings must also be brought within time limits. No relief against forfeiture under County Courts Act 1984, s. 138: *Artesian Residential Investments Ltd* v *Beck* (1999)

- Assured tenant must occupy the dwelling-house as his 'only or principal home': 1988 Act, s. 1. But tenant husband (Dick) who abandons wife will remain an assured tenant: *Brown* v *Draper* (1944). Occupation of wife is to be treated as occupation of the husband: Matrimonial Homes Act 1983, s. 1(6) as amended by Housing Act 1988, sch. 17, para. 33

- Harriet holding over as statutory periodic tenant: s. 5(2). Mr Wright can give two months' notice requiring possession of her flat: s. 21(3). But continued payment of weekly rent may give rise to inference of a new (assured shorthold) periodic tenancy

- Consider whether Mr Wright is a resident landlord based on his occupation of Brownleaves. Two-home landlord in Rent Act context: *Wolff* v *Waddington* (1989). But Mr Wright must show that he occupies Flat 3, Brownleaves, as his 'principal' home for Housing Act purposes

☼ Suggested answer

Flat 1, Greenleaves, is occupied by Tom on an assured monthly tenancy. Because he occupies as a contractual periodic tenant, his tenancy cannot be brought to an end by Mr Wright except by obtaining a court order for possession (s. 5(1) of the Housing Act 1988). In other words, a notice to quit by the landlord in relation to such a tenancy will be of no effect.

Before proceedings are commenced, Mr Wright must serve on Tom a s. 8 notice in the prescribed form. This must inform Tom of the ground(s) on which possession is sought and set out the time-scale of the action (s. 8(3)). Once this s. 8 notice is served,

Mr Wright must bring his proceedings within the time-limits set out in s. 8(3). Proceedings should not commence earlier than two weeks from the service of the s. 8 notice, unless possession is sought under grounds 1, 2, 5 to 7, 9 and 16, in which case proceedings should not commence earlier than two months from service and, if the tenancy is periodic, the date on which the tenancy could be terminated by notice to quit given on the date of service of the notice.

It seems that Mr Wright has three separate grounds for possession under sch. 2 — ground 8 (mandatory — at least three months' rent unpaid) and grounds 10 (some rent lawfully due) and 11 (persistent delay in paying rent), being both discretionary grounds — all relating to non-payment of rent. Accordingly, he may commence proceedings for possession after two weeks from the date of service of his s. 8 notice. It has been held that the terms of the 1988 Act expressly rule out a claim for forfeiture by the landlord (see s. 5(1) and s. 45(4)). In *Artesian Residential Investments Ltd* v *Beck* [1999] 22 EG 145, the Court of Appeal held that s. 7(3) is explicit in obliging the court mandatorily to order possession if the court is satisfied that any of the grounds in sch. 2 is established. There is no room, therefore, for an assured tenant applying for relief against forfeiture under s. 138 of the County Courts Act 1984.

If Tom decides to send a cheque for the full amount of the arrears a few days before the court hearing and this is accepted by Mr Wright, the district judge is entitled to adjourn the possession proceedings to allow time for the cheque to be cleared. The adjournment will only be for a short period (normally 7–14 days): *Day* v *Coltrane* [2003] 30 EG 146.

So far as Flat 1, Brownleaves, is concerned, Dick's assured tenancy expired by effluxion of time in January 1993 and he has recently separated from his wife and no longer lives with her at the premises. The question, therefore, arises as to whether Dick's statutory periodic tenancy (which automatically came into being upon the expiry of the fixed term: see s. 5(2)) continues to be assured under the 1988 Act. If not, Mr Wright may simply determine the statutory periodic tenancy by giving Dick the appropriate notice for the period of the tenancy (i.e., one month's notice in the case of a monthly tenancy). If, on the other hand, Dick retains his assured tenancy status (despite no longer living at the premises), Mr Wright would only be entitled to evict him by seeking possession on any of the grounds in sch. 2 and by serving the appropriate s. 8 notice on him. For the purposes of security of tenure, there is no distinction made between assured contractual periodic tenancies and assured statutory periodic tenancies.

As to Dick's status, it is evident that an assured tenant must 'occupy' the dwelling-house as his 'only or principal home' (s. 1): *Ujima Housing Association* v *Ansah* (1998) 30 HLR 831. The tenant husband who goes away for a time leaving his spouse in occupation will, as long as he intends to return to the house, remain an assured tenant (*Brown* v *Brash* [1948] 2 KB 247). The tenant who leaves with no intention to return (in other words, abandoning his wife) will also, nevertheless, remain an

assured tenant (*Brown* v *Draper* [1944] KB 309, in the Rent Act context). ...
Matrimonial Homes Act 1983, s. 1(6), as amended by the Housing Act 1988, sch. 17,
para. 33, provides that the occupation of the wife, in these circumstances, is to be
treated as the occupation of the husband. Accordingly, as long as Dick's wife continues to occupy the flat (and as long as she continues to be Dick's wife), the assured
tenancy will persist. She will be entitled to make rent payments herself (Matrimonial
Homes Act 1983, s. 1(5)). She may fail to do this, in which case Mr Wright will have
grounds for seeking possession (see grounds 8, 10 and 11, above).

Regarding Flat 2, Brownleaves, this was initially occupied by Harriet under an
assured shorthold tenancy, which we are told has now expired, but Harriet continues
to remain in occupation paying the weekly rent. Since the fixed term has expired by
effluxion of time, Mr Wright can obtain possession of the flat by giving Harriet two
months' notice (s. 5(2)). The fact that Harriet is holding over as a statutory periodic
tenant (by virtue of s. 5(2)) will not prejudice Mr Wright's position (s. 21(3)).
The court, on being satisfied that the tenancy was an assured shorthold, must order
possession. One problem which may arise, however, relates to the continued payment
of the weekly rent by Harriet. This may give rise to the inference that a *new* periodic
tenancy has been created by agreement following the expiry of the assured shorthold.
Normally, the expiry of the term will lead to the implication of a statutory periodic
tenancy. If, however, Harriet can point to the grant of another tenancy on the coming
to an end of the fixed term, that tenancy will not be a statutory periodic tenancy
(s. 5(4)); it will almost certainly be an assured (shorthold) tenancy under the 1988 Act
(s. 20(4)), and Mr Wright will have to satisfy the two months' notice requirement
under s. 21(1) in relation to that tenancy.

Harriet may also end her statutory periodic tenancy by serving an ordinary common law notice to quit (subject to the four-week minimum imposed by s. 5 of the
Protection from Eviction Act 1977): *Laine* v *Cadwallader* [2001] L & TR 8. Mr Wright is
also free to accept an offer of surrender from Harriet.

It seems, therefore, that Mr Wright may have difficulties in recovering possession
of Flats 1 and 2, Brownleaves. In order to avoid these difficulties, he may wish to
consider arguing that he is a resident landlord in respect of the flats at Brownleaves,
based on his residence of Flat 3 in that building for four nights a week (including
weekends). Assuming that the building is *not* a purpose-built block of flats, Mr Wright
must establish that he has occupied Flat 3 as his only or principal home. It has been
held, in the Rent Act context, that a landlord may have two homes for the purpose of
the resident landlord exclusion (*Wolff* v *Waddington* [1989] 47 EG 148) and that it is
possible to occupy a flat as a home despite spending only two or three nights there
(*Langford Property Co. Ltd* v *Tureman* [1949] 1 KB 29, involving a statutory tenant). In
the Housing Act 1988 context, however, assuming Mr Wright occupies both flats as
his home, the crucial question is whether he occupies Flat 3, Brownleaves, as his
principal home. Only then will he qualify for resident landlord status.

3

...oes the assured tenancy permit landlords to charge their tenants a
...hat is the position under an assured shorthold tenancy?

Co... ...ary

This is an easy question if you have studied the relevant provisions on rent in the Housing
Act 1988, as amended by the Housing Act 1996, s. 100.

Some landlord and tenant syllabuses may concentrate quite heavily on the rental aspects
of Pt I of the 1988 Act, although our experience is that lecture-time tends to be devoted
more to security of tenure. Our advice is to be guided by your lecturer and the emphasis he
or she places on different parts of the course.

- Landlord has no right to increase rent during fixed term (assured) tenancy:
  s. 13(1). Similarly, tenant has no right to apply for a rent reduction. But consider
  effect of rent review clause in tenancy

- Rent increases permissible in respect of statutory periodic tenancies, but tenant
  has no right to propose rent reduction

- Landlord also free (at any time) to invoke rent proposal provisions in respect of
  assured periodic tenancies: ss. 13 and 14

- Consider how the rent assessment committee makes its rent determination in
  respect of assured tenancies: s. 14

- No right to rent increase during initial fixed term of old assured shorthold
  tenancy, but tenant may apply for a rent reduction. Examine s. 22 procedure.
  After initial fixed term, landlord may propose a rent increase: s. 13. In respect of
  new assured shorthold tenancies (granted on or after 28 February 1987), tenant
  may apply for reduction during first six months of tenancy: Housing Act 1996,
  s. 100

☼ Suggested answer

The policy of Pt I of the Housing Act 1988 is to allow the landlord and tenant to enjoy
freedom of contract to stipulate the level of the rent, to agree upon a rent review
clause in appropriate cases, and to limit the degree of statutory intervention.

While a fixed term (assured) tenancy is continuing, the parties will be bound by the
contractual rent. Thus, the landlord is not entitled to increase the rent unilaterally or
to apply to the rent assessment committee for the rent to be increased (s. 13(1)). There
may, however, be a rent review clause in the lease which may permit upwards (or

downwards) rent reviews at stated intervals. Similarly, the tenant is bound by the terms of the lease and (in the absence of a review clause) has no right to apply for a rent reduction.

In the case of a statutory periodic tenancy (which will arise when an assured fixed-term tenancy comes to an end), the rent payable will continue at the same level as before (s. 5(3)). However, the landlord now has the right to propose a rent increase. The tenant, however, is given no corresponding right to propose that the rent be reduced.

In the case of a contractual (assured) *periodic* tenancy, the landlord is free (at any time) to invoke the Act's rent proposal provisions. These involve the landlord serving on the tenant a notice in prescribed form which proposes the new rent and the date it is to take effect. If the tenant wishes to contest the rent proposed, he must refer the notice to a rent assessment committee before the date on which the proposed rent is to take effect. If he fails to do so, the rent as proposed will take effect on the date shown in the notice (ss. 13 and 14).

Where the tenant refers the notice to the rent assessment committee, the committee must determine the rent at which they consider the dwelling-house might reasonably be expected to be let in the open market by a willing landlord under an assured tenancy having the same terms as the tenancy in question (s. 14(1)). In making the determination, the committee must disregard any effect on the rent attributable to the granting of a tenancy to a sitting tenant, any increase in value of the dwelling-house attributable to certain tenant's improvements (defined in s. 14(3)) and any reduction in value of the house attributable to the tenant's breach of covenant (s. 14(2)).

This formula is, of course, radically different from that which prevails in relation to Rent Act tenancies. In its attempt to free the private landlord from the shackles of letting at a 'fair rent' (which, by definition, was less than the market rent), and thereby revitalise the private rented sector, the 1988 Act places the responsibility in the hands of the rent assessment committees rather than rent officers. These committees must, in each case, consider the local market, the number of potential tenants for the particular property, and then assess the sum at which a 'willing landlord' (i.e., someone who wants to let, given a reasonable return on his or her property, being appraised of the market conditions) would reasonably expect the property to be rented. The committee may, in determining the rent under s. 14, refer to comparable assured tenancy rents in the vicinity, and the president of each rent assessment panel is placed under a duty to keep and make publicly available certain information with respect to rents under assured tenancies.

In the case of assured shorthold tenancies, the landlord has no right to seek an increase in rent during the initial fixed term. During that same fixed term, however, the tenant may apply to the rent assessment committee for a reduction in the rent. On such an application, the committee is required to determine the rent which, in its opinion, the landlord might reasonably be expected to obtain under the assured shorthold tenancy (s. 22(1)). If the tenant's application is successful, he may not apply again (s. 22(2)(a)). Moreover, once the initial fixed term has ended, the tenant no longer has the right to apply, even if he has not applied before and even if the landlord and tenant enter into a new fixed term assured shorthold agreement (s. 22(2)). These provisions are now modified in relation to new assured shorthold tenancies (granted on or after 28 February 1997, which do not have to comply with the requirement of a fixed term) by virtue of the Housing Act 1996, s. 22. In relation to new tenancies, the tenant is allowed to make his application for a reduction in rent during the first six months from the grant of the original tenancy.

Under the s. 22 procedure, the committee is directed not to make a determination at all unless it considers that there is a sufficient number of similar dwelling-houses in the locality let on assured tenancies (whether shorthold or not) (s. 22(3)(a)). In other words, the committee is not expected to tamper with the rent payable by the tenant: unless it considers that the rent he or she pays is 'significantly higher' than those with comparable tenancies, it should not make any determination at all (s. 22(3)(b)).

When the initial fixed term has expired, the landlord may propose an increase of rent under s. 13 of the 1988 Act. However, if the committee has made a determination under s. 22 on the tenant's application, the landlord will have to wait 12 months before he can make a rent proposal (s. 22(4)(c)). When the landlord is free to propose an increased rent, the procedure to be followed will be the same as for any assured tenancy (i.e., the committee must determine the rent at which the dwelling-house might reasonably be expected to be let in the open market by a willing landlord under an assured shorthold tenancy).

The inference to be drawn from these provisions is that a landlord who lets on an assured shorthold should not reasonably expect to obtain as high a rent as a landlord who lets on an assured tenancy which is not shorthold. The price to the landlord of conferring no security of tenure is a return on the property lower than that otherwise obtainable. However, much will depend on the way the market operates. If there are more potential tenants than available properties, the level of rents under assured shorthold tenancies will not be substantially lower than that for assured tenancies with security of tenure. In either case, the rent will be a market rent for that particular tenancy.

Q Question 4

To what extent has the *Mannai* principle been applied in the context of statutory notices served under Pt I of the Housing Act 1988? Is there a discernible trend in the case law?

Commentary

This is not an easy question. Although there have been a number of recent cases on the validity of s. 20 (and s. 21) notices under the Housing Act 1988, the extent to which the 'reasonable recipient' test (laid down in *Mannai*) applies in this context is still far from clear. There has been a lot of academic (and practitioner) literature on this subject and there is no doubt that it remains a topical area of study. The cases, however, are not easy to reconcile and the temptation is to refer simply to a few decisions without really trying to rationalise the appropriate tests used by the courts. To help you with this question, here are some useful articles: Blaker, G., 'Reasonable Notice' (2003) SJ 1070; Pawlowski, M., 'Assured Shorthold Tenancies: Section 20 Notices' [2001] JHL 34; Bedworth, G., 'Sounding the Retreat' (2004) SJ 43; Chapman, H., 'Landlords Take Note' (2003) SJ 1264; Webber, G., 'Caught Short' (2002) SJ 182 and Gaunt, J., 'Notices: When is a Defect not a Defect — Parts I and II?' (2002) NLJ 424 and 460.

- Explain *Mannai* 'reasonable recipient' test. Reformulation of the test in *York* v *Casey* (1998). New two-stage test applied to s. 20 notices: *Panayi* v *Roberts* (1993), *Andrews* v *Burrows* (1997) and *Clickex Ltd* v *McCann* (1999)

- More restrictive approach which stresses importance of complying with statutory requirements applied in *John Lyon Grammar School* v *Secchi* (1999) and *Speedwell Estates Ltd* v *Dalziel* (2002)

- Decision in *Ravenseft Properties Ltd* v *Hall* (2002) sees a return to a more pragmatic approach reflected in *Mannai*. Also evident in *B Osborn & Co. Ltd* v *Dior* (2003)

- But strict approach adopted in *McDonald* v *Fernandez* (2003) concerning the validity of a s. 21 notice. Language of statute more prescriptive here. Absence of any wording allowing the notice to be 'substantially to the same effect'. This explains difference in approach

:Q: Suggested answer

One of the prerequisites to the creation of an assured shorthold tenancy prior to the enactment of the Housing Act 1996 was the service by the landlord of a notice on the proposed tenant before the tenancy began, informing the tenant that the tenancy was to be a shorthold. Although the 1996 Act changed the law in this respect, the requirement of a 'starter' or preliminary notice has given rise to problems for many landlords seeking possession of premises in reliance on a tenancy agreement pre-dating the 1996 Act.

In *Mannai Investment Co. Ltd* v *Eagle Star Life Assurance Co. Ltd* [1997] AC 749, the majority of the House of Lords, applying the test enunciated in *Carradine Properties Ltd* v *Aslam* [1976] 1 WLR 442, concluded that the correct test for determining the validity of a contractual break notice was whether a reasonable recipient of the notice with knowledge of the terms of the lease would have been left in no doubt as to when the lease was to end. In *York* v *Casey* [1998] 2 EGLR 25, the Court of Appeal, dealing with a case involving a s. 20 notice under the Housing Act 1988, concluded that there was no material distinction between the approach adopted in *Mannai* (involving a notice in a contractual setting) and a statutory notice served by a landlord in the context of a residential lease. The Court, however, went on, in effect, to reformulate the *Mannai* approach into a two-stage test involving, initially, an examination of whether the error in the notice was obvious or evident and, secondly, whether notwithstanding that error, the notice in its context was sufficiently clear to leave a reasonable recipient in no reasonable doubt as to the terms of the notice. In *York* itself, the s. 20 notice incorrectly stated the termination date as September 6, a date preceding the actual start date of the tenancy. This error was considered to be so obvious that the reasonable recipient would not have been misled by it.

This two-stage approach stemmed from two earlier Court of Appeal cases, namely, *Panayi* v *Roberts* [1993] 2 EGLR 51 and *Andrews* v *Burrows* (1997) 30 HLR 203, both specifically concerned with s. 20 notices and decided prior to the House of Lords' ruling in *Mannai*. In *Panayi*, the Court held that the use of 'May' rather than 'November' in the s. 20 notice in respect of the month of termination of the tenancy was not an evident error or obvious slip. An 'evident error' in this context meant an error which would have been evident to a person with the ordinary qualities of the recipient. Moreover, the prescribed form required the insertion of the correct date for the tenancy and a notice with an incorrect date (as in this case) was held not to be 'substantially to the same effect' as a notice with a correct date. By contrast, in *Andrews*, the tenancy agreement was for a term of one year commencing on 29 May 1993. However, the s. 20 notice stated that the tenancy would commence on 29 May 1993 and end on 28 May 1993 (rather than 1994). Not surprisingly, the insertion of the wrong year was held to be an obvious clerical error, which would have been understood to be so by both parties and, therefore, did not invalidate the notice. There was no question of error, unlike in *Panayi*, giving rise to any 'perplexity' to an ordinary recipient of the notice.

The 'evident error' test was applied in *Clickex Ltd* v *McCann* [1999] 30 EG 96, where the dates in the s. 20 notice did not match the dates in the tenancy agreement. The Court of Appeal, applying the two-stage approach formulated in *York*, concluded that the error in the notice was not obvious or evident. Moreover, when the notice was read in the context of the tenancy agreement, a reasonable recipient would be in real doubt as to when the tenancy ended. The notice and tenancy agreement were in conflict with each other and it was impossible to say, looking at the documents alone, which one was correct.

It is generally accepted that the two-stage approach enunciated in *York* is at variance with the test laid down in *Mannai* and has the potential for producing confusion. As mentioned earlier, the House of Lords in *Mannai* reverted to a straighforward test for the validity of a notice put forward in *Carradine Properties*, namely, 'Is the notice quite clear to a reasonable tenant reading it?' Or putting it slightly differently: 'Is it plain that he cannot be misled by it?'

Another noticeable trend in the case law over the last few years has been an insistence on strict compliance with the relevant statutory requirements. In *Manel* v *Memon* [2000] 2 EGLR 40, the s. 20 notice omitted several aspects of the information specified in the 1988 Regulations. The Court of Appeal held that these omissions were fatal to the validity of the notice since this information contained important advice to the prospective tenant and sought to safeguard his position. Significantly, the reasonable recipient test was not mentioned by the Court. The importance of a party complying with statutory requirements has been stressed in other cases, mostly in the context of leasehold reform. In *John Lyon Grammar School* v *Secchi* (1999) 32 HLR 820, a tenant's notice served under s. 42 of the Leasehold Reform, Housing and Urban Development Act 1993 was held to be invalid as there had been a failure to comply with the statutory requirements. The *Mannai* test was unable to save the error in the notice. In *Speedwell Estates Ltd* v *Dalziel* [2002] EG 104, also involving a leasehold reform notice which did not comply with the statutory requirements, the court applied another two-stage test requiring the court (1) to identify what the relevant statute required of the notice and whether the notice 'adequately complied' with those requirements and (2) if the notice contained an error on its face, there could be scope for the application of the *Mannai* principle. This approach has been followed by the Court of Appeal in *Burman* v *Mount Cook Land Ltd* [2002] 06 EG 156 which also emphasised strict compliance with the relevant statutory provisions.

However, a move away from this somewhat restrictive approach was seen in *Ravenseft Properties Ltd* v *Hall* [2002] 11 EG 156, involving three defective notices under s. 20 of the 1988 Act. In one case, the commencement date of the tenancy was incorrect, in the second the termination date was incorrect and in the third the notice contained various errors in the text of the notes forming part of the prescribed form. The Court of Appeal rejected the two-stage test put forward in *Speedwell* and did not consider whether there had been a failure to comply with the mandatory requirements. Instead, the Court, applying the *Mannai* principle, upheld the notices on the basis that they were all 'substantially to the like effect' as the prescribed form. A move back to the more straightforward *Mannai* 'reasonable recipient' test can also be discerned from other recent cases: *Trafford Metropolitan Borough Council* v *Total Fitness (UK) Ltd* [2002] 44 EG 169, *Proctor & Gamble Technical Centres Ltd* v *Brixton Estates plc* [2003] 31 EG 69 and *Lay* v *Ackerman* [2004] EWCA Civ 184. In *McDonald* v *Fernandez* [2003] 42 EG 128, an assured shorthold tenant argued that the landlord's s. 21 notice did not validly terminate his statutory periodic tenancy because it did not specify a date that was the last day of a period of the tenancy: see, s. 21(4) of the 1988 Act. It merely gave a date upon which possession would be required. The Court of Appeal held that the notice was invalid because the statute was quite clear and specific as to what date was to be included in the s. 21 notice. It is submitted that, despite the outcome, the reasoning accords with the *Mannai* ruling. The Court of Appeal concluded that there was no room for a different date to be included in the notice on the basis that the reasonable recipient would have understood the purpose of the notice. The correct question was not 'what is the purpose of the notice?' but 'what does the statute require?' That question fell to be interpreted strictly. The difference then in approach between s. 21 and s. 20 notices can be explained on the basis that the information to be provided in a s. 21 notice is required by statute to be in clear and precise language. The *McDonald* and *Ravenseft* cases may, therefore, be reconciled if the application of *Mannai* in the context of s. 20 notices is understood as an interpretation of the words 'substantially to the same effect'.

Consistent with this approach, the most recent case dealing with a s. 20 notice favours the *Mannai* approach. In *B Osborn & Co. Ltd* v *Dior* (2003) 05 EG 144, the landlord's agent had served the s. 20 notices but left the spaces for the name, address and telephone number of the landlord blank. The equivalent particulars were, however, given at the end of the form. The court held that, even with the landlord's details absent, the notice was 'substantially to the same effect' in accomplishing the statutory purpose of the form. It seems, therefore, that the most recent trend is towards a return to the more pragmatic approach exemplified in *Mannai* in the specific context of the validity of s. 20 notices.

Further reading

Bedworth, G., 'Sounding the Retreat' (2004) SJ 43.

Blaker, G., 'Reasonable Notice' (2003) SJ 1070.

Chapman, H., 'Landlords Take Note' (2003) SJ 1264.

Colbey, R., 'Detecting a Sham' (2001) SJ 1612.

Gaunt, J., 'Notices: When is a Defect not a Defect — Parts I and II?' (2002) NLJ 424 and 460.

Murdoch, S., 'Notice the Similarity' [2003] EG 162.

Murdoch, S., 'Take it One Day at a Time' [2003] EG 125.

Pawlowski, M., and Brown, J., 'Assured Tenancies: Contracting Out?' (2001) SJ 448.

Pawlowski, M., 'Assured Shorthold Tenancies: Section 20 Notices' [2001] JHL 34.

Webber, G., 'Caught Short' (2002) SJ 182.

Leasehold enfranchisement

Introduction

By virtue of the Leasehold Reform Act 1967 and the Leasehold Reform, Housing and Urban Development Act 1993, certain tenants of long residential leases are conferred rights compulsorily to purchase the freehold reversion or compulsorily to acquire (for a premium) an extension of their lease.

Questions in this area may be of both essay and problem type. In this chapter, we have set out an example of each.

The Leasehold Reform Act 1967 confers on a tenant of a leasehold *house*, a right to acquire on fair terms the freehold or an extended (50-year) lease of the house, subject to certain conditions which have now been substantially modified under the Commonhold and Leasehold Reform Act 2002. The Leasehold Reform, Housing and Urban Development Act 1993, Pt I, on the other hand, gives most owners of long leases of *flats* a right either to collective enfranchisement (i.e., a collective right to buy the freehold of a block of flats), or an individual right to acquire a new 90-year lease. Here again, the 2002 Act has made significant changes to the qualifying conditions and valuation procedures. Most significantly, the low-rent and residency tests have now been abolished for both the 1967 and 1993 Acts thus making it far easier for long leaseholders to enfranchise. Both questions in this chapter fully incorporate the substantive amendments made by the 2002 Act. To help you to understand the new law, we have also included various articles on the 2002 amendments in the **Further Reading** at the end of this chapter.

Q Question 1

On 1 May 1990, the Earl of Westminster granted Tom a 40-year lease of a five-bedroomed terraced house in Central London. The ground rent is £550 per annum. Tom has always resided in the house during weekdays, spending weekends with his mother in Brighton. Since taking up the lease, he has also run a business from the two ground-floor rooms in the house. In July 2004, Tom inherited a family fortune and now wishes to acquire from the Earl the freehold title to the house.

Advise Tom as to whether he is able to claim a right of enfranchisement under the Leasehold Reform Act 1967 (as amended by the Commonhold and Leasehold Reform Act 2002). Assuming Tom is able to claim such a right, outline the procedure which must be followed under the Act.

Commentary

You should approach this question by, first, explaining the preconditions of enfranchisement under the 1967 Act (as amended) in the light of the interpretative case law which has developed since the enactment of the statute, and, secondly, outlining the requisite procedures for enfranchisement (i.e., the tenant's notice, the fixing of the price and the execution of the conveyance).

- Consider conditions for enfranchisement under Leasehold Reform Act 1967: (1) meaning of house and premises (2) long lease. Abolition of low rent and residency test under Commonhold and Leasehold Reform Act 2002. But Tom must satisfy new two-year ownership condition

- Absences from house not fatal: *Poland* v *Earl of Cadogan* (1980). Also use of house for mixed business and residential purposes does not preclude 1967 Act: *Tandon* v *Trustees of Spurgeons Homes* (1982). Much will depend on nature and extent of Tom's business user. Even if a business tenancy, Tom will qualify for enfranchisement if he satisfies new two-year residency test under 2002 Act

- Tom may serve notice of intention on Earl to acquire freehold of house. Binding contract of sale arises. Determination of price: s. 9.

- Once served with notice and price agreed, Earl obliged to convey fee simple to Tom: s. 8(1). Tom liable for Earl's conveyancing fees and valuation costs: s. 9(4)

:Q: Suggested answer

The Leasehold Reform Act 1967, as originally enacted, conferred on a tenant of a leasehold house, occupying the house as his residence, a right to acquire on fair terms the freehold (or an extended 50-year lease) of the house. Important changes to the qualifying conditions were made by the Commonhold and Leasehold Reform Act 2002, in particular, in relation to the residency and low-rent requirements under the 1967 Act. Before turning to these, it will be useful to examine the other pre-conditions for enfranchisement which remain unaltered.

A claim under the 1967 Act can only be made in respect of a 'house and premises' which, under s. 2(1), includes any building designed or adapted for living in and reasonably so called, notwithstanding that the building is not structurally detached, or was or is not solely designed or adapted for living in, or is divided horizontally into flats or maisonettes: *Collins* v *Howard de Walden Estates Ltd* [2003] 37 EG 137, applying the House of Lords ruling in *Malekshad* v *Howard de Walden Estates Ltd* [2002] 3 WLR 1881, where a town house and mews together constituted a building, but could not be treated as a 'house' because a vertically divided building was expressly excluded from being a house under s. 2(1)(b) of the 1967 Act.

Section 2(3) of the 1967 Act provides that the premises accompanying a house may, for the purposes of the 1967 Act, include garages, gardens, yards, outhouses and appurtenances which, at the relevant time, are let to the tenant with the house and are occupied and used for the purposes of the house or any part of it (*Gaidowski* v *Conville and Caius College Cambridge* [1975] 1 WLR 1066 and *Methuen-Campbell* v *Walters* [1979] QB 525). Section 3 of the 1967 Act provides that the lease must have originally been granted for a period exceeding 21 years as from its actual date of execution and delivery (*Roberts* v *Church Commissioners for England* [1972] 1 QB 278).

As mentioned earlier, prior to the 2002 Act, a low-rent requirement applied to enfranchisement claims under the 1967 Act. If the lease in question commenced before 1 April 1963, the rent had to be less than two-thirds of the letting value of the premises, or less than two-thirds of the rateable value on the appropriate day if the lease was entered into on or after 1 April 1963 but before 1 April 1990. If, on the other hand, the lease in question commenced on or after 1 April 1990 (as in the present case), the rent had to be less than £1,000 per annum for properties situated in London, or less than £250 in relation to properties situated elsewhere (see, s. 4 and s. 4A, as amended by the Leasehold Reform, Housing and Urban Development Act 1993, s. 65). Although the Housing Act 1996 (see, s. 106 and sch. 9) removed the low-rent test under the 1967 and 1993 Acts, this amendment only affected leases of houses and flats over 50 years (in the case of the 1967 Act) and over 35 years (in the case of the 1993 Act). The low-rent test continued to apply for leases of houses (as in the present case) between 21 years and 50 years. The current position, however, is that the 2002 Act has abolished the low-rent test almost entirely for freehold house claims.

Under the old law, it also had to be shown that the house was the tenant's only or main residence either for the last three years, or for periods amounting to three years out of the last 10 years. In *Poland* v *Earl of Cadogan* [1980] 3 All ER 544, however, it was held that a tenant could still be in occupation of a house as his residence, for the purposes of the 1967 Act, even though absent for substantial periods, provided that such a tenant could establish that he had evidenced a clear intention to maintain his occupation. Ultimately, it was a question of fact whether the tenant occupied the house as his main residence. In *Tandon* v *Trustees of Spurgeons Homes* [1982] AC 755, the House of Lords held that a house used for mixed business and residential purposes could fall within the 1967 Act. The current position is that the 2002 Act has virtually abolished the residency condition for making a claim to the freehold. However, a claimant (such as Tom) will still need to show that he has been tenant of the house for a minimum period of two years prior to any claim. Moreover, if his tenancy is characterised as falling within Pt II of the Landlord and Tenant Act 1954 (i.e., as a business tenancy), he must show he has occupied the whole or part of the house as his only or main residence for a continuous period of two years, or for periods amounting in aggregate to two years out of the 10-year period preceding his claim. Significantly also, the 2002 Act excludes, in their entirety, tenancies subject to Pt II of the 1954 Act unless they fulfil one of several conditions, the most important (in Tom's case) being that the tenancy was granted for an original term in excess of 35 years.

Assuming Tom satisfies the long lease and two-year ownership test, he will be able to enfranchise under the 1967 Act (as amended). To this end, the property in question (a terraced house) clearly falls within the statutory definition of 'house and premises' and there is no doubt that he has a qualifying lease which, as from its date of execution and delivery, exceeds 21 years. In fact, it was granted for a term of 40 years so that, even if his lease is to be treated as a business tenancy, he will not be excluded from the 1967 Act, provided he can establish the two-year residency test, referred to above. In this connection, despite his absences from the house at weekends, Tom will still be regarded as occupying the house as his only or main residence, unless it can be shown that he treated his mother's house in Brighton as his main residence — see, the *Poland* case, above. In any event, the *Tandom* case (above) shows that it is possible for a house with mixed business and residential user to fall outside Pt II of the 1954 Act if the business user is limited and merely incidental to residential occupation.

The facts do not show any grounds which might prevent Tom from enfranchising (i.e., the Earl is not an exempt landlord under the 1967 Act, nor is there anything to suggest that he has an intention to develop the property or that he requires possession for occupation by himself or an adult member of his family: ss. 17 and 18 of the 1967 Act, respectively).

Provided the necessary qualifying conditions are fulfilled, Tom may at any time serve on the Earl a notice of intention, in prescribed form, to acquire the freehold of the house. As soon as the notice has been served, a binding contract of sale is deemed to have come into existence. Tom can register this contract either by way of notice or caution (if the house is registered land), or (if the house is unregistered) as a Class C(iv) land charge, so as to bind any third party transferees. After service of the notice, Tom may seek a release from the agreement to enfranchise either freely or for a consideration payable to the Earl. Under the old law, Tom would be precluded from making a further claim for a period of three years. Under the 2002 Act, however, the period is reduced to 12 months.

The price payable will be fixed with reference to the value which the house, if sold on the open market by a willing seller, might be expected to realise on the basis of certain assumptions detailed in s. 9 of the 1967 Act, as amended by the 1993 Act, s. 66 and sch. 15. If marriage value forms part of the purchase price, the 2002 Act provides that the Earl's share of marriage value should be fixed at 50 per cent. In default of agreement, the price payable will be determined by a local Leasehold Valuation Tribunal, with a right of appeal to the Lands Tribunal.

By virtue of s. 8(1) of the 1967 Act, the Earl, once served with Tom's notice and after such time as the price has been agreed, is obliged to convey to Tom the house and premises in fee simple free from any incumbrances attaching to the freehold land, subject only to any leases and incumbrances thereon created by Tom (e.g., mortgages, subleases, etc.). By virtue of s. 9(4), Tom will be responsible for paying the Earl's legal and other professional fees incurred in investigating and verifying Tom's claim, the valuation costs and conveyancing fees.

Q Question 2

To what extent did the Leasehold Reform, Housing and Urban Development Act 1993 enable lessees of blocks of flats to enfranchise or acquire extended leases? How has the Commonhold and Leasehold Reform Act 2002 simplified this process?

Commentary

This question requires you to explain (in some depth) the statutory provisions on collective enfranchisement and leasehold extension contained in the Leasehold Reform, Housing and Urban Development Act 1993. Your answer should demonstrate a working knowledge of Pts I and II of the 1993 Act as well as the changes affected by the 2002 Act — no doubt, a daunting prospect for many students in view of the complexity of the statutory provisions!

- Requirements for collective enfranchisement under the 1993 Act. Meaning of qualifying tenant and long lease. Abolition of low rent and residency requirements under 2002 Act

- Procedure for making a claim altered by 2002 Act. Need for a company to exercise the right to collective enfranchisement. Participating members. Changes to valuation and marriage value

- Individual right to extend lease — qualifying conditions altered by 2002 Act — low rent and residency test abolished in favour of new two-year ownership requirement. Calculation of premium for extended lease. Change to marriage value

- Procedure for extended lease. Notices to reach agreement on terms and price. Dispute over terms resolved by court, disagreement on price referred to Leasehold Valuation Tribunal

:Q: **Suggested answer**

The Leasehold Reform, Housing and Urban Development Act 1993 received Royal Assent in 1993 and, in relation to its enfranchisement provisions, came into force on 1 November 1993. One of the most fundamental reforming measures introduced by Pt I of the Act was to give most owners of long leases of flats either a right to collective enfranchisement (i.e., a collective right to buy the freehold of a block of flats), or an individual right to acquire a new 90-year lease.

(1) Collective enfranchisment

For a building to qualify under the 1993 Act, as originally enacted, it had to fulfil certain conditions, namely:

(a) be an independent building or be part of a building which is capable of independent development;

(b) contain two or more flats held by 'qualifying tenants';

(c) not have a resident freeholder if the building is not a purpose-built block of flats and comprises less than four units;

(d) be in single freehold ownership; and

(e) have at least 90 per cent of the internal floor space occupied or intended to be occupied for residential purposes.

Some of these conditions have now been modified by virtue of the Commonhold and Leasehold Reform Act 2002, which came into force on 1 May 2002. Under condition (e) above, the amount of internal floor space which must be occupied for residential purposes has been reduced to 75 per cent. Minor changes have also been made to the definition of resident freeholder for the purposes of condition (c), above.

To be a qualifying tenant under the 1993 Act, the lessee had to have a long lease (i.e., a lease which, when originally granted, was for a term exceeding 21 years) at a low rent (i.e., a rent which, during the first year of the lease did not exceed either two-thirds of the letting value in that year (if the lease was granted before 1 April 1963), or two-thirds of the rateable value in that year (if the lease was granted on or after 1 April 1963 but before 1 April 1990), or £1,000 per annum for London properties or £250 per annum elsewhere (in any other cases). These low rent limits were removed under the Housing Act 1996 but only for leases over 35 years in the case of enfranchisement under the 1993 Act. Here again, the 2002 Act has made fundamental changes by abolishing the low-rent test altogether for collective claims.

Under the 1993 Act, the qualifying tenants had to comprise not less than one-half of all the flats in the building and at least one-half of them must have each lived in their respective flats as their only or principal home for at least one year, or periods amounting to three years out of the previous 10 years. The 2002 Act, however, has abolished this latter requirement so that no residency condition now attaches to a collective claim. The 2002 Act also amends the procedure for making a claim. Under the old law, the participating tenants had to agree on the vehicle by which to effect the purchase (i.e., a nominee purchaser), which usually was a management company set up by the tenant. This procedure has now changed under the 2002 Act. An initial notice to enfranchise must now be given by a private company limited by guarantee, one of whose objects must be the exercise of the right to collective enfranchisement of the building. This company is referred to as the 'Right to Enfranchise' (RTE) company. All the qualifying tenants of flats in the building are entitled to be members of such a company. A participating member of an RTE company includes any member of the company who has given a participation notice (i.e., a notice containing prescribed particulars stating that he wishes to become a participating member during the participation period). The participation period is a period of six months from the date of the initial notice to enfranchise, or the date of the sale contract, whichever is the earlier.

When an RTE company exercises its right to enfranchise, the number of participating members (being qualifying tenants of the flats in the building) must amount to at least one-half of all the flats in that building, except that in the case of a building with only two qualifying tenants, both must be participating tenants. Before the company can give an initial notice to enfranchise, it must invite each and every qualifying tenant who is not already a participating member to become so. A period of at least 14 days must elapse after the giving of this invitation before the company can serve the initial notice to enfranchise on the freeholder.

Significant changes have also been made to the method of valuation. Under the old law, the price to be paid for the purchase of the freehold was the aggregate of the building's investment value to the freeholder, not less than one-half of the marriage value (i.e., the increased value attributable to the freehold by virtue of the participating tenants being able to grant themselves extended leases at nil premium and a peppercorn rent), and compensation for loss in the value of other property owned by the freeholder. Now, the valuation date for the purposes of the collective claim is the date of the claim (i.e., the date of the initial notice to enfranchise) so as to make this consistent with claims under the Leasehold Reform Act 1967. The landlord's share of the marriage value has now been fixed at 50 per cent. Also, where a lease held by a participating member of an RTE company has, on the relevant date, an unexpired term of more than 80 years, no marriage value is now attributed to the potential ability of the participating member to extend his lease.

(a) Individual right to extend

All qualifying tenants of flats, subject to certain conditions, have an individual right to extend their leases under the 1993 Act. As originally drafted, the Act required the tenant, in order to qualify, to be a tenant of a flat held on a long lease at a low rent (the test being the same as for collective enfranchisement) which he had occupied as his only or principal home for three years or for periods amounting to three years out of the last 10 years. Here again, the 2002 Act has abolished the low-rent requirement for new lease claims so that the only primary condition now is that the lease be a long lease (i.e., for an original term exceeding 21 years). Thus, the residency condition is also abolished but the tenant must have been a qualifying tenant of the flat for a period of at least two years (i.e., he must have owned the lease for this period of time) before making the claim to an extension. The 2002 Act has also given personal representatives of a deceased qualifying tenant the right to make a claim.

As with collective enfranchisement, the valuation date for the purposes of an individual claim is now the date upon which the tenant gave notice of his claim. In terms of the valuation itself, the 2002 Act provides that the landlord's share of the marriage value is to be fixed at 50 per cent. As with collective enfranchisement, no marriage value is considered where the lease has an unexpired term exceeding 80 years. Otherwise, the premium to be paid by the tenant for new extended lease will comprise the diminution in the flat's investment value to the landlord, 50 per cent of the marketable value (i.e., the additional value released by replacing the existing lease with the extended lease), and compensation for loss in the value of other property owned by the freeholder.

The extended lease will be for a term expiring 90 years after the end of the current lease and will reserve a peppercorn rent. The landlord is entitled to oppose a claim for an extended lease on redevelopment grounds. The procedure to be followed for a claim to an extended lease is more straightforward than for collective enfranchisement. The qualifying tenant can serve a preliminary notice to obtain information from the landlord. Thereafter, he must serve his notice of claim which, *inter alia*, must state a description of the flat, sufficient particulars to establish that the lease and tenant qualify, the premium being offered (which must be a realistic figure: *Mount Cook Ltd* v *Rosen* [2003] 10 EG 165), the terms of the new lease, and a date by which the landlord must respond to the notice (being not less than two months). The provisions for notices under the 1993 Act are, however, procedural and, therefore, may be waived by the parties: *Latifi* v *Colherne Court Freehold Ltd* [2003] 12 EG 130.

Once the landlord has responded to the tenant's notice of claim, there follows a succession of procedural notices and counternotices between the parties to reach agreement on the terms of the sale and price. Any dispute over the terms are resolved by the court, whereas disagreement on price is referred to the Leasehold Valuation Tribunal with appeal to the Lands Tribunal. The 1993 Act provides no limit to the number of times that a qualifying tenant can exercise his right to a lease extension.

Further reading

Driscoll, J., and Radevsky, A., 'What is a House?' (2003) NLJ 64.

Driscoll, J., 'Flats and Houses: New Rights for Leaseholders' (2002) SJ 564.

Ezekiel, E., 'House Style' (2003) SJ 130.

Greenish, D., 'Tenants Gain A Collective Voice' [2002] EG 120.

Greenish, D., 'Extension Course' [2002] EG 145.

Business tenancies

Introduction

Here again, the subject lends itself to problem questions, although you may also find essay-type questions which ask you to consider, for example, what reforms have been recently introduced in this field (see Question 4).

Most business tenants have the benefit of two quite distinct statutory codes:

(a) the Landlord and Tenant Act 1954, Pt II (as amended by the Law of Property Act 1969 and, most recently, the Regulatory Reform (Business Tenancies) (England and Wales) Order 2003), which affords

    (i) security of tenure, and

    (ii) compensation for disturbance in certain cases where the landlord is entitled to possession; and

(b) the Landlord and Tenant Act 1927 (as amended by the 1954 Act), which entitles the tenant to compensation for improvements on quitting the holding.

Security of tenure under Pt II of the 1954 Act is afforded by:

(a) automatic continuance of the tenancy notwithstanding expiry of a fixed term or service of a notice to quit on a periodic tenant (s. 24);

(b) compelling a landlord who desires possession to establish one or more specific grounds (listed in s. 30(1)), having made a formal statement of the grounds relied on *either* by notice of termination complying with s. 25 *or* by notice of opposition (i.e., a counternotice) to a tenant's request for a new tenancy under s. 26;

(c) giving the tenant a right to apply for a new tenancy *either* pursuant to a request for a new tenancy under s. 26 *or* in response to a landlord's notice of termination served under s. 25. The right accrues once either procedure is initiated (s. 24).

The Regulatory Reform (Business Tenancies) (England and Wales) Order 2003, which came into force on 1 June 2004, now gives the landlord the right to apply to the court for an order terminating the tenancy if it can make out one or more of the specified grounds of opposition listed in s. 30(1). Like the tenant, it can also now apply to the court for a lease renewal pursuant to a s. 25 notice which must set out the landlord's proposals for the terms of the new tenancy (i.e., property, duration, rent and other terms).

The 2003 Order has also made other significant changes to the lease renewal procedures under Pt II. Thus, there is no longer an obligation on the tenant to serve a counternotice in response to a landlord's s. 25 notice of termination. The tenant is no longer required to issue his application not less than two months nor more than four months after the date of service of the s. 25 notice/s. 26 request. The tenant may now issue his application immediately upon receipt of the landlord's s. 25 notice of termination (but if it serves a s. 26 request then it must wait for two months from the date of the service, unless the landlord serves a counternotice opposing renewal earlier).

The 1954 Act leaves the parties free to agree extensions and renewals (s. 28) and imposes no restrictions on rent. The Act is, therefore, of no immediate importance to the parties unless and until either the landlord is opposed to a renewal (or continuation of a periodic tenancy), or negotiations for a renewal break down. In the former case, the landlord would normally take the initiative by service of a s. 25 notice of termination. In the latter case, the deadlock is invariably broken by either the landlord serving a s. 25 notice stating that he would not oppose an application for a new tenancy, or the tenant serving a request for a new tenancy under s. 26. This course, however, is not open to periodic tenants. Given that a tenancy continues under Pt II on the same terms as granted, it is usual for the landlord to take the initiative under s. 25. It would be otherwise if the tenant wished to regularise his position, for example, prior to selling his business.

We have included three problem and five essay-type questions in this Chapter. We have not included a question on the various methods by which a landlord may seek to avoid Pt II protection, although this is also a fertile source for a good examination question in this field. The reader is, however, referred to Pawlowski, M., 'Avoiding Protection under Pt II' [1996] RRLR vol. 16/2, pp. 29–35 for a summary of the various ways in which Pt II may be excluded. Be aware, however, that the Regulatory Reform (Business Tenancies) (England and Wales) Order 2003, see above, has abolished the need to make a joint application to court for a 'contracting out' order where the parties wish to enter into a lease that is excluded from the 1954 Act's security of tenure provisions. Instead, the landlord will now serve a prescribed form of notice on the tenant confirming that the new lease is to be excluded from the Act and the tenant will then sign a declaration confirming it has received the notice and understood its contents. Reference to the notice and declaration must be contained in or endorsed upon the new lease.

Other important changes have been made to the lease renewal procedures (including changes to interim rent applications), largely implementing the Law Commission's recommendations made in its 1992 Report. We have, therefore, included an essay question (substantially revised from the 2nd edition of this book) on this important topic.

Our general advice for all examinations holds good for this subject. Read the question carefully, prepare a rough plan, list the relevant cases and, above all, ANSWER THE QUESTION AS SET!

Q Question 1

Nigel is the landlord of business premises, the lease of which expires on 25 December 2005. The tenant has on several occasions paid the rent a few weeks late and is using the premises for a purpose other than that specified in the lease. In addition, Nigel has vague plans to demolish and reconstruct the premises, or alternatively to let them to his son who wants to set up a video business. Explain to Nigel:

(a) Which of the grounds under the Landlord and Tenant Act 1954, s. 30, are available to him in order to claim possession. In the case of each ground, you should consider what he will have to substantiate and the financial consequences of his choice of grounds.

(b) What steps he should take (and when) in order to claim possession, and what steps you would expect the tenant to take in response (assuming that the tenant does not wish to leave) and how the matter may eventually be resolved.

Commentary

This is a fairly typical problem question on the subject. There is a lot of ground to cover so you cannot afford to dwell on one point for too long at the expense of others. Remember that there are two parts to the question and your time is limited! Your answer should incorporate the various changes to the lease renewal procedure introduced by the Regulatory Reform (Business Tenancies) (England and Wales) Order 2003.

For a good overview of the workings of ground (f) (intention to redevelop), see Dean, B., and Clark, R., 'Into the Valley of Decision' [1996] EG 9644, 176 and Pawlowski, M., 'Three Bites at the Cherry?' [1996] RRLR vol. 16/3, pp. 7–13.

- Consider four possible grounds: (1) persistent delay in paying rent (s. 30(1)(b)); (2) substantial breach of tenancy obligation (s. 30(1)(c)); (3) intention to develop (s. 30(1)(f)); and (4) intention to occupy holding for business (s. 30(1)(g))

- Financial consequences relating to compensation for disturbance (s. 37) and for tenant's improvements (under Landlord and Tenant Act 1927)

- Service of s. 25 notice of termination. Requirements of notice/no provision for amendment

- Requirement for a tenant's counternotice abolished under Regulatory Reform (Business Tenancies) (England and Wales) Order 2003. Application to court — removal of time limits under 2003 Order. If Nigel successful, tenancy will end on 25 December 2005. If unsuccessful, court obliged to grant a new tenancy of the holding on terms as to duration, rent, etc

:Q: Suggested answer

(a) Four possible grounds present themselves on the facts. First, Nigel may seek to rely on s. 30(1)(b) of the 1954 Act (i.e., persistent delay in paying rent). Here, Nigel must show that a new tenancy ought not to be granted in view of the delay. In *Hopcutt* v *Carver* (1969) 209 EG 1069, the tenant had been consistently late in payments of rent during the preceding two years, at one time delaying for five months. No offer was made by the tenant for payment in advance in the future, nor was any security offered. On these facts, a new lease was refused. In *Hurstfell Ltd* v *Leicester Square Property Co. Ltd* [1988] 37 EG 109, the Court of Appeal reiterated that there was an obligation on the tenant to explain the reason for past failures and to satisfy the court that, if a new lease was granted, there would be no recurrence of the late payments. If, on the other hand, the landlord has accepted late payment of rent over a period of time so as to be estopped from insisting on timely payment, the landlord will be required to give reasonable notice in order to revert to strict compliance with the obligation to pay rent on time: *Haze* v *Akhtar* [2002] 07 EG 124. In the present case, it is unlikely that Nigel would succeed on this ground bearing in mind that the rent was paid only a few weeks late and (presumably) not 'persistently' in arrears.

Secondly, the tenant is using the premises for a purpose not specified in the lease. Here, Nigel can rely on s. 30(1)(c) of the 1954 Act (i.e., substantial breaches of obligations under the tenancy or any other reason connected with the use or management of the holding). Once again, this is a discretionary ground in so far as the breach of covenant must be such that a new tenancy ought not to be granted (*Eichner* v *Midland Bank Executor and Trustee Co. Ltd* [1970] 1 WLR 1120). It may be that, in the present case, the breach is not serious enough to warrant a refusal of a new lease.

Thirdly, we are told that Nigel has vague plans to demolish and reconstruct the premises. This may afford a basis for opposing a new tenancy under s. 30(1)(f) (i.e., intention to demolish or reconstruct, or effect substantial work of construction on the holding). In order to succeed, Nigel would need to establish that he has the necessary intention to demolish etc. at the date of the hearing and that he requires legal possession of the holding (i.e., the work could not be done satisfactorily unless he obtains exclusive occupation). A bare assertion of intention is not enough and Nigel will fail if serious difficulties (e.g., obtaining planning permission or finance) lie ahead (*Betty's Cafes* v *Phillips Furnishing Stores Ltd* [1959] AC 20, adopting the test laid down in *Cunliffe* v *Goodman* [1950] 2 KB 237 with regard to the similar provision in the Landlord and Tenant Act 1927, s. 18). It has been held, however, that lack of planning permission for the development need not be fatal under ground (f). It is sufficient if there is a reasonable prospect of obtaining permission, which is not fanciful or one that would be sensibly ignored by a reasonable landlord: see *Cadogan* v *McCarthy & Stone Developments Ltd* [1996] EGCS 94, *Aberdeen Steak Houses Group Ltd* v *Crown Estate Commissioners* [1997] 2 EGLR 107 and *Yoga for Health Foundation* v *Guest* [2002] All ER (D) 81.

The landlord's intention must be to effect the work on the termination of the current tenancy. In Nigel's case, we are told that he has only 'vague plans' to carry out redevelopment work. Unless Nigel can avail himself of a declaration under s. 31(2) (i.e., the near-miss provisions), he will not, it is submitted, succeed under this ground because of the lack of the requisite intention on his part.

Fourthly, Nigel is considering letting the premises to his son who wants to set up a video business. It would seem that s. 30(1)(g) has no application here since Nigel does not intend to occupy the holding for his own business or residence. In this connection, the intended business must be the landlord's business to be carried on by him in the holding (*Hunt* v *Decca Navigator Co. Ltd* (1972) 222 EG 625), except where the landlord is a trustee and the business is to be carried on by a beneficiary (s. 41(2)), or where the landlord has a controlling interest in a company and it is intended that the company will occupy (s. 30(3)), or where the landlord is a company and the business is to be carried on by another company in the same group (s. 42(3)). None of these exceptions seems to apply in the present case.

The financial consequence of Nigel relying on grounds (b) and (c) is that he will not be obliged to pay the tenant compensation for disturbance under s. 37 of the 1954 Act. The position is otherwise if Nigel successfully objects on grounds (f) or (g). The obligation to pay compensation for tenant's improvements carried out during the tenancy under the Landlord and Tenant Act 1927 will, however, apply in either case.

(b) Nigel will need to serve a s. 25 notice of termination on the tenant not more than 12 months and not less than six months before the termination date specified in the notice. The specified termination date must not be earlier than the date at which the tenancy would expire at common law (i.e., 25 December 2005). Nigel's notice must also state whether he would oppose an application to the court for a new tenancy and, if so, on which grounds (mentioned in s. 30(1)).

There appears to be no provision for amendment and so a landlord cannot depart from the grounds stated in his notice. Moreover, the withdrawal of a notice with a view to serving a fresh notice stating different grounds seems to be excluded by s. 24(1). Nigel should therefore be advised to state his grounds carefully, although the court will excuse minor slips so long as the tenant has fair warning of the case he has to answer (*Barclays Bank Ltd* v *Ascott* [1961] 1 WLR 717).

Nigel's tenant is no longer required to serve any counternotice in repsonse to Nigel's s. 25 notice of termination. This requirement was abolished under the

Regulatory Reform (Business Tenancies((England and Wales) Order 2003, which came into force on 1 June 2004. The only requirement now is that the tenant issue an application to the court for the grant of a new tenancy. Prior to the 2003 Order, it would have been incumbent on the tenant to issue its application not less than two months and not more than four months after the giving of the s. 25 notice. This requirement has also been removed so that the tenant is now free to issue his application immediately upon receipt of Nigel's s. 25 notice of termination. The date, however, by which the tenant's proceedings must be issued has also altered. Under the 2003 Order, Nigel's tenant has now until the termination date contained in the s. 25 notice (i.e., 25 December 2005) to make an application to court. The parties are, however, free to agree in writing to extend this deadline as often as they choose to facilitate a negotiated settlement.

As to how the matter may eventually be resolved, this will depend on whether Nigel is successful in opposing the grant of a new tenancy. If so, the tenancy will end on the date specified in the s. 25 notice (25 December 2005), or three months after the final disposal of the application by the court, whichever is the later (s. 64). If Nigel is unsuccessful, the court will be obliged to grant the tenant a new tenancy of the holding (s. 29). If the parties fail to agree on the terms of the new tenancy, the court will decide having regard to the guidelines laid down in s. 32 (the property), s. 33 (the duration), s. 34 (the rent), and s. 35 (other terms). Nigel should be made aware that, under the 2003 Order, either the landlord *or* the tenant can now make an application for an interim rent. Moreover, the maximum length the court will be able to award the tenant under s. 33 has been increased from 14 to 15 years.

Q Question 2

> 'In order for a tenancy to fall within section 23 of the Landlord and Tenant Act 1954, the property comprised in the tenancy must include premises which are "occupied by the tenant and are so occupied for the purposes of a business carried on by him or for those and other purposes". ' (s. 23(1)).

Discuss.

Commentary

Superficially this may appear a simple question, but in fact there is considerable opportunity for the well-prepared student to examine a number of different points and illustrate them by reference to the case law.

Apart from considering what constitutes 'occupation' for the purpose of s. 23(1), you should also examine the meaning of the word 'business' and, in particular, draw the distinction between bodies of persons where virtually any activity suffices, and an individual where engagement in a 'trade, profession or employment' is essential (s. 23(2)). The reference to 'those and other purposes' should also trigger a discussion of mixed business and residential user. Lastly, a brief reference to the meaning of the word 'premises' in s. 23(1) will gain additional marks.

You will obviously need to make reference to the House of Lords ruling in *Graysim Holdings Ltd v P & O Property Holdings Ltd* [1996] 1 AC 329, on the subject of 'dual occupation' of business premises.

The secret of a good answer, therefore, is to select the material which most directly addresses the question.

- **No continuance if tenant ceases to occupy at expiry of a fixed term:** *Esselte AB v Pearl Assurance plc* (1997). **But temporary vacation not fatal:** *Morrisons Holdings Ltd v Manders Property (Wolverhampton) Ltd* (1976)

- **Consider** *Graysim Holdings Ltd v P & O Property Holdings Ltd* (1996). **Dual occupation not permitted. Compare** *Bagettes Ltd v GP Estates Ltd* (1956) **and** *Lee-Verhulst (Investments) Ltd v Harwood Trust* (1973)

- **Occupation by servants or agents of the tenant:** *Chapman v Freeman* (1978). **Mixed business and residential user:** *Cheryl Investments Ltd v Saldanha/Royal Life Saving Society v. Page* (1978)

- **Meaning of the word 'business':** s. 23(2). **Contrast individuals with body of persons:** *Hawkesbrook Leisure Ltd v The Reece-Jones Partnership* (2003). **Also meaning of 'premises':** *Bracey v Read* (1963)

:Ǫ: Suggested answer

A tenant who wishes to qualify for protection under the Landlord and Tenant Act 1954, Pt II, must bring his tenancy within the requirements of s. 23(1). Thus, if the tenant ceases to occupy for the purposes of his business at the expiry of a fixed term, there can be no continuance of his tenancy under s. 24 (*Esselte AB v Pearl Assurance plc* [1997] 1 WLR 891 and *Surrey County Council v Single House Properties Ltd* [2002] 4 All ER 143, where it was held that, if a tenant following a request for a new tenancy vacates the premises before the contractual term date, the tenancy will determine on the contractual term date and the landlord's s. 25 notice will not extend the term beyond that date. If a business tenant temporarily vacates the premises while they are being repaired or following a fire, he will not lose his protection under Pt II provided that he has the intention to return as soon as the premises are fit for occupation (*Morrisons Holdings Ltd v Manders Property (Wolverhampton) Ltd* [1976] 1 WLR 533; *I. and H. Caplan Ltd v Caplan (No. 2)* [1963] 1 WLR 1247) and *Webb v Sandown Sports Club Ltd* [2000] EGCS 13. He must show that he has a reasonable prospect of bringing this about in that the premises will be reinstated in the near or reasonable future

(*Flairline Properties Ltd* v *Hassan* [1998] 169 EGCS 169). In most cases the tenant will be in personal occupation of the premises, but it has been held that a tenant who occupies a building for the sole purpose of sub-letting parts falls outside the section (*Bagettes Ltd* v *GP Estates Ltd* [1956] Ch 290). Such an occupation, although for a 'business', is not one to which Pt II applies since it involves the progressive elimination of the holding. The position is otherwise, however, if the tenant retains a sufficient degree of control over the occupied parts (*Lee-Verhulst (Investments) Ltd* v *Harwood Trust* [1973] QB 204 and *William Boyer & Sons Ltd* v *Adams* (1976) 32 P & CR 89).

In *Graysim Holdings Ltd* v *P & O Property Holdings Ltd* [1996] 1 AC 329, the House of Lords ruled that intermediate landlords who are not themselves in occupation of the premises are not protected under Pt II because the 1954 Act makes no provision for dual occupation of premises (i.e., a business tenant and his sub-tenant cannot enjoy statutory protection under Pt II in respect of the same premises). The House of Lords, however, did not rule out the possibility that, in exceptional cases, the rights reserved by the tenant might be so extensive that he would remain in occupation of the property for the purposes of Pt II. The crux of the matter lies in the distinction between the two earlier cases (mentioned above), namely, *Bagettes* and *Lee-Verhulst*. In the former, the residential flats were let unfurnished and, although the tenant provided hot water for the sub-tenants and cleaned the common parts, the 'service' element was negligible: see also, *Bassairi Ltd* v *Camden London Borough Council* [1998] EGCS 27. By contrast, in *Lee-Verhulst*, the lettings comprised furnished rooms with substantial services (i.e., supply of bedlinen, daily cleaning of rooms and regular change of linen, and provision of light meals if required). The Court of Appeal held that, in view of the degree of control and extent of the services provided, the tenant 'occupied' the entire premises for the purposes of its business, namely that of 'providing furnished accommodation and services for those residing there'. In *Graysim* itself, it was held that where the letting takes the form of a *sub-tenancy*, the sub-tenant will be entitled to exclusive possession of the sub-let part and, hence, will be the 'occupier' to the exclusion of the tenant. At the other end of the spectrum, however, where the occupancy takes the form of a *licence*, there will often be more room for argument that the tenant retains occupation of the property because the rights granted by a licence will be less extensive than those comprised in a sub-tenancy. The key elements in the *Lee-Verhulst* case were the provision of services to the occupants (who were characterised as licensees) and the unrestricted entry to each room necessary to perform those services: see also, *Linden* v *Department of Health and Social Security* [1986] 1 WLR 164, to the same effect, involving eight self-contained flats managed by the district health authority. By contrast, in *Graysim*, neither the tenant nor his agents had any right of access to the units, nor did they have keys or means of access. All the occupants had exclusive possession and each was a sub-tenant in respect of his unit.

Occupation preparatory to carrying on business is sufficient (e.g., occupying a seaside cafe during the winter months) (*Artemiou* v *Procopiou* [1966] QB 878, *per* Salmon LJ at p. 890). Occupation by servants of the tenant may also be sufficient, provided the premises are occupied for a purpose necessary to the furtherance of the business and not merely for its convenience (*Chapman* v *Freeman* [1978] 1 WLR 129). Where the tenancy is held on trust, occupation by all or any of the beneficiaries under the trust, and the carrying on of a business by all or any of the beneficiaries, falls to be treated for the purposes of s. 23 as equivalent occupation or the carrying on of a business by the tenant (*Frish Ltd* v *Barclays Bank Ltd* [1951] 2 QB 541, *per* Lord Evershed MR at pp. 549).

In *Cafeteria (Keighley) Ltd* v *Harrison* (1956) 168 EG 668, Denning LJ expressly declared that business premises could be occupied by an agent or manager of the tenant. See also *Hills (Patents) Ltd* v *University College Hospital Board of Governors* [1956] 1 QB 90, where Denning LJ observed that while 'possession in law is, of course, single and exclusive . . . occupation may be shared with others or had on behalf of others'. In *Ross Auto Wash Ltd* v *Herbert* (1978) 250 EG 971, Fox J held that a tenant company could be in occupation of business premises even though another company was acting as its manager. Moreover, s. 42 of the 1954 Act provides, *inter alia*, that the occupation and carrying on of a business by one member of a group of companies of which the tenant is a member is deemed to be the occupation and conduct of the business of the tenant. For these purposes, a company is a member of another if it is a subsidiary of the other or of a third body corporate.

It is possible for the character of a tenancy to change from residential to business. A tenancy of residential premises will be a business tenancy if the tenant's business activity is a significant purpose of the occupation and is not merely incidental to the residential occupation (*Cheryl Investments Ltd* v *Saldanha; Royal Life Saving Society* v *Page* [1978] 1 WLR 1329). Contrast *Gurton* v *Parrott* [1991] 18 EG 161, where it was held that the tenant occupied the premises for the purpose of her residence only and that the running of the business of dog kennels was merely incidental, being something akin to a hobby (see also *Wright* v *Mortimer* (1996) 72 P & CR D36, where the business purposes were held not to be a significant element in the occupation). If business user ceases and the 1954 Act ceases to apply, the tenancy will not move into the relevant residential code unless there is evidence of communication between the parties that amounts to a contractual variation of the user covenant in the lease: *Tomkins* v *Basildon District Council* [2002] 43 EG 208.

The word 'business' is defined in s. 23(2). Where bodies of persons are concerned, 'any activity' suffices (*Addiscombe Garden Estates* v *Crabbe* [1958] 1 QB 513, lawn tennis club). However, it has been held that the activity for this purpose must be something which is correlative to the conceptions involved in the words 'trade, profession or employment' (*Hillil Property & Investment Co. Ltd* v *Naraine Pharmacy Ltd* (1979) 252 EG 1013). In that case, a company tenant who used premises simply for dumping waste building materials from another property was held not to be indulging in an 'activity' within s. 23(2). Most recently, in *Hawkesbrook Leisure Ltd* v *The Reece-Jones Partnership* (2003) EWHC 3333 (Ch), it was held that the extended definition of 'business' in s. 23(3) given by the case law meant that many activities were entitled to statutory protection even though they were not carried on commercially. In this case, the claimant had a corporate structure, a number of employees, dealt with accounting matters in the usual way, advertised its facilities and was registered for VAT. The fact that it was running a business without the predominant intention of making a profit (but simply maintaining sports facilities) was considered irrelevant. See also *Wandsworth LBC* v *Singh* [1991] 62 P&CR 219.

On the other hand, where individuals are concerned, they must be engaged in a 'trade, profession or employment' (*Abernethie* v *A.M. & J. Kleiman Ltd* [1970] 1 QB 10, carrying on of a Sunday school held to be a gratuitous, spare-time activity). See also *Lewis* v *Weldcrest Ltd* [1978] 1 WLR 1107 (taking in of lodgers where no commercial advantage involved held insufficient).

It should be stressed that Pt II does not apply where the tenant is carrying on a business use in breach of covenant, unless the immediate landlord or his predecessor in title has consented thereto or the immediate landlord has acquiesced therein (s. 23(4) and *Bell* v *Alfred Franks and Bartlett Co. Ltd* [1980] 1 WLR 340).

Lastly, the word 'premises' in s. 23(1) has been held to include the letting of incorporeal hereditaments together with land (*Stumbles* v *Whitley* [1930] AC 544, fishing rights). In *Bracey* v *Read* [1963] Ch 88, it was held that premises were not confined to buildings but included the land on which the buildings were erected. Thus, the letting of gallops was held to come within Pt II. Contrast, however, *Land Reclamation Ltd* v *Basildon District Council* (1979) 250 EG 549, where it was held that a right of way, which stood by itself and was not the subject of a more comprehensive demise including a corporeal hereditament, fell outside Pt II.

Q Question 3

John has a 10-year lease which will expire on 30 June 2005. The premises consist of a ground floor shop with a flat above and a basement. John occupies the shop for the purpose of his video rental business and lives in the flat. He has sub-let the basement to a nearby solicitor on a monthly tenancy for the purpose of storing old files. John's landlord, Bill, bought the freehold in 2001.

In August 2004, John received a notice in proper form in respect of the whole premises from Bill, specifying 30 June 2005 as the termination date and stating that he would oppose any renewal of John's lease under the Landlord and Tenant Act 1954, s. 30(1)(f) and (g). Bill intends to refurbish the property and has vague plans to turn it into a wine bar, which he hopes to run himself. John wants to remain in the premises.

(a) Advise John as to the steps he should take to protect his position and as to the likelihood of his obtaining a new lease. If he does so, what principles will govern the establishment of its terms? [15 marks]

(b) How would your advice differ if John was the lessee but ran his business through a company, Visionhire Ltd, in which he owned all the shares? [10 marks]

Commentary

This question should provide few problems for the student who has revised business tenancies thoroughly. Part (a) calls for a broad outline of the statutory machinery for termination, including the guidelines for determining the terms of a new tenancy by the court. Part (b) is more specific and requires you to consider whether a business tenant can occupy the premises through a company which is wholly owned by him.

You should be aware that the Regulatory Reform (Business Tenancies) (England and Wales) Order 2003 has made significant changes to both the statutory machinery for renewal and the provisions in the 1954 Act concerning ownership and control of businesses. You must make reference to these changes in order demonstrate to the examiner your awareness of the new legislation.

For a summary of the cases interpreting occupation through a company under the 1954 Act (prior to its revision by the 2003 Order), see Pawlowski, M., 'Business Occupation through Third Parties' [1988] EG 8840, 25. It is important to refer to some of this case law in your answer to show what anomalies existed prior to the 2003 Order coming into force (1 June 2004).

- No longer any requirement to serve a counternotice: Regulatory Reform (Business Tenancies) (England and Wales) Order 2003. Apply to court for the grant of a new tenancy. Time limits for application abolished

- Can Bill invoke s. 30(1)(f)? Bare assertion of intention not enough: *Gregson* v *Cyril Lord* (1963). Bill cannot rely on s. 30(1)(g) since he purchased the freehold during last five years: s. 30(2). In any event, need to prove genuine intention and reasonable prospect of bringing about occupation: *Dolgellau Golf Club* v *Hett* (1998)

- If Bill unsuccessful, court must grant new tenancy of the holding. Consider terms of new tenancy: (1) meaning of holding (2) duration (3) rent and (4) other terms

- Occupation through a company not permitted under old law: *Pegler* v *Craven* (1952). Alter ego argument also failed in *Christina* v *Seear* (1985) and *Nozari-Zadeh* v *Pearl Assurance plc* (1987)

- Consider position if company is the agent or manager of the tenant: *Cafeteria (Keighley) Ltd v Harrison* (1956) and *Ross Auto Wash Ltd v Herbert* (1978). Consider also effect of s. 41 of the 1954 Act. Rely now on changes introduced by 2003 Order

:Q: Suggested answer

(a) John is no longer required to serve a counternotice (stating that he is not willing to give up possession) in response to Bill's s. 25 notice of termination in order to preserve his legal position. The Regulatory Reform (Business Tenancies) (England and Wales) Order 2003, which came into force on 1 June 2004, has abolished this requirement. However, John must apply to the court for the grant of a new tenancy in order to activate the lease renewal procedure under the 1954 Act.

Prior to the 2003 Order, John was obliged to issue his application for the grant of a new tenancy not less than two months and not more than four months after the giving of the s. 25 notice of termination: see, s. 29(3). This time-limit has now also been removed under the 2003 Order. Instead, John may issue his application immediately upon receipt of the s. 25 notice. (If he had served a s. 26 request for a new tenancy thereby initiating the renewal procedure himself, the new Order would have required him to wait for two months from the date of service of his request, unless Bill had served a counternotice opposing renewal earlier).

John can, however, postpone issuing his application to the court until the termination date specified in the s. 25 notice (i.e., 30 June 2005), if he so wishes. John and Bill are also free (under the 2003 Order) to agree in writing to extend this date further, if they so want, in order to facilitate a negotiated settlement without incurring significant court costs.

As to the likelihood of John obtaining a new lease, this will depend on whether Bill can successfully object to the grant of a new tenancy on the ground specified in his s. 25 notice. In order to succeed under s. 30(1)(f), Bill must show that:

(a) he intends to demolish, or reconstruct or effect substantial work of construction on the *holding* on the termination of the tenancy; and

(b) he requires legal possession of the *holding* (i.e., the work could not be done satisfactorily unless he obtains exclusive occupation).

A bare assertion of intention is not enough and Bill will need to establish that he has a reasonable prospect of obtaining the requisite planning permission, finance, builders etc. in order to carry out his refurbishment plans (*Reohorn v Barry Corporation* [1956] 1 WLR 845, *Gregson v Cyril Lord* [1963] 1 WLR 41, *Cadogan v McCarthy & Stone Developments Ltd* [1996] EGCS 94 and *Yoga for Health Foundation v Guest* [2002] All ER (D81).).

The word 'holding' is defined in s. 23(3) of the 1954 Act as meaning the property comprised in the tenancy, there being excluded any part thereof which is occupied neither by the tenant nor by any person employed by the tenant and so employed for the purposes of the business by reason of which the tenancy is one to which Pt II applies. Thus, it would seem that Bill would not be entitled to possession of the basement in any event since this does not form part of the holding for the purposes of s. 23(3).

It is surprising that Bill has relied on s. 30(1)(g) (i.e., intention to occupy the holding for landlord's business) in his s. 25 notice of termination. It is to be noted that Bill purchased the freehold during the last five years ending with the termination of the tenancy and thus falls foul of the exclusion to ground (g) under s. 30(2) (*Diploma Laundry Ltd* v *Surrey Timber Co. Ltd* [1955] 2 QB 604 and *VCS Carpark Management Ltd* v *Regional Railways North East Ltd* [2000] 1 All ER 403 (CA)). In any event, in order to have succeeded under this ground, Bill would need to have shown not only that he had a genuine *bona fide* intention to occupy the holding but also, on an objective test, that he had a reasonable prospect of bringing about this occupation by his own act or volition (*Gregson* v *Cyril Lord Ltd* [1963] 1 WLR 41 and *Zarvos* v *Pradham* [2003] EWCA Civ 208). The wisdom or long-term viability of the landlord's proposed business are irrelevant in determining the requisite intention under s. 30(1)(g). Moreover, it appears that the absence of detailed plans, permissions and consents will also not necessarily denote lack of intention. The crucial factor in all cases is the reality of the landlord's intention to start the proposed business, not the likelihood of its ultimate success (*Dolgellau Golf Club* v *Hett* [1998] 34 EG 87 and *Gatwick Parking Services Ltd* v *Sargent* [2000] 25 EG 141, where it was held that the landlord must show that he has a real, not merely fanciful, chance of obtaining planning permission). As already mentioned, however, ground (g) is not open to Bill in view of his purchase of the freehold in 2001.

Assuming that Bill is unsuccessful in opposing John's application for a new tenancy, then the court must grant a new tenancy (s. 29). If the parties are unable to agree the terms of the new tenancy, the court will set them, subject to various limits as to property, duration, rent and other terms.

As a general rule, the grant must be of the *holding* as existing at the date of the order, nothing more and nothing less (s. 32). That being the case, John will be granted a new tenancy of the ground floor shop and flat only to the exclusion of the basement premises (*Narcissi* v *Wolfe* [1960] Ch 10). However, Bill may insist on the grant of the entire premises comprised in the current lease, if so minded (s. 32(2)). Unless the parties agree otherwise, John will be entitled to the re-grant of easements or profits enjoyed under the current lease (s. 32(3)).

As to duration, the court is empowered to grant such term as is reasonable, subject to an upper limit of 15 years (s. 33) as amended by the 2003 order. However, the court has full discretion to order a short term where the landlord fails to establish grounds

(d) to (g) but persuades the court that he is likely to be able to establish such grounds in the near future (see, e.g., *Upsons Ltd* v *E. Robins Ltd* [1956] 1 QB 131). Instead of granting a short term, the court may insert a break clause allowing the landlord to determine the lease when ready to redevelop (*McCombie* v *Grand Junction Co. Ltd* [1962] 1 WLR 581). This may be of relevance to Bill who may not be able to establish the requisite intention at the specified date of termination.

The rent to be determined is an open market rent disregarding prestige (or adverse image) attaching to the holding, goodwill and certain tenant's improvements (s. 34).

As to the other terms, s. 35 directs the court to have regard to the terms of the current tenancy and to all relevant circumstances in determining the terms of the new tenancy other than duration and rent. The basic principle is that the landlord is not entitled without justification to the insertion of terms in the new tenancy which are more onerous than the terms in the current tenancy (*Gold* v *Brighton Corporation* [1956] 1 WLR 1291 and *Cardshops Ltd* v *Davies* [1971] 1 WLR 591). The burden of persuading a court to change the terms of the current tenancy is on the party proposing them, and the court must be satisfied that they are fair and reasonable in all the circumstances (*O'May* v *City of London Real Property Co. Ltd* [1983] 2 AC 726). Thus, for example, the burden is squarely on the landlord to justify the inclusion of an automatic right to require an authorised guarantee agreement on assignment in the alienation covenant to be included in the new lease: *Wallis Fashion Group Ltd* v *CGU Life Assurance Ltd* (2001) 81 P & CR 28, where it was held that such a guarantee should be required only 'where reasonable'.

(b) If John was the lessee but ran his business through a company in which he owned all the shares, it could be argued that he was not in occupation of the holding for the purpose of his business within the meaning of s. 23(1). In *Pegler* v *Craven* [1952] 2 QB 69, the claimant was the tenant of premises comprising living accommodation and a shop. The business of the shop was carried on by a company, half the shares of which were held by the tenant, and he was the managing director. The Court of Appeal held that he was not the occupier of the shop since the business of the shop was the business of the company and was not the tenant's business. Lord Evershed MR, however, left open the question whether, in some circumstances, it could be argued that a company in actual occupation was but the *alter ego* of the tenant, particularly where the tenant was the beneficial owner of all (or substantially all) the shares issued in the company so that the tenant remained in legal theory in occupation of the premises.

The point was taken up in *Christina* v *Seear* (1985) 275 EG 898, where the tenants owned all the shares in the company and therefore controlled it. They argued that the premises were occupied by them for the purposes of a business carried on by them within s. 23(1), in that the company was a mere vehicle or *alter ego* through which the business was carried on by them. The Court of Appeal, rejecting this argument, held that the tenants did not bring themselves within s. 23(1). The same result was reached in *Nozari-Zadeh* v *Pearl Assurance plc* (1987) 283 EG 457, where it was also intimated that the position might be different if the company in question was merely the agent or manager of the tenant. In this connection, it has been expressly declared that business premises could be occupied by an agent or manager (*Cafeteria (Keighley) Ltd* v *Harrison* (1956) 168 EG 668, *per* Denning LJ). In *Ross Auto Wash Ltd* v *Herbert* (1978) 250 EG 971, Fox J held that a tenant company could be in occupation of business premises even though another company was acting as its manager.

Reference may also be made to s. 41 of the 1954 Act, which provides, *inter alia*, that when a tenancy is held on trust, occupation by all or any of the beneficiaries under the trust, and the carrying on of a business by all or any of the beneficiaries, shall be treated as equivalent occupation or the carrying on of a business by the tenant. This provision, therefore, could be used to overcome the difficulty that arose in the *Pegler, Christina* and *Nozari-Zadeh* line of cases; but it should be noted that s. 41 can be used only if the terms of the tenant's lease permit the actual entry into occupation and carrying on of the business by the company.

Fortunately, most of the difficulties highlighted by the above case law have been removed by virtue of the Regulatory Reform (Business Tenancies) (England and Wales) Order 2003. This Order, as mentioned earlier, came into force on 1 June 2004. As from this date, the definition of 'tenant' will be extended so that an individual (such as John) and any company in which he has a controlling interest will be treated as one and the same person for the purposes of deciding whether the 'tenant' occupied the premises for the purpose of his business. In addition, companies controlled by one individual are to be treated as members of a group of companies. In view of these recent substantive changes, John will not be prejudiced in making an application for a lease renewal simply because the business is being run not by him personally but through his wholly-owned company.

Q Question 4

'The Law Commission's analysis of the workings of Pt II of the 1954 Act supports the view that both abolition, at one extreme, and changing to a different scheme of statutory protection at the other are undesirable. Instead, the proposals address areas of the 1954 Act, both substantive and procedural, which have caused difficulties or anomalies.'

What recent changes have been introduced to Pt II of the 1954 Act? Do these address the areas of 'substance and procedure' identified by the Law Commission which have caused 'difficulties or anomalies'?

Commentary

This question seeks to test your knowledge of the broader issues governing the workings of the Landlord and Tenant Act 1954, Pt II in the light of the recent amendments introduced by the Regulatory Reform (Business Tenancies) (England and Wales) Order 2003 which came into force on 1 June 2004.

You should be aware that the Law Commission published its final proposals for reform in this area in 1992: see, 'Business Tenancies: A Periodic Review of the Landlord and Tenant Act 1954 Pt II', Law Com. No. 208 (1992). Prior to this, the Commission published a working paper on Pt II of the 1954 Act (Working Paper No. 111, 1988). You should refer to these, where appropriate, in your answer.

- **Changes to contracting out provisions — no need for court application Safeguards for tenant**

- **Changes to notice timetables and applications to court**

- **Interim rent applications now available to either landlord or tenant**

- **Changes to tenant's notice of termination and s. 40 notices requiring information. Also provisions relating to ownership and control of businesses altered**

- **Amendments have brought about a quicker, easier, fairer and cheaper renewal process and reflect the recommendations of the Law Commission in its 1998 Report**

The Regulatory Reform (Business Tenancies) (England and Wales) Order 2003, which came into force on 1 June 2004, addresses several concerns over the working of Pt II of the 1954 Act which have arisen over the years. The last revision of Pt II took place in 1969, which made limited amendments (e.g., the introduction of interim rents): see, Law of Property Act 1969.

One of the major changes introduced under the 2003 Order relates to contracting out of Pt II. It will no longer be necessary for the landlord and tenant to apply to court for a contracting out order where they wish to enter into a lease that is excluded from the 1954 Act's security of tenure provisions. Instead, the landlord is now required to serve a prescribed form of notice on the tenant confirming the new lease is to be excluded from the Act and the tenant will then sign a declaration confirming that it has received the notice and understood its contents. The landlord's notice must be served at least 14 days before the date on which the tenant enters into the new lease or, if earlier, becomes contractually bound to do so. The tenant must then sign the prescribed declaration prior to entering into the new lease (or agreement for lease) and a reference to the notice and the declaration must be contained in or endorsed upon the lease (or agreement). Where there is not enough time to wait for 14 days before the parties enter into the transaction, they can still use the notice procedure so long as the prescribed notice is served on the tenant at any time before the contract is signed and the tenant makes a *statutory* declaration in the prescribed form. These provisions apply similarly to agreements to surrender leases that are protected under Pt II.

The unsatisfactory nature of the joint court application procedure to contract out was identified by the Law Commission in its final proposals for amendment of the 1954 Act in November 1992. Prior to that (in 1988, it had published a Working Paper analysing the practical problems of the 1954 Act's operations and procedures.) The Commission felt that the joint application procedure was unnecessarily complicated and should be abolished and replaced by compliance with a series of formalities avoiding any court application. The 2003 Order reflects the rationale of the Commission's views by the introduction of the landlord's 'health warning notice' and a tenant's declaration confirming that the landlord's notice has been served, that the tenant agrees that security of tenure should be excluded and that he accepts the consequences of so doing.

The 2003 Order has also brought about changes to the service of s. 25 notices and s. 26 requests in line with the recommendations of the Law Commission. Apart from various minor amendments to other statutory notices, the Commission felt that no practical purpose would be achieved by the retention of a tenant's counter-notice indicating whether he is willing to give up possession. In reality, this is served virtually automatically by tenants regardless of their plans. On the other hand, it can work unfairly to deprive ill-advised or disorganised tenants of statutory protection. Accordingly, under the 2003 Order, there is now no longer an obligation on the tenant to serve a counternotice in response to a landlord's s. 25 notice of termination. A landlord, however, remains obliged to serve a counternotice within two months of a tenant's s. 26 request if it opposes renewal (the grounds of opposition remaining unchanged). Moreover, if the landlord is not opposing renewal, it must now confirm its proposals as to the terms of the new tenancy (i.e., the property being either the whole or part of the property comprised in the existing tenancy), the rent to be payable and the other terms (which will usually be stated as being the same as the existing terms).

The Law Commission also expressed the view (in its Working Paper) that steps should be taken to reduce the number of court applications which were commenced simply to safeguard the tenant's rights. It proposed, therefore, that a *landlord* should be able to make an application under the Act and that this should take one of two forms. The landlord could apply simply for the termination of the current tenancy, a procedure that would be adopted in cases where the landlord was opposing renewal on one of the statutory grounds. Alternatively, a landlord could apply for the renewal of the tenancy, a process which would mirror the tenant's right to make a similar application. The 2003 Order reflects these recommendations. Both the tenant and the landlord are now able to apply to the court for a renewal of the existing tenancy. If the landlord is opposing renewal, it may now also apply to the court to terminate the tenancy if it can make out one of the grounds of opposition. The time for making applications to the court have also changed. The requirement that the tenant must issue its application not less than two months nor more than four months after the date of service of the s. 25 notice/s. 26 request has been removed altogether. The tenant will now be able to issue his application immediately upon receipt of the s. 25 notice, but if it serves a s. 26 request then it must wait for two months from the date of service, unless the landlord serves a counternotice opposing a renewal earlier. The landlord will also be able to issue the proceedings as soon as the s. 25 notice/s. 26 request has been served, unless a s. 26 request has been served and it is opposing renewal in which case it may issue after serving its counternotice opposing renewal.

The date by which the renewal proceedings must be issued has now also changed to the termination/renewal date contained in the s. 25 notice/s. 26 request. In addition, the parties are now free to agree in writing to extend this date as often as they choose so as to enable them to avoid court proceedings and reach a negotiated settlement without being concerned about rigid time-constraints and escalating court costs.

A crucial change proposed by the Law Commission related to interim rent. It recommended that either a landlord or a tenant should be able to apply for interim rent so as to eradicate the unfair practice of a landlord dragging out the statutory procedures in order to ensure that the tenant continues to pay a contractual rent which exceeds current market levels. This change has now been implemented under the 2003 Order so that either the landlord or the tenant can make the application at any time following service of the s. 25 notice/s. 26 request but must be made no later than six months 'after the termination of the relevant tenancy'. As the date in the s. 25 notice/s. 26 request is the termination date for the current tenancy, it seems that the Order requires either side to make their application to the court for an interim rent no later than six months after that date. Given, however, that the new rules have sought to remove the unnecessary deadlines for the issue of renewal proceedings, it seems rather strange that they have also introduced a new deadline requiring the parties to litigate if either wish an interim rent to be set and cannot agree it in time. The 2003 Order also makes important changes to the determination of the amount of the interim rent. At present, interim rent is calculated by reference to the rent under the new lease but having regard to the rent payable under the old expiring lease and on the assumption that a new lease would be granted from year to year. Assuming a rising market, this method has tended to 'cushion' the tenant from the full impact of the current market rent. The new rules effectively remove this automatic cushioning effect where the landlord is not opposing a new tenancy of the whole premises.

Minor changes have also been made to the tenant's s. 27(1) notice of termination. Previously, where a fixed-term lease had expired and was being continued by the 1954 Act but lease renewal proceedings were not on foot, the tenant could give notice to determine of at least three months' length expiring on a quarter day. From 1 June 2004, the notice can end on any date so that expiry on a quarter day is no longer required. The maximum term length the court is able to award under s. 33 of the 1954 Act has been increased from 14 to 15 years to reflect the change in practice since 1954 of granting leases in multiples of five years rather than seven years. Minor changes have also been made to the tenant's right to claim compensation for disturbance.

Another area of dissatisfaction recognised by the Law Commission related to the workings of s. 40 of the 1954 Act. The problem with s. 40 notices (which seek certain basic information from the tenant or landlord) was that, whilst they stated on their face that they had to be replied to within a month, there was no method of enforcing this requirement. The 2003 Order now makes it possible for either party to apply to the court to force a response to the notice and, if loss has been suffered as a result of the failure to respond, claim damages.

Finally, the Commission recognised that anomalies existed in the current interpretation of the occupation of property for the purposes of a business. The existing provisions in the 1954 Act did not work consistently since an individual tenant had no protection if a company which he controlled traded on the premises (*Chrsitina* v *Seear* (1985) 275 EG 898), while an individual landlord could oppose renewal on the basis that the company that he controlled was intending to trade from the premises (s. 30(3)). These anomalies have now been addressed in the 2003 Order. The definition of 'tenant' will, from 1 June 2004, be extended so that an individual and any company in which he has a controlling interest will be treated as one and the same for the purposes of deciding whether the 'tenant' occupies the premises. In addition, companies controlled by one individual are to be treated as members of a group of companies. The same will apply to landlords, except where the landlord has acquired its controlling interest in the relevant company less than five years prior to the date contained in the s. 25 notice/s. 26 request in which case that landlord/company would not satisfy the five year test when attempting to rely on the own-occupation ground if the landlord is opposing renewal.

The rationale underlying all these changes is to make procedures under Pt II of the 1954 Act quicker, easier, fairer and cheaper. There is no doubt that the changes to the contracting-out procedures will make it cheaper and quicker for the parties to exclude Pt II. Concerns have been expressed, however, that these provisions (requiring the service of notices within a prescribed timetable) will provide new scope for technical challenges to purported exclusion on the grounds of procedural non-compliance. The changes to the notice timetables, on the other hand, are likely to cut down considerably on the current practice of 'game playing' that has been common in respect of lease renewals in recent years. One of the great concerns with the existing provisions was that the tenant could lose his rights to a new tenancy on purely procedural mistakes. The new provisions which abolish the tenant's counternotice go some way to avoid this in the future. However, the date for the tenant's application to court is still crucial and, although this can be modified by the parties, it will inevitably give rise to errors and mistakes potentially nullifying the renewal process. The ability, however, of the parties to hold-off taking the matter to court will undoubtedly increase the potential for lease renewal disputes to come to a negotiated settlement. The change to the interim rent provisions will also make the whole process fairer by allowing either landlord or tenant to apply for an interim rent. In addition, the landlord's ability to apply to court for a new lease will create a fairer process. All in all, therefore, the 2003 Order is to be welcomed, not least because it implements virtually all of the Law Commission's proposals put forward in its 1992 Report.

Q Question 5

In what circumstances will a business tenant be eligible for compensation for improvements undertaken to the demised premises? How does this form of compensation differ from compensation for disturbance?

Commentary

This is a relatively easy essay question on a business tenant's compensation rights. It is the sort of question which should leave you in no doubt as to whether it is 'on' or not. The subject matter is immediately clear and you have either revised this topic or not! If you are lucky enough to have studied the subject prior to the exam, this is a 'give-away' question and you should have no difficulty in scoring high marks.

Notice that there are really two parts to this question — you must, therefore, give a *balanced* answer which shows the examiner that you understand the differences between the two types of compensation.

The rules governing the amount of compensation payable for disturbance are quite complex. For a good summary, see McLoughlin, P., 'Compensation for Disturbance of Business Tenants' [1990] EG 9033, 22. On the subject of compensation for improvements, see Pawlowski, M., 'Compensation for Improvements' [1992] RRLR vol. 13/2, p. 110 and, more recently, Anyamene, R., 'Recovery Programme' [1999] 9926 EG 148, containing a useful diagram of the relevant procedures.

- Meaning of 'improvement' under Landlord and Tenant Act 1927. Tenant must serve notice on landlord of intention to effect the improvement. Possible objections by landlord

- Improvement must be completed within time agreed or fixed by the court. Once works completed, tenant entitled to certificate of improvement. Tenant must give notice to landlord of his claim for compensation: s. 47. Amount of compensation fixed by agreement or by court

- Compensation for disturbance intended to compensate for loss of goodwill attached to the holding. Available if landlord successfully objects on grounds (e), (f) or (g) of s. 30(1) of 1954 Act

- Amount of compensation for disturbance calculated by reference to rateable value of holding. Provisions restricting or excluding right to compensation: s. 38 and *Bacchiocchi* v *Academic Agency Ltd* (1998)

:Q: Suggested answer

The right to compensation for improvements is governed by the Landlord and Tenant Act 1927, Pt I (as amended by the Landlord and Tenant Act 1954). In relation to improvements, Pt I applies to any premises held under a lease used wholly or partly for carrying on any trade, profession or business (except a lease of agricultural holdings), mining leases, or written leases where the tenant is expressly the holder of an office or employment under the landlord (s. 17).

The tenant is entitled to compensation only at the termination of the tenancy and upon quitting the demised premises. In addition, the tenant must have complied with a number of pre-conditions. First, the tenant must show an 'improvement' on his holding made by him or his predecessors in title. In order to qualify, the improvement must:

(a) be of such a nature as to be calculated to add to the letting value of the holding at the termination of the tenancy;

(b) be reasonable and suitable to the character of the holding, and

(c) not diminish the value of any other property belonging to the same landlord or to any superior landlord.

Secondly, the tenant must have served on the landlord a notice of intention to effect the improvement. The notice of intention must be served on the landlord prior to the commencement of the works and contain a specification and plan showing the proposed improvement and the part of the premises affected. If the landlord makes no objection to the proposed improvement, the tenant may go ahead and carry out the works without recourse to litigation. If, on the other hand, the landlord, within three months after service of the tenant's notice, serves on the tenant a notice of objection, the tenant must then apply to the court for a certificate that the improvement is a proper one if he wishes to proceed with the works. The landlord may object to the proposed improvement on a variety of different grounds. For example, he may seek to argue that the proposed works do not comprise an 'improvement' within the meaning of the 1927 Act, or that the tenant is outside the scope of the Act. In particular, the landlord may object on the ground that he has offered to execute the improvement himself in consideration of a reasonable increase in rent, or of an increase to be determined by the court. If the landlord carries out the works, no compensation is payable under the 1927 Act, but if he defaults the court may then issue a certificate that the improvement is a proper one and compensation will be available. It has been held recently that a tenant is free to change his mind and withdraw his notice of intention to effect an improvement. In these circumstances, the landlord cannot insist on carrying out the improvements himself in return for a reasonable increase in rent: *Norfolk Capital Group Ltd* v *Cadogan Estates Ltd*, (2004), unreported, available on Lawtel.

Thirdly, the tenant must have completed the improvement within the time agreed with the landlord or fixed by the court. Once the tenant has executed the improvement, he is entitled to request the landlord to furnish him with a certificate that the improvement has been duly executed. If the landlord fails or refuses, the court may grant the certificate.

Lastly, the tenant must give notice to the landlord of his claim for compensation. There are detailed time limits specified in s. 47 of the 1954 Act as to the service of the tenant's notice. The amount of compensation is fixed by agreement between the parties or, in default of agreement, by the court.

The right to compensation for disturbance differs in a number of respects. This form of compensation is essentially intended to compensate the tenant for the loss of goodwill attached to the holding. It is available to the tenant where the landlord successfully objects to the grant of a new tenancy on grounds (e), (f) or (g) of s. 30(1) of the 1954 Act (s. 37(1)). (There is also now a right to compensation when there is no renewal of the tenancy following a successful opposition by the landlord to the grant of a new tenancy on the ground that it is the intention that a company under its control should occupy the property: Regulatory Reform (Business Tenancies) (England and Wales) Order 2003.) The tenant will be entitled to compensation under s. 37(1) even if, at time of serving its s. 26 request, it had no intention of actually seeking a renewal but wanted simply to qualify for statutory compensation: *Sun Life Assurance plc* v *Thalesl Tracs Ltd* [2001] 34 EG 100, where it was held that the s. 26 request does not require the tenant to have any particular state of mind. The compensation is recoverable from the landlord from the date that the tenant quits the holding.

There are complicated rules for determining the amount of compensation. In the case of existing tenancies where the landlord's s. 25 notice of termination was served before 1 April 1990, the level of compensation remains at three times the rateable value of the holding, or (if the tenant can show continuous occupation as a business tenant over a period of 14 years immediately preceding termination of the tenancy) six times the rateable value (at the date of the service of the notice). Personal occupation during the 14-year period is not, however, essential where all the previous occupants were predecessors in the same business (s. 37(2)).

On 1 April 1990, the rating revaluation of commercial properties came into effect resulting in an average increase in rateable values of eight times. To coincide with this change, the multiplier used to compute compensation for disturbance was reduced from three to one. Thus now, where the s. 25 notice is served after 31 March 1990, the level of compensation is one or two times the rateable value of the holding at the date of service of the notice. However, some tenants have the option to require compensation at eight (or 16) times the rateable value of 31 March 1990 instead of one (or two times) the current rateable value.

It is apparent that the 14-year period of occupation has to be satisfied up to the date of termination of the tenancy specified in the landlord's s. 25 notice. In *Sight & Sound Education Ltd* v *Books etc. Ltd* [1999] 43 EG 161, the tenant gave up possession by the contractual term date (thereby ceasing to enjoy Pt II protection) and, consequently, was not entitled to compensation based on twice the rateable value.

As a result of a 1969 amendment to the 1954 Act, it is not necessary for the tenant to go through the motions of applying for a new tenancy to preserve his claim for disturbance. For example, if the landlord specifies grounds (e), (f) or (g) in his s. 25 notice or opposition to a s. 26 request, and the tenant sees little chance of a successful application, his claim under s. 37 will be unaffected by a decision to quit the holding on the specified termination date (cf. *Lloyds Bank Ltd* v *City of London Corporation* [1983] Ch 192).

Agreements restricting or excluding compensation for disturbance are void except where, looking back from the date that the tenant quit the holding, there was less than five years' continuous business occupation by the tenant or his predecessors in business (s. 38). When determining whether the business tenant has occupied for the whole of the five-year period, the courts are reluctant to find that a business occupancy has ceased where the business premises are empty for only a short period, whether mid-term or before or after trading at either end of the lease, provided always that during that period there existed no rival for the role of business occupant and that the premises were not being used for some other non-business purpose. However, if the premises are left vacant for a period of months, the courts are more likely to conclude that the reason for that period of closure was not an incident in the ordinary course of business life and that the 'thread of continuity' had been broken (*Bacchiocchi* v *Academic Agency Ltd* [1998] 2 All ER 241, where the tenant was held to have been in business occupation despite the premises standing empty for 12 days prior to termination of the lease). The decision has been the subject of much criticism: see, for example, Bennion, F., (1998) 148 NLJ 953 and 986.

Equally, the right to compensation for improvements cannot be excluded by contract unless it was made before 9 February 1927. However, the court may give effect to a contract depriving the tenant of the right to claim compensation for improvements provided it was made between 8 February 1927 and 10 December 1953, and for valuable consideration.

Q Question 6

In 1965, Property UK Ltd acquired the freehold of a block of 25 flats in Chelsea. Daniel has, since 1992, held a fixed-term lease of the premises, which he uses for his property business. He lives in one of the flats in the block and lets out the rest on six-month assured shorthold tenancies. Daniel retains a key to each of the flats and cleans the common parts, landings and stairwells once a week.

Last month, Daniel read through the terms of his head lease and realised that it is due to expire in two years' time. He is keen to keep his lucrative letting business and does not wish to give up possession of the block.

Advise Daniel as to what rights (if any) he may have under Pt II of the Landlord and Tenant Act 1954.

Commentary

This question is concerned primarily with the House of Lords decision in *Graysim Holdings Ltd* v *P & O Property Holdings Ltd* [1996] 1 AC 329, on the meaning of business occupation under Pt II of the 1954 Act. A good answer will outline the relevant qualifying conditions for statutory protection under Pt II and consider specifically whether Daniel's business of sub-letting the flats within the block precludes him from seeking a statutory renewal of his tenancy. For further reading, see: Haley, M., 'Business Tenancies: Parting with Occupation' [1997] Conv 139, Higgins, S., 'The Continuation Conundrum: Pt II of the Landlord and Tenant Act 1954' [1997] Conv 119 and Pawlowski, M., 'Business Occupation under Pt II — An Update' [1998] RRLR vol. 18/3, pp. 239–46.

• Tenant occupying for the sole purpose of sub-letting parts falls outside s. 23(1). Consider *Graysim Holdings Ltd* v *P & O Property Holdings Ltd* (1996). Case applied to residential sub-lettings: *Bassairi Ltd* v *Camden London Borough Council* (1998)

• But rights reserved to tenant may be so extensive as to justify conclusion that tenant still in occupation: *Lee-Verhulst (Investments) Ltd* v *Harwood Trust* (1973). Contrast *Bagettes Ltd* v *GP Estates Ltd* (1956)

• Tenant must be in occupation of the holding at expiry of the contractual term: *Esselte AB* v *Pearl Assurance plc* (1997). If not, there can be no continuance of the tenancy under s. 24. Daniel's business involves progressive elimination of the holding and, hence, not in occupation for purposes of s. 24

• Daniel should change nature of his business so as to grant licences (as opposed to tenancies) in the future. If he alters his business in this way, he will be in a better position to argue that he is in business occupation under Pt II

:Ọ: **Suggested answer**

A business tenant under Pt II of the 1954 Act enjoys the benefit of a large measure of security of tenure following the expiry of his contractual lease. Under s. 24(1) of the 1954 Act, a tenancy to which Pt II applies cannot come to an end except in the manner provided by the Act. The most important effects are that a fixed term continues after its contractual expiry date and a periodic tenancy cannot be determined by a normal notice to quit. A business tenancy which is continued in this way (i.e., under s. 24) can be assigned and is capable of transmission on death (and bankruptcy) in the normal way. The only feature which is changed is the mode of termination. The continuation tenancy can be terminated only in accordance with the statutory machinery for termination prescribed by the Act.

This machinery is complex. A landlord who desires possession must establish one or more specific grounds (listed in s. 30), having made a formal statement of the grounds relied on either by notice of termination complying with s. 25 or by a notice of opposition to a tenant's request for a new tenancy under s. 26. A tenant who wishes to renew his business tenancy must apply for renewal either pursuant to a request for a new tenancy under s. 26, or in response to a landlord's notice of termination served under s. 25. If he is successful, the court is bound to order the grant of a new tenancy and will determine the terms of the new tenancy in default of agreement between the parties. If, on the other hand, the tenant is unsuccessful in his application to renew, he will be eligible to be paid compensation for disturbance and for tenant's improvements to the premises in certain circumstances.

The qualifying conditions for Pt II security are set out in s. 23 of the1954 Act, which provides that Pt II applies to any tenancy where the property comprised in the tenancy is or includes premises 'which are occupied by the tenant and are so occupied for the purposes of a business carried on by him . . .'. Where the tenant is an individual (as in the present case), he must be engaged in a trade, profession or employment in order to qualify under Pt II. There is no doubt that Daniel is engaged in a business within the meaning of s. 23. However, it has been held that a tenant occupying a building for the sole purpose of sub-letting parts nevertheless falls outside s. 23(1). In *Graysim Holdings Ltd* v *P & O Property Holdings Ltd* [1996] 1 AC 329, the House of Lords held that intermediate landlords who are not themselves in actual physical occupation of the premises are not within the class of persons protected by Pt II, which is concerned to protect tenants in their occupation of property for the purpose of their business, not to give protection to tenants in respect of income from sub-lettings. Moreover, Pt II makes no provision for 'dual occupation' of premises. In other words, it looks through a sub-letting to the occupying sub-tenant and affords him statutory protection (assuming he is in business occupation), not the mesne landlord.

Although the *Graysim* case involved the letting of a market hall, it has since been applied in the context of residential sub-lettings. In *Bassairi Ltd* v *Camden London*

Borough Council [1999] 48 & TR 45, the existence of the sub-lettings (which were, significantly, assured shorthold tenancies) was enough to prevent the tenant from being able to claim it occupied the premises for the purposes of a business under Pt II.

It is important, however, to bear in mind that the House of Lords did not rule out the possibility that, in exceptional cases, the rights reserved by the tenant might be so extensive that he would remain in occupation of the property for the purposes of Pt II. In *Lee-Verhulst (Investments) Ltd* v *Harwood Trust* [1973] 1 QB 204, for example, the occupancies comprised furnished rooms with substantial services (i.e., supply of blankets, bed linen and towels, daily cleaning, regular change of linen and provision of light meals if required). The Court of Appeal held that, in view of the degree of control and extent of the services provided, the tenant 'occupied' the entire premises for the purpose of its business, namely, that of 'providing furnished accommodation and services for those residing there'. By contrast, in *Bagettes Ltd* v *G.P. Estates Ltd* [1956] Ch 290, the residential flats were let unfurnished and, although the tenant provided hot water for the sub-tenants and cleaned the common parts, the 'service' element was negligible. Not surprisingly, the tenant was held not to be in occupation of the holding.

In *Graysim* itself, it was suggested that where the letting takes the form of a *sub-tenancy*, the sub-tenant will be entitled to exclusive possession of the sub-let part and, hence, will be the 'occupier' to the exclusion of the tenant. At the other end of the spectrum, however, where the occupancy takes the form of a *licence* to occupy, there will often be more scope for argument that the tenant retains occupation of the property because the rights granted by a licence to the occupier will be less extensive than those comprised in a sub-tenancy. The key elements in the *Verhulst* case were the provision of services to the occupants (who were characterised as licensees) and the unrestricted access to each room necessary to perform those services: see also, *Linden* v *Department of Health and Social Security* [1986] 1 WLR 164, involving eight self-contained flats managed by a district health authority. By contrast, in *Graysim*, neither the tenant nor his agents had any right of access to the units, nor did they have keys or means of access. All the occupants had exclusive possession and each was a sub-tenant in respect of his unit.

Central, therefore, to the application of Pt II is the notion that a business tenant must be in *occupation* of the premises for the purposes of his business at the contractual expiry date of the lease. If he does not occupy at that date, there can be no continuance of his tenancy under s. 24 (see *Esselte AB* v *Pearl Assurance plc* [1997] 1 WLR 891). Daniel will, therefore, need to satisfy this requirement of s. 23 in order to qualify for protection under Pt II.

Unfortunately for Daniel, as we have seen, the authorities do not assist him in his current position. Although he clearly carries on a business, this is not one to which Pt II applies since it involves the progressive elimination of the holding. By sub-letting all the flats in the block, he has effectively excluded the sub-let accommodation from the holding and thus cannot be said to be *occupying* any significant part of the holding for the purposes of a business. In the present context, the term 'occupation' connotes some business activity by the tenant on the property in question; in other words, some physical use of the property for the purposes of a business carried on by him.

Exceptionally, however, where the tenant grants a genuine licence, the rights reserved by the tenant may be so extensive as not to rule out the possibility of statutory protection under Pt II. In the residential context, it may be open to a tenant to argue that its degree of control over third-party occupants is sufficiently great to come within the *Lee-Verhulst* ruling, referred to above. As things stand at the moment, Daniel clearly does not fall within this exception, but he may be well-advised to alter the nature of his business so as to do so. This would involve granting licences (as opposed to tenancies) in the future and ensuring that he has a right of unrestricted access to the flats in question in order to provide requisite attendance and services. If he alters his business in this way over the next two years, he will be in a good position to argue that he is in business occupation for the purposes of Pt II and, hence, be eligible to renew his lease under s. 26 of the Act.

Q Question 7

What is meant by PACT? What is the contemporary significance of the PACT scheme in the light of Lord Woolf's reforms to the English civil justice system?

Commentary

This essay question is concerned with the PACT system for settling disputes as to new lease terms in the context of lease renewal proceedings under the Landlord and Tenant Act 1954, Pt II. A good answer will consider the nature of the PACT scheme in the context of the changes brought about by the Civil Procedure Rules (CPR). For further reading, see King, Vivien M., 'The 1954 Act Goes PACT' [1997] RRLR vol. 17/4, pp. 322–27, Myers, A., 'Justice on a Faster Track' [1999] 9912 EG 160 and 'Renewals under Woolf', [1999] 9914 EG 147, Webber, G., 'Lease Renewals and the CPR', (2000) 144 SJ 136 and 170, pp. 136–37 and 170–72 and Francis, P., 'The Woolf Reforms — How Will They Impact on Property Disputes under the Landlord and Tenant Act 1954?' [1999] RRLR 237.

- Scheme allows disputes over terms of a new business tenancy to be settled by arbitration or independent expert instead of litigation. Appointment of PACT arbitrators and experts

- Aims of scheme. Main advantage is flexibility and less delay over court proceedings. In what situations is it used?

- If PACT appointee an arbitrator, he will sit in a quasi-judicial capacity and be bound by provisions of the Arbitration Act 1996. Contrast role and functions of appointee sitting as an expert

- Aims of Lord Woolf's changes to civil justice. Change in culture of dispute resolution. PACT scheme consistent with this ideology

- Drawback of PACT is that it requires consent of both parties. No pre-action protocol in relation to lease renewal cases. Potential conflict between CPR rules seeking to avoid the necessity for the start of proceedings and the requirement under the 1954 Act that tenant commence his application for the grant of a new tenancy at an early stage of negotiations for renewal. This now avoided largely by the Regulatory Reform (Business Tenancies) (England and Wales) Order 2003

;Q: Suggested answer

PACT stands for 'Professional Arbitration on Court Terms'. It is a method of alternative dispute resolution which was put forward by the RICS and Law Society to be used in the context of business tenancy renewal proceedings under the Landlord and Tenant Act 1954, Pt II. At present, the scheme provides a means by which disputes over the terms of a new lease (which has been renewed in accordance with Pt II of the 1954 Act) can be dealt with by way of arbitration or the use of an independent expert, rather than litigation. The scheme does not currently apply to an application for a new lease which is opposed by the landlord on one of the grounds contained in s. 30(1)(a)–(g) of the 1954 Act (although it may be so extended in the future). The appointment of a PACT arbitrator or expert may be made by either the Royal Institute of Chartered Surveyors (RICS) or Law Society upon the application of both the landlord and tenant. Such arbitrators and experts are specialists in the area of commercial leases and the workings of the 1954 Act and have been specifically trained under the PACT scheme. It is estimated that there are approximately 60 PACT appointees to date, appointed from the ranks of both solicitors and surveyors.

In essence, the PACT scheme vests in a PACT appointee the same statutory discretion as a judge has in court when determining lease terms under ss. 29–35 of the 1954 Act. In this regard, PACT represents a system of dispute resolution which is an alternative to litigation.

The stated aim of the scheme is to increase the effectiveness and flexibility of the legal system and to give a greater choice both to landlords and tenants and to their legal advisers. The scheme is very much in keeping with the spirit of Lord Woolf's civil law reforms as contained in his Report, *Access to Justice*. In this vein, the scheme encourages parties to view litigation as a last resort, and to view professional arbitration as a cheaper and speedier option for settling disputes over new lease terms.

The PACT system is intended to be more flexible than the current court system, in that the parties are able to adapt their own rules to their very specific requirements and choose whether the adjudicator is to be a solicitor or surveyor sitting as an arbitrator or expert. It is intended that the PACT system will avoid delays — which have been a common complaint about the system of settling lease terms under the current renewal procedures. If PACT proves more speedy, then it is hoped that wasted costs will be avoided. In this connection, under PACT, the parties have a choice as to the type of PACT dispute resolution method to use, namely, arbitration with an oral hearing, arbitration on paper submissions, or the use of an independent expert.

It is noteworthy, however, that PACT can be adopted as a mean of settling a dispute as to new lease terms only where *both* parties consent to the referral. In this context, PACT can be used in one of two instances: first, where the landlord does not *per se* oppose the lease renewal but the parties cannot reach agreement over the terms of the new lease; and, secondly, where the landlord has sought, but failed, to obtain possession and the parties (having failed to reach agreement over the new lease terms) decide to adjourn matters so as to allow a PACT appointee to determine the lease terms. The adjournment of the court proceedings and reference of the matter to a PACT appointee would ordinarily be done by a consent order.

When using PACT, the parties are free to choose their own type of appointee (i.e., solicitor or surveyor). Either type of appointee is feasible. If the dispute regarding the new lease terms is valuation or rental based then a surveyor would probably be the more appropriate expert. If the dispute relates to the wording of new clauses in a renewed lease then a solicitor would be more suitable.

The parties may present their submissions to the PACT appointee by way of either written or oral submissions. If agreement cannot be reached on these procedural matters, the appointee may choose the relevant route as to how to determine the case and directions as to how matters should proceed. The parties can represent themselves, or have professional representation in the form of a lawyer or surveyor.

If the parties choose to engage a PACT appointee as an arbitrator then he will sit in a quasi-judicial capacity and will be bound by the provisions of the Arbitration Act 1996. A PACT appointee sitting as an expert, on the other hand, will not be so bound, and the rules of evidence do not apply to expert determinations. Conversely, an arbitrator has, by virtue of the 1996 Act, a discretion as to whether to apply the rules of evidence (s. 34(2)(f) and s. 34(2)(d)). An arbitrator also has power to decide whether any, and if so what, documents or classes of documents should be disclosed by the parties. In contrast, experts have no power to order disclosure, and can only decide matters on the documents presented to them by the parties.

Once a decision has been made as to the new lease terms, the PACT appointee must formally record his decision, and in so doing apply the criteria as set out in the appropriate sections of the 1954 Act as regards the property to be comprised in the new lease, the rent to be paid, duration, and other terms of the new lease. In this connection, the starting point for determining the terms of the new lease will be the terms of the old lease, and the burden of showing any detraction from the old terms is on the party seeking change (see *O'May* v *City of London Real Property Co. Ltd* [1983] 1 AC 726).

The PACT scheme has attracted a new significance in the light of Lord Woolf's changes to civil justice. The recommendations for reform of the civil justice system have largely been embodied in the Civil Procedure Rules (CPR) which came into force on 26 April 1999. The rules have sought to effect a change in the culture of dispute resolution and there are two broad objectives: (i) to make litigation a matter of last resort and to make the courts more accessible for those who genuinely need assistance; and (ii) to make litigation quicker and cheaper. By virtue of the rules, the courts are obliged to promote settlement of disputes wherever possible. The PACT scheme, as we have already seen, already operates in the context of uncontested 1954 Act lease renewals, where the main source of dispute is the terms to be included in a new lease. Thus far, PACT has not been widely used, the main problem being that its use depends on the consent of *both* parties. It is often in one party's interest to delay the resolution of matters and not resort to the quicker and cheaper facility of the PACT scheme. However, since the introduction of the Woolf reforms, with their emphasis on speed, cost effectiveness and alternative dispute resolution, it is likely that a party who chooses not to use the PACT facility will be regarded by the court as having unreasonably refused to comply with the aims of the CPR and be penalised in costs. In this respect, it may be worthwhile for the party seeking to use PACT to write formally to the other party suggesting use of the scheme, while reserving the right to refer the matter to the court on the issue of costs in the event of the other party refusing consent.

Although there is, as yet, no pre-action protocol in relation to lease renewal cases, the parties are, nevertheless, required 'to act reasonably in exchanging information and documents relevant to the claim and generally in trying to avoid the necessity for the start of proceedings' (CPR, PD Protocols, para. 4). The inherent difficulty, however, with applying this latter principle in the context of business renewal is that the 1954 Act has required the tenant to commence his application for the grant of a new tenancy at an early stage of negotiations for renewal in order to preserve his security under Pt II. Under CPR, once proceedings are issued, there are limited options for the parties to adjourn pending negotiations for renewal of the lease. This problem, however, has now been largely addressed by the Regulatory Reform (Business Tenancies) (England and Wales) Order 2003, which came into force on 1 June 2004. The date by which renewal proceedings must be issued has now been changed to the termination/renewal date contained in the s. 25 notice or s. 26 request. Moreover, for the purpose of issuing the court proceedings, the parties are now free to agree in writing to extend this date as often as they wish so as to provide them with the ability to avoid the court process altogether in order to achieve a negotiated settlement without the concern of rigid time constraints and escalating court costs.

Q Question 8

What kind of building works qualify under s. 30(1)(f) of the Landlord and Tenant Act 1954 so as to entitle the landlord to oppose a tenant's application for a new tenancy on the ground of redevelopment? Must the intended work involve the structure of the premises in the sense of load-bearing elements? Does the recent case law provide a consistent answer to this question?

Commentary

We have included this question so as to provide you with some understanding of recent cases on the nature of the intended works falling within para. (f). Two recent cases, in particular, have concerned development schemes involving alterations to internal partitions and removal of non-load-bearing walls: *Ivorygrove Ltd* v *Global Grange Ltd* [2003] EWHC 1409 (Ch) and *Global Grange Ltd* v *Marazzi* [2002] EWHC 3010 (Ch), concerning adjacent premises owned by the same landlord. It was unfortunate that these two cases were not heard together at county court level since they both raised similar issues regarding the nature and extent of the proposed works. The upshot is that the cases have produced different results on largely similar facts.

   We are conscious that this question may be of more interest to our surveying (as opposed to law) students. However, the issues raised will be of concern to legal advisers practising in the commercial lease field.

* Nature of works falling within s. 30(1)(f) — demolition, reconstruction, substantial work of construction of the premises comprised in the holding. Meaning of 'substantial part' of the premises: *Romulus Trading Co. Ltd* v *Henry Smith's Charity Trustees* (1990)

* What is the character of the physical work? Meaning of reconstruction: *Joel v. Swaddle* (1957) and *Percy E. Cadle & Co. Ltd* v *Jacmarch Properties Ltd* (1957)

* Do the works have to involve load-bearing elements? *Bewlay (Tobacconists) Ltd* v *British Bata Shoe Company Ltd* (1959) and *Barth* v *Pritchard* (1990). Consider 'eggshell' premises: *Pumperninks of Picadilly Ltd* v *Land Securities plc* (2002)

* Contrast decision in *Ivorgrove* (2003) with *Global Grange* (2002). Ultimately, divergence in outcome due to factual differences in the two cases

ⵞ Suggested answer

In order for a landlord successfully to oppose a tenant's application for a new tenancy under s. 30(1)(f) of the 1954 Act, he must show that he has the requisite intention to do any one (or more) of the following:

(i) *demolish* or *reconstruct* the premises comprised in the holding;

(ii) demolish or reconstruct a *substantial part* of the premises comprised in the holding; or

(iii) carry out *substantial work of construction* on the whole (or part) of the holding.

The question of what is 'substantial' is one of fact and degree and the cases demonstrate that an appellate court will not interfere with the discretion of the trial judge unless his decision was clearly wrong or one to which no person could reasonably come: *Atkinson* v *Bettison* [1955] 1 WLR 1127. As the Court of Appeal observed in *Romulus Trading Co. Ltd* v *Henry Smith's Charity Trustees* [1990] 2 EGLR 75, 'ultimately it is a question for the jury'. It is also evident that the proposed works must be looked at as a whole and that demolition on its own (without reconstruction) is enough.

Although the time and cost of the works are relevant considerations, the real issue is the true character of the physical work. In this connection, reconstruction work must involve an interference with the structure of the premises coupled with a rebuilding of that part of the premises which has been affected by interference with the structure: *Joel* v *Swaddle* [1957] 1 WLR 1095 and *Percy E. Cadle & Co. Ltd* v *Jacmarch Properties Ltd* [1957] 1 QB 323. In this context, therefore, rebuilding involves substituting structurally something different from that which was there before the interference. What, however, has remained unclear until recently is whether s. 30(1)(f) applies when the proposed work, however extensive, does not involve the structure of the premises in the sense of load-bearing elements.

In *Romulus Trading*, mentioned earlier, Farquharson LJ expressed the view that structure was not necessarily confined to outside or other load-bearing walls and works of preparation ancillary to such works could properly be included as works of reconstruction or construction. His Lordship also included within para. (f) work closely associated with the completion of works of construction (e.g., plastering and decorating of new walls, rewiring, laying of cables and drains, etc.).

In *Bewlay (Tobacconists) Ltd* v *British Bata Shoe Company Ltd* [1959] 1 WLR 45, the work involved the amalgamation of two shops into one by removing three-quarters of the dividing walls with consequential alterations to some of the pillars supporting the ceiling, putting in a new double shop-front, a small amount of reconstruction of lavatory accommodation and the filling in of a recessed portion of a wall. This was held to constitute reconstruction of a substantial part of the premises. Lord Evershed MR accepted that removal of part of a non-loading-bearing wall was 'demolition' within s. 30(1)(f) and that the replacement of the wall by screens could be called 'reconstruction'. By contrast, in *Barth* v *Pritchard* [1990] 1 EGLR 109, Stocker LJ expressed the view that 'substantial work of construction' required some form of building work which involved the structure and that wooden partitions, however extensive, did not fall within the definition of 'construction'. He did recognise, however, that it was ultimately a question of fact depending on the circumstances of the given case.

In *Graysim Holdings Ltd* v *P & O Property Holdings Ltd* [1993] 1 EGLR 96, the deputy judge held expressly that demolition and/or construction need not be confined to load-bearing walls. In *Pumperninks of Picadilly Ltd* v *Land Securities plc* [2002] 3 All ER 609, the Court of Appeal held that an 'eggshell (i.e., premises comprising solely of the internal skin of the building with all load-bearing parts excluded) is capable of being demolished and/or reconstructed within the meaning of ground (f). It was left open, however, whether the same result would follow where the demised property included load-bearing or structural parts.

Two recent cases have shed light on this important question. In *Ivorygrove Ltd* v *Global Grange Ltd* [2003] EWHC 1409 (Ch), the proposed works involved the conversion of a number of houses into a hotel by making connections between them at all levels. The redevelopment would also create 43 bedrooms with en-suite facilities from 73 existing bedrooms. For this purpose, doorways were to be blocked up and internal walls demolished. Only a minority of the internal walls were load-bearing. Much of the existing partitioning was to be removed and replaced by new partitions stiffened by plywood, insulated and plastered. The existing partitions were characterised as substantial requiring to be knocked down by a sledgehammer thereby disturbing the skirting, walls, and ceiling finishes. A larger shaft was also to be installed replacing the existing lift service and two steel beams inserted in the basement. The total cost of the scheme was estimated at £4.2 million and would take approximately 44 weeks to carry out. Not surprisingly, the trial judge held that the scheme qualified under s. 30(1)(f) as being works of demolition and reconstruction of a substantial part of the premises and also a substantial work of construction of the holding. The decision was upheld on appeal by Lawrence Collins J, who concluded, from an extensive review of the authorities, that there was nothing in para. (f) which required the demolition or construction of load-bearing features as a condition of its applicability. In his view, therefore, whether the relevant parts of the premises were load-bearing was simply one of the factors to be taken into account in determining the 'jury question' of whether there is demolition or construction. In particular, with regard to partitioning, para. (f) would, clearly, not apply to temporary and moveable office screens. But in other cases where the partitioning was of a more substantial nature, much would depend on the nature of the work, the role of the partitions and the purpose behind the development scheme.

A different conclusion, however, was reached in another case involving (coincidentally) adjacent premises owned by the same landlord. In *Global Grange Ltd* v *Marazzi* [2002] EWHC 3010 (Ch) the intention was to upgrade an existing two-star hotel into more luxurious four-star premises with fewer bedrooms but all with en-suite facilities. The total cost was estimated at around £2 million and the works would take 12 months to complete. Some of these works clearly involved demolition and reconstruction (i.e., removal of the basement wall and its replacement by a steel beam, installation of a lift, removal and restoration of part of the staircase and opening up of access in party walls). However, none of this affected a substantial part of the premises. Although the works also involved the creation of stud partitions, these were characterised by the trial judge as merely making convenient divisions to enable use of the premises to suit the particular requirements of the tenants rather than being part of the essential structure of the premises. As such, their function was no different from that of temporary partitions found in office buildings. Thus, according to the trial judge, although structure did not necessarily mean load-bearing elements, it had to include the basic fabric of the building which gave it its essential form and character as a building. On the facts, therefore, he held that the proposed scheme did not constitute work of demolition or reconstruction of a substantial part of the premises.

The decision was upheld on appeal by Park J (see, [2002] EWHC 3010 (Ch)), essentially on the ground that it was one which a judge could properly reach on the facts. In particular, his Lordship confirmed the view that installing new partitions was not construction but merely altering the internal layout. Ultimately, it was a question of degree and if the plans had been more extensive, for example, to gut the whole interior of the hotel and rebuild it, that 'obviously' would be reconstruction. What, therefore, is significant in *Marazzi* is that the essence of the internal structure remained the same. Interestingly, however, Park J did recognise that a different judge might have taken an opposite view on the facts.

The divergence of result between the *Ivorygate* and *Marazzi* decisions may be explained on the basis of the factual differences in the two cases. However, this is not entirely convincing. Indeed, Lawrence Collins J in *Ivorgate* felt distinctly uneasy in trying to answer this difficulty by simply saying that, where the question is one of fact and degree, different judges can come to different conclusions on substantially similar facts. Since an appellate court, as we have seen, will rarely interfere with the trial judge's evaluation of the evidence (unless it is plainly wrong), this has meant that both decisions have been upheld.

Further reading

Bignell, J., and Dray, M., 'The Future of the Landlord and Tenant Act 1954, Pt II: Continuing the Debate' (2001) 5 L & T Rev 66.

Colby, A., Wallis, A., and Fenn, K., '1954 Act Changes to Business Leases' [2004] EG 29 May, 132, 5 June, 116.

Furber, J., 'The New Regime of Business Tenancy Renewal' NLJ, 28 May 2004, 796.

Haley, M., 'Business Tenancies: Parting with Occupation' [1997] Conv 139.

Haley, M., 'Business Tenancies: Renewal and Authorised Guarantee Agreements' [2000] Conv 566.

Hewitson, R., 'Reform of Business Tenancies Legislation' [2002] Conv 261.

Higgins, S., 'The Continuation Conundrum: Pt II of the Landlord and Tenant Act 1954' [1997] Conv 119.

Martin. J., 'Business Tenancies Reforms — Should We Have Expected More? (2004) L & T Rev [52].

Neuberger, D., 'Our Not So Flexible Friend' [2000] EG 139.

Pawlowski, M., 'New Consultation on Termination of Tenancies for Tenant Default' (2003) L & T Rev 32.

Pawlowski, M., 'Three Bites at the Cherry' [1996] 16 RRLR 7.

Smith, C., and Reekie, P., 'A Healthier Alternative' [2004] EG 137.

Webber, G., 'LTA 1954 Reforms (1), (2), (3), (4) and (5) (2004) SJ 520, 522, 566, 617 and 651.

Agricultural tenancies

Introduction

In this chapter, you will find four questions — two on agricultural holdings, one on agricultural tied cottages and one on the Agricultural Tenancies Act 1995.

The subject of agricultural holdings is complex in so far as it is regulated by highly detailed statutory provisions. The legislative code which continues to apply in respect of agricultural tenancies granted before 1 September 1995 is the Agricultural Holdings Act 1986, which consolidated a number of earlier enactments. On 1 September 1995, the Agricultural Tenancies Act 1995 came into force and introduced the farm business tenancy. The Act does not generally apply to any tenancy granted before this date, so that rights acquired by agricultural tenants under the 1986 Act remain intact.

Most landlord and tenant courses do not deal with this topic in any great depth and, consequently, exam questions tend to be of the essay type, requiring only a broad knowledge of the area. For a good summary of the 1986 and 1995 statutory codes, see Smith, P. F., *The Law of Landlord and Tenant*, 6th edn, London: Butterworths, 2002, Chs 26 and 27.

The subject of agricultural tied cottages tends also to be given little emphasis, and hence we have included only one question on this topic. Occupiers of agricultural tied cottages who are agricultural workers are governed, in principle, by one of two statutory codes. If the occupation arose under an agreement entered into before 15 January 1989, it will be governed by the Rent (Agriculture) Act 1976. If, on the other hand, the occupation arose under an agreement entered into on or after this date, it will be an assured agricultural occupancy under the Housing Act 1988, Pt I, Ch. III. Essentially, this latter form of occupancy is treated as an assured tenancy under the 1988 Act.

Q Question 1

'An agricultural holding is defined in s. 1(1) of the Agricultural Holdings Act 1986 as being the aggregate of the land (whether agricultural land or not) comprised in a contract of tenancy which is a contract for an agricultural tenancy . . .'

Discuss.

Commentary

This is a highly technical question on the definition of an agricultural holding for the purposes of the 1986 Act. To score high marks, you need to refer not only to the appropriate statutory provisions but also the relevant case law interpreting the same.

Essentially, you should cover three main areas, namely:

(a) the meaning of 'agricultural land';

(b) the definition of 'contract of tenancy'; and

(c) the two main exceptions to s. 2 of the Act (i.e., grazing/mowing agreements and licences).

- Agricultural land defined as land used for agriculture which is so used for the purpose of a trade or business: s. 1(1). Consider mixed user: *Blackmore* v *Butler* (1954). Business need not be agricultural: *Rutherford* v *Maurer* (1962)

- Meaning of 'contract of tenancy': s. 1(5). Cases when agreement *deemed* to be for a tenancy from year to year: s. 2. Status of tenancy 'for more than one year but less than two years' — not protected either under Pt II of the Landlord and Tenant Act 1954 or Agricultural Holdings Act 1986: *Gladstone* v *Bower* (1960)

- Consider two main exceptions to s. 2 of 1986 Act: (1) grazing/mowing agreements and (2) licences: *Lory* v *Brent London Borough Council* (1971) and *Stone* v *Whitcombe* (1980)

☼ Suggested answer

Essentially, the Agricultural Holdings Act 1986 applies to contracts of tenancy of agricultural holdings. The term 'agricultural holding' is defined in s. 1(1) of the 1986 Act and, in simple terms, means the aggregate of the agricultural land comprised in a contract of tenancy which is not a service tenancy.

It may be convenient to begin with the phrase 'agricultural land'. This is defined by s. 1(4) as meaning land used for agriculture which is so used for the purpose of a trade or business. The word 'agriculture' is further defined in s. 96(1) as including horticulture, fruit growing, seed growing, dairy farming, livestock breeding and keeping, market gardening and the use of land as grazing or meadow land.

Where there is a mixed use, the test is one of dominant user so that the tenancy must be in substance agricultural. There is no question of severance, so that the Act either applies to all of the land or to none of it (*Howkins* v *Jardine* [1951] 1 KB 614). In *Blackmore* v *Butler* [1954] 2 QB 171, a cottage and garden (let for use in connection with a farm) were held to constitute 'land used for agriculture'. The same test is applied where there is a mixed agricultural and business use. For example, in *Dunn* v *Fidoe* [1950] 2 All ER 685, an inn, which was used both as an inn and as a farmhouse let with 12 acres of agricultural land, was held to be an agricultural holding. (See also, *Bracey* v *Read* [1963] Ch 88; *Monson* v *Bound* [1954] 1 WLR, 1321 and *Jewell* v *McGowan* [2002] EWCA Civ 145.).

Given that the land is used for agriculture, it is immaterial that the business is not agricultural (*Rutherford* v *Maurer* [1962] 1 QB 16). In this case, the Court of Appeal held that the words 'trade or business' in the Agricultural Holdings Act 1948, s. 1(2) (predecessor to the 1986 Act) could not be limited in their meaning to any specific trade or business such as agriculture. Hence, since the field in question was used for grazing (and, therefore, for agriculture) and was so used for the purpose of a trade or business (namely, a riding school), it was agricultural land within s. 1(2) of the 1948 Act. (See also, *Gold* v *Jacques Amand Ltd* [1992] 27 EG 140).

However, an agricultural tenancy will cease to be agricultural if, during the tenancy and before service of any notice to quit, agricultural activity is wholly or substantially abandoned, regardless of the landlord's consent (*Wetherall* v *Smith* [1980] 1 WLR 1290).

The phrase 'contract of tenancy' is defined by s. 1(5) of the 1986 Act as meaning 'a letting of land, or agreement for letting land, for a term of years or from year to year'. For the purposes of this definition, a lease for life or lives within the Law of Property Act 1925, s. 149(6), is deemed to be a letting for a term of years.

Under s. 2 of the 1986 Act, if land is let for agricultural use for an interest less than a tenancy from year to year (s. 2(2)(a)), or a person is granted a licence to occupy land for agricultural use (s. 2(2)(b)), the agreement is *deemed* to be for a tenancy from year to year. In order, however, for a licence to fall within s. 2(2)(a), it must confer exclusive possession of the land on the licensee (*Bahamas International Trust Co. Ltd* v *Threadgold* [1974] 1 WLR 1514).

A tenancy for more than one year but less than two is a tenancy for a 'term of years' within the meaning of s. 1(5) of the 1986 Act. It is not, however, a tenancy for a term of 'two years or more' (within s. 3 of the 1986 Act), nor does it qualify as an 'interest less than a tenancy from year to year' (within s. 2(2) of the 1986 Act) (*Gladstone* v *Bower* [1960] 2 QB 384). The consequence, therefore, is that such a tenancy is not protected against termination either by the Landlord and Tenant Act 1954, Pt II (dealing with business tenancies), or by the Agricultural Holdings Act 1986 (*EWP Ltd* v *Moore* [1992] 1 QB 460). By contrast, in *Bernays* v *Prosser* [1963] 2 QB 592, it was held that a tenancy for one year certain was less than a tenancy from year to year, so that a tenant holding under such a tenancy fell within s. 2 and the tenancy took effect as if it were a tenancy from year to year. In *Calcott* v *J. S. Bloor (Measham) Ltd* [1998] 40 EG 180, the landlord entered into an agreement to let the land for a term of 13 months from 1 November 1992. The agreement was not, however, signed until 11 June 1993, by which time there was less than a year to run. Because a term cannot be granted retrospectively (see *Keen* v *Holland* [1984] 1 EGLR 9), the agreement was converted into a yearly tenancy. Moreover, that yearly tenancy was held to run from 11 June (when the agreement was signed) and not 30 November (when the purported 13-month term came to an end).

Section 2 of the 1986 Act will also not apply to an agreement for the letting of land (or the granting of a licence to occupy land) which is made:

(a) in contemplation of the use of the land only for grazing or mowing (or both) during some specified period of the year (s. 2(3)(a)); or

(b) by a person whose interest in the land is less than a tenancy from year to year and has not taken effect as such a tenancy by virtue of s. 2 (*Rutherford* v *Maurer* [1962] 1 QB 16).

Where a tenancy is granted for one year (less one day) of agricultural land which is to be kept as grassland and is partially used for ploughing and raising crops, the tenancy is not made 'in contemplation of the use of land only for grazing . . . during some specified period of the year' within s. 2(3)(a) of the 1986 Act, and accordingly the tenancy will take effect as a tenancy from year to year of an agricultural holding under that section (*Lory* v *Brent London Borough Council* [1971] 1 WLR 823). However, an agreement for grazing rights only during the grazing season (i.e., from April to October) will fall within the exclusion contained in s. 2(3)(a) (*Stone* v *Whitcombe* (1980) 40 P & CR 296, where it was held that it was not necessary for specified dates to be agreed for the agreement to relate to 'specified' periods if the parties have agreed exclusive occupation of the land only during a particular season). Similarly, in *Watts* v *Yeend* [1987] 1 WLR 323, it was held that a licence granted in contemplation of the use of land for grazing was a seasonal grazing licence which was understood in agricultural circles as referring to a period of less than a year.

Lastly, it may be mentioned that for the protection of the 1986 Act to apply, the agricultural holding must be comprised in a single contract of tenancy (*Blackmore* v *Butler* [1954] 2 QB 171).

Q Question 2

(a) To what extent is it possible to contract out of the security of tenure provisions of the Agricultural Holdings Act 1986? (Illustrate your answer by reference to decided cases.)

(b) How may an agricultural tenant oppose a landlord's notice to quit the holding?

Commentary

The first part of this question is quite specific and requires you to consider several important cases on devices for avoiding security of tenure under the 1986 Act. The leading case is now the House of Lords decision in *Barrett* v *Morgan* [2000] 2 AC 264.

The second part of the question is much wider in scope and should give you no problems provided you have a good working knowledge of the security of tenure provisions of the 1986 Act. Since this is only half the question, you will need to be succinct in your answer — the examiner will not expect you to go into great detail.

- Covenant in lease purporting to prevent an agricultural tenant from serving a counternotice invalid as being contrary to public policy: *Johnson* v *Moreton* (1980) and *Featherstone* v *Staples* (1986).

- Notice to quit served by landlord on head tenants with their agreement not to serve a counternotice will take effect as a notice to quit (and not a surrender) and will terminate a subtenancy of the holding: *Barrett* v *Morgan* (2000). Thus, unilateral act (i.e., notice to quit) will destroy the subtenancy. But if head tenancy determined by consensual act (i.e., by surrender), subtenancy unaffected: *Pennell* v *Payne* (1995).

- Tenant may serve counternotice on landlord requiring that notice to quit shall not take effect unless Agricultural Land Tribunal consents: s. 26.

- Right of tenant to serve counternotice excluded in certain cases: s. 26(2). Referral of notice to arbitration. Powers of the Tribunal and grounds for consent to operation of landlord's notice to quit: s. 27(3).

:Q: Suggested answer

(a) The Agricultural Holdings Act 1986 does not in terms expressly prohibit contracting out of the right to serve a counternotice, but s. 26(1) of the Act (which confers security of tenure on the tenant) has been held to be mandatory and to override any contrary stipulation in the tenancy.

Thus, a covenant in a lease of an agricultural holding purporting to prevent a tenant from serving a counternotice in response to a landlord's notice to quit under s. 25(1) of the Agricultural Holdings Act 1986 will be invalid as being contrary to public policy. This was established by the House of Lords in *Johnson* v *Moreton* [1980] AC 37, where a clause in the lease provided that the tenant was to give up possession of farm premises to the landlords upon the determination of the term, and not to serve a counternotice or take any other steps to claim the benefit of any statutory provision granting security of tenure. The House of Lords concluded that the policy of the

Agricultural Holdings Act 1948 (predecessor to the 1986 Act) made it clear that an agricultural tenant could not by agreement deprive himself of the option to serve a counternotice in advance. Accordingly, the clause was held unenforceable.

Reference may also be made to *Featherstone* v *Staples* [1986] 1 WLR 861. In this case, it was held that, where an agricultural tenancy is granted to joint tenants, including a company wholly owned by the landlord, who farm the land as a partnership, a clause in the partnership agreement purporting to prevent the joint tenants serving a counternotice without the consent of the company will be void and unenforceable. The general rule, however, is that a valid counternotice cannot be served without the concurrence of all the joint tenants (*Newman* v *Keedwell* (1977) 35 P & CR 393).

Most recently, the House of Lords have held that a notice to quit an agricultural holding served by the landlord on the head tenants with their agreement not to serve a counternotice under the 1986 Act took effect as notice to quit (and not as a surrender) and consequently was effective to terminate a sub-tenancy of the holding. In *Barrett* v *Morgan* [2000] 2 AC 264, the claimant freeholders were seeking possession of farm land from the defendant sub-tenant. A head-lease of the farm had been granted by the claimants' predecessor to his two sons. As part of a scheme to evict the sub-tenant, the claimants, as head landlords, served a notice to quit on the two sons, who then abstained from exercising their statutory right to serve a counternotice. In this way, it was argued, the claimants had effectively determined the head-lease which, in turn, gave them the right to possession against the defendant sub-tenant.

The point was addressed in the earlier case of *Sparkes* v *Smart* [1990] 2 EGLR 245, where on very similar facts, the Court of Appeal concluded that the actions of the tenant were collusive with the freeholder with a view to putting an end to the sub-lease and giving the freeholder vacant possession. The upshot of the *Sparkes* decision was that the notice to quit effectively determined the head-lease but not the sub-lease. In the Court of Appeal in *Barrett* ([1998] 4 All ER 179), their Lordships followed the *Sparkes* decision and held that the mechanism employed by the claimant freeholders of serving a notice to quit on the footing that no counternotice would be served was tantamount to a consensual surrender and could not, therefore, result in the determination of the defendant's sub-tenancy.

The House of Lords, on appeal, reversed this finding. According to Lord Millett, who gave the leading speech, service of a notice to quit by either a tenant or a landlord by pre-arrangement with the other was *not* tantamount to surrender of the tenancy, as unlike a surrender it did not need the consent of the receiving party to have effect. In the *Barrett* case, although the tenants had consented to the service of the notice to quit, their consent was unnecessary and the freeholders were only doing with their consent what they were entitled to do without it. In his Lordship's view, it would be an extraordinary result if a tenant could determine a sub-tenancy by the unilateral act of serving a notice to quit on the landlord but could not achieve the same result by telling the landlord that he would not object to a notice to quit served by him. The defendant's sub-tenancy was, therefore, determined, not by any collusive agreement but by the natural expiry of the tenancy from which the defendant's sub-tenancy was derived.

In reaching this conclusion, the House essentially applied the earlier Court of Appeal decision in *Pennell* v *Payne* [1995] QB 192, where it was held that an immediate tenant who serves notice to quit on the head landlord does an act which on the expiry of the notice to quit will determine not only his own tenancy but also any sub-tenancy that he may have granted. The upshot of the House of Lords ruling is, therefore, that if the termination of the head tenancy is brought about by a *unilateral* act (i.e., notice to quit), this will destroy the sub-tenancy. If, on the other hand, the head tenancy is determined by the *consensual* act (i.e., by surrender) then the sub-tenancy is unaffected. The decision in *Sparkes* is, accordingly, no longer good law.

(b) Where a notice to quit is served on the tenant, he or she may within one month serve a counternotice on the landlord requiring that the notice to quit shall not take effect unless the Agricultural Land Tribunal consents to its operation (s. 26). If no such counternotice is served in time, the consent of the Tribunal is not required. In this connection, the landlord is under no statutory or implied duty to the tenant to set out his (or her) right to serve a counternotice (*Crawford* v *Elliott* [1991] 13 EG 163).

The right of the tenant to serve a counternotice is excluded if the notice to quit is given on any of the Cases set out in sch. 3, Pt I to the Act (i.e., Case A (smallholdings); Case B (planning consent); Case C (certificate of bad husbandry); Case D (non-compliance with notice to pay rent or to remedy breaches); Case E (irremediable breaches); Case F (insolvency); Case G (death of tenant) and Case H (ministerial certificates): s. 26(2)). It has been held recently that the statutory exclusion of the tenant's right to serve a counternotice does not infringe the European Convention on Human Rights 1952: *Lancashire County Council* v *Taylor* [2004] EWHC 776.

Where a notice to quit is given specifying Case A, B, D or E, a tenant who wishes to contest the reason stated may refer the notice to arbitration. The tenant's notice requiring arbitration must be given within one month of the service of the landlord's notice to quit (see, e.g., *Parrish* v *Kinsey* (1983) 268 EG 1113, where it was held that the time limit was inflexible). This procedure is somewhat modified if the tenant has committed a breach of the terms of the tenancy (e.g., a failure to repair) and has been served with a notice to do work as a prerequisite to a notice to quit served under Case D. Here, the tenant, if he wishes to contest a reason stated, must, within one month of service of the landlord's notice to do work, serve a written notice specifying the items in respect of which he denies liability and requiring arbitration. In addition, despite non-compliance with a notice to do work, the tenant may, under s. 28, by counternotice within one month of the landlord's notice to quit under Case D or an arbitration award, require consent of the Tribunal to the Case D notice. By s. 28(5), the Tribunal must consent to the operation of the notice unless it appears to them that a fair and reasonable landlord would not insist on possession, having regard to:

(a) the extent of the tenant's failure to comply with the notice to do work;

(b) the consequences of his failure to comply in any respect; and

(c) the circumstances surrounding the failure.

Where the tenant is entitled to serve a counternotice and does so, the Tribunal will consent to the operation of the landlord's notice to quit if satisfied that one of the grounds in s. 27(3) exists, unless it appears that, in all the circumstances, a fair and reasonable landlord would not insist on possession (s. 27(2)). The grounds may be summarised as follows:

(a) that the carrying out of the purpose for which the landlord proposes to end the tenancy is desirable in the interests of good husbandry as respects the land to which the notice relates, treated as a separate unit;

(b) that the landlord's purpose in ending the tenancy is in the interests of sound management of the estate of which the land in question forms part;

(c) that the landlord's purpose in ending the tenancy is desirable for agricultural research, education, experiment or demonstration, or for the purpose of enactments relating to smallholdings or allotments;

(d) greater hardship would be caused by withholding than by giving consent to the operation of the notice; and

(e) that the landlord intends to end the tenancy for the purpose of the land being used for a non-agricultural use not falling within Case B.

The Tribunal has power, under s. 27(4), to impose such conditions as appear to them requisite for securing that the land to which the notice relates will be used for the purpose for which the landlord proposes to terminate the tenancy.

Lastly, it may be mentioned that a landlord's notice to quit will be invalid and unenforceable if it contains a false statement made fraudulently by the landlord (*Rous* v *Mitchell* [1991] 1 All ER 676).

Q Question 3

What security of tenure is available to an occupier of an agricultural tied cottage?

Commentary

This is a 'give-away' question if you have revised this particular topic for the exam. You should refer both to the Rent (Agriculture) Act 1976 (which continues to apply to agreements entered into before 15 January 1989) and to the Housing Act 1988, Pt I, Ch. III (which applies to agreements entered into on or after this date) as amended by the Housing Act 1996 (which applies to agreements made on or after 28 February 1997). Note that you are not asked to specify the conditions which must be satisfied in order to come within the statutory codes. The question is directed solely at the *security of tenure* provisions of the two Acts.

- Rent (Agriculture) Act 1976 confers security of tenure similar to that under Rent Act 1977. Thus, protected occupier will become a statutory tenant provided residence condition satisfied: s. 4(1)

- Succession rights and landlord's grounds for possession. Consider both discretionary and mandatory grounds

- Consider assured agricultural occupancy under Housing Act 1988. Meaning of statutory periodic tenancy and agricultural worker condition. Recovery of possession

- Amendments made under Housing Act 1996 in respect of tenancies granted on or after 28 February 1997. Problem with 'agricultural worker condition' in this context

☼ Suggested answer

The Rent (Agriculture) Act 1976 conferred on agricultural workers security of tenure (and a considerable degree of rent protection) with respect to their tied cottages. Largely modelled on the provisions of the Rent Act 1977, the 1976 Act was necessary as many agricultural workers would be excluded from being Rent Act protected tenants, their tenancies either being at a low rent or being within the agricultural holding exemption. Indeed, many would not be tenants at all but mere licensees.

The 1976 Act continues to apply in respect of agreements entered into before 15 January 1989. However, the Housing Act 1988, Pt I, Ch. III, phased out the statutory scheme of the 1976 Act in respect of agreements entered into on or after this date. The 1988 Act seeks to retain security of tenure for agricultural workers, while allowing the landlord to charge a market rent. The new tenure which was introduced to cater for these persons was the assured agricultural occupancy.

The 1976 Act confers security of tenure in a similar manner to that conferred on protected and statutory tenants by the Rent Act 1977. Thus, upon the termination of the tenancy or licence, a protected occupier under the 1976 Act automatically becomes a statutory tenant in his or her own right (s. 2(4)) provided that he or she occupies the dwelling-house as his or her residence at all material times (s. 4(1)). Generally speaking, all burdens and benefits of the original (contractual) agreement will continue to apply to the statutory tenancy. However, by agreement the parties have the right to vary many of the terms of a statutory tenancy.

A single succession to a tenancy or relevant licence is allowed under the 1976 Act (ss. 3 and 4). If, however, the original occupier dies after 15 January 1989, leaving no surviving spouse but a family member who has resided in the dwelling-house for two years before death, then the succession of the family member is to an assured agricultural occupancy under the 1988 Act. If more than one family member qualifies, the county court is to choose one in default of agreement. Moreover, common-law spouses are entitled to succeed and will have priority over other members of the occupier's family.

A statutory tenancy will also come into being where a notice of increase of rent is served on the occupier (s. 16 of the 1976 Act).

The landlord of a protected occupier is able to recover possession only on proof of one or more statutory grounds (s. 6 and sch. 4 of the 1976 Act). The grounds for possession are, as with the Rent Act 1977, divided into discretionary and mandatory grounds. As with the 1977 Act, in the case of a discretionary ground, the court cannot make an order for possession under the 1976 Act unless it is reasonable to do so (s. 7(2)). The discretionary grounds resemble corresponding Rent Act 1977 grounds. In the case of the mandatory grounds, there is, as with the 1977 Act, no overriding discretion in the court to refuse to make an order for possession once a ground is made out by the landlord. These grounds are:

(a) recovery of possession by the landlord as an owner-occupier following a notice to quit to the tenant;

(b) a retirement ground; and

(c) an overcrowding ground.

The landlord may also recover possession under a discretionary ground (Case 1) where he is able to show that suitable alternative accommodation is available to the tenant.

Where the landlord wishes to obtain possession of the dwelling-house with a view to housing an employee of his in agriculture and that person's family, and no other suitable accommodation can be provided by the landlord by reasonable means, he may apply to the relevant housing authority for alternative accommodation to be provided for the occupier under s. 27. If satisfied of the above, and that it ought, in the interests of efficient agriculture, to provide the alternative accommodation, the authority will be under a statutory duty, enforceable by an action for damages, to use its best endeavours to provide the accommodation.

Under the Housing Act 1988, the assured agricultural occupancy is treated as if it were an assured tenancy even though it may not be a tenancy at all (s. 24(3)). If the assured agricultural occupancy is for a fixed-term tenancy, it will become a statutory periodic tenancy once the fixed term comes to an end (s. 25(1)(b)). That statutory periodic tenancy will, however, remain an assured agricultural occupancy so long as the agricultural worker condition is fulfilled (i.e., the occupier must be either a qualifying worker, or someone who is incapable of work in agriculture in consequence of a qualifying injury or disease, and the dwelling-house must be in qualifying ownership).

The recovery of possession of an assured agricultural occupancy differs only in two respects from other assured tenancies. First, the discretionary ground of possession in ground 16 of sch. 2 (tenant having ceased to be in the landlord's employment, dwelling-house having been let in consequence of his employment) would, if available, make a nonsense of the protective code. Accordingly, the landlord cannot use it (s. 25(2)). Secondly, the rehousing provisions of Pt IV of the 1976 Act will apply to a dwelling-house let on an assured agricultural occupancy (see above). If the landlord is able to use this procedure to secure suitable alternative accommodation for the occupier, he will be able to argue that it is reasonable for the court to order possession of the dwelling-house, producing a certificate from the local authority as conclusive evidence of the availability of the suitable alternative accommodation for the tenant when the order takes effect (s. 7(4) of the 1988 Act).

Substantial amendments to Pt I of the Housing Act 1988 were made by the Housing Act 1996 (which came into force on 28 February 1997). In respect of tenancies granted on or after this date, a landlord is no longer required to serve a notice of assured shorthold on a tenant and it is no longer a requirement that the assured shorthold tenancy be for at least six months. Essentially, the emphasis has been reversed so that, in most cases, new tenancies granted on or after 28 February 1997, and which fall within the provisions of the Housing Act 1988, will be assured shortholds. However, the 1988 Act (see para. 9 of sch. 2A) provides that one of the circumstances in which a tenancy will not automatically take effect as an assured shorthold is where the agricultural worker condition is 'for the time being' fulfilled. It seems, therefore, that if at the commencement date of the tenancy the agricultural condition is *not* fulfilled, the tenancy will start and (presumably) continue as an assured shorthold. It has been suggested, however, that any tenancy granted to an agricultural worker who subsequently satisfies the agricultural worker condition will switch to being an assured agricultural tenancy (Johnstone, M., 'Countryside Contradictions [1997] EG 9709, pp. 150–51). This is because, it is argued, a tenancy cannot be an assured shorthold tenancy if 'for the time being' the agricultural worker condition is satisfied. One way of avoiding this difficulty is for the landlord to ensure that there is a written agreement containing an express statement that the tenancy is to be an assured shorthold. If this is done, the tenancy will not switch in the way described above.

Q Question 4

To what extent has the Agricultural Tenancies Act 1995 altered the law in respect of the statutory regulation of agricultural tenancies? What were the main objectives of the new legislation?

Commentary

This question requires you to give a discursive account of the workings of the 1995 Act with particular reference to the principal objectives of the new law. You will gain more marks if you approach your answer from a comparative standpoint — to what extent is the 1995 Act an improvement on the 1986 Act regime? You may find the following literature helpful in answering this question: McNully, S. and Evans, D., 'The Agricultural Revolution' [1995] EG 9530, 82–85; Yates, R., 'Pastures New', (1995) 145 NLJ, pp. 1372–74; (Mainly for Students) 'Agricultural Lettings' [1995] EG 9525, 153–54 and Jessel, C., 'Drafting Farm Business Leases' [1995] EG 9545, 126–27. See also, generally Evans, D., *The Agricultural Tenancies Act 1995* (London: Sweet & Maxwell), and Sydenham A., and Mainwaring, N., *Farm Business Tenancies* (London: Jordan Publishing Limited).

- Aims of 1995 Act. Basic rationale to allow parties freely to negotiate a contract of tenancy within a statutory framework, which provides some security of tenure to the farm tenant. Contrast heavy regulation under Agricultural Holdings Act 1986

- Nature of the farm business tenancy. To qualify, tenancy must meet the business conditions and *either* the agricultural condition *or* notice condition

- Security of tenure radically different from 1986 Act. New rules relating to repairing obligations. Outline statutory review machinery

- Continuing application of 1986 Act alongside 1995 Act has given rise to anomalies. Consider, for example, tenant's right to compensation for disturbance under both Acts

☼ Suggested answer

The Agricultural Tenancies Act 1995 received Royal Assent on 1 September 1995 and introduced the novel concept of the farm business tenancy. Agricultural tenancies granted before this date remain within the Agricultural Holdings Act 1986 regime and are unaffected by the 1995 Act changes. The 1986 Act will also continue to apply to any tenancy which is a succession tenancy on death or retirement pursuant to the Act.

The main aims of the new legislation were to: (i) deregulate the number of agricultural lettings and to simplify agricultural legislation; (ii) increase the number of agricultural lettings and allow them to be freely negotiated between the parties; and (iii) provide a statutory framework which would enable farmers to adapt to future changes in policy and market conditions.

The basic rationale of the new legislation is, therefore, to permit the parties freely to negotiate a contract of tenancy upon terms which are acceptable to both landlord and tenant, but within a statutory framework which provides some degree of security of tenure to the farm tenant. This is in sharp contrast to the old regime under the Agricultural Holdings Act 1986, where an agricultural tenant can expect (subject to limited exceptions) lifetime security of tenure and succession rights on death and retirement for up to two generations (in respect of tenancies granted before 12 July 1984). Moreover, a landlord, under the 1986 Act, has very limited scope for recovering his property and the complexity of the notice procedures gives rise to unfairness and expensive litigation for both parties. The statutory regime was regarded by many as contributing to a reluctance on the part of landlords to make land available on anything other than specific short-term lettings outside the security of tenure provisions of the 1986 Act. The new scheme sought to address this difficulty.

The central feature of the 1995 Act is the farm business tenancy. To qualify as such, the tenancy must meet the business conditions and *either* the agricultural condition *or* the notice condition. The business conditions are that all or part of the land in the tenancy is farmed for the purposes of a trade or business and has been so farmed since the tenancy began. The agricultural condition requires that the character of the tenancy is primarily or wholly agricultural having regard to the tenancy terms, use of the land, the nature of any commercial activities conducted on the land and any other relevant circumstances. The alternative notice condition is that the landlord and tenant each gave the other written notice before the tenancy began stating that they intended the tenancy to be and remain a farm business tenancy and identifying the land concerned (so long as at the beginning of the tenancy its character was primarily or wholly agricultural).

There is no specific minimum term for a farm business tenancy, unlike under Pt I of the 1986 Act in relation to agricultural holdings. Whereas the 1986 Act converts licences into tenancies within the scope of the Act, the 1995 Act does not, leaving scope for a genuine licence outside the Act. A tenancy at will is expressly excluded from the 1995 Act's definition of a tenancy.

The tenant's security of tenure is radically different from that under the 1986 Act. The tenant of a farm business tenancy does not have enduring statutory protection. Instead, a tenant of more than two years has merely the certainty of one full agricultural cycle's notice that his tenancy is to be terminated. He is entitled to at least 12 months' (and not more than 24 months') notice in writing from his landlord to take effect at the end of a year of the tenancy unless it has been given to take effect on the term date of the tenancy itself. The tenant has a similar right to give written notice of termination on his landlord. Significantly, no grounds are needed by the landlord to regain possession. Until terminated by notice, the tenancy will continue from year to year at the expiry of the contractual term. If the farm business tenancy is for two years or less, its termination is governed solely by the parties' agreement or, in the absence of express provision for termination, by the common law.

Another significant feature of the new law relates to repairing obligations. The 1986

Act contains substantial controls that limit the repairing obligations of both the land-lord and tenant. By contrast, under the 1995 Act, repairing obligations are left to the agreement of the parties. So far as rent is concerned, a statutory review machinery applies unless expressly excluded by the tenancy, or the tenancy provides for the variation of the statutory rent review by fixed amounts or in accordance with a formula, provided that the formula allows the possibility of the rent going down as well as up and does not require or permit anyone to exercise a discretion or judgment in determining the rent (s. 9). The rent review procedure in the Act sets out the machinery for a statutory review notice and the appointment of an arbitrator. Undoubtedly, these provisions bring the determination of rent review more into line with commercial rent determinations. For example, the parties are free to agree the frequency of rent reviews (otherwise they will be three-yearly).

The 1995 Act also provides for a non-excludable right to compensation for improve-ments made by the tenant with the landlord's consent. In addition, the tenant is entitled, subject to certain exceptions, to remove any fixtures erected by him during the tenancy or at any time after when he remains in possession as a tenant. The tenant is not obliged to give notice to his landlord that he intends to remove a fixture, neither is he obliged to comply fully with the conditions of the tenancy before he is entitled to remove a fixture.

There is no doubt that the 1995 Act represents a marked shift away from the heavy statutory regulation of the 1986 Act towards a system which encourages free negotiation of terms as between agricultural tenant and landlord. The original aims of the Agricultural Holdings Act 1948 which preceded the 1986 Act (and which sought to safeguard tenants and enhance food production in post-war Britain) have little relevance today where the emphasis is on encouraging diversification of business by tenants and making more farmland available for letting on commercial terms.

Although the 1995 Act has been welcomed by most, the continuing application of the 1986 Act alongside the 1995 Act has given rise to some anomalies. For example, an agricultural tenant under the 1986 Act may be able to claim substantial com-pensation for disturbance on quitting the holding pursuant to his landlord's notice to quit (s. 60 of the 1986 Act), but a tenant of a farm business tenancy is unable to claim such compensation unless specifically provided for in the tenancy. Such anomalies, however, will eventually disappear as 1986 Act agricultural holdings become fewer in number.

The radical reduction in legislative interference reflected in the 1995 Act has prompted both lawyers and surveyors to rethink the way in which they negotiate and draft agricultural tenancies: see Jessel, C., 'Drafting Farm Business Leases' [1995] EG 9545, 126–27. Undoubtedly, the trend is to produce agreements for farm business tenancies which resemble leases for other forms of investment property without the former strictures of a complex statutory agricultural regime.

Further reading

Dawson, I., 'Notices to Quit, the Agricultural Holdings Legislation, and Order' [2000] Conv 344.

Murdoch, S., 'Insecure Tenancies' [2000] EG 166.

Secure tenancies

Introduction

Most tenants (and some licensees) of public sector residential accommodation are conferred security of tenure by virtue of the Housing Act 1985, Pt IV. The Housing Act 1985 also deals with other important areas of housing law (e.g., homelessness, right to buy etc.) which are outside the scope of this book.

By s. 79(1) of the 1985 Act, a tenancy under which a dwelling-house is let as a separate dwelling is a secure tenancy at any time when both the landlord and tenant conditions are satisfied. The landlord condition is that the interest of the landlord belongs to one of the authorities or bodies listed in s. 80 of the Act (i.e., a local authority, a new town corporation, the Development Board for Rural Wales, the Housing Corporation, a housing trust which is a charity, and certain housing associations and housing cooperatives). The condition will not be satisfied where only one of two joint landlords complies with it (*R* v *Plymouth City Council and Cornwall City Council, ex parte Freeman* (1987) 19 HLR 328). The tenant condition is that the tenant is an individual and occupies the dwelling-house as his or her only or principal home, or, where the tenancy is a joint tenancy, that each of the joint tenants is an individual and at least one of them occupies the dwelling-house as his or her only or principal home (s. 81 and *Crawley Borough Council* v *Sawyer* (1987) 20 HLR 98).

The provisions of Pt IV of the 1985 Act apply in relation to a licence to occupy a dwelling-house (whether or not granted for a consideration) as they apply in relation to a tenancy (s. 79(3)). However, security does not apply to a licence granted as a temporary expedient to a person who entered the dwelling-house (or any other land) as a trespasser (whether or not, before the grant of that licence, another licence to occupy that or another dwelling-house had been granted to him) (s. 79(4)). A licence will not be secure if there is no exclusive possession of the subject premises (*Family Housing Association* v *Miah* (1982) 5 HLR 94; *The Royal Borough of Kensington and Chelsea* v *Hayden* (1985) 17 HLR 114; *Westminster City Council* v *Clarke* [1992] 1 All ER 695 and *Shepherds Bush Housing Association Ltd* v *HATS Co-operative* [1992] 24 HLR 176). In addition, a number of tenancies and licences are not secure, and these are listed in sch. 1 to the 1985 Act.

Since the last edition of this book, the concept of the 'tolerated trespasser' has been firmly established by the courts. In *Pemberton* v *Southwark London Borough Council* [2000] 1 WLR 1672, the Court of Appeal held that a former secure tenant, who had been allowed to stay on in her flat after a conditional order for possession had been made against her, had a sufficient interest in the property to bring an action in nuisance and negligence against the local authority arising from an infestation of cockroaches in the flat. See further, Wilkinson, H.W., 'Tolerated and Non-tolerated Trespassers' (2000) NLJ Practitioner 1301.

In this chapter, you will find two questions dealing with security of tenure, terms of a secure tenancy and succession rights. In view of the impending Law Commission's Final Report on *Renting Homes* (and draft Bill), we have included a final question on the Commission's far-reaching proposals which are intended to substantially overhaul existing housing law.

Q Question 1

In 1998, the Burberry District Council granted Mark and his wife, Michelle, a weekly tenancy of a flat in a block of flats on its housing estate at a rent of £50 per week. Upon their taking up possession of the flat, the Council provided them with a rent book detailing the terms of their tenancy. Condition 2(a) provides '. . . the tenants covenant at all material times to use the premises in a tenant-like manner'.

The couple's marriage is an unhappy one and Mark and Michelle frequently row. They have broken the door, smashed a front window and damaged the bathroom. They have also been abusive to other tenants on the estate, engaging in anti-social behaviour including the revving of their car engine and slamming of the car doors in the early hours of the morning. Mark and Michelle have also fallen into rent arrears. At present, six months' rent arrears are outstanding. Despite their estrangement, the couple continue to live in the flat with their 19-year-old daughter, Yvette.

The Council has plans in the near future to demolish the block of flats to make way for a new housing estate.

Advise the Council which wishes to evict Mark and Michelle.

Commentary

This is a straightforward question on the security of tenure provisions of the Housing Act 1985, Pt IV. You should begin your answer by outlining the requisite preconditions for a secure tenancy and then consider what grounds (under sch. 2 to the Act) are available to the Council to obtain possession of the flat. The relevant statutory procedures for obtaining possession should also be mentioned.

- **Tenancy qualifies as a secure periodic tenancy under the 1985 Act. Landlord and tenant conditions satisfied**

- Council must serve statutory notice and seek an order for possession. Consider different categories of grounds for possession

- Breach of express covenant to use the premises in a tenant-like manner: *Warren* v *Keene* (1954). Also, rent arrears. Both breaches give Council a discretionary ground for possession under ground 1. Consider likelihood of suspended possession order

- Council may also invoke ground 2 (as replaced by Housing Act 1996, s. 144) based on conduct of tenants: *Woking Borough Council* v *Bystram* (1993). Here again, suspended order likely

- Alternatively, rely on mandatory ground 10 provided that suitable alternative accommodation will be available for the tenants and their family. Need to establish settled intention to carry out development work within reasonable time of possession order: *Wansbech District Council* v *Marley* (1988)

☼ Suggested answer

It would seem from the facts that Mark and Michelle have a secure periodic tenancy under the Housing Act 1985, Pt IV. By s. 79(1) of the 1985 Act, a tenancy under which a dwelling-house is let as a separate dwelling is a secure tenancy at any time when both the landlord and tenant conditions are satisfied. The landlord condition requires that the interest of the landlord belongs to one of the bodies listed in s. 80 of the Act, and this includes a local authority. The tenant condition requires that the tenant is an individual and occupies the dwelling-house as his or her only or principal home, or, where there is a joint tenancy (as in the present case) that each of the joint tenants is an individual and at least one of them occupies the dwelling house as his or her only or principal home (s. 81). Both these conditions appear to be satisfied in the present case. Moreover, the couple's tenancy does not appear to fall within any of the excluded tenancies listed in sch. 1 to the 1985 Act.

A periodic secure tenancy cannot be brought to an end by a landlord's common law notice to quit (s. 82(1)). Instead, the landlord must serve a statutory notice, under s. 83(2) of the Act, on the secure tenant(s). Moreover, the landlord must obtain an order for possession and the secure tenancy will end only on the date specified in the court order. The statutory notice (which must be in prescribed form) must be in force when the proceedings for possession are issued and must specify the ground(s) for possession relied on.

There are three categories of grounds, which are contained in sch. 2 to the 1985 Act. Grounds 1–8 (contained in sch. 2, Pt I) are subject to an overriding requirement that it must be reasonable to make an order for possession. The term 'reasonable' means reasonable having regard to the interests of both the parties and the public (*London Borough of Enfield* v *McKeon* (1986) 18 HLR 330). An example of a ground falling within this category relates to rent arrears or breaches of obligation of the tenancy (ground 1). Grounds 9–11 (contained in sch. 2, Pt II) are subject to a requirement that when the order takes effect suitable alternative accommodation will be available to the tenant and his family (s. 84(2)(b) and sch. 2, Pt IV). Ground 10 (in this category) gives the landlord a ground for possession where demolition or reconstruction works are intended in relation to the premises. Grounds 12–16 (contained in sch. 2, Pt III) are subject to both the requirement of reasonableness and the availability of suitable alternative accommodation. This last category is not relevant to the problem.

In this case, Mark and Michelle, by deliberately damaging the premises, are in breach of their express covenant to use the premises in a tenant-like manner. The phrase 'tenant-like manner' has been judicially defined as giving rise to an obligation to take proper care of the property and not to damage it, wilfully or negligently (*Warren* v *Keen* [1954] 1 QB 15, *per* Denning LJ, at p. 20). We are also told that Mark and Michelle have fallen into rent arrears. Both these breaches of covenant provide the Council with a discretionary ground for possession under ground 1 (above). If the Council is successful, the court may make an immediate order for possession, suspend the order, or adjourn matters generally. In *Haringey London Borough Council* v *Stewart* (1991) 2 EGLR 252, the tenant's poor record for persistent late payment of rent, coupled with no proposals for paying off the arrears, justified an order for possession. By contrast, in *Woodspring District Council* v *Taylor* (1982) 4 HLR 95, the amount of arrears of rent (£557) was not considered substantial enough to justify an outright possession order. In the present case, much will depend on how the county court judge views the damage to the property (i.e., its extent and cost of repair) and the reasons why the arrears have fallen due. On balance, a suspended order for possession is the most likely outcome (i.e., a possession order suspended on terms that Mark and Michelle make good the damage to the property and pay off the arrears by instalments, within a specified time-scale).

In addition, the Council should seek to invoke ground 2 of sch. 2 (as replaced by s. 144 of the Housing Act 1996) based on the conduct of the tenants which causes (or is likely to cause) a nuisance or annoyance to 'persons residing, visiting or otherwise engaging in a lawful activity in the locality'. This new terminology replaces the former reference to 'neighbours' under the 1985 Act: see *Northampton Borough Council* v *Lovatt* [1998] 07 EG 142. We are told that Mark and Michelle have been abusive to other tenants on the estate and engaged in various acts of anti-social behaviour. It is evident, therefore, that their conduct falls within this ground, but here again, it is unlikely that the Council will obtain an outright possession order: see *Woking Borough Council* v *Bystram* [1993] EGCS 208 (complaints by neighbours relating to abusive and foul language by the tenants — suspended possession order granted).

In view of the unlikelihood of obtaining an outright possession order under grounds 1 and 2, the Council should consider relying on ground 10 as an additional basis for obtaining possession of the house. Ground 10 is mandatory in the sense that it is not subject to the overriding requirement of reasonableness (see earlier). However, the Council must show that, when the possession order takes effect, suitable alternative accommodation will be available to Mark and Michelle and their family.

One difficulty with relying on this ground is that the Council must establish the requisite settled intention to carry out development work within a reasonable time of obtaining possession of the flat (*Wansbech District Council* v *Marley* (1988) 20 HLR 247). Although a resolution of the Council passed by its appropriate committee is not essential, there must be clear evidence proving a definite intention (*Poppet's (Caterers) Ltd* v *Maidenhead BC* [1971] 1 WLR 69 and *Betty's Cafes Ltd* v *Phillips Furnishing Stores Ltd* [1959] AC 20, applying *Cunliffe* v *Goodman* [1950] 2 KB 237). In addition to showing the requisite intention, the Council must establish that it cannot reasonably carry out the demolition and reconstruction works without obtaining possession of the flat.

Lastly, regarding the requirement of suitable alternative accommodation, since the court cannot make an order for possession under ground 10 unless it is satisfied that suitable alternative accommodation will be available for 'the tenant and his family', it follows that Mark and Michelle's daughter, Yvette, who is 19 and living in the premises, is a person with a potential interest in the possession proceedings and must be joined as party to those proceedings (*Wandsworth London Borough Council* v *Fadayomi* [1987] 3 All ER 474).

Q Question 2

(a) What terms are imposed in a secure tenancy under the Housing Act 1985? [15 marks]

(b) Mary, a widow with two (foster) boys, Derek and Ian, was granted a monthly secure tenancy of a three-bedroomed family house by the local authority in 1986. In 1988, Mary invited her gay lover, Judy, to move into the house with her. Derek got married in 1989 and moved away. Mary has recently died, leaving Ian, now aged 16, and Judy living in the house.

Advise Derek, Ian and Judy whether any of them has any rights in relation to the house. [10 marks]

Commentary

This two-part question requires you to demonstrate your knowledge of the terms of a secure tenancy and succession rights under the Housing Act 1985. Part (a) covers familiar ground and should not pose any real problems. Part (b), on the other hand, raises a number of issues, not all of which may be readily apparent even to the well-prepared student. Your answer should, of course, refer to the House of Lords ruling in *Fitzpatrick* v *Sterling Housing*

Association Ltd [2001] 1 AC 27 on succession rights of same-sex partners and the subsequent House of Lords decision in *Mendoza* v *Ghaidan* [2004] UKHL 30 applying the European Convention on Human Rights. The reference to the two children being foster boys seems a little unsporting since the point has been judicially considered only at county court level (*Reading Borough Council* v *Isley* [1981] CLY 1323). The fact that Ian is a minor also raises the question whether (and if so, how) he can succeed to the secure tenancy during his minority. The difficulty lies in the fact that a legal estate in land does not vest in a minor but is held in trust for him (or her) until majority: see, para. 2 of sch. 1 to the Trusts of Land and Appointment of Trustees Act 1996. The upshot of this is that Ian will acquire only an equitable interest in the secure tenancy pending his majority. There are two cases on this point which should be mentioned in your answer: *Kingston upon Thames RLBC* v *Prince* (1999) 31 HLR 794 and, more recently, *Newham LBC* v *R* [2004] EWCA Civ 41. See further, Mills, S., and Joss, N., 'Children and Secure Tenancies (2001) 5 L & T Rev 53.

- Section 91 prohibits assignments of all or part of the dwelling-house. But consider exceptions and s. 92 under which tenant may assign to another secure tenant with consent of landlord. Consider limited grounds for refusal: sch. 3, 1985 Act

- Ability to take in lodgers. Provisions dealing with subletting of part and whole of premises: ss. 93 and 94

- Repair scheme: s. 96(1). Ability to carry out improvements: ss. 97–101. Enfranchisement rights under Pt V

- Preconditions for succession to secure tenancy: s. 87. House of Lords held that same-sex partner entitled to succeed as member of the tenant's family but not as surviving spouse of tenant: *Fitzpatrick* v *Sterling Housing Association Ltd* (2001). This now incompatible with Human Rights Act 1988: *Ghaidan* v *Godin-Mendoza* [2004] UKHL 30. Thus, Judy will be entitled to succeed to Mary's tenancy

- Derek has moved away from the house and, therefore, cannot succeed. Ian has lived at the house at all material times and the fact that he is a foster child should not affect his right to succession: *Reading Borough Council* v *Isley* (1981). Whilst a minor, he will hold an equitable tenancy: *Kingston upon Thames RLBC* v *Prince* (1998)

☼ Suggested answer

(a) The Housing Act 1985 imposes a variety of terms into secure tenancies. Sections 91–101 contain complex provisions which place varying levels of restrictions on the ability of secure tenants to take in lodgers, to sublet or assign their leasehold interests to third parties, or to exchange their lettings with other secure tenants, and to carry out repairs or improvements to the premises. The aim of these provisions is to establish a framework so as to enable secure tenants to carry out various activities which, prior to the legislation, often amounted to a breach of covenant.

Save for a few limited exceptions (e.g., where there is an exchange, or where a succession has occurred on the death of a secure tenant, or where the tenancy is transferred to the spouse of a secure tenant following divorce or judicial separation), s. 91 prohibits assignments of all or part of the dwelling-house: *Burton v Camden London Borough Council* [2000] 2 AC 399 (HL). Section 92, however, provides that it is a term of every secure tenancy that the tenant may, with the written consent of the landlord, assign the tenancy to another secure tenant. In such cases, only limited grounds for refusal exist. These grounds are set out in sch. 3 to the 1985 Act and include situations where:

(a) one of the tenants is being evicted for non-payment of rent or breach of any other obligation of the tenancy; or

(b) one of the tenants would be acquiring premises which were substantially greater than his or her own family's needs; or

(c) one of the tenants does not intend to use the premises for housing purposes; or

(d) the landlord in question provides accommodation for people with specific needs and the exchange would bring in occupiers outside this purpose.

Section 93(1)(a) is concerned with the ability of secure tenants to take in lodgers. The subsection provides that it is a term of every secure tenancy that the tenant may allow any persons to reside as lodgers in the dwelling-house.

It is also a term of every secure tenancy that the tenant will not, without the written consent of the landlord, sub-let or part with possession of *part* of the dwelling-house (s. 93(1)(b)). If the tenant parts with possession of the dwelling-house or sublets the *whole* of it, the tenancy ceases to be a secure tenancy. The landlord cannot unreasonably withhold his consent, and the onus is on the landlord to show that the withholding of consent was not unreasonable (s. 94(2)). In determining this question, the fact that consent would lead to overcrowding of the dwelling-house, or that the landlord proposes to carry out works on the dwelling-house which would affect the accommodation likely to be used by the proposed sub-tenant, may be taken into account. If a landlord fails to reply to a tenant's request, this is deemed to be an unreasonable refusal.

Section 96(1), as re-enacted by the Leasehold Reform, Housing and Urban Development Act 1993, provides for the Secretary of State to formulate a scheme whereby secure tenants may serve a notice informing the landlord of repairs the landlord is responsible for. The current repair scheme requires that the tenant serves a notice on the landlord stating that 'qualifying repairs' need to be carried out. The landlord must respond with a counternotice specifying the nature of the proposed repair, the name of the contractor who will undertake the work and the date when it will be carried out. If the work is not completed in time, a second contractor must be nominated by the landlord. If the second contractor fails to execute the works, the landlord is liable to pay the tenant compensation, enforceable in the county court.

Sections 97–101 are concerned with the issue of improvements. As a general rule, a secure tenant cannot carry out improvements (including alterations, additions and external decorative work), unless consent has been obtained from the landlord. Here again, as with the rules governing partial sub-letting, the landlord must not unreasonably withhold his consent, and if unreasonably withheld it is treated as given (s. 97(3)). There is also provision for the landlord to reimburse the tenant the cost of his improvements (s. 100).

Both the landlord and the tenant may vary the terms of the secure tenancy (ss. 102–103).

Part V of the Housing Act 1985 confers on secure tenants who have been in occupation of their properties for over three years, the right either to purchase the freehold of their house, or to acquire a long lease of 125 years, subject to generous discounts.

(b) The succession rights on the death of a secure tenant are contained in the Housing Act 1985, ss. 87–90.

Under s. 87, a person is qualified to succeed if he or she occupies the dwelling-house as his or her only or principal home at the time of the secure tenant's death and either:

(a)　he or she is the tenant's spouse; or

(b)　he or she is another member of the tenant's family and has resided with the tenant throughout the period of 12 months ending with the tenant's death (*Peabody Donation Fund Governors* v *Grant* (1982) 264 EG 925).

Section 113(1) of the 1985 Act defines the phrase 'member of the tenant's family' as including a person living with the tenant as husband and wife, the tenant's parent, grandparent, child, grandchild, brother, sister, uncle, aunt, nephew or niece.

The House of Lords in *Fitzpatrick* v *Sterling Housing Association Ltd* [2001] 1 AC 27 held that a same-sex partner may be entitled to succeed to a statutory tenancy under the Rent Act 1977 on the ground that he (or she) was a member of the original tenant's family, provided that the relationship was stable and permanent. The House, however, also confirmed the earlier case of *Harrogate Borough Council* v *Simpson* [1986] 2 FLR 91 (involving a lesbian couple) decided under the provisions of the 1985 Act, that a same-sex partner could not succeed to a tenancy as the surviving spouse of the original tenant. This is because the word 'spouse' meant a person who was legally the husband or wife of the original tenant, and the extended definition (of a person living with him 'as his or her wife or husband') only applied to those persons who, though not legally husband and wife, lived *as such* without being married. Such words were gender specific, connoting a relationship between a man and a woman, so that the man had to show that the woman was living with him as 'his' wife, and the woman had to show that the man was living with her as 'her' husband. However, the point has now been reconsidered by both the Court of Appeal and House of Lords from a human rights standpoint. In *Ghaidan v Mendoza* [2002] 4 All ER 1162, the claimant sought to succeed to a Rent-Act protected tenancy as the same-sex partner of the deceased tenant. He relied upon para. 2 of sch. 1 to the Rent Act 1977 as a person living with the tenant as 'his or her wife or husband'. Despite the previous House of Lords' ruling in *Fitzpatrick*, the Court of Appeal concluded that to construe para. 2 other than to include same-sex partners was incompatible with the Human Rights Act 1988. The Court of Appeal ruling has been confirmed recently on appeal to the House of Lords so that para. 2 must now be read as though the survivor of a homosexual couple living together was the surviving spouse of the original tenant: [2004] UKHL 30.

Judy, therefore, will be entitled to succeed to Mary's secure tenancy as a member of her family provided that their relationship was a stable, close, and loving one. This seems apparent from the fact that Mary and Judy had lived together for a number of years prior to the former's death. She will also be entitled to succeed as a surviving spouse in the light of the *Mendoza* ruling.

We are told that Derek got married in 1989 and moved away from the house. He, clearly, cannot succeed to his mother's secure tenancy because he cannot fulfil the necessary 12-month residence requirement. Ian, on the other hand, appears to qualify as a successor, having lived in the house at all material times. The fact that Ian is a foster child should not affect this conclusion. In *Reading Borough Council v Isley* [1981] CLY 1323, three foster boys, who were never formally adopted by the tenant, were held entitled to succeed to a secure tenancy. The undisputed evidence was that they had always been treated in all respects as the natural children of the tenant (and her husband). Although Ian is still a minor, he may still hold an equitable tenancy of the property (*Kingston upon Thames RLBC v Prince* (1999) 31 HLR 794 (CA), where it was held that the security provisions of the 1985 Act did extend to minors. The point has been considered more recently in *Newham London Borough Council v R* [2004] EWCA Civ 41, where the minor had resided with her mother until the latter's death in 2001. The mother had left (in her will) her entire net estate to be held upon trust for the minor and appointed her aunt as sole executor and trustee. The minor was clearly a person qualified to succeed to her mother's secure periodic tenancy. The Court of Appeal, applying *Prince*, held that the legal tenancy vested in the child's aunt by virtue of her mother's will. Moreover, the 1985 Act did not prevent the aunt from holding the tenancy in this way despite the fact that she was not someone who could qualify to succeed to the tenancy herself.

Q Question 3

What are the principal features of the Law Commission's current proposals to reform housing law? What are the main themes underlying the Commission's new approach to the landlord and tenant relationship?

Commentary

This is a very topical question given that the Law Commission is about to publish its Final Report in early 2005. Your syllabus will, no doubt, contain some reference to the Commission's proposals, which undoubtedly will have very far-reaching consequences for both the private and public-rented sector. We refer you to the **Further Reading** at the end of this chapter for articles summarising the Commission's recommendations. Note that the question requires you to not only summarise the principal features of the new scheme, but also explain the Commission's thinking and rationale.

- Scope of the new scheme — what tenancies will be included? Key proposal is the introduction of two new types of occupation agreement

- Nature of type I and type II occupation agreements. How will existing tenancies fit into this scheme?

- Another key aspect of the proposals is the 'consumer approach' to tenancy agreements. All the parties' rights to be contained in tenancy agreement. Fairness and transparency — application of Unfair Contract Terms in Consumer Regulations 1994. Model agreements — key terms, compulsory minimum terms and negotiable/default terms

- Ultimate aims of the reform to provide a more simple, comprehensible and more flexible statutory framework

☼ Suggested answer

In November 2003, the Law Commission published its Report *Renting Homes* (Law Com. No. 284), marking an entirely new approach to the way in which the private and public-rented sector of the housing market should be regularised in the future. It is intended that the new scheme shall have retrospective effect (except for Rent Act tenancies) and that it should apply to all contracts for a rent which confer a right to occupy premises as a home. This means, for example, that licences will be included in the scheme, but there will also be several types of occupancy which will be excluded (e.g., leases for 21 years or more, business tenancies and agricultural holdings) in order to prevent overlap with other statutory codes. Certain special arrangements will also fall under the new scheme (e.g., holiday lets, agreements where the accommodation is shared with the landlord and certain agreements for temporary accommodation).

A key proposal in the Commission's report is that there should be just two types of occupation agreement covering the bulk of renting situations. The type I agreement (the 'secure home rental agreement') will be modelled on the current secure tenancy (currently under Pt IV of the Housing Act 1985) and will give extensive statutorily prescribed security of tenure. This means that the landlord would have to establish grounds for possession and the possession order would be at the court's discretion. In this connection, it is proposed to give courts more specific guidance as to when it is reasonable to make an order. The principal discretionary ground for possession will be breach of the occupation agreement. In addition, there will be a number of grounds which may be broadly described as 'estate management' grounds whereby, if a court thinks it reasonable and if the landlord can provide suitable alternative accommodation, it will be possible for a landlord to regain possession. There will be no mandatory grounds and the landlord will be obliged to serve a notice (in prescribed form) on the tenant indicating the reasons for possession and encouraging the tenant to take legal advice. The form of notice will be similar to the notice of seeking possession currently required under the Housing Acts 1988 and 1985. In view of the current technicalities associated with the service of such notices on assured/shorthold and secure tenancies, the Commission envisages simplifying the process of service. Thus, notices will not have to commence or end on a particular day. Personal service will be dispensed with and notices will be validly served if simply left at the premises. These requirements will all be set out in the tenancy agreement itself. Powers to suspend possession orders will also be retained but the notion of the 'tolerated trespasser' will be abolished.

The type II agreement ('the contractual home rental agreement'), on the other hand, will be modelled on the assured shorthold tenancy (under, what is now, Pt I of the Housing Act 1988). This second form of agreement will give much less statutory protection but will be able to be enhanced by the tenancy agreement itself. Under a type II agreement, a landlord would be entitled to obtain a possession order provided the appropriate notice procedure had been followed. Here again, the Commission is anxious to introduce some simplification into the current procedures. Thus, for example, the requirement under s. 21(4) of the Housing Act 1988 that the notice end on the last day of a period of a tenancy will be removed. Where fixed-term tenancies are concerned, the landlord will be entitled to end the tenancy if the tenant is in breach of covenant. It is proposed that a mandatory ground for possession will be made available if two months' rent is in arrears. At present, assured shorthold tenancies cannot be determined (in the absence of tenant default) until after six months after the commencement of the tenancy. This moratorium on the ability of the court to order possession will be abolished.

It is envisaged that social landlords will, in most cases, be required to use the type I agreement, whereas most private landlords will want to use type II agreements. Unlike the present law, therefore, the identity of the landlord will no longer play a key role in the definition of the agreement type. The Commission is anxious to do away with inflexibility in the renting sector. Thus, in its view, landlord neutrality would enable a private landlord to provide housing on exactly the same terms as those offered by the public sector. This would have the additional benefit of allowing the private and public sectors to work more closely in partnership. For example, a flexible framework would also permit social landlords to opt for a type II agreement thereby allowing them to charge market (as opposed to social) rents. This would go some way, it is envisaged, in providing social landlords with the necessary financial resources to improve their housing stock. In order for the new scheme to work properly, the intention is that the new provisions will operate retrospectively so that all existing tenancies (except, possibly, Rent Act tenants) will be converted into either a type I or type II agreement.

Conversion in respect of most types of existing tenancies is unlikely to prove problematic. Thus, secure and assured tenants will become type I tenants. Introductory and assured shorthold tenants will become type II tenants. It is envisaged that other tenants, currently wholly excluded from the residential codes, may be brought within one or other of the two types of agreement.

A second prominent feature of the Law Commission's rationale is the promotion of a 'consumer approach' to the provision of rental housing. Misconceptions and lack of understanding between the parties of the rights and responsibilities of landlord and tenant is seen as a major flaw in the current law. In the Commission's view, there should be transparency and fairness in landlord and tenant relations. Thus, it is envisaged that all the parties' rights will be set out expressly in the tenancy agreement. In this connection, the obvious difficulty with the current law is that the tenancy agreement does not set out the true legal position because many terms are superimposed by complex legislation. In order to introduce greater fairness into bargain, it is also proposed that terms will be subject to the provisions of the Unfair Terms in Consumer Contracts Regulations 1999. This will ensure the use of clear language and avoid the inclusion of unfair terms. Failure to provide a copy of the agreement in writing will not invalidate the tenancy but will attract (non-criminal) sanctions. For example, tenants without written agreements will (after two weeks) be entitled to withhold rent (up to a maximum of two months) and will be able to go to court to force the landlord to provide a written agreement.

Because all the essential elements of the agreement (including the circumstances in which proceedings for possession could be taken) will be set out in the agreement itself, the Commission also proposes that there should be made available a limited range of model agreements, drawn up by the Secretary of State, following consultation with landlords' and tenants' groups. These model agreements would be prescribed in regulations. It is proposed that all such tenancy agreements will comprise three parts. Part A will set out the key terms (i.e., the parties' names, address of the property, the rent and term). Part B will consist of the compulsory minimum terms, which define when a landlord may seek possession and other duties which are currently implied into a tenancy by law (e.g, the covenant for quiet enjoyment and the landlord's repairing obligations under s. 11 of the Landlord and Tenant Act 1985). Part C will comprise various default or negotiable terms. Here, the parties will be free to negotiate their own terms, but if they fail to do so, default terms will apply automatically.

Ultimately, the aims of the Commission are that housing law should be simpler, more comprehensible and more flexible. It is acknowledged that this has not been an easy task and that more work needs to be done, in particular, to ensure that the model occupation agreements are appropriately user-friendly.

Further reading

Dymond, A., 'Security of Tenure: The Way Forward' (2002) SJ 616.

Mills, S., and Joss, S., 'Children and Secure Tenancies' (2001) 5 L & T Rev 53.

Murdoch, S., 'All Tenants Are Equal' [2002] EG 137.

Partington, M., 'Renting Homes — New Opportunities: A Personal View' (2004) 8 L & T Rev 25.

Partington, M., 'The Reform of Housing Law: Interim Progress Report' (2003) 7 L & T Rev 60.

Partington, M., 'Law Commission: Renting Homes, A Progress Report' (2002) 6 L & T Rev 98

Partington, M., 'Reforming Housing Law: The Law Commission' (2001) 5 L & T Rev 95.

Probert, R., 'Tenancies and Same-sex Couples' (2002) NLJ 1801.

Wilkinson, H.W., 'Tolerated and Non-tolerated Trespassers' (2000) NLJ Practitioner 1301.

Pick and mix questions

Introduction

In this chapter, we have set out six questions which mix a number of different topics in landlord and tenant law.

Most students tend to shy away from such questions because they are perceived as being more complicated than single topic questions. Our experience is that most students will have revised *some* of the topics covered in the question but, invariably, not all. If you are faced with a mixed topic question and cannot answer all the areas, it is best not to attempt it — move on to another question which covers more familiar ground which you have revised more fully.

If you do decide to attempt such a question, our advice is to read the question very carefully and pick out all the various issues before putting pen to paper. If you feel you can take on all the topics, then you will need to structure your answer so that the various areas are dealt with in a logical, coherent whole. One advantage to mixed topic questions is that the examiner will not expect you to cover each topic in the same detail as you would a single topic question, but you should, nevertheless, be able to display a command of a wide area of knowledge, not superficially, but incisively and with depth in the given area.

Q Question 1

(a) To what extent is the classification of tenancies into specific and periodic an over-simplification?

(b) Explain the legal position of a tenant who withholds payment of rent on the ground that his landlord has failed to execute repairs for which he (the landlord) is responsible.

Commentary

This is a good example of a two-part question where the two parts are wholly unrelated in subject-matter.

Part (a) requires you to consider those tenancies which do *not* fall neatly into the two-fold classification of specific or periodic. In other words, you should examine (i) the tenancy at will, (ii) the tenancy at sufferance, and (iii) the tenancy by estoppel. If you merely give a list of the different types of fixed-term and periodic tenancies, you are not answering the question.

Part (b) requires you to examine equitable set-off against rent (*British Anzani (Felixstowe) Ltd* v *International Marine Management (UK) Ltd* [1980] QB 637) and the common law right to deduct repairing costs from rent (*Lee-Parker* v *Izzet* [1971] 1 WLR 1688 and *Asco Developments Ltd* v *Gordon* (1978) 248 EG 683). For further reading, see Rank, P. M., 'Repairs in Lieu of Rent' (1976) 40 Conv 196, and Waite, A., 'Repairs and Deduction from Rent' (1981) 45 Conv 199. This is an interesting question in view of the number of cases where the right to set-off and to make a deduction was considered in the context of an express exclusion that rent should be payable 'without any deduction' (*Connaught Restaurants Ltd* v *Indoor Leisure Ltd* [1994] 4 All ER 834 (CA); *Famous Army Stores* v *Meehan* [1993] 09 EG 114; *Electricity Supply Nominees Ltd* v *IAF Group Ltd* [1993] 1 WLR 1059; *Star Rider Ltd* v *Inntrepreneur Pub Co.* [1998] EGLR 53; and *Unchained Growth plc* v *Granby Village (Manchester) Management Co. Ltd* [2000] 1 WLR 739. For an interesting article on the Unfair Terms in Consumer Contracts Regulations 1999 as they apply to leases, see Heppinstall, A., 'A New Weapon for Tenants' (2002) SJ 59.

- **Tenancy at will creates relationship of tenure without estate. Circumstances when such a tenancy may arise: (1) express agreement (2) tenant holds over (3) tenant takes possession under a void lease and (4) purchaser let into possession before completion**

- **Tenancy at sufferance where tenant holds over and landlord has neither consented nor objected to occupation. Legal effect of this relationship will depend on subsequent events**

- **Tenancy by estoppel where landlord purports to grant tenancy of premises of which he is not the lawful owner. Tenant cannot deny his leasehold obligations nor can landlord set up want of title as a basis for repudiating the lease. Feeding the estoppel and statutory protection**

- **Consider equitable set-off: *British Anzani (Felixstowe) Ltd* v *International Marine Management (UK) Ltd* (1980)**

- **Consider also common law right to deduct repairing cost from rent: *Lee-Parker* v *Izzet* (1971) and *Asco Developments Ltd* v *Gordon* (1978)**

- **Neither right excluded where obligation to pay rent is expressly stated to be 'without any deduction': *Connaught Restaurants Ltd* v *Indoor Leisure Ltd* (1994).**

Consider application of Unfair Contract Terms Act 1977, sch. 1, para. 1(b): *Elecrticity Supply Nominees Ltd* v *IAF Group Ltd* (1993). Consider also impact of Unfair Terms in Consumer Contracts Regulations 1999

:Ö: **Suggested answer**

(a) Not all tenancies fall neatly into the two-fold classification of specific (i.e., fixed term) or periodic. For example, a tenancy at will creates a relationship of tenure without estate and arises where the occupier is more than a licensee (i.e., he enjoys exclusive possession with the consent of the owner) but the conduct of the parties allows for no inference as to quantum of interest. Because the permitted occupation is for an uncertain period, it is not a 'term of years absolute' within the Law of Property Act 1925, s. 205(1)(xxvii), so that a tenancy at will may be determined at any time by a demand for possession or by any other act which, by implication of law, negates any continuing consent given by the landlord.

Such a tenancy may arise:

(a) by express agreement (see, e.g., *Manfield & Sons Ltd* v *Botchin* [1970] 2 QB 612 and *Hagee (London) Ltd* v *Erikson (A.B.) and Larson* [1976] QB 209);

(b) where the tenant holds over with the landlord's consent and a periodic tenancy has not yet arisen (see, e.g., *Wheeler* v *Mercer* [1957] AC 416, where there was a holding over pending agreement on the new rent);

(c) where the tenant takes possession under a void lease; or;

(d) where a purchaser is let into possession before completion. The courts, however, are generally disinclined to infer a tenancy at will from an exclusive occupation of indefinite duration (*Heslop* v *Burns* [1974] 1 WLR 1241).

A tenant at will is entitled to the protection of the Rent Act 1977 where applicable (*Chamberlain* v *Farr* [1942] 2 All ER 567), but a tenant at will of business premises cannot claim the protection of the Landlord and Tenant Act 1954, Pt II (*Hagee (London) Ltd* v *Erikson (A.B.) and Larson* (express tenancy at will) and *Wheeler* v *Mercer* (implied tenancy at will)).

Another example of a tenancy not falling within the two-fold classification is a tenancy at sufferance. This denotes the relationship of owner and occupier where the tenant holds over on the expiry of his lease and the landlord has neither consented to nor expressed objection to the occupation. The absence of the landlord's consent negatives any relationship of tenure. The legal effects of this relationship will depend on subsequent events, namely:

(a) if the landlord requires the tenant to quit, the tenant becomes a trespasser and (by the doctrine of trespass by relation) the landlord can claim mesne profits from the date that the tenant's possession ceased to be lawful until possession is given up; or

(b) if the landlord signifies his consent (e.g., by a demand for rent) the tenant becomes a tenant at will, and if rent is paid with reference to a particular period the tenant becomes a periodic tenant; or

(c) if the landlord simply acquiesces, he will be statute barred if he fails to re-assert his title within 12 years from the date that the tenant's possession ceased to be lawful (Limitation Act 1980, s. 15).

Reference may also be made to a tenancy by estoppel. The doctrine of estoppel precludes parties, who have induced others to rely upon their representations, from denying the truth of the facts represented. For the purposes of landlord and tenant law, this means that neither the landlord nor the tenant can question the validity of the lease granted once possession has been taken up. Thus, even if the landlord is not the lawful owner of the estate out of which the tenant is granted his lease, the tenant cannot deny any of his leasehold obligations to the landlord by arguing that the grant was not effectively made. In other words, the tenant is estopped from suggesting that, due to the defect in the landlord's title, he is released from his lease-hold obligations (*Industrial Properties (Barton Hill) Ltd* v *Associated Electrical Industries Ltd* [1977] QB 580). Similarly, the landlord cannot set up his want of title as a ground for repudiating the lease (*EH Lewis* v *Morelli* [1948] 2 All ER 1021 and *Mackley* v *Nutting* [1949] 2 KB 55).

If, after the purported creation of a tenancy by means of the estoppel doctrine, the landlord acquires the legal estate out of which the tenancy could be created (e.g., as where he purchases the freehold), this feeds the estoppel and the tenancy becomes good in interest. On this occurrence, the tenant acquires a legal tenancy founded upon the landlord's newly acquired legal estate (*Church of England Building Society* v *Piskor* [1954] Ch 553).

A tenancy by estoppel may be a protected tenancy under the Rent Act 1977 (*Stratford* v *Syrett* [1958] 1 QB 107) and a business tenancy subject to protection under Pt II of the Landlord and Tenant Act 1954 (*Bell* v *General Accident Fire & Life Assurance Corporation Ltd* [1998] 17 EG 144).

(b) A tenant has two distinct arguments he can put forward to justify his with-holding of rent in this type of case.

By way of self-help, the tenant may decide to do the repairs himself and deduct the expense from current or future rent. On being sued for unpaid rent by his landlord, the tenant will be able to rely on his own counterclaim against the landlord for breach of the landlord's repairing covenant as effecting a complete defence by way of an equitable set-off to the claim for rent (*British Anzani (Felixstowe) Ltd* v *International Marine Management (UK) Ltd* [1980] QB 137). Equitable set-off can be used to pay for the cost of repairs the landlord is required to carry out but fails to, and for any reasonable consequential losses arising from the landlord's default. Set-off will, therefore, be important to a tenant where the failure to repair has led to expenditure, not only to get the work done but also to put right damage caused to the tenant's property as a result of the failure to repair.

Alternatively, the tenant has a common law right to deduct the repairing cost from the rent where, having given notice to the landlord, the tenant carries out the repairs which are the landlord's responsibility. In *Lee-Parker* v *Izzet* [1971] 1 WLR 1688, Goff J held that there is an 'ancient common law right' to recover the cost of repairs out of rent payable and, in any action for non-payment of rent, to raise the withholding of rent as a defence because, as a matter of law, that money is not owed to the landlord. The principle was approved by Sir Robert Megarry VC in *Asco Developments Ltd* v *Gordon* (1978) 248 EG 683, who allowed the cost of repairs to be recovered by reduction of rent arrears already in existence.

The ancient common law right can be used only to recover the cost of repair, whereas set-off is wider (as mentioned above) because it enables the tenant to get back, for example, the cost of repairing or replacing furniture damaged by water coming into the premises because of the landlord's default. In *British Anzani* (above), Forbes J suggested that the ancient common law right was appropriate for claiming ascertainable sums spent on repairs which the landlord could not really dispute, whereas the wider right of set-off should be used if more than the basic cost of repair is claimed. Interestingly, it has been held that rent 'lawfully due' from an assured tenant, for the purposes of grounds 8 and 10 of sch. 2 to the Housing Act 1988, is the rent *after* the deduction of any equitable set-off of damages claimed by the tenant against the landlord for the latter's breach of covenant to repair: *Baygreen Properties Ltd* v *Gil* [2002] 49 EG 126. Equitable set-off can also be invoked where the landlord is exercising his remedy of distress in respect of unpaid rent: *Fuller* v *Happy Shopper Markets Ltd* [2001] 25 EG 159.

The right to set-off and to make a deduction will not be excluded even where the obligation to pay rent is expressly stated to be 'without any deduction' (*Connaught Restaurants Ltd* v *Indoor Leisure Ltd* [1994] 4 All ER 834, where the Court of Appeal held that the expression 'without any deduction' was insufficient by itself, in the absence of any context suggesting the contrary, to operate by implication as an exclusion of a tenant's equitable right of set-off against rent). Contrast *Famous Army Stores* v *Meehan* [1993] 09 EG 114, which was disapproved. However, such an exclusion, where operative (e.g., by the use of words 'without any deduction *or set off whatsoever'*), does not fall foul of the Unfair Contract Terms Act 1977 since sch. 1, para. 1(b) to the Act expressly states that the provisions of the Act are not applicable to 'any contract so far as it relates to the creation or transfer of an interest in land or the termination of such an interest'. In *Electricity Supply Nominees Ltd* v *IAF Group Ltd* [1993] 1 WLR 1059, it was held that the words 'relates to' in sch. 1 to the 1977 Act were sufficiently wide to contemplate the inclusion of all the lease covenants which were integral to the lease which itself created the interest in land. See also, *Star Rider Ltd* v *Inntrepreneur Pub Co.* [1998] EGLR 53 and *Unchained Growth plc* v *Granby Village (Manchester) Management Co. Ltd* [2000] 1 WLR 739 (CA).

However, reference must also now be made to the Unfair Terms in Consumer Contracts Regulations 1999, which came into force on 1 October 1999 and apply to any terms entered into on or after 1 July 1995. The Regulations apply to a 'seller or supplier' acting in a business capacity and to a 'consumer' acting for purposes which are outside a trade, business or profession. Whilst, therefore, this definition appears to exclude business tenants, it will cover all residential tenants. If a particular term falls to be characterised as unfair, it will be unenforceable against the consumer (reg. 8(1)). It is evident that a number of leasehold terms may potentially fall foul of the Regulations. For example, an absolute prohibition against assigning, sub-letting or parting with possession or occupation of the premises could be treated as unfair in so far as it causes a significant detriment to the tenant who may have good reasons for assigning or sub-letting. Similarly, a forfeiture clause which entitles the landlord to determine the lease without any prior warning when the rent is, say, only 14 days late, is likely to be struck down. Clauses which fetter the tenant's right of set-off or deduction could also be held unenforceable on similar grounds: see para. 1(b) of sch. 2 to the 1999 Regulations, which specifically refers to 'inappropriately excluding . . . the option of offsetting a debt owed to the [supplier] against any claim which the consumer may have against him'.

Q Question 2

In 1980, Dracula Properties Ltd (Dracula) demised a newsagent's shop to David for a term of 25 years from 25 December 1980. By the lease, David covenanted (*inter alia*):

(a) not to assign, underlet or part with possession of the premises or any part thereof;

(b) not to use the premises (nor suffer or permit the same to be used) for any unlawful or immoral purposes;

(c) not to make any alterations or additions to the premises.

It has come to Dracula's attention that:

(a) David's wife, Sarah, has recently been in trouble with the police for selling obscene magazines and videos in the shop. David has actively encouraged his wife in this new venture. Dracula became aware of these facts in early May 2004;

(b) Miss Smith is occupying the basement of the premises as a sub-tenant. There is strong evidence that she is using this accommodation for the purpose of prostitution and that David and his wife have turned a blind eye to this. These facts came to light in August 2004;

(c) The frontage of the premises has been substantially altered. This fact came to light only last week.

The rent due on 24 June 2004 in advance was duly paid by Sarah on behalf of her husband. No other rent has been demanded or accepted.

Advise Dracula on the legal consequences of these events under common law and statute.

Commentary

This question combines the topic of forfeiture with the termination of a business tenancy under the Landlord and Tenant Act 1954, Pt II. Notice that the lease is due to expire on 24 December 2005, which makes it possible for the landlord to invoke the statutory machinery for termination under Pt II instead of bringing an action for forfeiture.

For further reading, see Williams, D., 'Landlord and Tenant Act 1954 Part II — The Operation of Sections 30(1)(b) and (c)' [1990] EG 9049, 40 and Brown, J., 'Waiver' [1997] EG 9702, 119.

- Does acceptance of rent for June quarter waive the breach of user covenant? Acceptance of rent from David's wife constitutes an act of waiver. But breach of user covenant a continuing breach: *Segal Securities* v *Thoseby* (1963). Fresh right of forfeiture arises on next rent day

- Dracula must serve s. 146 notice as a prelude to forfeiture. Breach incapable of remedy so landlord can proceed with little delay: *Van Haarlam* v *Kasner Charitable Trust* (1992). Relief from forfeiture unlikely: *Egerton* v *Esplanade Hotels, London Ltd* (1947)

- Subtenancy also in breach of absolute covenant against assignment, subletting etc. Prostitution also breach of David's covenant not to suffer or permit any part of premises to be used for immoral purpose. No waiver and relief against forfeiture unlikely

- Alteration to frontage breach of covenant which is capable of remedy: *Savva* v *Houssein* (1996)

- Consider using machinery for termination of Landlord and Tenant Act 1954, Pt II, instead of forfeiture proceedings

☼ Suggested answer

The fact that David's wife, Sarah, has been selling obscene magazines and videos in the shop constitutes prima facie a breach of the user covenant in the lease under which David (as lessee) covenanted not to suffer or permit the premises to be used for any unlawful/immoral purposes. But does the acceptance of rent for the June quarter preclude Dracula from forfeiting the lease for this breach? A waiver by acceptance of rent is sufficient if payment is accepted from a person on behalf of the tenant in satisfaction of the rent under the lease (*Pellatt* v *Boosey* (1862) 31 LJ CP 281). The fact, therefore, that the rent has been accepted from David's wife on his behalf will constitute an act of waiver of forfeiture. However, a breach of a user covenant is classified, as a matter of law, as a *continuing* breach (*Doe d Ambler* v *Woodbridge* (1829) 9 B & C 376 and *Segal Securities Ltd* v *Thoseby* [1963] 1 QB 887), so that despite the acceptance of rent in June 2004 with knowledge of the breach, there will be a continually recurring cause of forfeiture and the waiver (by the acceptance of rent for the June quarter) will operate only in relation to past breaches. Because the breach is continuing, a fresh right of forfeiture will arise after the next rent day (i.e., 29 September 2004).

In order to pursue its remedy of forfeiture, Dracula must serve on David a notice pursuant to the Law of Property Act 1925, s. 146, specifying the breach complained of and, 'if the breach is capable of remedy', requiring the tenant to remedy it within a reasonable period of time (s. 146(1)). A breach of a negative covenant which leaves a stigma on the demised premises is generally incapable of remedy (*Governors of Rugby School* v *Tannahill* [1935] 1 KB 87). Thus, if the breach is irremediable (as in the present case), the landlord does not have to stipulate in its s. 146 notice that the breach be remedied and may proceed to execute its right of forfeiture (whether by action or physical re-entry) with little delay (*Dunraven Securities Ltd* v *Holloway* (1982) 264 EG 709 and *DR Evans & Co.* v *Chandler* (1969) 211 EG 1381, use of premises for the sale of pornographic material). In *Van Haarlam* v *Kasner Charitable Trust* [1992] 36 EG 135, a case involving a breach of covenant not to use the premises for any illegal or immoral purposes, 30 days' notice was held reasonable. Furthermore, since the breach is technically incapable of remedy, David's only recourse is to seek relief from forfeiture under s. 146(2) of the 1925 Act. Whether such relief will be granted is debatable in view of the fact that relief from forfeiture is normally refused where the tenant has permitted immoral or illegal user of the premises (*Egerton* v *Esplanade Hotels, London Ltd* [1947] 2 All ER 88). In an appropriate case, however, where the tenant is genuinely ignorant of the facts, relief may be granted (*Glass* v *Kencakes Ltd* [1966] 1 QB 611 and *Ropemaker Properties Ltd* v *Noonhaven Ltd* (1989) 2 EGLR 50).

Miss Smith's occupation of the basement as a sub-tenant is also in clear breach of the terms of David's lease. The lease contains an absolute covenant against assignment, sub-letting etc., so that the provisions of the Landlord and Tenant Act 1927,

306 PICK AND MIX QUESTIONS

s. 19(1) (which impose a proviso that the landlord's consent shall not be unreasonably withheld) do not apply (*FW Woolworth and Co. Ltd* v *Lambert* [1937] Ch 37, *per* Romer LJ at pp. 58–59). Assuming the basement premises are being used for prostitution, this will also constitute a breach of David's covenant not to suffer or permit any part of the premises to be used for an unlawful/immoral purpose.

We are told that these facts came to light in August 2004, so that there is no question of Dracula waiving these breaches by the acceptance of rent in June 2004 when it had no knowledge of the same. In this connection, a waiver of forfeiture can only occur where the landlord does some unequivocal act recognising the continued existence of the lease with knowledge of the facts upon which its right of re-entry arises (*Matthews* v *Smallwood* [1910] 1 Ch 777, at p. 786 and, more recently, *Cornillie* v *Saha* (1996) 28 HLR 561 (CA)). Here again, Dracula will need to particularise the breaches complained of in his s. 146 notice as a preliminary to forfeiting the lease by physical re-entry or proceedings for possession. Moreover, because a breach of a covenant not to assign, underlet or part with possession is an irremediable breach (*Scala House & District Property Co. Ltd* v *Forbes* [1974] QB 575), David is not in a position to avoid the forfeiture by ceasing the action which constitutes the breach. Once again, his only recourse is to seek relief from forfeiture under s. 146(2) of the 1925 Act, which (as mentioned earlier) is problematical in view of the immoral nature of the breach.

The alteration to the frontage of the shop also constitutes a breach of the covenant not to make any alterations or additions to the demised premises. As Dracula became aware of this only last week, no question of waiver arises. It will be necessary, however, for Dracula to include particulars of this breach in its s. 146 notice. In *Savva* v *Houssein* [1996] 47 EG 138, the Court of Appeal held that all breaches of covenant were capable of remedy if the mischief caused by the breach can be removed. In the case of a covenant against alterations, the mischief can be removed by restoring the property to the state it was in before the alterations. Dracula's s. 146 notice, therefore, must require David to remedy the breach.

Since David's lease constitutes shop premises, it is likely that it qualifies as a business tenancy under the Landlord and Tenant Act 1954, Pt II. Section 24 of the Act expressly preserves various common law methods of termination, including forfeiture of the lease. Alternatively, Pt II of the Act prescribes statutory machinery for termination of a business tenancy. In this case, it would be open to Dracula, as an alternative to forfeiting the lease, to serve on David a notice of termination of his tenancy under s. 25 of the 1954 Act. This must be in a prescribed form (or substantially to like effect) and must specify the date at which the existing tenancy is to come to an end. The notice itself must be given not more than 12 months and not less than six months before the termination date specified in the notice, which must not be earlier than the date at which the tenancy would expire or could be brought to an end by the landlord at common law. In David's case, the earliest termination date is the date of the expiry of his lease (i.e., 24 December 2005). In addition, Dracula's notice must state whether Dracula would oppose a tenant's application to the court for the grant of a new tenancy and, if so, on which of the seven grounds specified in s. 30(1) of the Act.

On the facts, Dracula may rely on ground (c) of s. 30(1), namely, substantial breaches of obligations under the tenancy. The ground (like grounds (a) and (b)) is discretionary in the sense that, although proof of a breach of covenant is essential, the landlord must also show that a new tenancy ought not to be granted by reason of the substantial breaches of obligations. In this connection, the court is entitled to consider the whole of the tenant's conduct and not merely matters specified in the landlord's notice of opposition (*Eichner* v *Midland Bank Executor and Trustee Co. Ltd* [1970] 1 WLR 1120). If Dracula is successful in opposing David's application for a new tenancy, the existing tenancy will come to an end on the date specified in the s. 25 notice (i.e., 24 December 2005), or three months after the final disposal of the application by the court, whichever is the later (s. 64). It is important to bear in mind that the tenant's right to compensation for disturbance is limited to cases where the landlord successfully objects to the grant of a new tenancy on grounds (e), (f) or (g) of s. 30(1) (s. 37(1)). The tenant's right to compensation for improvements, however, will not be affected.

Q Question 3

In March 1995, Joshua granted Peter (who runs a car parking and vehicle storage business) a 20-year lease of a two acre car parking and vehicle storage area. The lease provided that the rent was £15,000 per annum payable quarterly in advance and that Joshua would 'keep in good repair and structural condition' the boundary wall surrounding the demised premises.

In 2002, Peter discovered that the boundary wall was subsiding due to inadequate foundations. In the same year, the entrance to the car park was shut off by building contractors employed by the local water authority who were carrying out major excavations to a local sewage system. Peter wrote to Joshua in relation to both these matters requesting that Joshua repair the boundary wall and put pressure on the authority to reorganise their works so as to free up the entrance to the car park. Joshua ignored both these requests.

As a result of the water authority's works, the entrance to the car park remained blocked for two years, rendering the car park inoperable during this period.

In March 2004, Peter eventually abandoned the premises. Joshua has now written to Peter demanding the outstanding rent for the June and September quarters.

Advise Peter.

Commentary

The essential issue in this question is whether Peter is still bound under the terms of his lease to pay the rent. One approach is to argue that Joshua was guilty of a repudiatory breach by failing to remedy the defective boundary wall and that Peter, by accepting the repudiation by quitting the premises in 2004, effectively terminated the lease. But does the remedial work to the wall constitute a work of repair within the meaning of the landlord's repairing covenant? Moreover, are the defects sufficiently fundamental to constitute a repudiatory breach? Even assuming the facts warrant a repudiatory breach, does this doctrine apply to a business tenancy governed by the Landlord and Tenant Act 1954, Pt II?

Alternatively, it may be possible to argue that the lease was discharged by frustration (i.e., by the actions of the water authority denying Peter the substantial benefit of the letting). Here again, it is doubtful on the facts whether the event in question was sufficiently serious to warrant the operation of the doctrine.

A third possibility is that the lease was effectively surrendered upon Peter abandoning the premises.

The likelihood of Joshua forfeiting the lease for non-payment of rent should also be considered.

See also, Question 4, **Chapter 9**.

- Consider doctrine of repudiatory breach: *Hussein* v *Mehlman* (1992) and *Chartered Trust plc* v *Davies* (1997). Does the condition of the boundary wall constitute a disrepair within the meaning of Joshua's repairing covenant?: *Brew Bros Ltd* v *Snax (Ross) Ltd* (1970)

- Are the defects sufficiently fundamental to constitute a repudiatory breach? If so, does the doctrine of repudiatory breach apply in the context of a business tenancy?

- Application of the doctrine of frustration: *National Carriers Ltd* v *Panalpina Northern Ltd* (1981). Consider also doctrine of frustratory mitigation

- Has the lease been effectively surrendered by operation of law? Landlord does not appear to have accepted the surrender: *Preston Borough Council* v *Fairclough* (1982). Peter continues to be liable for rent until lease formally brought to an end (e.g., by forfeiture)

☼ Suggested answer

The question whether Peter is bound to pay the rent will depend on whether or not the lease has effectively been brought to an end. One possibility is that the lease has been terminated by operation of the doctrine of repudiatory breach. It was once thought that this doctrine had no universal application to leases. In *Total Oil Great Britain Ltd* v *Thompson Garages (Biggin Hill) Ltd* [1972] 1 QB 318, Lord Denning MR was of the opinion that because a lease was a demise conveying an interest in land, it did not come to an end like an ordinary contract on repudiation and acceptance. This view no longer represents the law. In *Hussein* v *Mehlman* [1992] 32 EG 59, it was reaffirmed that a lease could come to an end by the tenant's acceptance of his land-lord's repudiatory conduct. In that case, the defendant landlord granted the claimant tenants a three-year assured shorthold tenancy of a dwelling-house subject to the covenants to repair implied on the part of the landlord by the Landlord and Tenant Act 1985, s. 11. From the commencement of the term, the claimants made several complaints to the defendant regarding the disrepair of the premises. The defendant refused to carry out these repairs and eventually the claimants returned the keys and vacated the dwelling-house. On the evidence, the court held that the defendant had been guilty of a repudiatory breach (in so far as the defects were such as to render the house as a whole unfit to be lived in) and the claimants, by vacating the premises and returning the keys, had accepted that repudiation as putting an end to the tenancy. The decision in *Hussein* was treated as apparently correct, without argument, by the Court of Appeal in *Chartered Trust plc* v *Davies* [1997] 2 EGLR 83, where, although the lease had still about 20 years left to run, the landlord's conduct in derogating from grant resulted in substantial interference with the tenant's business driving her to bankruptcy. This, in itself, was considered sufficient to deprive the tenant of the whole benefit of her contract and constitute a repudiation of the lease regardless of the unexpired term of the lease.

In the present case, we are told that the boundary wall was subsiding due to inadequate foundations. Does this come within Joshua's covenant to repair? Although the term 'repair' includes the obligation to remedy inherent defects in design or construction of the premises, the question in all cases is one of fact and degree (*Brew Bros Ltd* v *Snax (Ross) Ltd* [1970] 1 QB 612 and *Ravenseft Properties Ltd* v *Davstone (Holdings) Ltd* [1980] QB 12). In *Smedley* v *Chumley & Hawke Ltd* (1981) 261 EG 775, for example, the lease of a restaurant contained a landlord's covenant to keep the main walls and roof in good structural condition and repair through-out the tenancy. A few years after the commencement of the lease, it became evident that the foundations of the restaurant were defective. There were no piles under part of the concrete raft on which the building was constructed, with the result that the raft tilted, causing damage to the walls and roof. The Court of Appeal held that the landlords were liable under their covenant.

Assuming that remedial work to the boundary wall constitutes repair, are the defects sufficiently fundamental to constitute a repudiatory breach? In *Hussein* v *Mehlman* (above) the defects in question rendered the dwelling-house uninhabitable, thereby depriving the tenant of the essential part of what he had contracted for, namely, a house in which all rooms were usable and in which ceilings were not collapsed or collapsing and into which rain, wind and cold did not penetrate through the various defects in the structure. It is submitted that the present case is distinguishable in that the car park was probably capable of operating without hindrance despite the defects to the boundary wall. On the facts therefore, it is difficult to argue that Peter has been deprived of substantially the whole of his bargain: *Nynehead Developments Ltd* v *RH Fibreboard Containers* Ltd [1999] O2 EG 139. Another distinguishing feature is that in *Hussein* v *Mehlman* there was clear evidence that the tenant had accepted the repudiation by vacating the premises and handing back the keys. In the present case, we are told that Peter merely abandoned the premises after two years. This delay may possibly constitute an affirmation of the contract and deny Peter the right to terminate for its breach.

A more fundamental difficulty lies in the fact that it may be open to question whether the doctrine of repudiatory breach applies at all in the context of a business tenancy protected under the Landlord and Tenant Act 1954, Pt II. In this connection, s. 24 of the Act is quite specific in setting out certain non-statutory (common law) methods of termination (i.e., notice to quit given by tenant, surrender, forfeiture, agreement for a new tenancy etc.). It is doubtful whether termination by acceptance of a landlord's repudiatory breach falls within any of these heads.

Alternatively, it may be possible to argue that the lease was discharged by a frustrating event, namely, the actions of the water authority in shutting off the entrance to the car park. In *National Carriers Ltd* v *Panalpina Northern Ltd* [1981] AC 675, the House of Lords held that the contractual doctrine of frustration was applicable to leases, but the actual circumstances in which a lease could be frustrated would be rare. In that case, access to a warehouse demised to the defendants for a term of 10 years was closed up for a period of 20 months by the local authority in order for essential works to be carried out to a neighbouring warehouse. During that period, the demised warehouse was rendered useless for the tenants' purpose and they claimed that the lease had been frustrated by the events which had happened. The House of Lords held that, having regard to the likely length of continuance of the lease after the interruption of user in relation to the term originally granted, the tenants had failed to raise a triable issue. A similar conclusion would, it is submitted, be reached in the present case. Although the disruption was for a period of two years, it is important to bear in mind that the lease has another 10 years left to run before its expiry in March 2015.

It has been suggested by one commentator that there is a doctrine of 'frustratory mitigation' which may apply to leases: see Morgan, J. [1995] Conv 74. In contrast to frustration, an event giving rise to frustratory mitigation merely *suspends* the operation of the relevant covenant until such time as it can be performed, or it becomes evident that performance will never be possible and it is properly frustrated. It is unlikely, however, that this doctrine (if it exists) would provide a defence for an action for non-payment of rent against Peter. Despite the fact that he may not be getting what he bargained for as a result of the water authority's works, the payment of rent will still be possible even if the anticipated use of the premises is not.

Another possibility is that the lease was effectively surrendered by operation of law. Although a mere temporary abandonment of possession by the tenant will not of itself justify an inference that the lease has been impliedly surrendered, a permanent abandonment of possession will suffice, particularly where the tenant having left with the unequivocal intention of not returning, the landlord accepts his implied offer for a surrender by changing the locks and re-letting the premises to another person (*R v London Borough of Croydon, ex parte Toth* (1986) 18 HLR 493). The position, however, may be otherwise if the tenant (as in the present case) simply abandons possession but the landlord has not formally accepted the surrender and ended the lease nor re-let the premises (*Preston Borough Council v Fairclough* (1982) 8 HLR 70).

It seems, therefore, that Peter continues to be liable to pay the rent until such time as the lease is formally ended. One possibility is that Joshua will seek to forfeit the lease for non-payment of rent. Abandonment of the premises by the tenant does not of itself entitle a landlord to forfeit the lease unless it amounts to a breach of a covenant (e.g., non-payment of rent) or condition in the lease: *Thatcher v Pearce & Sons Ltd* [1968] IWLR 278. Apart from relying on the law of forfeiture, Joshua may have resort to the Distress for Rent Act 1737, s. 16, which provides a means by which a landlord may, in certain circumstances, recover possession of premises left uncultivated or unoccupied. In view, however, of the cumbersome nature of this procedure, the landlord's remedy of forfeiture is to be preferred.

Q Question 4

(a) What are the essential attributes of rent? What is meant by the doctrine of certainty of rent? [10 marks]

(b) In August 1992, Norman granted Harriet an assured weekly tenancy of a dwelling-house known as 'The Mews'. At that time, the property was occupied by Harriet and her husband, Nick. In October 1993, Norman assigned his reversionary interest to Sheila subject to Harriet's tenancy. In December 2003, Harriet divorced Nick and, in the course of the proceedings for ancillary relief, she undertook to transfer the tenancy to Nick. Nothing, however, was done to implement the undertaking, and in fact Harriet continues to occupy the property. Nick has recently moved out and found accommodation elsewhere.

Since the divorce proceedings, no rent has been paid under the tenancy. Sheila now wishes to obtain possession of the property and recover the arrears of rent.
    Advise Sheila. [15 marks]

Commentary

This is a two-part question which raises a mixed bag of topics.

Part (a) requires you to write a mini-essay on the meaning of 'rent' and the doctrine of certainty of rent. To score good marks, you should illustrate your answer, wherever possible, by reference to case law.

Part (b) is more complicated since it requires you to assimilate the various issues and produce a coherent, succinct piece of advice in a relatively short time-span. The danger is that you will run out of time before completing your answer. There is quite a lot of ground to cover:

(a) the ability of an assignee landlord (Sheila) to sue upon breaches of covenant occurring after the assignment;

(b) the requisite legal formalities for the assignment of a weekly tenancy; and

(c) the statutory machinery for termination under the Housing Act 1988, Pt I.

Note that part (b) of the question carries more marks than part (a). Your answer should, therefore, reflect this imbalance.

- Meaning of rent as recompense for the use of land. Doctrine of certainty of rent requires that rent is calculable with certainty at such time as payment becomes due: *Greater London Council* v *Connolly* (1970)

- Harriet's liability to pay rent continues because benefit of covenant to pay rent passes with the reversionary estate: Law of Property Act 1925, s. 141(1) and *Re King, Deceased, Robinson* v *Gray* (1963). Sheila can thus claim the rent

- Assignment of weekly tenancy must be by deed: *Crago* v *Julian* (1992). Thus, Harriet continues to be tenant of the premises

- Sheila should be advised to bring proceedings against Harriet under the Housing Act 1988, Pt I, for possession of the premises and recovery of the arrears. Need for court order: s. 5(1). Also, requirement of s. 8 notice. Consider grounds 8, 10 and 11 relating to non-payment of rent

;Q: Suggested answer

(a) Rent is a profit issuing out of and derived from land payable by a tenant to a landlord as a compensation or consideration for possession of the land demised during a given term. In paying rent, a tenant implicitly acknowledges his landlord's title. In *CH Bailey* v *Memorial Enterprises Ltd* [1974] 1 WLR 728, Lord Denning cited with approval Holdsworth's *History of English Law* (1900), Vol. VII, p. 262, which states that '. . . in modern law, rent is not conceived of as a thing, but rather as a payment which a tenant is bound by his contract to make to his landlord for the use of the land'. Similarly, in *Bradshaw* v *Pawley* (1980) 253 EG 693, Sir Robert Megarry V-C observed (at p. 695) that rent was essentially the periodical monetary compensation payable by the tenant in consideration for the grant of a lease of land.

Rent is, accordingly, a contractual sum which the landlord is entitled to receive from the tenant in return for the latter's use and occupation of his land. Rent may be contrasted with a rentcharge, the latter being charged on land in perpetuity or for a term, with an express power of distress, but the owner of the rentcharge has no reversion on the land charged. By the Rentcharges Act 1977, s. 2, rentcharges cannot generally be created after 22 August 1977. Rent may also be contrasted with a premium or fine. These are capital sums payable as a lump sum (or in instalments) at or from the commencement of a lease, or on its subsequent assignment.

The House of Lords has recently ruled that money paid under a mistake of law can be recovered by the payer even where payment had been made under a settled understanding of the law at the time, or where payment had been received by the payee under an honest belief of an entitlement to retain the money (*Kleinwort Benson Ltd* v *Lincoln City Council* [1998] 3 WLR 1095 (HL)). The case has huge potential consequences in respect of overpayments of rent, service charges and other periodical payments payable under a lease. For example, in *Nurdin & Peacock plc* v *DB Ramsden & Co. Ltd (No. 2)* [1999] 1 All ER 941, the Court of Appeal held that various overpayments of rent under a commercial lease were paid under a mistake of law and, hence, under the *Kleinwort* principle, recoverable by the payer. (See also, *Universities Superannuation Scheme Ltd* v *Marks & Spencer plc* [1990] 04 EG 158, involving underpayments of service charges made by the tenant.)

The doctrine of certainty of rent requires that the rent payable by a tenant to his landlord is calculable with certainty at such time as payment becomes due. In *Greater London Council* v *Connolly* [1970] 2 QB 100, the claimant Council increased the rents of the tenants of some quarter of a million houses by amounts averaging 7s 6d a week. The rent books of the tenants contained printed conditions of the tenancies. By condition 2, the rent was 'liable to be increased or decreased on notice being given'. The Court of Appeal held that although the amount of rent was dependent on an act of the landlord, it could be calculated with certainty at the time when payment became due and so was not uncertain. A rent calculated by reference to the index of retail prices has also been held as sufficiently certain: (*Blumenthal* v *Gallery Five Ltd* (1971) 220 EG 483). Similarly, a sum representing 10 per cent of the turnover of a business has been upheld as certain (*Smith* v *Cardiff Corporation (No. 2)* [1955] Ch 159).

In regard to rent review clauses, the rent does not necessarily have to be certain when it falls due, provided that it is ascertained in due course under a rent review procedure (*CH Bailey Ltd* v *Memorial Enterprises Ltd*, above).

(b) We are told that in October 1993 the reversionary interest was assigned to Sheila subject to the benefit of Harriet's tenancy. Despite the assignment, Harriet's liability will have continued because the rent reserved under the tenancy and the benefit of every covenant having reference to the subject-matter of the tenancy will have passed with the reversionary estate under the Law of Property Act 1925, s. 141(1). The effect of s. 141(1) is that once the reversion has been assigned it is only the assignee of the reversion (Sheila) who can sue on the real covenants contained in the tenancy, whether the breach took place before or after the assignment (*Re King, Deceased, Robinson* v *Gray* [1963] Ch 459 and *London & County (A. & D.) Ltd* v *Wilfred Sportsman Ltd* [1971] Ch 764, at pp. 782–4).

We are also told that in December 2003, Harriet divorced Nick and undertook to transfer the weekly tenancy to him, but this was never implemented. A similar situation arose in *Crago* v *Julian* [1992] 1 WLR 372, where the Court of Appeal held that, although the Law of Property Act 1925, s. 54(2) excepted the creation of a lease for a term not exceeding three years at a full market rent from the requirement of s. 53(1)(a) that the creation of an interest in land had to be in writing, it did not extend to the *assignment* of such leases which, therefore, had to be in writing. Moreover, the exception in s. 54(2) from the requirement of a deed for leases not required to be in writing applied only to their creation, and subsequent dispositions by assignment (or otherwise) had to be by deed unless otherwise exempted. The upshot of the foregoing so far as the present case is concerned is that, since there has been no formal assignment of the weekly tenancy in writing, Harriet continues to remain the tenant of the property. (Interestingly, had Harriet's tenancy been a secure tenancy under the Housing Act 1985, any purported transfer of her interest to Nick would also have been ineffective under s. 91(1) of the 1985 Act, which provides that a secure periodic tenancy is not capable of being assigned (*Burton* v *Camden London Borough Council* [2000] 2 WLR 427 (HL).)

Since the rent is in arrears, Sheila should be advised to commence proceedings against Harriet in the county court under the Housing Act 1988, Pt I (to which the tenancy is subject), for possession of the premises and recovery of the arrears. Since the assured tenancy is periodic, it cannot be brought to an end except by obtaining an order from the court (s. 5(1)). A notice to quit by the landlord in relation to such a tenancy will be of no effect.

Before proceedings are commenced, Sheila must serve on Harriet a notice under s. 8 of the 1988 Act, informing her of the ground(s) on which possession is sought and setting out the time-scale of the action (s. 8(3)). The proceedings should not commence earlier than two weeks from the service of the s. 8 notice.

The court is restricted in the granting of a possession order in relation to a dwelling let on an assured tenancy. It must not make a possession order unless it is satisfied that certain grounds, listed in sch. 2, have been established. In the present case, Sheila should be advised to rely on grounds 8, 10 and 11. Ground 8 is a mandatory ground which would entitle Sheila to an order for possession as of right (i.e., the court does not have a discretion to adjourn proceedings or suspend the operation of the possession order once it is satisfied that the ground has been established). To succeed under ground 8, Sheila must show that at least three months' rent is unpaid both at the date of the service of the s. 8 notice and at the date of the hearing. In this connection, there is always the danger that Harriet will pay off all the arrears prior to the hearing.

Grounds 10 and 11 are discretionary grounds which will not entitle Sheila to possession as of right; the court may only make an order for possession if it considers it reasonable to do so, and has wide powers to adjourn proceedings or suspend the operation of a possession order. Ground 10 requires Sheila to establish that some rent lawfully due from Harriet is unpaid on the date on which proceedings for possession are begun and was in arrears at the date of the service of the s. 8 notice. Here again, Harriet may thwart the proceedings by paying off the arrears before the hearing. However, ground 11 will apply whether or not any rent is in arrears on the date on which proceedings for possession are begun, provided Sheila can show that Harriet has persistently delayed paying rent which has become lawfully due.

Q Question 5

You have been asked by a client landlord to draft a short lease for use in respect of residential premises.

(a) Outline the form and contents of your draft.

(b) Explain what obligations would be imposed by law if your client chose to proceed in the absence of such a lease.

Commentary

This is a question which requires you to draw on a number of different areas of landlord and tenant law. The danger is that you will concentrate on one or two topics in detail at the expense of other areas. Try to give a broad outline of the contents of your draft, referring to the more important landlord and tenant covenants as appropriate. The question also asks you to describe the various implied obligations in the absence of express agreement. Here again, you are only expected to give a broad outline of the legal position.

You may assume that the two parts of the question carry an equal distribution of marks. Bear this in mind, when writing your answer.

- Five parts to a lease: (1) the premises (2) habendum (3) reddendum (4) covenants and (5) forfeiture clause

- Outline tenant's covenants: to pay rent, repair, covenant against assignment subletting, etc., user, making of alterations, permitting landlord and agents access to demised property and insurance. Landlord's covenant for quiet enjoyment

- Tenant's implied covenants to pay rent and other outgoings and not to deny landlord's title. Landlord's implied covenant for quiet enjoyment and not to derogate from grant

- Consider also implied repairing obligations on the part of both landlord and tenant at common law and under statute

:Q: Suggested answer

(a) Although no precise form is required by law for a lease, a fairly standard layout is invariably adopted as a matter of conveyancing practice. A lease by deed usually consists of five parts.

The 'premises' comprises the date of the lease, the names and description of the parties, the recitals (if any), the rent or premium, the operative words of demise, the description of the parcels demised, and any exceptions and reservations. My client may wish to limit the physical extent of the grant by excluding from it some part of the premises (e.g., the garden). This can be done by means of an exception. On the other hand, the landlord may wish to reserve some right newly created out of the subject-matter of the demise. For example, he may wish to reserve himself a right of way over the demised premises.

The 'habendum' specifies the quantity and quality of the estate demised and is usually identified by the words 'to hold' or 'to have and to hold'. The habendum fixes the commencement date and duration of the term.

The 'reddendum' fixes the rent payable under the lease and indicates with certainty that rent is payable by words such as 'yielding and paying'. Invariably, the rent will be reserved throughout the term or for a fixed period, followed by a reference to a rent review provision. Because a short lease is envisaged in the problem, I would not consider inserting a rent review clause in my draft.

The 'covenants' are the various obligations of the landlord and tenant, and these will be set out after the reddendum. So far as the tenants covenants are concerned, I would envisage including the following:

    (a)   covenant to pay rent;

    (b)   covenant to repair;

    (c)   covenant against assigning, sub-letting, charging or parting with possession. Such a covenant would take a fully qualified form (i.e., not to assign, underlet etc. 'without the landlord's consent such consent not to be unreasonably withheld') so as to anticipate the provisions of the Landlord and Tenant Act 1927, s. 198(1);

(d) user covenant limiting user of the demised premises to a private dwelling-house and residence only;

(e) a qualified covenant against the making of alterations or additions to the demised premises without prior consent of the landlord;

(f) covenant permitting the landlord and his agents to enter upon the premises for the purpose of inspecting the state and condition thereof. This would be coupled with a provision entitling the landlord to serve notice on the tenant to effect repairs, and the right of the landlord to execute such repairs himself (in the event of a failure to repair by the tenant) and to claim the cost from the tenant as a debt or rent arrears. Such a clause would permit the landlord to recoup the cost of the repairs without the necessity of serving a notice under the Law of Property Act 1925, s. 146(1), or complying with the procedures contained in the Leasehold Property (Repairs) Act 1938 (*Colchester Estates (Cardiff)* v *Carlton Industries plc* [1986] Ch 80) and *Jervis* v *Harris* [1996] 1 EGLR 78 (CA).

(g) covenant to insure.

So far as the landlord's covenants are concerned, I would limit these to just the covenant for quiet enjoyment.

Following the covenants, I would insert an appropriate proviso for re-entry for non-payment of rent (whether formally demanded or not) or other breaches of the tenant's covenants. The proviso (or forfeiture clause) provides the landlord with a contractual remedy against the tenant whereby he can terminate the lease.

Lastly, my draft would contain a number of schedules dealing with various matters, for example, a detailed description of the premises demised, a list of fixtures and fittings, and a set of regulations regarding the tenant's use of the premises (e.g., a prohibition on keeping animals on the premises, committing acts of nuisance etc.), and a schedule of condition in connection with the tenant's covenant to repair which obliges him to keep the premises in repair to a defined standard.

(b) In the absence of a written lease, a number of covenants will be implied under the common law and by statute into an oral tenancy. (Presumably, it is envisaged that such a tenancy would be either periodic or for a term not exceeding three years at the best rent with immediate possession so as to fall within the exception of a formal deed under the Law of Property Act 1925, s. 54(2).)

A covenant to pay rent will be implied from the mere contractual relationship of landlord and tenant. There is also an implied liability on the part of the tenant to pay charges in respect of the property (e.g., council tax, water rates and sewerage charges). It is also an implied condition of every lease, fixed term or periodic, that the tenant is not expressly or impliedly to deny the landlord's title or prejudice it by any acts which are inconsistent with the existence of the tenancy.

So far as the landlord is concerned, there is implied into every lease a covenant entitling the tenant to the quiet enjoyment of the demised premises. Under this covenant, the tenant is entitled peacefully to enjoy the premises without interruption from the landlord or persons claiming under him. The implied covenant, however, terminates with the landlord's interest (*Baynes & Co.* v *Lloyd & Sons* [1895] 2 QB 610). A landlord is also subject to an implied covenant not to derogate from his grant (*Harmer* v *Jumbil (Nigeria) Tin Areas Ltd* [1921] 1 Ch 200 and *Aldin* v *Latimer Clark, Muirhead & Co.* [1894] 2 Ch 437).

In addition to the above, a number of obligations relating to the state and condition of the premises will be implied on the part of the landlord. At common law, in relation to furnished lettings, there is an implied condition that the premises will be fit for human habitation at the commencement of the tenancy (see, e.g., *Smith* v *Marrable* (1843) 11 M & W 5). Where the essential means of access to units in a building in multiple occupation are retained in the landlord's control, the landlord is also impliedly obliged to maintain those means of access to a reasonable standard (*Liverpool City Council* v *Irwin* [1977] AC 239). This principle, however, appears to be confined to the special circumstances of a high-rise building in multiple occupation where the essential means of access to the units are retained in the landlord's occupation (*Duke of Westminster* v *Guild* [1985] QB 688).

An obligation to repair may also be implied on the landlord in order to match a correlative obligation on the part of the tenant (*Barrett* v *Lounova (1982) Ltd* [1990] 1 QB 348; but see *Adami* v *Lincoln Grange Management Ltd* [1998] 17 EG 148, in which the Court of Appeal concluded that the *Barrett* case was decided on its own special facts and contained no general principle requiring the implication of an obligation on a landlord to keep the structure of a building in good repair).

There are also a number of repairing obligations imposed on a landlord by statute. The Landlord and Tenant Act 1985, s. 8 (formerly the Housing Act 1957, s. 6), implies terms as to fitness for human habitation throughout the term of the tenancy. However, the section applies only to residential lettings within certain low rent limits (see s. 8(4).). More importantly, the Landlord and Tenant Act 1985, s. 11 (formerly the Housing Act 1961, s. 32), as amended by the Housing Act 1988, s. 116, implies covenants on the part of the landlord in relation to residential lettings under seven years, to keep in repair the structure and exterior of the dwelling-house and to keep in repair and proper working order the installations in the dwelling-house for the supply of water, gas and electricity, and for sanitation and space and water heating. If the lease is of a flat, the landlord's duty extends to any part of the structure or exterior of the building in which the landlord has an estate or interest (s. 11(1A)(a)). In the case of installations, where the landlord lets only part of the building, the landlord must keep in repair and proper working order an installation which directly or indirectly serves the flat, provided that the installation is in part of a building in which the landlord has an estate or interest, or which is owned or controlled by him (s. 11(1A)(b)). These extended obligations apply only if the disrepair or failure to maintain affect the tenant's enjoyment of the flat or common parts (s. 11(1B)).

So far as the tenant is concerned, his implied obligations in relation to the state and condition of the premises are limited to not committing waste and using the premises in a tenant-like manner (*Warren* v *Keen* [1954] 1 QB 15).

Q Question 6

Janet and Arnold hold the freehold title to a four-bedroomed house in Sussex. Last year, they decided to move to another property in Cornwall. Eleven months ago, the couple allowed Stanley to take up occupation of the Sussex property. Stanley duly entered into occupation of the property and, upon being handed the front door keys, signed an agreement entitled 'Occupation Agreement'. This agreement stated, *inter alia*, that Stanley would pay Janet and Arnold £450 per month and that the latter could nominate a third party to share occupation with Stanley, if they so chose.

Three months ago, Janet and Arnold fell into a disagreement about the property in Sussex. Janet wished to sell the property with vacant possession, being keen to use the proceeds of sale for her own business purposes. Arnold, however, was very resistant to the idea of any sale because he felt that the property was producing a good financial return. Two months ago, without Arnold's concurrence or consent, Janet served on Stanley a month's written notice to quit, purportedly terminating the Occupation Agreement. The notice was duly served by Janet on the relevant monthly anniversary date.

Stanley immediately telephoned Arnold complaining about the notice. Arnold told Stanley that he should keep paying the £450 per month as normal, as Arnold took the view that Janet did not really mean to end the agreement. To date, Stanley has made one payment of £450 since the notice was served, but his cheque for this amount was promptly returned by Janet.

Advise Stanley as to his rights in relation to his occupation of the Sussex property, in particular, as to the validity of Janet's notice both at common law and under statute.

Commentary

This question is concerned with the law relevant to the lease/licence distinction, and the common law and statutory rules governing the validity of notices to quit. Although there is no direct authority dealing with the service of a notice by one joint landlord, reference should be made to the analagous position in respect of joint tenants: *Hammersmith and*

Fulham London Borough Council v *Monk* [1992] 1 AC 478 and *Crawley Borough Council* v *Ure* [1995] 1 FLR 806. For further reading, see: Goulding, S. [1992] Conv 279, Dewar, J. (1992) 108 LQR 375 and Shorrock, K. [1995] Conv 424.

A consideration of the statutory code relating to assured shorthold tenancies under the Housing Act 1988 is also essential, especially in the light of the amendments introduced by the Housing Act 1996.

- Consider whether Stanley has been granted exclusive possession under the agreement: *Street* v *Mountford* (1985). The nomination clause will be treated as a sham if not genuinely exercised: *Antoniades* v *Villiers* (1990)

- No deed required as Stanley holds on a monthly tenancy granted in possession: Law of Property Act 1925, s. 54(2)

- Periodic tenancy can be brought to an end at common law by service of notice to quit by one joint tenant: *Hammersmith and Fulham LBC* v *Monk* (1992) and *Greenwich London Borough Council* v *McGrady* (1982). Effect of Housing Act 1988, s. 45(3)

- Decision in *Monk* (above) applied in *Crawley Borough Council* v *Ure* (1995) where Court of Appeal held that there was no duty of consultation between co-tenants under Law of Property Act 1925, s. 26(3). Janet's notice valid at common law despite being served without Arnold's concurrence

- But Stanley almost certainly an assured shorthold tenant under the Housing Act 1988, as amended by the Housing Act 1996. Under 1988 Act, landlord has automatic right to possession on giving two months' notice of seeking possession: s. 21(1)(b). Permissible for one out of joint tenants to serve s. 21 notice. But Janet has only given one month's notice so her notice is invalid. Open to her, however, to serve fresh notice in compliance with s. 21

☼ Suggested answer

It is first necessary to determine whether Stanley holds a tenancy or a contractual licence of the Sussex property. Whereas a tenancy of residential property attracts some measure of statutory protection, a licence will not. If Stanley has been granted a tenancy, it is likely that this will be an assured shorthold under the Housing Act 1988 (as amended by the Housing Act 1996). If he has a licence then the Act will not apply.

The agreement itself does not provide any clues as to the nature of the arrangement. In any event, since the House of Lords' ruling in *Street* v *Mountford* [1985] AC 809, the labels placed on the agreement are not of real importance in determining the legal relationship between the parties. According to *Street*, the test as to whether an occupancy agreement is a tenancy or a licence is whether, on the true construction of the agreement, the occupier has been granted exclusive possession of the accommodation, for a fixed or periodic term, at a stated rent. If these conditions are satisfied, the agreement will be held to create a tenancy, except where the circumstances surrounding the relationship negate the inference of a tenancy (e.g., where the occupier falls to be classified as a 'lodger' in the sense that the landlord provides attendance or services which require the landlord to exercise unrestricted access to and use of the premises, or where, from the outset, there is no intention to create legal relations, or where possession is granted pursuant to a contract of employment or sale).

Does Stanley have exclusive possession of the property, for a term, at a rent? Clearly, Stanley has a term, albeit periodic in nature, since the payment of £450 is treated by the parties as being referable to a monthly period. It is monthly by virtue of the fact that, in the absence of any contrary agreement, the payment is tendered and accepted on a monthly basis (see *Adler* v *Blackman* [1952] 2 All ER 945). He clearly pays a consideration, which falls to be construed as rent. But does Stanley have exclusive possession? The central aspect of any landlord and tenant relationship is the notion of exclusive possession (i.e., the occupier has the legal right to exclude everyone, including the landlord, from the demised premises). In this connection, the nomination clause reserved in the agreement in favour of Janet and Arnold suggests, at first glance, that Stanley lacks the requisite 'monopoly of control' over the property so as to confer exclusive possession on him. However, such clauses have been held to be shams if not genuinely exercised by the grantor. For example, in *Antoniades* v *Villiers and Another* [1990] 1 AC 417, a nomination clause in an occupation agreement was held to constitute a sham and a pretence. It was seen by the court as merely an attempt to deny the occupier exclusive possession and permit the owner to circumvent the statutory protection afforded to residential occupiers. In the present case, if the nomination clause has been *genuinely* exercised by Janet and Arnold then it may be valid. On the facts, however, there is no such suggestion and, therefore, I would conclude that the clause is of no effect and that Stanley falls to be characterised as a monthly tenant.

Being a monthly tenancy granted in possession, for a term not exceeding three years, at the best rent available without taking a fine, it will be a valid legal lease despite the absence of a deed (s. 54(2) of the Law of Property Act 1925). Moreover, despite the potential for the tenancy to continue for more than three years before being determined, it falls to be treated as being within s. 54(2) because the length of each period of the tenancy (i.e., one month) is less than three years (see *Ex Parte Voisey* (1882) 21 ChD 442). Accordingly, Stanley holds the Sussex property on a valid monthly periodic tenancy.

Periodic tenancies continue until such time as either the landlord or the tenant serves a valid notice to quit bringing the tenancy to end. The basic rule, at common law, is that one full period of notice must be given. Moreover, where there are joint tenants so that there is co-ownership at law of the leasehold estate (in the sense that the joint tenants hold the estate collectively as one legal unit), a valid notice to quit can be served on the landlord by *one* tenant alone so as to determine the tenancy (see *Hammersmith and Fulham LBC* v *Monk* [1992] 1 AC 478 (HL) and *Greenwich London Borough Council* v *McGrady* (1982) 6 HLR 36 (CA)). The notice must, however, be a genuine notice to quit terminating the tenancy at the end of a period of the tenancy, otherwise it may be construed as a surrender which requires the concurrence of all joint tenants (*Leek and Moorlands Building Society* v *Clark* [1952] 2 QB 788 (CA) and *Hounslow London Borough Council* v *Pilling* [1994] 1 All ER 432 (CA)). Although the *Monk* and *McGrady* cases both dealt with secure tenancies under the Housing Act 1985, there is no reason to suppose that they do not apply in the context of assured tenancies under the Housing Act 1988. In this connection, it seems also that the common law position regarding the service of a notice to quit by one joint assured tenant is unaffected by s. 45(3) of the Housing Act 1988, which provides that any reference in the Act to the landlord or tenant is a reference to all persons jointly constituting the landlord and/or tenant. There is no case, however, directly in point so the matter remains an open one.

The decision in *Monk* was applied by the Court of Appeal in *Crawley Borough Council* v *Ure* [1995] 1 FLR 806, which also considered the related issue of whether the joint tenant who serves notice is under a duty to consult his co-tenant under s. 26(3) of the Law of Property Act 1925, which provides that statutory trustees for sale 'shall so far as practicable consult the persons of full age for the time being beneficially interested in possession . . .'. The Court of Appeal concluded that s. 26(3) did not apply to the service of a notice to quit and, therefore, there was no obligation of consultation. The Trusts of Land and Appointment of Trustees Act 1996 has not affected this aspect of the law: *Notting Hill Housing Trust* v *Brackley* [2001] 35 EG 106. In that case, it was held that a joint tenant, in serving a notice to quit, was not acting as a trustee so no duty under s. 11 of the 1996 Act (successor to s. 26(3) of the 1925 Act) could arise. Giving notice merely expressed a joint tenant's intention that he (or she) no longer consented to the joint tenancy.

In the present case, the notice to quit served by Janet (as joint landlord) on Stanley is for a full period and *prima facie* seems valid at common law. In the light of the *Monk* ruling, referred to above, and by parity of reasoning, it is probably valid at common law despite the fact that it was served by Janet without Arnold's concurrence. As Janet has accepted no rent since Stanley received the notice, it is also arguably that no waiver of the notice to quit has occurred.

However, this does not conclude the matter since Stanley is almost certainly an assured shorthold tenant entitled to statutory protection under the Housing Act 1988 (as amended by the Housing Act 1996). The 1996 Act has substantially altered the assured shorthold tenancy scheme originally set up by the Housing Act 1988. As from

28 February 1997 (being the date when the relevant provisions of the 1996 Act came into force), any tenancy which before this date would have been an assured tenancy under the 1988 Act is now deemed to be an assured shorthold unless the parties otherwise agree. In order to qualify as an assured shorthold tenancy, there must be a letting (as opposed to a licence) of a dwelling, which is let as a separate dwelling, to an individual (or group of individuals) who occupies the dwelling as his/her only or principal home and it is not a tenancy which falls within one or other of the exceptions set out in sch. 1 of the Housing Act 1988. These exceptions include tenancies entered into before the commencement of the 1988 Act, tenancies of high rateable value (or if granted after 1 April 1990, high rents in excess of £25,000 per annum), tenancies after 1 April 1990 at an annual rent of less than £250 per annum, business tenancies, students lettings, holiday lets, tenancies granted by resident landlords, Crown lettings, and lettings by public sector landlords. None of these exceptions, of course, apply to Stanley's tenancy. The upshot of the foregoing, therefore, is that Stanley's tenancy, being created after 27 February 1997, will be an assured shorthold.

Under the 1988 Act, landlords are given an automatic right to possession of assured shorthold tenancies on giving two months' written notice of seeking possession (see s. 21 of the 1988 Act as amended by s. 96 of the Housing Act 1996). Under s. 21(1)(b), it is permissible for one out of joint landlords to serve the requisite s. 21 notice on the tenant so no difficulty arises from the fact that, in the present case, Janet has served notice without the concurrence of her co-owner, Arnold. It is evident, however, that Janet has only given one month's notice requiring possession. Her notice is, accordingly, invalid under the Act and a fresh two months' notice will need to be given by Janet, on the relevant anniversary day, in order to determine Stanley's assured shorthold tenancy properly. If, upon expiry of the notice, Stanley refuses to vacate, it will be necessary for Janet to bring proceedings for possession of the Sussex property in the local county court. She will not be entitled to evict him without a court order.

Further reading

Dewar, J., 'When Joint Tenants Part' (1992) 108 LQR 375.

Goulding, J., 'Service of a Notice to Quit by One Joint Tenant' [1992] Conv. 279.

Heppinstall, A., 'A New Weapon for Tenants' (2002) SJ 59.

Morgan, J., 'Suspending Leasehold Covenants: A Doctrine of Frustratory Mitigation?' [1995] Conv 74.

Riley, A., 'The Model Package for 21st Century, Leases' [2003] EG 142.

Shorrock, K., 'Notice to Quit by One Periodic Lessee of Residential Property — Time for Statutory Intervention?' [1995] Conv. 424.

Wilkinson, H.W., 'A Clearer, Fairer Deal for Private Tenants' (2002) NLJ 1002.

Index